CHILTON BOOK COMPANY

REPAIR & TUNE-UP GUIDE

TOYOTA CAMRY 1983-86

All U.S. and Canadian models of Toyota Camry

— omit

— add in note

President LAWRENCE A. FORNASIERI
Vice President and General Manager JOHN P. KUSHNERICK
Executive Editor KERRY A. FREEMAN, S.A.E.
Senior Editor RICHARD J. RIVELE, S.A.E.
Editor JOHN M. BAXTER, S.A.E.

CHILTON BOOK COMPANY
Radnor, Pennsylvania
19089

SAFETY NOTICE

Proper service and repair procedures are vital to the safe, reliable operation of all motor vehicles, as well as the personal safety of those performing repairs. This book outlines procedures for servicing and repairing vehicles using safe, effective methods. The procedures contain many NOTES, CAUTIONS and WARNINGS which should be followed along with standard safety procedures to eliminate the possibility of personal injury or improper service which could damage the vehicle or compromise its safety.

It is important to note that repair procedures and techniques, tools and parts for servicing motor vehicles, as well as the skill and experience of the individual performing the work vary widely. It is not possible to anticipate all of the conceivable ways or conditions under which vehicles may be serviced, or to provide cautions as to all of the possible hazards that may result. Standard and accepted safety precautions and equipment should be used when handling toxic or flammable fluids, and safety goggles or other protection should be used during cutting, grinding, chiseling, prying, or any other process that can cause material removal or projectiles.

Some procedures require the use of tools specially designed for a specific purpose. Before substituting another tool or procedure, you must be completely satisfied that neither your personal safety, nor the performance of the vehicle will be endangered.

Although information in this guide is based on industry sources and is as complete as possible at the time of publication, the possibility exists that the manufacturer made later changes which could not be included here. While striving for total accuracy, Chilton Book Company cannot assume responsibility for any errors, changes, or omissions that may occur in the compilation of this data.

PART NUMBERS

Part numbers listed in this reference are not recommendations by Chilton for any product by brand name. They are references that can be used with interchange manuals and aftermarket supplier catalogs to locate each brand supplier's discrete part number.

SPECIAL TOOLS

Special tools are recommended by the vehicle manufacturer to perform their specific job. Use has been kept to a minimum, but where absolutely necessary, are they referred to in the text by the part number of the tool manufacturer. These tools can be purchased, under the appropriate part number, from Kent-Moore Corporation, 29784 Little Mack, Roseville, Michigan 48066. For Canada, contact Kent-Moore of Canada, Ltd., 2395 Cawthra Mississauga, Ontario, Canada L5A 3P2 or an equivalent tool can be purchased locally from a tool supplier or parts outlet. Before substituting any tool for the one recommended, read the SAFETY NOTICE at the top of this page.

ACKNOWLEDGMENTS

The Chilton Book Company expresses appreciation to Toyota Motor Sales, U.S.A., Inc., 2055 W. 190th Street, Torrance, California 90504, Biscotte Toyota, 2062 W. Main Street, Norristown, Pennsylvania 19401 and Mainline Toyota, Devon, Pennsylvania 19333 for their generous assistance.

Manufactured in the United States of America
1234567890   6543210987

Chilton's Repair & Tune-Up Guide: Toyota Camry 1983–86
ISBN 0-8019-7740-1 pbk.
Library of Congress Catalog Card No. 86-47722

CONTENTS

Quick Reference Specifications For Your Vehicle

Fill in this chart with the most commonly used specifications for your vehicle. Specifications can be found in Chapters 1 through 3 or on the tune-up decal under the hood of the vehicle.

Tune-Up

Firing Order_____

Spark Plugs:

    Type_____

    Gap (in.)_____

Torque (ft. lbs.)_____

Idle Speed (rpm)_____

Ignition Timing (°)_____

    Vacuum or Electronic Advance (Connected/Disconnected)_____

Valve Clearance (in.)

    Intake_____   Exhaust_____

Capacities

Engine Oil Type (API Rating)_____

    With Filter Change (qts)_____

    Without Filter Change (qts)_____

Cooling System (qts)_____

Manual Transmission (pts)_____

    Type_____

Automatic Transmission (pts)_____

    Type_____

Front Differential (pts)_____

    Type_____

Rear Differential (pts)_____

    Type_____

Transfer Case (pts)_____

    Type_____

FREQUENTLY REPLACED PARTS

Use these spaces to record the part numbers of frequently replaced parts.

PCV VALVE	OIL FILTER	AIR FILTER	FUEL FILTER
Type_____	Type_____	Type_____	Type_____
Part No._____	Part No._____	Part No._____	Part No._____

General Information and Maintenance

HOW TO USE THIS BOOK

Chilton's Repair and Tune-Up Guide for the Toyota Camry is designed for the car owner who wishes to do some of the service on his/her own car. Included are step-by-step instructions for maintenance, troubleshooting and repair or replacement of many of the components on your car.

The first two chapters will be the most used, since they contain maintenance and tune-up information and procedures. Studies have shown that a properly tuned and maintained car can get at least 10% better gas mileage (which translates into lower operating costs) and periodic maintenance will catch minor problems before they turn into major repair bills. The other chapters deal with the more complex systems of your car. Operating systems from engine through brakes are covered to the extent that the average do-it-yourselfer becomes mechanically involved. This book will not explain such things as rebuilding the differential for the simple reason that the expertise required and the investment in special tools make this task impractical and uneconomical. It will give you the detailed instructions to help you change your own brake pads and shoes, tune-up the engine, replace spark plugs and filters, and do many more jobs that will save you money, give you personal satisfaction and help you avoid expensive problems.

A secondary purpose of this book is a reference guide for owners who want to understand their car and/or their mechanics better. In this case, no tools at all are required. Knowing just what a particular repair job requires in parts and labor time will allow you to evaluate whether or not you're getting a fair price quote and help decipher itemized bills from a repair shop.

Before attempting any repairs or service on your car, read through the entire procedure outlined in the appropriate chapter. This will give you the overall view of what tools and supplies will be required. There is nothing more frustrating than having to walk to the bus stop on Monday morning because you were short one gasket on Sunday afternoon. So read ahead and plan ahead. Each operation should be approached logically and all procedures thoroughly understood before attempting any work. Some special tools that may be required can often be rented from local automotive jobbers or places specializing in renting tools and equipment. Check the yellow pages of your phone book.

All chapters contain adjustments, maintenance, removal and installation procedures, and overhaul procedures. When overhaul is not considered practical, we tell you how to remove the failed part and then how to install the new or rebuilt replacement. In this way, you at least save the labor costs. Backyard overhaul of some components (such as the alternator or water pump) is just not practical, but the removal and installation procedure is often simple and well within the capabilities of the average car owner.

Two basic mechanic's rules should be mentioned here. First, whenever the LEFT side of the car or engine is referred to, it is meant to specify the DRIVER'S side of the car. Conversely, the RIGHT side of the car means the PASSENGER'S side. Second, all screws and bolts are removed by turning counterclockwise, and tightened by turning clockwise.

Safety is always the most important rule. Constantly be aware of the dangers involved in working on or around an automobile and take proper precautions to avoid the risk of personal injury or damage to the vehicle. See the section in this chapter, Servicing Your Vehicle Safely, and the SAFETY NOTICE on the acknowledgment page before attempting any service procedures and pay attention to the instructions provided. There are 3 common mistakes in mechanical work:

1. Incorrect order of assembly, disassembly or adjustment. When taking something apart or putting it together, doing things in the wrong order usually just costs you extra time; however it CAN break something. Read the entire procedure before beginning disassembly. Do everything in the order in which the instructions say you should do it, even if you can't immediately see a reason for it. When you're taking apart something that is very intricate (for example a carburetor), you might want to draw a picture of how it looks when assembled at one point in order to make sure you get everything back in its proper position. We will supply exploded views whenever possible, but sometimes the job requires more attention to detail than an illustration provides. When making adjustments (especially tune-up adjustments), do them in order. One adjustment often affects another and you cannot expect satisfactory results unless each adjustment is made only when it cannot be changed by any other.

2. Overtorquing (or undertorquing) nuts and bolts. While it is more common for overtorquing to cause damage, undertorquing can cause a fastener to vibrate loose and cause serious damage, especially when dealing with aluminum parts. Pay attention to torque specifications and utilize a torque wrench in assembly. If a torque figure is not available remember that, if you are using the right tool to do the job, you will probably not have to strain yourself to get a fastener tight enough. The pitch of most threads is so slight that the tension you put on the wrench will be multiplied many times in actual force on what you are tightening. A good example of how critical torque is can be seen in the case of spark plug installation, especially where you are putting the plug into an aluminum cylinder head. Too little torque can fail to crush the gasket, causing leakage of combustion gases and consequent overheating of the plug and engine parts. Too much torque can damage the threads or distort the plug, which changes the spark gap at the electrode. Since more and more manufacturers are using aluminum in their engine and chassis parts to save weight, a torque wrench should be in any serious do-it-yourselfer's tool box.

There are many commercial chemical products available for ensuring that fasteners won't come loose, even if they are not torqued just right (a very common brand is Loctite®). If you're worried about getting something together tight enough to hold, but loose enough to avoid mechanical damage during assembly, one of these products might offer substantial insurance. Read the label on the package and make sure the product is compatible with the materials, fluids, etc. involved before choosing one.

3. Crossthreading. This occurs when a part such as a bolt is screwed into a nut or casting at the wrong angle and forced, causing the threads to become damaged. Crossthreading is more likely to occur if access is difficult. It helps to clean and lubricate fasteners, and to start threading with the part to be installed going straight in, using your fingers. If you encounter resistance, unscrew the part and start over again at a different angle until it can be inserted and turned several times without much effort. Keep in mind that many parts, especially spark plugs, use tapered threads so that gentle turning will automatically bring the part you're threading to the proper angle if you don't force it or resist a change in angle. Don't put a wrench on the part until it's been turned in a couple of times by hand. If you suddenly encounter resistance and the part has not seated fully, don't force it. Pull it back out and make sure it's clean and threading properly.

Always take your time and be patient; once you have some experience, working on your car will become an enjoyable hobby.

TOOLS AND EQUIPMENT

The service procedures in this book presuppose a familiarity with hand tools and their proper use. However, it is possible that you may have a limited amount of experience with the sort of equipment needed to work on an automobile. This section is designed to help you assemble a basic set of tools that will handle most of the jobs you may undertake.

In addition to the normal assortment of screwdrivers and pliers, automotive service

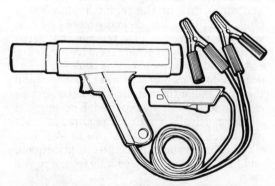

An inductive pickup simplifies timing light connection to the spark plug wire

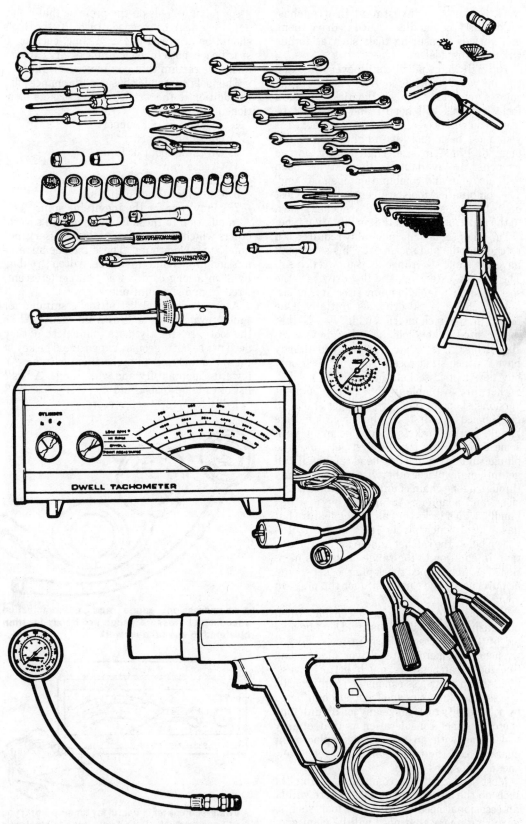

You need only a basic assortment of hand tools for most maintenance and repair jobs

work requires an investment in wrenches, sockets and the handles needed to drive them, and various measuring tools such as torque wrenches and feeler gauges.

You will find that virtually every nut and bolt on your Toyota is metric. Therefore, despite a few close size similarities, standard inch-size tools will not fit and must not be used. You will need a set of metric wrenches as your most basic tool kit, ranging from about 6mm to 17mm in size. High quality forged wrenches are available in three styles: open end, box end, and combination open/box end. The combination tools are generally the most desirable as a starter set; the wrenches shown in the illustration are of the combination type.

The other set of tools inevitably required is a ratchet handle and socket set. This set should have the same size range as your wrench set. The ratchet, extension, and flex drives for the sockets are available in many sizes; it is advisable to choose a ⅜″ drive set initially. One break in the inch/metric sizing war is that metric-sized sockets sold in the U.S. have inch-sized drive (¼, ⅜, ½, etc.). Thus, if you already have an inch-sized socket set, you need only buy new metric sockets in the sizes needed. Sockets are available in six and twelve point versions; six point types are stronger and are a good choice for a first set. The choice of a drive handle for the sockets should be made with some care. If this is your first set, take the plunge and invest in a flex-head ratchet; it will get into many places otherwise accessible only through a long chain of universal joints, extensions, and adapters. An alternative is a flex handle, which lacks the ratcheting feature but has a head which pivots 180°; such a tool is shown below the ratchet handle in the illustration. In addition to the range of sockets mentioned, a rubber-lined spark plug socket should be purchased. The correct size for the plugs in your Toyota's engine is $\frac{13}{16}$″.

The most important thing to consider when purchasing hand tools is quality. Don't be misled by the low cost of bargain tools. Forged wrenches, tempered screwdriver blades, and fine tooth ratchets are much better investments than their less expensive counterparts. The skinned knuckles and frustration inflicted by poor quality tools make any job an unhappy chore. Another consideration is that quality tools come with an unbeatable replacement guarantee, if the tool breaks, you get a new one, no questions asked.

Most jobs can be accomplished using the tools on the accompanying lists. There will be an occasional need for a special tool, such as snap ring pliers; that need will be mentioned in the text. It would not be wise to buy a large

assortment of tools on the premise that someday they will be needed. Instead, the tools should be acquired one at a time, each for a specific job, both to avoid unnecessary expense and to be certain that you have the right tool.

The tools needed for basic maintenance jobs, in addition to the wrenches and sockets mentioned, include:
1. Jackstands, for support
2. Oil filter wrench
3. Oil filter spout or funnel
4. Grease gun
5. Battery post and clamp cleaner
6. Container for draining oil
7. Many rags for the inevitable spills

In addition to these items there are several others which are not absolutely necessary, but handy to have around. These include a transmission funnel and filler tube, a drop (trouble) light on a long cord, an adjustable (crescent) wrench, and slip joint pliers.

A more advanced list of tools, suitable for tune-up work, can be drawn up easily. While the tools are slightly more sophisticated, they need not be outrageously expensive. The key to these purchases is to make them with an eye towards adaptability and wide range. A basic list of tune-up tools could include:
1. Tachometer/dwell meter

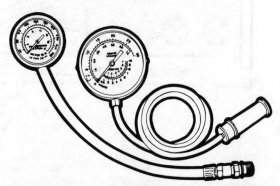

A compression gauge and a combination vacuum/fuel pressure gauge are handy for troubleshooting and tune-up work

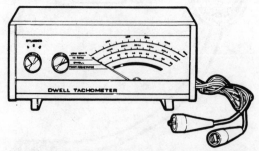

A dwell/tachometer is useful for tune-up work; you won't need a dwell meter if your car has electronic ignition

2. Spark plug gauge and gapping tool
3. Feeler gauges for valve adjustment
4. Timing light

You will need both wire-type and flat-type feeler gauges, the former for the park plugs and the latter for the valves. The choice of a timing light should be made carefully. A light which works on the DC current supplied by the car battery is the best choice; it should have a xenon tube for brightness. Since most late model cars have electronic ignition, and since nearly all cars will have it in the future, the light should have an inductive pickup which clamps around the number one spark plug cable (the timing light illustrated has one of these pickups). In addition to these basic tools, there are several other tools and gauges which you may find useful. These include:

1. A compression gauge. The screw-in type is slower to use, but eliminates the possibility of a faulty reading due to escaping pressure
2. A manifold vacuum gauge
3. A test light
4. A combination volt/ohmmeter
5. An induction meter, used to determine whether or not there is current flowing in a wire, an extremely helpful tool for electrical troubleshooting.

Finally, you will find a torque wrench necessary for all but the most basic of work. The beam-type models are perfectly adequate. The newer click-type (breakaway) torque wrenches are more accurate, but are much more expensive, and must be periodically recalibrated.

SERVICING YOUR CAR SAFELY

It is virtually impossible to anticipate all of the hazards involved with automotive maintenance and service, but care and common sense will prevent most accidents. The rules of safety for mechanics range from, don't smoke around gasoline, to, use the proper tool for the job. The trick to avoiding injuries is to develop safe work habits and take every possible precaution.

Dos

• Do keep a fire extinguisher and first aid kit within easy reach.
• Do wear safety glasses or goggles when cutting, drilling, grinding or prying. If you wear glasses for the sake of vision, they should be made of hardened glass that can serve also as safety glasses, or wear safety goggles over your regular glasses.
• Do shield your eyes whenever you work around the battery. Batteries contain sulphuric acid. In case of contact with the eyes or skin, flush the area with water or a mixture of water and baking soda and get medical attention immediately.
• Do use safety stands for any undercar service. Jacks are for raising vehicles; safety stands are for making sure the vehicle stays raised until you want it to come down. Whenever the car is raised, block the wheels remaining on the ground and set the parking brake.
• Do use adequate ventilation when working with any chemicals or hazardous materials. Like carbon monoxide, the asbestos dust resulting from brake lining wear can be poisonous in sufficient quantities.
• Do disconnect the negative battery cable when working on the electrical system. The secondary ignition system can contain up to 40,000 volts.
• Do follow manufacturer's directions whenever working with potentially hazardous materials. Both brake fluid and antifreeze are poisonous is taken internally.
• Do properly maintain your tools. Loose hammerheads, mushroomed punches and chisels, frayed or poorly grounded electrical cords, excessively worn screwdrivers, spread open end wrenches, cracked sockets, slipping ratchets, or faulty droplight sockets can cause accidents.
• Do use the proper size and type of tool for the job being done.
• Do when possible, pull on a wrench handle rather than push on it, and adjust your stance to prevent a fall.
• Do be sure that adjustable wrenches are tightly closed on the nut or bolt and pulled so that the face is on the side of the fixed jaw.
• Do select a wrench or socket that fits the nut or bolt. The wrench or socket should sit straight, not cocked.
• Do strike squarely with a hammer; avoid glancing blows.
• Do set the parking brake and block the drive wheels if the work requires the engine running.

Always support the car securely with jackstands; never use cinder blocks, tire changing jacks or the like

Don'ts

• Don't run an engine in a garage or anywhere else without proper ventilation – EVER! Carbon monoxide is poisonous; it takes a long time to leave the human body and you can build up a deadly supply of it in your system by simply breathing in a little every day. You may not realize you are slowly poisoning yourself. Always use power vents, windows, fans or open the garage doors.

• Don't work around moving parts while wearing a necktie or other loose clothing. Short sleeves are much safer than long, loose sleeves; hard-toed shoes with neoprene soles protect your toes and give a better grip on slippery surfaces. Jewelry such as watches, fancy belt buckles, beads or body adornment of any kind is not safe working around a car. Long hair should be hidden under a hat or cap.

• Don't use pockets for toolboxes. A fall or bump can drive a screwdriver deep into your body. Even a wiping cloth hanging form the back pocket can wrap around a spinning shaft or fan.

• Don't smoke when working around gasoline, cleaning solvent or other flammable material.

• Don't smoke when working around the battery. When the battery is being charged, it gives off explosive hydrogen gas.

• Don't use gasoline to wash your hands; there are excellent soaps available. Gasoline may contain lead, and lead can enter the body through a cut, accumulating in the body until you are very ill. Gasoline also removes all the natural oils from the skin so that bone dry hands will suck up oil and grease.

• Don't service the air conditioning system unless you are equipped with the necessary tools and training. The refrigerant, R-12, is extremely cold when compressed, and when released into the air will instantly freeze any surface it contacts, including your eyes. Although the refrigerant is normally non-toxic, R-12 becomes a deadly poisonous gas in the presence of an open flame. One good whiff of the vapors from burning refrigerant can be fatal.

HISTORY

In 1933, the Toyota Automatic Loom Works started an automobile division. Several models, mostly experimental, were produced between 1935 and 1937. Automobile production started on a large scale in 1937 when the Toyota Motor Co. Ltd. was founded. The name for the automobile company was changed from the family name. Toyoda, to Toyota, because a numerologist suggested that this would be a more auspicious name to use for this endeavor. It must have been; by 1947, Toyota had produced 100,000 vehicles. Today Toyota is Japan's largest producer or motor vehicles and ranks among the largest in world production.

It was not until the late 1950s, that Toyota began exporting cars to the United States. Public reception of the Toyopet was rather cool. The car was heavy and under-powered by U.S. standards. Several other models were exported, including the almost indestructible Land Cruiser. It was not until 1965, however, with the introduction of the Corona sedan, that Toyota enjoyed a real success on the U.S. market.

Continual product improvement, a good dealer network, and an ability to blanket the economy end of the market are responsible for this success. Today, Toyota produces a full range of models, from the economical to the luxurious.

SERIAL NUMBER IDENTIFICATION

Vehicles

All models have the vehicle identification number (VIN) stamped on a plate which is attached to the left side of the instrument panel. This plate is visible through the windshield.

The VIN is also stamped on a plate in the engine compartment which is usually located on the firewall.

Through 1980 the serial number consists of a series identification number (see the chart below) followed by a six-digit production number.

Beginning with 1981 models the serial number consists of seventeen symbols (letters and numbers).

Engine

The engine serial number consists of an engine series identification number, followed by a six-digit production number.

VIN plate on the firewall

Engine Identification

Year	Displacement (cc/cu in.)	Number of Cylinders	Type	Engine Series Identification
1983–84	1995/121.7	4	SOHC	2S-E
1984	1839/112.2	4	SOHC	1C-TL
1985	1995/121/7	4	SOHC	2S-E
	1839/112.2	4	SOHC	1C-TL
1986	1995/121.4	4	SOHC	2S-E
	1974/120.4	4	SOHC	2C-T

Vehicle Identification

Engine Type/ Model/ Trans.	Year	Series Identification Number*
Gasoline Eng.	1983–84	SV
Diesel Eng.	1984	CV
Gasoline Eng.	1985	
DLX Sedan		SV12E
LE Sedan		SV16E
DLX Liftback		SV12H
LE Liftback		SV16H
Diesel Eng.		
Seden		CV12E
	1986	
DLX Sedan		SV12E
LE Sedan		SV16E
LE Liftback		SV16H
Diesel		
Sedan DLX		CV13E

The serial numbers are stamped on the right side of the cylinder block, below the oil filter.

ROUTINE MAINTENANCE

Air Cleaner

The air cleaners used on Toyota vehicles are of the dry element, disposable type. They should never be washed or oiled.

Clean the element every 3,000 miles, or more often under dry, dusty conditions, by using low pressure compressed air. Blow from the inside toward the outside.

CAUTION: *Never use high air pressure to clean the element, as this will probably damage it.*

Replace the element every 30,000 miles or more often under dry, dusty conditions. Be sure to use the correct one; all Toyota elements are of the same type but they come in a variety of sizes.

To remove the air cleaner element, unfasten the wing nut(s) and clips (if so equipped) on top of the housing and lift off the top section. Set it aside carefully since the emission system hoses are attached to it on some models. Unfasten these hoses first (if so equipped), to remove it entirely from the car. Lift the air cleaner element out for service or replacement.

Installation is the reverse of removal.

PCV Valve

The positive crankcase ventilation (PCV) valve should be replaced every 30,000 miles or 24 months. (California models, 1980 and later, every 60,000 miles).

NOTE: *For PCV valve removal and installation, See Chapter 4.*

Charcoal Canister

The charcoal canister vacuum lines, fittings, and connections should be checked every 6,000 miles for clogging, pinching, looseness, etc. Clean or replace components as necessary. If the canister is clogged, it may be cleaned using low pressure compressed air, as shown.

The entire canister should be replaced every five years/60,000 miles.

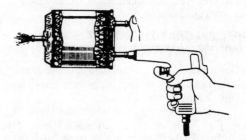

Using compressed air to clean the charcoal canister

Battery

FLUID LEVEL (EXCEPT MAINTENANCE FREE BATTERIES)

Check the battery electrolyte level at least once a month, or more often in hot weather or

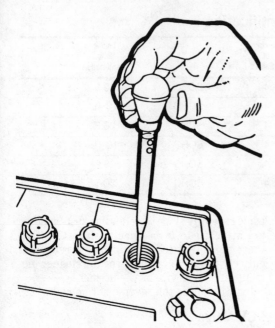

The specific gravity of the battery can be checked with a simple float-type hydrometer

during periods of extended car operation. The level can be checked through the case on translucent polypropylene batteries; the cell caps must be removed on other models. The electrolyte level in each cell should be kept filled to the split ring inside, or the line marked on the outside of the case.

If the level is low, add only distilled water, or colorless, odorless drinking water, through the opening until the level is correct. Each cell is completely separate from the others, so each must be checked and filled individually.

If water is added in freezing weather, the car should be driven several miles to allow the water to mix with the electrolyte. Otherwise, the battery could freeze.

SPECIFIC GRAVITY (EXCEPT MAINTENANCE FREE BATTERIES)

At least once a year, check the specific gravity of the battery. It should be between 1.20 and 1.26 at room temperature.

The specific gravity can be checked with the use of an hydrometer, an inexpensive instrument available from many sources, including auto parts stores. The hydrometer has a squeeze bulb at one end and a nozzle at the other. Battery electrolyte is sucked into the hydrometer until the float is lifted from its seat. The specific gravity is then read by noting the position of the float. Generally, if after charging, the specific gravity between any two cells varies more than 50 points (.050), the battery is bad and should be replaced.

It is not possible to check the specific gravity in this manner on sealed (maintenance free) batteries. Instead, the indicator built into the top of the case must be relied on to display any signs of battery deterioration. If the indicator is dark, the battery can be assumed to be OK. If the indicator is light, the specific gravity is low, and the battery should be charged or replaced.

CABLES AND CLAMPS

Once a year, the battery terminals and the cable clamps should be cleaned. Loosen the clamps and remove the cables, negative cable first. On batteries with posts on top, the use of a puller specially made for the purpose is recommended. These are inexpensive, and available in auto parts stores. Side terminal battery cables are secured with a bolt.

Clean the cable clamps and the battery terminal with a wire brush, until all corrosion, grease, etc. is removed and the metal is shiny. It is especially important to clean the inside of the clamp thoroughly, since a small deposit of foreign material or oxidation there will prevent a sound electrical connection and inhibit either starting or charging. Special tools are available for cleaning these parts, one type for conventional batteries and another type for side terminal batteries.

Before installing the cables, loosen the battery holddown clamp or strap, remove the battery and check the battery tray. Clear it of any debris, and check it for soundness. Rust should

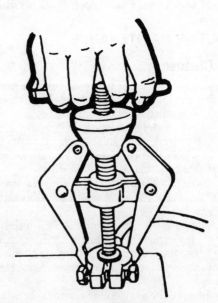

Special pullers are available to remove cable clamps

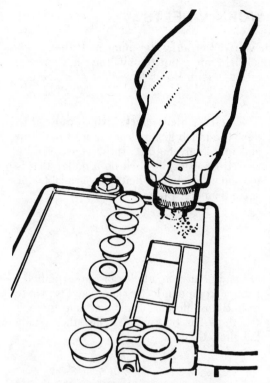

Clean the battery posts with a wire brush, or the special tool shown

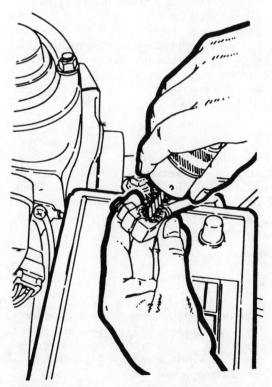

Clean the inside of the clamps with a wire brush, or the special tool

be wire brushed away, and the metal given a coat of anti-rust paint. Replace the battery and tighten the holddown clamp or strap securely, but be careful not to over-tighten, which will crack the battery case.

After the clamps and terminals are clean, re-install the cables, negative cable last; do not hammer on the clamps to install. Tighten the clamps securely, but do not distort them. Give the clamps and terminals a thin external coat of grease after installation, to retard corrosion.

Check the cables at the same time that the terminals are cleaned. If the cable insulation is cracked or broken, or if the ends are frayed, the cable should be replaced with a new cable of the same length and gauge.

NOTE: *Keep flame or sparks away from the battery; it gives off explosive hydrogen gas. Battery electrolyte contains sulphuric acid. If you should splash any on your skin or in your eyes, flush the affected area with plenty of clear water; if it lands in your eyes, get medical help immediately.*

REPLACEMENT

When it becomes necessary to replace the battery, select a battery with a rating equal to or greater than the battery originally installed. Deterioration, embrittlement and just plain aging of the battery cables, starter motor, and associated wires makes the battery's job harder in successive years. The slow increase in electrical resistance over time makes it prudent to install a new battery with a greater capacity than the old. Details on battery removal and installation are covered in Chapter 3.

Belts

INSPECTION

The belts which drive the engine accessories such as the alternator or generator, the air pump, power steering pump, air conditioning compressor and water pump are of either the V-belt design or flat, serpentine design. Older belts show wear and damage readily, since their basic design was a belt with a rubber casing. As the casing wore, cracks and fibers were readily apparent. Newer design, caseless belts do not show wear as readily, and many untrained people cannot distinguish between a good, serviceable belt and one that is worn to the point of failure.

It is a good idea, therefore, to visually inspect the belts regularly and replace them, routinely, every two to three years.

ADJUSTING

Belts are normally adjusted by loosening the bolts of the accessory being driven and moving

HOW TO SPOT WORN V-BELTS

V-Belts are vital to efficient engine operation—they drive the fan, water pump and other accessories. They require little maintenance (occasional tightening) but they will not last forever. Slipping or failure of the V-belt will lead to overheating. If your V-belt looks like any of these, it should be replaced.

This belt has deep cracks, which cause it to flex. Too much flexing leads to heat build-up and premature failure. These cracks can be caused by using the belt on a pulley that is too small. Notched belts are available for small diameter pulleys.

Cracking or weathering

Oil and grease on a belt can cause the belt's rubber compounds to soften and separate from the reinforcing cords that hold the belt together. The belt will first slip, then finally fail altogether.

Softening (grease and oil)

Glazing is caused by a belt that is slipping. A slipping belt can cause a run-down battery, erratic power steering, overheating or poor accessory performance. The more the belt slips, the more glazing will be built up on the surface of the belt. The more the belt is glazed, the more it will slip. If the glazing is light, tighten the belt.

Glazing

The cover of this belt is worn off and is peeling away. The reinforcing cords will begin to wear and the belt will shortly break. When the belt cover wears in spots or has a rough jagged appearance, check the pulley grooves for roughness.

Worn cover

This belt is on the verge of breaking and leaving you stranded. The layers of the belt are separating and the reinforcing cords are exposed. It's just a matter of time before it breaks completely.

Separation

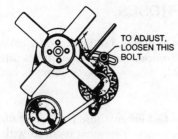

Fan belt adjustment

TO ADJUST, LOOSEN THIS BOLT

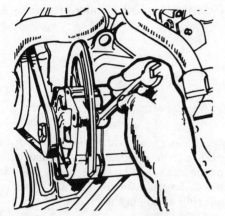

To adjust belt tension or to replace belts, first loosen the component's mounting and adjusting bolts slightly

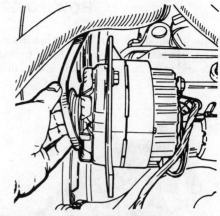

Slip the new belt over the pulley

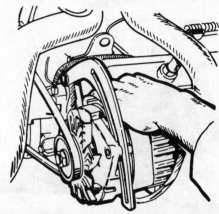

Pull outward on the component and tighten the mounting bolts

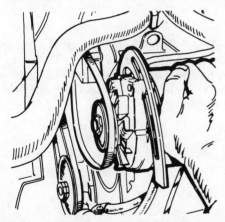

Push the component toward the engine and slip off the belt

that accessory on its pivot points until the proper tension is applied to the belt. The accessory is held in this position while the bolts are tightened. To determine proper belt tension, you can purchase a belt tension gauge or simply use the deflection method. To determine deflection, press inward on the belt at the midpoint of its longest straight run. The belt should deflect (move inward) ⅜ to ½″ (9.525–12.7mm). Some long V-belts and most serpen-

tine belts have idler pulleys which are used for adjusting purposes. Just loosen the idler pulley and move it to take up tension on the belt.

REMOVAL AND INSTALLATION

To remove a drive belt, simply loosen the accessory being driven and move it on its pivot point to free the belt. Then, remove the belt. If an idler pulley is used, it is often necessary, only, to loosen the idler pulley to provide enough slack the remove the belt.

It is important to note, however, that on engines with many driven accessories, several or all of the belts may have to be removed to get at the one to be replaced.

Hoses

REMOVAL AND INSTALLATION

Radiator hoses are generally of two constructions, the preformed (molded) type, which is custom made for a particular application, and the spring-loaded type, which is made to fit

HOW TO SPOT BAD HOSES

Both the upper and lower radiator hoses are called upon to perform difficult jobs in an inhospitable environment. They are subject to nearly 18 psi at under hood temperatures often over 280°F., and must circulate nearly 7500 gallons of coolant an hour—3 good reasons to have good hoses.

A good test for any hose is to feel it for soft or spongy spots. Frequently these will appear as swollen areas of the hose. The most likely cause is oil soaking. This hose could burst at any time, when hot or under pressure.

Swollen hose

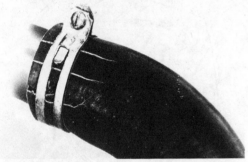

Cracked hoses can usually be seen but feel the hoses to be sure they have not hardened; a prime cause of cracking. This hose has cracked down to the reinforcing cords and could split at any of the cracks.

Cracked hose

Weakened clamps frequently are the cause of hose and cooling system failure. The connection between the pipe and hose has deteriorated enough to allow coolant to escape when the engine is hot.

Frayed hose end (due to weak clamp)

Debris, rust and scale in the cooling system can cause the inside of a hose to weaken. This can usually be felt on the outside of the hose as soft or thinner areas.

Debris in cooling system

several different applications. Heater hoses are all of the same general construction.

Hoses are retained by clamps. To replace a hose, loosen the clamp and slide it down the hose, away from the attaching point. Twist the hose from side to side until it is free, then pull it off. Before installing the new hose, make sure that the outlet fitting is as clean as possible. Coat the fitting with non-hardening sealer and slip the hose into place. Install the clamp and tighten it.

Air Conditioning System

NOTE: *This book contains simple testing and charging procedures for your car's air conditioning system. More comprehensive testing, diagnosis and service procedures may be found in CHILTON'S GUIDE TO AIR CONDITIONING SERVICE AND REPAIR, book part number 7580, available at your local retailer.*

OPERATION

The air conditioning system is designed to cycle a compressor on and off to maintain the desired cooling within the passenger compartment. Passenger compartment comfort is maintained by the temperature liver located on the control head. The system is also designed to prevent the evaporator from freezing.

When an air conditioning mode is selected, electrical current is sent to the compressor clutch coil. The clutch plate and the hub assembly is then drawn rearward which engages the pulley. The clutch plate and the pulley are then locked together and act as one unit. This in turn drives the compressor shaft which compresses low pressure refrigerant vapor from the evaporator into high pressure. The compressor also circulates refrigerant oil and refrigerant through the air conditioner system. On certain models, the compressor is equipped with a cut-off solenoid which will shut the compressor off momentarily under certain condi-

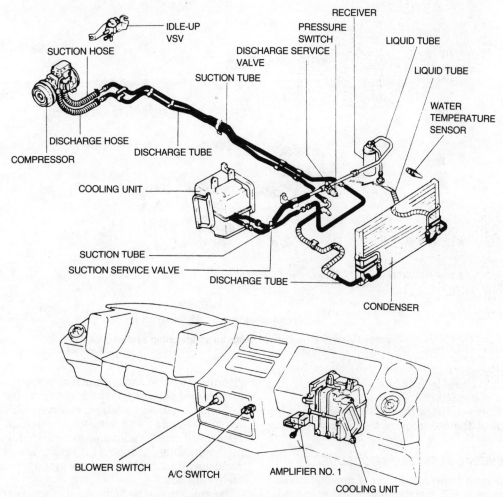

Exploded view of a typical manual air conditioning system

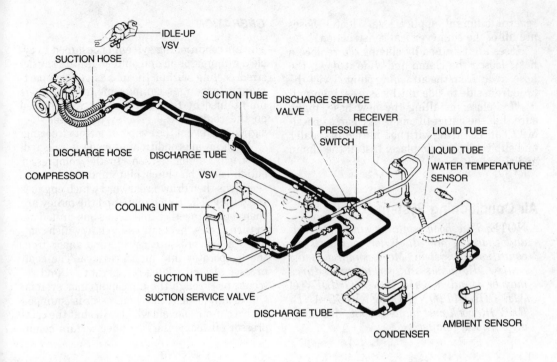

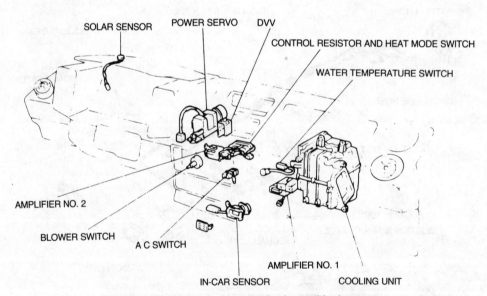

Exploded view of a typical automatic air conditioning system

tions. These include wide-open throttle and low idle speeds.

The switches on the control head are used to control the operation of the air conditioning system.

GENERAL SERVICING PROCEDURES

The most important aspect of air conditioning service is the maintenance of pure and adequate charge of refrigerant in the system. A refrigeration system cannot function properly if a significant percentage of the charge is lost. Leaks are common because the severe vibration encountered in an automobile can easily cause a sufficient cracking or loosening of the air conditioning fittings. As a result, the extreme operating pressures of the system force refrigerant out.

The problem can be understood by considering what happens to the system as it is operated with a continuous leak. Because the expansion valve regulates the flow of refrigerant to the evaporator, the level of refrigerant there is fairly constant. The receiver-drier stores any excess of refrigerant, and so a loss will first appear there as a reduction in the level of liquid. As this level nears the bottom of the vessel, some refrigerant vapor bubbles will begin to appear in the stream of liquid supplied to the expansion valve. This vapor decreases the capacity of the expansion valve very little as the valve opens to compensate for its presence. As the quantity of liquid in the condenser decreases, the operating pressure will drop there and throughout the high side of the system. As the R-12 continues to be expelled, the pressure available to force the liquid through the expansion valve will continue to decrease, and, eventually, the valve's orifice will prove to be too much of a restriction for adequate flow even with the needle fully withdrawn.

At this point, low side pressure will start to drop, and severe reduction in cooling capacity, marked by freeze-up of the evaporator coil, will result. Eventually, the operating pressure of the evaporator will be lower than the pressure of the atmosphere surrounding it, and air will be drawn into the system wherever there are leaks in the low side.

Because all atmospheric air contains at least some moisture, water will enter the system and mix with the R-12 and the oil. Trace amounts of moisture will cause sludging of the oil, and corrosion of the system. Saturation and clogging of the filter-drier, and freezing of the expansion valve orifice will eventually result. As air fills the system to a greater and greater extend, it will interfere more and more with the normal flows of refrigerant and heat.

A list of general precautions that should be observed while doing this follows:

1. Keep all tools as clean and dry as possible.

2. Thoroughly purge the service gauges and hoses of air and moisture before connecting them to the system. Keep them capped when not in use.

3. Thoroughly clean any refrigerant fitting before disconnecting it, in order to minimize the entrance of dirt into the system.

4. Plan any operation that requires opening the system beforehand in order to minimize the length of time it will be exposed to open air. Cap or seal the open ends to minimize the entrance of foreign material.

5. When adding oil, pour it through an extremely clean and dry tube or funnel. Keep the oil capped whenever possible. Do not use oil that has not been kept tightly sealed.

6. Use only refrigerant 12. Purchase refrigerant intended for use in only automotive air conditioning system. Avoid the use of refrigerant 12 that may be packaged for another use, such as cleaning, or powering a horn, as it is impure.

7. Completely evacuate any system that has been opened to replace a component, other than when isolating the compressor, or that has leaked sufficiently to draw in moisture and air. This requires evacuating air and moisture with a good vacuum pump for at least one hour.

If a system has been open for a considerable length of time it may be advisable to evacuate the system for up to 12 hours (overnight).

8. Use a wrench on both halves of a fitting that is to be disconnected, so as to avoid placing torque on any of the refrigerant lines.

ADDITIONAL PREVENTIVE MAINTENANCE CHECKS

Antifreeze

In order to prevent heater core freeze-up during A/C operation, it is necessary to maintain permanent type antifreeze protection of +15°F. or lower. A reading of −15°F. is ideal since this protection also supplies sufficient corrosion inhibitors for the protection of the engine cooling system.

NOTE: *The same antifreeze should not be used longer than the manufacturer specified.*

Radiator Cap

For efficient operation of an air conditioned car's cooling system, the radiator cap should have a holding pressure which meets manufacturer's specifications. A cap which fails to hold these pressure should be replaced.

Condenser

Any obstruction of or damage to the condenser configuration will restrict the air flow which is essential to its efficient operation. It is therefore, a good rule to keep this unit clean and in proper physical shape.

NOTE: *Bug screens are regarded as obstructions.*

Condensation Drain Tube

This single molded drain tube expels the condensation, which accumulates on the bottom of the evaporator housing, into the engine compartment.

If this tube is obstructed, the air conditioning performance can be restricted and condensation buildup can spill over onto the vehicle's floor.

SAFETY PRECAUTIONS

Because of the importance of the necessary safety precautions that must be exercised when working with air conditioning systems and R-12 refrigerant, a recap of the safety precautions are outlined.

1. Avoid contact with a charged refrigeration system, even when working on another part of the air conditioning system or vehicle. If a heavy tool comes into contact with a section of copper tubing or a heat exchanger, it can easily cause the relatively soft material to rupture.

2. When it is necessary to apply force to a fitting which contains refrigerant, as when checking that all system couplings are securely tightened, use a wrench on both parts of the fitting involved, if possible. This will avoid putting torque on refrigerant tubing. (It is advisable, when possible, to use tube or line wrenches when tightening these flare nut fittings.)

3. Do not attempt to discharge the system by merely loosening a fitting, or removing the service valve caps and cracking these valves. Precise control is possibly only when using the service gauges. Place a rag under the open end of the center charging hose while discharging the system to catch any drops of liquid that might escape. Wear protective gloves when connecting or disconnecting service gauge hoses.

4. Discharge the system only in a well ventilated area, as high concentrations of the gas can exclude oxygen and act as an anesthesia. When leak testing or soldering, this is particularly important, as toxic gas is formed when R-12 contacts any flame.

5. Never start a system without first verifying that both service valves are backseated, if equipped, and that all fittings are throughout the system are snugly connected.

6. Avoid applying heat to any refrigerant line or storage vessel. Charging may be aided by using water heated to less than 125°F to warm the refrigerant container. Never allow a refrigerant storage container to sit out in the sun, or near any other source of heat, such as a radiator.

7. Always wear goggles when working on a system to protect the eyes. If refrigerant contacts the eye, it is advisable in all cases to see a physician as soon as possible.

8. Frostbite from liquid refrigerant should be treated by first gradually warming the area with cool water, and then gently applying petroleum jelly. A physician should be consulted.

9. Always keep refrigerant can fittings capped when not in use. Avoid sudden shock to the can which might occur from dropping it, or from banging a heavy tool against it. Never carry a can in the passenger compartment of a car.

10. Always completely discharge the system before painting the vehicle (if the paint is to be baked on), or before welding anywhere near the refrigerant lines.

TEST GAUGES

Most of the service work performed in air conditioning requires the use of a set of two gauges, one for the high (head) pressure side of the system, the other for the low (suction) side.

The low side gauge records both pressure and vacuum. Vacuum readings are calibrated from 0 to 30 inches and the pressure graduations read from 0 to no less than 60 psi.

The high side gauge measures pressure from 0 to at last 600 psi.

Both gauges are threaded into a manifold that contains two hand shut-off valves. Proper

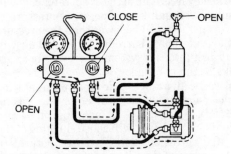

Installation of manifold guages for charging

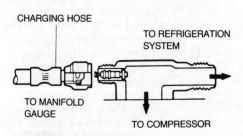

Charging hose connections

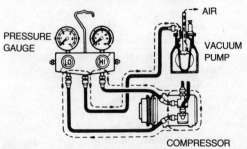

Installation of the A/C manifold guages for evacuation

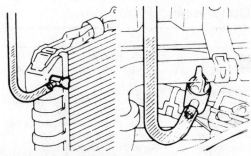

Installing the service hoses

manipulation of these valves and the use of the attached test hoses allow the user to perform the following services:

1. Test high and low side pressures.
2. Remove air, moisture, and contaminated refrigerant.
3. Purge the system (of refrigerant).
4. Charge the system (with refrigerant).

The manifold valves are designed so that they have no direct effect on gauge readings, but serve only to provide for, or cut off, flow of refrigerant through the manifold. During all testing and hook-up operations, the valves are kept in a close position to avoid disturbing the refrigeration system. The valves are opened only to purge the system or refrigerant or to charge it.

INSPECTION

CAUTION: *The compressed refrigerant used in the air conditioning system expands*

into the atmosphere at a temperature of − 21.7°F (−29.833°C) or lower. This will freeze any surface, including your eyes, that it contacts. In addition, the refrigerant decomposes into a poisonous gas in the presence of a flame. Do not open or disconnect any part of the air conditioning system.

Sight Glass Check

You can safely make a few simple checks to determine if your air conditioning system needs service. The tests work best if the temperature is warm (about + 70°F [+21.1°C]).

NOTE: *If your vehicle is equipped with an aftermarket air conditioner, the following system check may not apply. You should contact the manufacturer of the unit for instructions on systems checks.*

1. Place the automatic transmission in Park or the manual transmission in Neutral. Set the parking brake.
2. Run the engine at a fast idle (about 1,500 rpm) either with the help of a friend or by temporarily readjusting the idle speed screw.
3. Set the controls for maximum cold with the blower on High.
4. Locate the sight glass in one of the system lines. Usually it is on the left alongside the top of the radiator.
5. If you see bubbles, the system must be recharged. Very likely there is a leak at some point.
6. If there are no bubbles, there is either no refrigerant at all or the system is fully

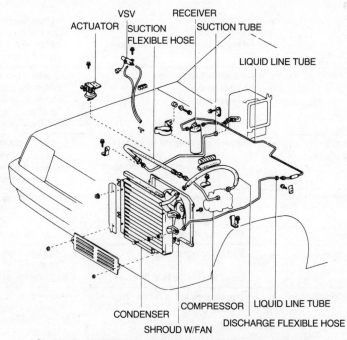

Condenser installation and related components—typical

Troubleshooting Basic Air Conditioning Problems

Problem	Cause	Solution
There's little or no air coming from the vents (and you're sure it's on)	• The A/C fuse is blown • Broken or loose wires or connections • The on/off switch is defective	• Check and/or replace fuse • Check and/or repair connections • Replace switch
The air coming from the vents is not cool enough	• Windows and air vent wings open • The compressor belt is slipping • Heater is on • Condenser is clogged with debris • Refrigerant has escaped through a leak in the system • Receiver/drier is plugged	• Close windows and vent wings • Tighten or replace compressor belt • Shut heater off • Clean the condenser • Check system • Service system
The air has an odor	• Vacuum system is disrupted • Odor producing substances on the evaporator case • Condensation has collected in the bottom of the evaporator housing	• Have the system checked/repaired • Clean the evaporator case • Clean the evaporator housing drains
System is noisy or vibrating	• Compressor belt or mountings loose • Air in the system	• Tighten or replace belt; tighten mounting bolts • Have the system serviced

Sight glass condition
  Constant bubbles, foam or oil streaks
  Clear sight glass, but no cold air
  Clear sight glass, but air is cold
  Clouded with milky fluid
	
	• Undercharged system
	
	• No refrigerant at all
	• System is OK
	• Receiver drier is leaking dessicant
		
		• Charge the system
		
		• Check and charge the system
		
		• Have system checked

Large difference in temperature of lines	• System undercharged	• Charge and leak test the system
Compressor noise	• Broken valves • Overcharged • Incorrect oil level • Piston slap • Broken rings • Drive belt pulley bolts are loose	• Replace the valve plate • Discharge, evacuate and install the correct charge • Isolate the compressor and check the oil level. Correct as necessary. • Replace the compressor • Replace the compressor • Tighten with the correct torque specification
Excessive vibration	• Incorrect belt tension • Clutch loose • Overcharged • Pulley is misaligned	• Adjust the belt tension • Tighten the clutch • Discharge, evacuate and install the correct charge • Align the pulley
Condensation dripping in the passenger compartment	• Drain hose plugged or improperly positioned • Insulation removed or improperly installed	• Clean the drain hose and check for proper installation • Replace the insulation on the expansion valve and hoses
Frozen evaporator coil	• Faulty thermostat • Thermostat capillary tube improperly installed • Thermostat not adjusted properly	• Replace the thermostat • Install the capillary tube correctly • Adjust the thermostat
Low side low—high side low	• System refrigerant is low • Expansion valve is restricted	• Evacuate, leak test and charge the system • Replace the expansion valve
Low side high—high side low	• Internal leak in the compressor—worn	• Remove the compressor cylinder head and inspect the compressor. Replace the valve plate assembly if necessary. If the compressor pistons, rings or

Troubleshooting Basic Air Conditioning Problems (cont.)

Problem	Cause	Solution
Low side high—high side low (cont.)		cylinders are excessively worn or scored replace the compressor
	• Cylinder head gasket is leaking	• Install a replacement cylinder head gasket
	• Expansion valve is defective	• Replace the expansion valve
	• Drive belt slipping	• Adjust the belt tension
Low side high—high side high	• Condenser fins obstructed	• Clean the condenser fins
	• Air in the system	• Evacuate, leak test and charge the system
	• Expansion valve is defective	• Replace the expansion valve
	• Loose or worn fan belts	• Adjust or replace the belts as necessary
Low side low—high side high	• Expansion valve is defective	• Replace the expansion valve
	• Restriction in the refrigerant hose	• Check the hose for kinks—replace if necessary
	• Restriction in the receiver/drier	• Replace the receiver/drier
	• Restriction in the condenser	• Replace the condenser
Low side and high side normal (inadequate cooling)	• Air in the system	• Evacuate, leak test and charge the system
	• Moisture in the system	• Evacuate, leak test and charge the system

charged. Feel the two hoses going to the belt-driven compressor. If they are both at the same temperature, the system is empty and must be recharged.

7. If one hose (high-pressure) is warm and the other (low-pressure) is cold, the system may be all right. However, you are probably making these tests because you think there is something wrong, so proceed to the next step.

8. Have an assistant in the car turn the fan control on and off to operate the compressor clutch. Watch the sight glass.

9. If bubbles appear when the clutch is disengaged and disappear when it is engaged, the system is properly charged.

10. If the refrigerant takes more than 45 seconds to bubble when the clutch is disengaged, the system is overcharged. This usually causes poor cooling at low speeds.

CAUTION: *If it is determined that the system has a leak, it should be corrected as soon as possible. Leaks may allow moisture to enter and cause a very expensive rust problem.*

NOTE: *Exercise the air conditioner for a few minutes, every two weeks or so, during the cold months. This avoids the possibility of the compressor seals drying out from lack of lubrication.*

TESTING THE SYSTEM

1. Connect a gauge set.
2. Close (clockwise) both gauge set valves.
3. Mid-position both service valves.
4. Park the car in the shade. Start the en-gine, set the parking brake, place the transmission in NEUTRAL and establish an idle of 1,500 rpm.

5. Run the air conditioning system for full cooling, but NOT in the MAX or COLD mode.

6. Insert a thermometer into the center air outlet.

7. Use the accompanying performance chart for a specifications reference. If pressures are abnormal, refer to the accompanying Pressure Diagnosis Chart.

ISOLATING THE COMPRESSOR

On cars with service valves, it is not necessary to discharge the system for compressor removal. The compressor can be isolated from the rest of the system, eliminating the need for recharging.

1. Connect a manifold gauge set.

2. Close both gauge hand valves and mid-position (crack) both compressor service valves.

3. Start the engine and turn on the air conditioning.

4. Turn the compressor suction valve slowly clockwise towards the front-seated position. When the suction pressure drops to zero, stop the engine and turn off the air conditioning. Quickly front-seat the valve completely.

5. Front-seat the discharge service valve.

6. Loosen the oil level check plug to remove any internal pressure.

The compressor is now isolated and the service valves can now be removed.

AIR CONDITIONING CHARGING LOCATIONS

The low pressure service hose is connected to the suction service valve on the compressor, while the high pressure hose is connected to the discharge service valve.

DISCHARGING PROCEDURE

1. Connect the red charging hose (high pressure side) of the manifold gauge to the service valve on the liquid line. Connect the blue charging hose (low pressure side) to the suction line.

2. Place the free end of the center hose into a suitable closed container.

3. Slowly open the high pressure hand valve to adjust the refrigerant flow. Open the valve slightly.

NOTE: *If refrigerant is allowed to escape too fast, compressor oil will be drawn out of the system.*

4. Check the container to make sure no oil is being discharged. If there is oil present, partially close the hand valve.

5. After the manifold gauge reading drops below 50 psi, slowly open the low pressure valve.

6. As the system pressure drops, gradually open both high and low valves until both gauges read 0 psi.

EVACUATING AND CHARGING PROCEDURE

1. Connect the manifold gauge set to the compressor according to the manufacturers instructions.

2. Connect the center hose to the vacuum pump inlet.

3. Turn the vacuum pump on and open both hand valves.

4. Allow the vacuum pump to operate for approximately 10 minutes. Check that the low pressure gauge reads more than 600mm Hg (23.62 in. Hg. 80.0 kPa) of vacuum.

NOTE: *If the reading on the gauges is not more than 600 mmHg, close both valves and shut off the vacuum pump. Inspect the system for leaks and repair as necessary.*

5. After the low pressure gauge show a vacuum of more than 700mm Hg, continue evacuating for approximately 15 minutes.

6. Close the manifold gauge valves and shut off the vacuum pump.

7. Install the refrigerant container tap valve.

8. Connect the center hose to the valve fitting.

9. Turn the handle clockwise to make a hole in the sealed tap.

10. Turn the handle fully counterclockwise to fill the center hose with air. Do not open the high and low pressure valves.

11. Loosen the center hose nut connected to center fitting of the manifold gauge until a hiss can be heard. Allow air to escape for a few seconds, and then tighten the nut.

NOTE: *After finishing the evacuation of the system, check the system for leaks.*

12. Install the refrigerant can tap valve.

13. Open the high pressure valve to charge the system with refrigerant vapor.

14. When the low pressure gauge reads 1 kg/cm^2 (14 psi), close the high pressure valve.

15. Using the halide gas leak detector, propane torch, or electric leak detector, check the system for leaks. If a leak is found, repair the faulty component or connection.

LEAK TESTING

Some leak tests can be performed with a soapy water solution. There must be at least a ½lb charge in the system for a leak to be detected. The most extensive leak tests are performed with either a Halide flame type leak tester or the more preferable electronic leak tester.

In either case, the equipment is expensive, and, the use of a Halide detector can be **extremely** hazardous!

Cooling System

Dealing with the cooling system can be a dangerous matter unless the proper precautions are observed. It is best to check the coolant level in the radiator when the engine is cold. This is done by removing the radiator cap, on models without an expansion tank, and seeing that the coolant is within two inches of the bottom of the filler neck. On models with an expansion tank, if coolant visible above the MIN mark on the tank, the level is satisfactory. Always be certain that the filler caps on both the radiator and the reservoir are tightly closed.

CAUTION: *When draining the coolant, keep in mind that cats and dogs are attracted by the ethylene glycol antifreeze, and are quite likely to drink any that is left in an uncovered container or in puddles on the ground. This will prove fatal in sufficient quantity. Always drain the coolant into a sealable container. Coolant should be reused unless it is contaminated or several years old.*

In the event that the coolant level must be checked when the engine is warm on engines without the expansion tank, place a thick rag over the radiator cap and slowly turn the cap counterclockwise until it reaches the first detent. Allow all the hot steam to escape. This will allow the pressure in the system to drop

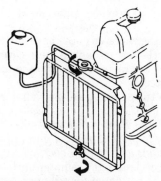

Open the radiator cap and radiator drain petcock to change the coolant

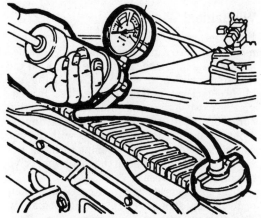

Pressurize the cooling system with the special tool shown to check for leaks

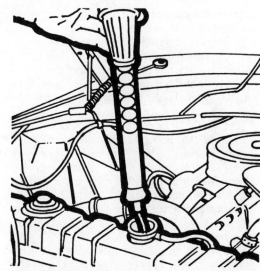

Coolant protection quality can be checked with an inexpensive float-type tester

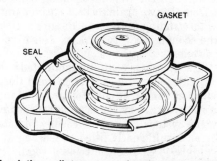

Check the radiator cap seal and gasket condition

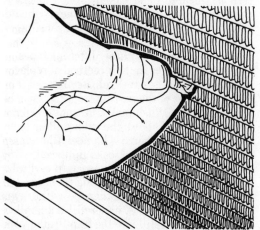

Clean the radiator fins of any debris which impedes air flow

gradually, preventing an explosion of hot coolant. When the hissing noise stops, remove the cap the rest of the way.

If the coolant level is low, add equal amounts of ethylene glycol based antifreeze and clean water. On models without an expansion tank, add coolant through the radiator filler neck. Fill the expansion tank to the MAX level on cars with that system.

CAUTION: *Never add cold coolant to a hot engine unless the engine is running, to avoid cracking the engine block.*

If the coolant level is chronically low or rusty, refer to the Troubleshooting chapter for diagnosis of the problem.

The radiator hoses and clamps and the radiator cap should be checked at the same time as the coolant level. Hoses which are brittle, cracked, or swollen should be replaced. Clamps should be checked for tightness (screwdriver tight only. Do not allow the clamp to cut into the hose or crush the fitting). The radiator cap gasket should be checked for any obvious tears, cracks or swelling, or any signs of incorrect seating in the radiator neck.

COOLANT CHANGES

Once every 24 months or 24,000 miles, the cooling system should be drained, thoroughly flushed, and refilled. This should be done with the engine cold.

1. Remove the radiator cap.

2. There are usually two drain plugs in the cooling system; one at the bottom of the radiator and one at the rear of the driver's side of the engine. Both should be loosened to allow the coolant to drain.

CAUTION: *When draining the coolant, keep in mind that cats and dogs are attracted by the ethylene glycol antifreeze, and are quite likely to drink any that is left in an uncovered container or in puddles on the ground. This will prove fatal in sufficient quantity. Always drain the coolant into a sealable container. Coolant should be reused unless it is contaminated or several years old.*

3. Turn on the heater inside the car to its hottest position. This ensures that the heater core is flushed out completely. Flush out the system thoroughly by refilling it with clean water through the radiator opening as it escapes from the two drain cocks. Continue until the water running out is clear. Be sure to clean out the coolant recovery tank as well if your car has one.

4. If the system is badly contaminated with rust or scale, you can use a commercial flushing solution to clear it out. Follow the manufacturer's instructions. Some causes of rust are air in the system, caused by a leaky radiator cap or an insufficiently filled or leaking system; failure to change the coolant regularly; use of excessively hard or soft water; and failure to use a proper mix of antifreeze and water.

5. When the system is clear, allow all the water to drain, then close the drain plugs. Fill the system through the radiator with a 50/50 mix of ethylene glycol type antifreeze and water.

6. Start the engine and top off the radiator with the antifreeze and water mixture. If your car has a coolant recovery tank, fill it half full with the coolant mix.

7. Replace the radiator and coolant tank caps, and check for leaks. When the engine has reached normal operating temperature, shut it off, allow it to cool, then top off the radiator or coolant tank as necessary.

Cooling System Bleeding

Procedure

CAUTION: *Do not remove the radiator cap while the engine and radiator are still hot. A sudden release of the cooling system pressure may cause the coolant to boil over causing personal injury.*

1. With the engine shut off, add sufficient coolant which provides corrosion and freezing protection.

2. Fill the radiator to the base of the radiator fill neck. Add coolant to the recovery tank as required to raise the level to the full mark as indicated.

3. Run the engine with the radiator cap removed until the upper hoses becomes hot.

CAUTION: *Rubber insulated gloves should be worn to prevent personal injury from any hot coolant which could overflow.*

4. Add coolant to the radiator until the level reaches the bottom of the fill neck.

5. Install the radiator cap after coolant bubbling subsides.

Windshield Wipers

For maximum effectiveness and longest element life, the windshield and wiper blades should be kept clean. Dirt, tree sap, road tar and so on will cause streaking, smearing and blade deterioration if left on the glass. It is advisable to wash the windshield carefully with a commercial glass cleaner at least once a month. Wipe off the rubber blades with the wet rag afterwards. Do not attempt to move the wipers by hand; damage to the motor and drive mechanism will result.

If the blades are found to be cracked, broken or torn, they should be replaced immediately. Replacement intervals will vary with usage, although ozone deterioration usually limits blade life to about one year. If the wiper pattern is smeared or streaked, or if the blade chatters across the glass, the elements should be replaced. It is easiest and most sensible to replace the elements in pairs.

There are basically three different types of refills, which differ in their method of replacement. One type has two release buttons, approximately ⅓ of the way up from the ends of the blade frame. Pushing the buttons down releases a lock and allows the rubber filler to be removed from the frame. The new filler slides back into the frame and locks in place.

The second type of refill has two metal tabs which are unlocked by squeezing them together. The rubber filler can then be withdrawn from the frame jaws. A new refill is installed by inserting the refill into the front frame jaws and sliding it rearward to engage the remaining frame jaws. There are usually four jaws, be certain when installing that the refill is engaged in all of them. At the end of its travel, the tabs will lock into place on the front jaws of the wiper blade frame.

The third type is a refill made from polycarbonate. The refill has a simple locking device at one end which flexes downward out of the

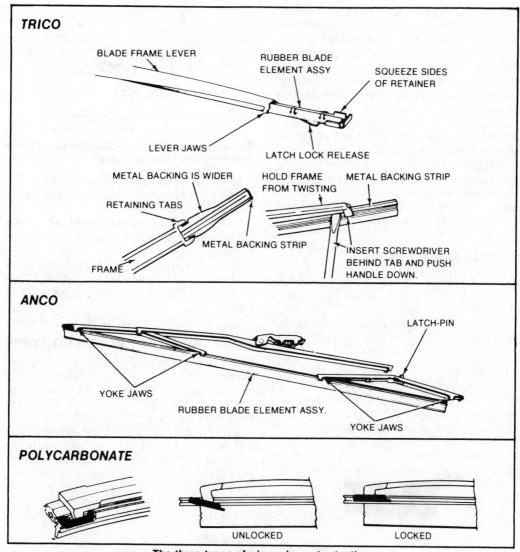

TRICO

BLADE FRAME LEVER

RUBBER BLADE ELEMENT ASSY

SQUEEZE SIDES OF RETAINER

LEVER JAWS

LATCH LOCK RELEASE

METAL BACKING IS WIDER

HOLD FRAME FROM TWISTING

METAL BACKING STRIP

RETAINING TABS

METAL BACKING STRIP

FRAME

INSERT SCREWDRIVER BEHIND TAB AND PUSH HANDLE DOWN.

ANCO

LATCH-PIN

YOKE JAWS

RUBBER BLADE ELEMENT ASSY.

YOKE JAWS

POLYCARBONATE

UNLOCKED

LOCKED

The three types of wiper element retention

groove into which the jaws of the holder fit, allowing easy release. By sliding the new refill through all the jaws and pushing through the slight resistance when it reaches the end of its travel, the refill will lock into position. Regardless of the type of refill used, make sure that all of the frame jaws are engaged as the refill is pushed into place and locked. The metal blade holder and frame will scratch the glass if allowed to touch it.

Fluid Level Checks
ENGINE OIL

The engine oil level should be checked at regular intervals; for example, whenever the car is refueled. Check the oil level, if the red oil

warning light comes on or if the oil pressure gauge shows an abnormally low reading.

It is preferable to check the oil level when the engine is cold or after the car has been

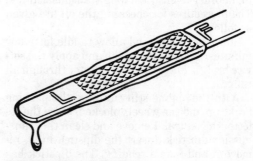

Typical engine oil dipstick

standing for a while. Checking the oil immediately after the engine has been running will result in a false reading. Be sure that the car is on a level surface before checking the oil level.

Remove the dipstick and wipe it with a clean rag. Insert it again (fully) and withdraw it. The oil level should be a at the F mark (Full) or between the F and the L (Low) marks. Do not run the engine if the oil level is below the L.

Add oil, as necessary. Use only oil which carries the API designation SF.

CAUTION: *Do not use unlabeled oil or a lower grade of oil which does not meet SF specifications.*

See the chart in the lubrication section of this chapter for proper oil viscosities. Do not overfill.

MANUAL TRANSMISSION

The oil in the manual transmission should be checked every 30,000 miles or 24 months, whichever occurs first.

To check the oil level, remove the transmission filler plug. This is always the upper plug, the lower plug being the drain.

The oil level should reach the bottom of the filler plug. If it is lower than this, add API grade GL-4 SAE 90 oil.

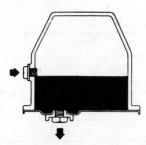

Manual transmission oil level should be up to the bottom of the filler (upper) plug

AUTOMATIC TRANSMISSION

Check the level of the transmission fluid every 3,000 miles and replace it every 30,000 miles. It is important that these figures be adhered to, in order to ensure a long transmission life. The procedures for checking the oil are given as follows:

Start the engine and allow to idle for a few minutes. Set the handbrake and apply the service brakes. Move the gear selector through all ranges.

With the engine still running, the parking brake on and the wheels blocked, place the selector in Neutral. Remove and clean the transmission dipstick. Insert the dipstick fully, remove it and take a reading. The dipstick has two ranges.

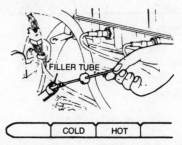

Three-speed automatic transmission dipstick location—insert shows ranges

1. COLD The fluid level should fall in this range when the engine has been running for only a short time.
2. HOT The fluid level should fall in this range when the engine has reached normal running temperatures.
3. Replenish the fluid through the filler tube with type F fluid, to the top of the COLD or HOT range, depending upon engine temperature.

CAUTION: *Do not overfill the transmission.*

BRAKE AND CLUTCH MASTER CYLINDERS

The brake and clutch (manual transmission) master cylinder reservoirs are made of a translucent plastic so that the fluid level can be checked without removing the cap. Check the fluid level frequently.

If the fluid is low, fill the reservoir with DOT 3 fluid, pouring so bubbles do not form in the reservoir. Use care not to spill any fluid on the car's paint, damage may result.

CAUTION: *Do not use a lower grade of brake fluid and never mix different types. Either could result in a brake system failure.*

COOLANT

The coolant level should be checked at least once a week or when the temperature gauge registers HOT (H).

CAUTION: *Allow the engine to cool before removing the radiator cap.*

Because the cooling system is under pressure, check the coolant level with the engine cold to prevent injury from high pressure, hot water.

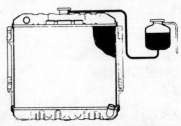

Check the coolant level in the expansion tank on models with a closed cooling system

The level should be ¾″ below the filler neck, when the engine is cold. Replenish with clean, non-alkaline water. If antifreeze is being added, use a type approved for aluminum (ethylene glycol). Most Toyota models have alloy heads.

CAUTION: *Never add cold water to a hot engine; damage to the cooling system and engine block could result.*

Some models are equipped with a closed cooling system, with a tube running from the radiator to a thermal expansion tank. On these models, check the level of the coolant in the expansion tank. The main radiator cap should only be removed when cleaning or draining the cooling system or if the expansion tank is empty.

CAUTION: *The cap on the main radiator is not a pressure/vacuum safety cap. Never remove it when the engine is hot. Severe injury could result.*

The expansion tank should be about ¾ full or coolant should reach the FULL mark. Add coolant as outlined.

NOTE: *The bottom plug is the drain.*

The oil level should reach to the bottom edge of the filler hole. If low, replenish with API grade GL-5 gear oil of the proper viscosity. The viscosity is determined by the ambient temperature range. If the temperature averages above 10° F, use SAE 90 gear oil. If the temperature averages below 10°F, use SAE 80 oil. Always check for leaks when checking the oil level.

POWER STEERING RESERVOIR

Check the level of the power steering fluid periodically. The fluid level should fall within the crosshatched area of the gauge attached to the reservoir cap. If the fluid level is below this, add DEXRON®II ATF fluid. Remember to check for leaks.

BATTERY

Check the electrolyte level in the battery frequently. The level should be between the upper and lower level lines marked on the battery case or just to the bottom of the filler well, depending on type. Use distilled water to correct the electrolyte level.

CAUTION: *Do not overfill the battery. It could leak and damage the car finish and battery bracket.*

Tires

INFLATION PRESSURE

Tire inflation is the most ignored item of auto maintenance. Gasoline mileage can drop as

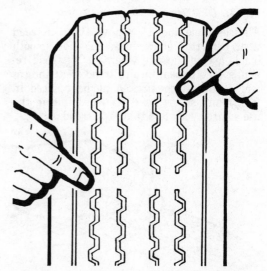

Tread wear indicators will appear when the tire is worn out

much as 0.8% for every 1 pound per square inch (psi of under inflation.

Two items should be a permanent fixture in every glove compartment; a tire pressure gauge and a tread depth gauge. Check the tire air pressure (including the spare regularly with a pocket type gauge. Kicking the tires won't tell you a thing, and the gauge on the service station air hose is notoriously inaccurate.

The tire pressures recommended for your care are usually found on the glove box door, on the door jam, or in the owners manual. Ideally, inflation pressure should be checked when the tires are cool. When the air becomes heated it expands and the pressure increases. Every 10 degree rise (or drop) in temperature means a difference of 1 psi, which also explains why the tire appears to lose air on a very cold night. When it is impossible to check the tires cold, allow for pressure build-up due to heat. If the hot pressure exceeds the cold pressure by more than 15 psi, reduce your speed, load or both. Otherwise internal heat is created in the tire. When the heat approaches the temperature at which the tire was cured, during manufacture, the tread can separate from the body.

CAUTION: *Never counteract excessive pressure build-up by bleeding off air pressure (letting some air out). This will only further raise the tire operating temperature.*

Before starting a long trip with lots of luggage, you can add about 2–4 psi to the tires to make them run cooler, but never exceed the maximum inflation pressure on the side of the tire.

TREAD DEPTH

All tires made since 1968, have 8 built-in tread wear bars that show up as ½″ wide smooth bands across the tire when $\frac{1}{16}″$ of tread remains. The appearance of tread wear indicators means that the tires should be replaced. In fact, many states have laws prohibiting the use of tires with less than $\frac{1}{16}″$ tread.

Tread depth can also be checked with an inexpensive gauge

A penny works as well as anything for checking tread depth; when the top of Lincoln's head is visible, it's time for new tires

You can check your own tread depth with an inexpensive gauge or by using a Lincoln head penny. Slip the Lincoln penny into several tread grooves. If you can see the top of Lincoln's head in 2 adjacent grooves, the tires have less than $\frac{1}{16}″$ tread left and should be replaced. You can measure snow tires in the same manner by using the tails side of the Lincoln penny. If you can see the top of the Lincoln memorial, it's time to replace the snow tires.

TIRE ROTATION

Tire wear can be equalized by switching the position of the tires about every 6000 miles. Including a conventional spare in the rotation pattern can give up to 20% more tire life.

CAUTION: *Do not include the new Space-Saver or temporary spare tires in the rotation pattern.*

There are certain exceptions to tire rotation, however. Studded snow tires should not be rotated, and radials should be kept on the same side of the car (maintain the same direction of rotation). The belts on radial tires get set in a pattern. If the direction of rotation is reversed, it can cause rough ride and vibration.

NOTE: *When radials or studded snows are taken off the car, mark them, so you can maintain the same direction of rotation.*

TIRE STORAGE

Store the tires at proper inflation pressures if they are mounted on wheels. All tires should be kept in a cool, dry place. If they are stored in the garage or basement, do not let them stand on a concrete floor; set them on strips of wood.

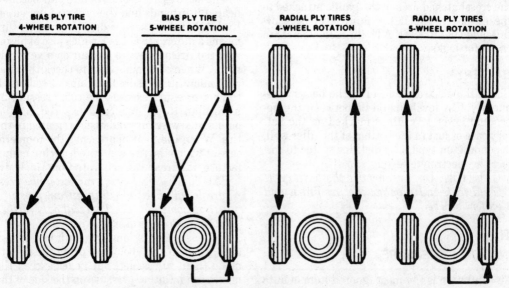

Tire rotation diagrams; note that radials should not be cross-switched

Troubleshooting Basic Tire Problems

Problem	Cause	Solution
The car's front end vibrates at high speeds and the steering wheel shakes	• Wheels out of balance • Front end needs aligning	• Have wheels balanced • Have front end alignment checked
The car pulls to one side while cruising	• Unequal tire pressure (car will usually pull to the low side) • Mismatched tires • Front end needs aligning	• Check/adjust tire pressure • Be sure tires are of the same type and size • Have front end alignment checked
Abnormal, excessive or uneven tire wear See "How to Read Tire Wear"	• Infrequent tire rotation • Improper tire pressure • Sudden stops/starts or high speed on curves	• Rotate tires more frequently to equalize wear • Check/adjust pressure • Correct driving habits
Tire squeals	• Improper tire pressure • Front end needs aligning	• Check/adjust tire pressure • Have front end alignment checked

Tire Size Comparison Chart

"Letter" sizes			Inch Sizes	Metric-inch Sizes		
"60 Series"	"70 Series"	"78 Series"	1965–77	"60 Series"	"70 Series"	"80 Series"
		Y78-12	5.50-12, 5.60-12 6.00-12	165/60-12	165/70-12	155-12
		W78-13	5.20-13	165/60-13	145/70-13	135-13
		Y78-13	5.60-13	175/60-13	155/70-13	145-13
			6.15-13	185/60-13	165/70-13	155-13, P155/80-13
A60-13	A70-13	A78-13	6.40-13	195/60-13	175/70-13	165-13
B60-13	B70-13	B78-13	6.70-13	205/60-13	185/70-13	175-13
			6.90-13			
C60-13	C70-13	C78-13	7.00-13	215/60-13	195/70-13	185-13
D60-13	D70-13	D78-13	7.25-13			
E60-13	E70-13	E78-13	7.75-13			195-13
			5.20-14	165/60-14	145/70-14	135-14
			5.60-14	175/60-14	155/70-14	145-14
			5.90-14			
A60-14	A70-14	A78-14	6.15-14	185/60-14	165/70-14	155-14
	B70-14	B78-14	6.45-14	195/60-14	175/70-14	165-14
	C70-14	C78-14	6.95-14	205/60-14	185/70-14	175-14
D60-14	D70-14	D78-14				
E60-14	E70-14	E78-14	7.35-14	215/60-14	195/70-14	185-14
F60-14	F70-14	F78-14, F83-14	7.75-14	225/60-14	200/70-14	195-14
G60-14	G70-14	G77-14, G78-14	8.25-14	235/60-14	205/70-14	205-14
H60-14	H70-14	H78-14	8.55-14	245/60-14	215/70-14	215-14
J60-14	J70-14	J78-14	8.85-14	255/60-14	225/70-14	225-14
L60-14	L70-14		9.15-14	265/60-14	235/70-14	
	A70-15	A78-15	5.60-15	185/60-15	165/70-15	155-15
B60-15	B70-15	B78-15	6.35-15	195/60-15	175/70-15	165-15
C60-15	C70-15	C78-15	6.85-15	205/60-15	185/70-15	175-15
	D70-15	D78-15				
E60-15	E70-15	E78-15	7.35-15	215/60-15	195/70-15	185-15
F60-15	F70-15	F78-15	7.75-15	225/60-15	205/70-15	195-15
G60-15	G70-15	G78-15	8.15-15/8.25-15	235/60-15	215/70-15	205-15
H60-15	H70-15	H78-15	8.45-15/8.55-15	245/60-15	225/70-15	215-15
J60-15	J70-15	J78-15	8.85-15/8.90-15	255/60-15	235/70-15	225-15
	K70-15		9.00-15	265/60-15	245/70-15	230-15
L60-15	L70-15	L78-15, L84-15	9.15-15			235-15
	M70-15	M78-15				255-15
		N78-15				

Note: Every size tire is not listed and many size comparisons are approximate, based on load ratings. Wider tires than those supplied new with the vehicle, should always be checked for clearance.

Troubleshooting Basic Wheel Problems

Problem	Cause	Solution
The car's front end vibrates at high speed	• The wheels are out of balance • Wheels are out of alignment	• Have wheels balanced • Have wheel alignment checked/adjusted
Car pulls to either side	• Wheels are out of alignment • Unequal tire pressure • Different size tires or wheels	• Have wheel alignment checked/adjusted • Check/adjust tire pressure • Change tires or wheels to same size
The car's wheel(s) wobbles	• Loose wheel lug nuts • Wheels out of balance • Damaged wheel • Wheels are out of alignment • Worn or damaged ball joint • Excessive play in the steering linkage (usually due to worn parts) • Defective shock absorber	• Tighten wheel lug nuts • Have tires balanced • Raise car and spin the wheel. If the wheel is bent, it should be replaced • Have wheel alignment checked/adjusted • Check ball joints • Check steering linkage • Check shock absorbers
Tires wear unevenly or prematurely	• Incorrect wheel size • Wheels are out of balance • Wheels are out of alignment	• Check if wheel and tire size are compatible • Have wheels balanced • Have wheel alignment checked/adjusted

Fuel Filter

CAUTION: *The pressure in the fuel system must be bled before removal of filter. Do not smoke while servicing the fuel filter. Vapors trapped in it could ignite.*

REMOVAL AND INSTALLATION

This filter should be replaced every 30,000 miles or 2 years, or if the filter appears clogged or dirty.

1. Place a drain pan under the fuel filter to catch the gasoline.

2. Slowly loosen the lower fitting (or the one coming from the fuel tank) on the fuel fitting.

3. After the pressure and the gasoline has bled off, remove and replace the filter in the normal manner.

4. Remove the hose clamps from the inlet and outlet hoses.

5. Work the hoses off the filter necks.

6. Snap the filter out of its bracket.

4. Installation is performed in the reverse order of removal. Be sure to install the filter in the proper direction. The arrow on top should point toward the engine.

LUBRICATION

Oil Recommendation

Use a good quality motor oil of a known brand, which carries the API classification SF. The

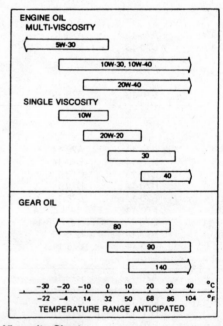

Oil Viscosity Chart

proper viscosity of the oil depends on the climate and temperature your car is operated in.

CAUTION: *Do not use unlabeled oil or a lower grade of oil which does not meet SF specifications. If 5W, 10W, or 5W-20 oil is used, avoid prolonged high-speed driving.*

Change the oil at the intervals recommended. If the vehicle is being used in severe service such as trailer towing, change the oil at more frequent intervals.

It is especially important that the oil be changed at the proper intervals in emission controlled engines, as they run hotter than non-controlled, thus causing the oil to break down faster.

Fuel Recommendations

All Camry models are equipped with a catalytic converter and, therefore, must use unleaded gasoline.

Oil Changes

ENGINE

The oil should be changed at the intervals specified. The amount of oil required for each engine and model may be found in the Capacities chart.

NOTE: *All new cars should have an oil change after the first 1,000 miles. The filter should also be changed at this time.*

To change the oil, proceed in the following manner:

1. Warm the oil by running the engine for a short period of time; this will make the oil flow more freely from the oil pan.

2. Park on a level surface and put on the parking brake. Stop the engine. Remove the oil filler cap from the top of the valve cover.

3. Place a pan of adequate capacity below the drain plug.

NOTE: *If the crankcase holds five quarts, a two quart mile container will not be suitable. A large flat pan makes a good container to catch oil.*

4. Use a wrench of the proper size (not pliers) to remove the drain plug. Loosen the drain plug while maintaining a slight upward force on it to keep the oil from running out around it. Allow the oil to fully drain into the container under the drain hole.

5. Remove the container used to catch the oil and wipe any excess oil from the area around the hole.

6. Install the drain plug, complete with its gasket. Be sure that the plug is tight enough that the oil does not leak out, but not tight enough to strip the threads.

NOTE: *Replace the drain plug gasket at every fourth oil change with a new one.*

7. Add clean, new oil of the proper grade and viscosity through the oil filler on the top of the valve cover. Be sure that the oil level registers near the F (full) mark on the dipstick.

All Camrys use a spin-off oil filter. Thise should be changed at the first 1,000 mile oil

Remove the oil filter with a strap wrench

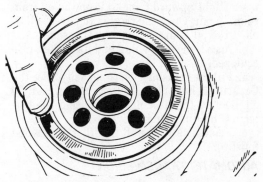

Coat the new oil filter gasket with clean oil

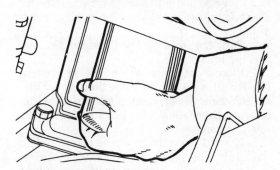

Install the new filter by hand

change and at the interval specified. The filter should be replaced during the engine oil change procedure. To replace the filter, proceed as follows:

1. Drain the engine oil as previously outlined. Place a container under the oil filter to catch any excess oil.

2. Use a spin-off (band) wrench to remove the filter unit. Turn the filter counterclockwise in order to remove it.

3. Wipe off the filter bracket with a clean rag.

4. Install a new filter and gasket, after first lubricating the gasket with clean engine oil.

CAUTION: *Do not use the wrench to tighten the filter. Tighten it by hand.*

5. Add engine oil as previously outlined in the appropriate section. Check for leaks.

MANUAL TRANSMISSION

The transmission oil should be replaced every 30,000 miles or 24 months, whichever occurs first. To change the transmission oil, proceed as follows:

1. Park the car on a level surface and put on the parking brake.
2. Remove the oil filler (upper) plug.
3. Place a container, of a large enough capacity to catch all of the oil, under the drain (lower) plug. Use the proper size wrench to loosen the drain plug slowly, while maintaining a slight upward force to keep the oil from running out. Once the plug is removed, allow all of the oil to drain from the transmission.
4. Install the drain plug and its gasket, if so equipped.
5. Fill the transmission to capacity. (See the Capacities chart.) Use API grade GL4 SAE 90 oil. Be sure that the oil level reaches the bottom of the filler plug.
6. Remember to install the filler plug when finished.

AUTOMATIC TRANSMISSION

Change the fluid in the automatic transmission every 30,000 miles or 25 months, whichever occurs first. To change the fluid, proceed as follows:

1. Park the car on a level surface. Set the parking brake.
2. Place a container, which is large enough to catch all of the transmission fluid, under the transmission oil pan drain plug. Unfasten the drain plug and allow all of the fluid to run out into the container.
3. Check the condition of the transmission fluid. If it is burnt, discolored, or has particles in it, the transmission needs to be overhauled. Consult your local Toyota dealer.
4. Install the drain plug in the transmission oil pan. Be sure that it is tight enough to prevent leakage, but not tight enough to strip the threads.
    CAUTION: *Fill the transmission with DEXRON®II ATF.*
5. Fill the transmission through the filler tube, after removing the dipstick, with DEXRON®II ATF fluid.
    NOTE: *It may be a good idea to fill to less than the recommended capacity (see the Capacities chart) as some of the fluid will remain in the torque converter.*
6. Start the engine and check the transmission fluid level, as outlined under Fluid Level Checks. Add fluid, if necessary, but do not overfill.

Chassis Greasing

The chassis lubrication for these models is limited to lubricating the front ball joints every

Ball joint grease fitting

30,000 miles or 24 months, whichever occurs first. To lubricate the ball joints, proceed as follows:

1. Remove the screw plug from the ball joint. Install a grease nipple.
2. Using a hand-operated grease gun, lubricate the ball joint with NGLI No. 1 molybdenum-disulphide lithium-based grease.
    CAUTION: *Do not use multipurpose or chassis grease.*
3. Remove the nipple and reinstall the screw plug.
4. Repeat for the other ball joint(s).

Body Lubrication

There is no set period recommended by Toyota for body lubrication. However, it is a good idea to lubricate the following body points at least once a year, especially in the fall before cold weather.

Lubricate with engine oil:
    Door lock latches
    Door lock rollers
    Station wagon tailgate hinges
    Door, hood, and hinge pivots
Lubricate with Lubricate:
    Trunk lid latch and hinge
    Glove box door latch
Lubricate with silicone spray:
    All rubber weather stripping
    Hood stops

When finished lubricating a body part, be sure that all the excess lubricant has been wiped off, especially in the areas of the car which may come in contact with clothing.

Wheel Bearings

Refer to the appropriate section in Chapter 9 for wheel bearing assembly and packing procedures.

PUSHING

Push-start a car with manual transmission when the engine will not turn over; do not attempt to start the car by towing it.

CAUTION: *If the car is tow-started, it may run into the back of the towing vehicle when it starts.*

To push-start the car, turn the ignition switch to ON. Fully depress the clutch pedal and shift into Second or Third gear. When the car reaches 10 mph, let the clutch pedal up slowly until the engine catches.

NOTE: *It is impossible to push-start models equipped with automatic transmission.*

JACKING

There are certain safety precautions which should be observed when jacking the vehicle. They are as follows:

1. Always jack the car on a level surface.
2. Set the parking brake if the front wheels are to be raised. This will keep the car from rolling backward off the jack.
3. If the rear wheels are to be raised, block the front wheels to keep the car from rolling forward.
4. Block the wheel diagonally opposite the one which is being raised.

NOTE: *The tool which is supplied with Toyota passenger cars includes a wheel block.*

5. If the vehicle is being raised in order to work underneath it, support it with jackstands. Do not place the jackstands against the sheet metal panels beneath the car or they will become distorted.

CAUTION: *Do not work beneath a vehicle supported only by a tire-changing jack.*

6. Do not use a bumper jack to raise the vehicle; the bumpers are not designed for this purpose.

HOW TO BUY A USED CAR

Many people believe that a two or three year old, or older, car is a better buy than a new one. This may be true. The new car suffers the heaviest depreciation in the first few years, but is not old enough to present a lot of costly repairs. Whatever the age of the used car you want to buy, this section and a little patience will help you select one that should be safe and dependable.

Shopping Tips

1. First, decide what model you want and how much you want to spend.
2. Check the used car lots and your local newspaper ads. Privately owned cars are usually less expensive, however, you will not get a warranty that, in most cases, comes with a used car purchased from a dealer.

3. Never shop at night. The glare of the lights makes it easy to miss defects in the paint and faults in the body caused by accident or rust repair.
4. Once you've found a car that you're interested in, try to get the name and phone number of the previous owner. Contact that person for details about the car. If he or she refuses information about the car, shop elsewhere. A private seller can tell you about the car and its maintenance history, but there are few laws requiring honesty from private citizens who are selling used vehicles. There are laws forbidding the tampering with or turning back a vehicle's odometer mileage reading. These laws apply to both a private seller as well commercial dealers. The law also requires that the seller, or anyone transferring ownership of a vehicle, must provide the buyer with a signed statement indicating the mileage on the odometer at the time of transfer.
5. Write down the year, model and serial number of the car before you buy it. Then, dial 1–800–424–9393, the toll-free number of the National Highway Traffic Safety Administration, and ask if the car has ever been included on any manufacturer's recall list. If so, make sure the necessary repairs were made.
6. Use the Used Car Checklist in this section, and check all the items on the used car that you are considering. Some items are more important than others. You've already determined how much money you can afford for repairs, and, depending on the price of the car, you should consider doing some of the needed repairs yourself. Beware, however, of trouble in areas involving operation, safety or emissions. Problems in the Used Car Checklist are arranged as follows:

1–8: Two or more problems in this segment indicate a lack of maintenance. You should reconsider your selection.

9–13: Indicates a lack of proper care, however, these can usually be corrected with a tune-up or relatively simple parts replacement.

14–17: Problems in the engine or transmission can be very expensive. Walk away from any car with problems in these areas.

7. If you are satisfied with the apparent condition of the car, take it to an independent diagnostic center or mechanic for a complete checkout. If your state has a state inspection program, have it inspected immediately before purchase, or specify on the invoice that purchase is conditional on the car's passing a state inspection.
8. Road test the car. Refer to the Road Test Checklist in this section. If your original evaluation, and the road test agree, the rest is up to you.

Used Car Checklist

NOTE: *The numbers on the illustration correspond to the numbers in this checklist.*

1. **Mileage:** Average mileage is about 12,000 miles per year. More than average may indicate hard usage. Catalytic converter equipped models may need converter service beyond the 50,000 mile mark.

2. **Paint:** Check around the tailpipe, molding and windows for overspray, indicating that the car has been repainted.

3. **Rust:** Check fenders, doors, rocker panels, window moldings, wheelwells, flooring and in the bed, for signs of rust. Any rust at all will be a problem. There is no way to stop the spread of rust, except to replace the part or panel.

4. **Body Appearance:** Check the moldings, bumpers, grille, vinyl roof, glass, doors, tail gate and body panels for overall condition. Check for misalignment, loose holddown clips, ripples, scratches in the glass, rips or patches in the top. Mismatched paint, welding in the bed, severe misalignment of body panels or ripples may indicate crash work.

5. **Leaks:** Get down under the car and take a good look. There are no "normal" leaks, other than water from the air conditioning condenser drain tube.

6. **Tires:** Check the tire air pressure. A common trick is to pump the tires up hard to make the car roll more easily. Check the tread wear and the spare tire condition. Uneven wear is a sign that the front end is, or was, out of alignment.

7. **Shock Absorbers:** Check the shocks by forcing downward sharply on each corner of the car. Good shocks will not allow the car to rebound more than twice after you let go.

8. **Interior:** Check the entire interior. You're looking for an interior condition that agrees with the overall condition of the car. Reasonable wear can be expected, but be suspicious of new seatcovers on sagging seats, new pedal pads, and worn armrests. These indicate an attempt to cover up hard usage. Pull back the carpets and/or mats and look for signs of water leaks or flooding. Look for missing hardware, door handles, control knobs, etc. Check lights and signal operations. Make sure that all accessories, such as air conditioner, heater, radio, etc., work. Air conditioning, especially automatic temperature control units, can be very expensive to repair. Check the operation of the windshield wipers.

9. **Belts and Hoses:** Open the hood and check all belts and hoses for wear, cracks, or weak spots. Check around hose connections for stains, indicating leaks.

10. **Battery:** Low electrolyte level, corroded terminals and/or a cracked battery case, indicate a lack of maintenance.

11. **Radiator:** Look for corrosion or rust in the coolant, indicating a lack of maintenance.

12. **Air Filter:** A dirty air filter element indicates a lack of maintenance.

13. **Spark Plug Wires:** Check the wires for cracks, burned spots or wear. Worn wires will have to be replaced.

14. **Oil Level:** If the level is low, chances are that the engine either uses an excessive amount of oil, or leaks. If the oil on the dipstick appears foamy or tan in color, a leakage of cool-

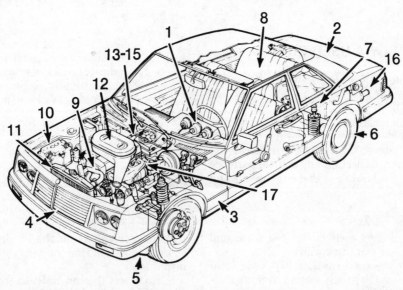

You should check these points when buying a used car. The "Used Car Checklist" gives an explanation of the numbered items

ant into the oil is indicated. Stop here, and go elsewhere for your car. If the oil appears thin or has the smell of gasoline, stop here and go elsewhere for your car.

15. **Automatic Transmission:** Pull the transmission dipstick out when the engine is running in PARK. If the fluid is hot, the dipstick should read FULL. If the fluid is cold, the level will show about one pint low. The fluid itself should be bright red and translucent, with no burned odor. Fluid that is brown or black and has a burned odor is a sign that the transmission needs major repairs.

16. **Exhaust:** Check the color of the exhaust smoke. Blue smoke indicates excessive oil usage, usually due to major internal engine problems. Black smoke can indicate burned valves or carburetor problems. Check the exhaust system for leaks. A leaky system is dangerous and expensive to replace.

17. **Spark Plugs:** Remove one of the spark plugs. An engine in good condition will have spark plugs with a light tan or gray deposit on the electrodes. See the color Tune-Up section for a complete analysis of spark plug condition.

Road Test Check List

1. **Engine Performance:** The car should have good accelerator response, whether cold or warm, with adequate power and smooth acceleration through the gears.

2. **Brakes:** Brakes should provide quick, firm stops, with no squealing, pulling or fade.

3. **Steering:** Sure control with no binding, harshness or looseness, and no shimmy in the wheel should be encountered. Noise or vibration from the steering wheel means trouble.

4. **Clutch:** Clutch action should be quick and smooth with easy engagement of the transmission.

5. **Manual Transmission:** The transmission should shift smoothly and crisply with easy change of gears. No clashing and grinding should be evident. The transmission should not stick in gear, nor should there be any gear whine evident at road speed.

6. **Automatic Transmission:** The transmission should shift rapidly and smoothly, with no noise, hesitation or slipping. The transmission should not shift back and forth, but should stay in gear until an upshift or downshift is needed.

7. **Differential:** No noise or thumps should be present. No external leakage should be present.

8. **Driveshaft, Universal Joints:** Vibration and noise could mean driveshaft problems. Clicking at low speed or coast conditions means worn U-joints.

9. **Suspension:** Try hitting bumps at different speeds. A car that bounces has weak shock absorbers. Clunks mean worn bushings or ball joints.

10. **Frame:** Wet the tires and drive in a straight line. Tracks should show two straight lines, not four. Four tire tracks indicates a frame bent by collision damage. If the tires can't be wet for this purpose, have a friend drive along behind you and see if the car appears to be traveling in a straight line.

Capacities

Year	Crankcase (qts)		Transmission (qts)		Drive Axle (qts)	Fuel Tank (gal)	Cooling System w/heater (qts)
	w/filter	w/o filter	Manual	Automatic *			
1983–84	4.2 ①	3.7 ①	2.7	6.3	②	13.8	7.4 ③
1985	4.2 ①	3.8 ①	2.7	2.5	1.7 ④	14.5	7.4 ⑤
1986	4.2 ①	3.8 ①	2.7	2.5 ⑥	1.7 ④	14.5	7.4 ⑤

① Diesel 4.5 w/Filter; 4.0 w/o
② Manual trans—2.7; Automatic—2.1
③ Diesel—8.0
④ Only automatic models have a separate differential
⑤ Diesel—8.9
⑥ Diesel—2.1

Tune-Up and Performance Maintenance

T2

TUNE-UP PROCEDURES

In order to extract the full measure of performance and economy from your engine it is essential that it be properly tuned at regular intervals. A regular tune-up will keep your car's engine running smoothly and will prevent the annoying minor breakdowns and poor performance associated with an untuned engine.

A complete tune-up should be performed every 12,000 miles or twelve months, whichever comes first. This interval should be halved if the car is operated under severe conditions, such as trailer towing, prolonged idling, continual stop and start driving, or if starting or running problems are noticed. It is assumed that the routine maintenance described in Chapter 1 has been kept up, as this will have a decided effect on the results of a tune-up. All of the applicable steps of a tune-up should be followed in order, as the result is a cumulative one.

If the specifications on the tune-up sticker in the engine compartment disagree with the Tune-Up Specifications chart in this chapter, the figures on the sticker must be used. The sticker often reflects changes made during the production run.

Spark Plugs

The job of the spark plug is to ignite the air/fuel mixture in the cylinder as the piston approaches the top of the compression stroke. The ignited mixture then expands and forces the piston down on the power stroke. This turns the crankshaft which then turns the remainder of the drive train.

The average life of a spark plug, if the engine is run on leaded fuel, is 12,000 miles, while on unleaded fuel, it may be considerably longer. Spark plug life also depends upon the mechanical condition of the engine and the type of driving you are doing. Plugs usually last longer and stay cleaner if most of your driving is done on long trips at high speeds.

The electrode end of the spark plug (the end that goes into the cylinder) is also a very good indicator of the mechanical condition of your engine. If a spark plug should foul and begin to misfire, you will have to find the condition that caused the plug to foul and correct it. It is also a good idea to occasionally give all the plugs the once-over to get an idea how the inside of your engine is doing. A small amount of deposit on a spark plug, after it has been in use for any period of time, should be considered normal. But a black liquid deposit on the plugs indicates oil fouling. You should schedule a few free Saturday afternoons to find the source of it. Because the combustion chamber is supposed to be sealed from the rest of the engine, oil on the spark plug means your engine is hemorrhaging.

The interval for spark plug changes is 30,000 miles.

1. If the spark plug wires are not numbered as to their cylinder, place a piece of masking tape on each wire and number it.

2. Grasp each wire by the rubber boot at the end. Pull the wires from the spark plugs. If the boots stick to the plugs, remove them with a twisting motion. Do not attempt to remove the spark plug wires from the plugs by pulling on the wire itself as this will damage the spark plug wires.

3. Clean any foreign material from around the spark plugs before removing them. Use the spark plug wrench supplied in the tool kit or a ratchet with an extension (if necessary) and a $\frac{13}{16}''$ plug socket.

Compare the condition of the spark plugs to the plugs shown in the Color Insert section. It should be remembered that any type of deposit will decrease the efficiency of the plug. If the plugs are not to be replaced, they should be

Troubleshooting Engine Performance

Problem	Cause	Solution
Hard starting (engine cranks normally)	• Binding linkage, choke valve or choke piston	• Repair as necessary
	• Restricted choke vacuum diaphragm	• Clean passages
	• Improper fuel level	• Adjust float level
	• Dirty, worn or faulty needle valve and seat	• Repair as necessary
	• Float sticking	• Repair as necessary
	• Faulty fuel pump	• Replace fuel pump
	• Incorrect choke cover adjustment	• Adjust choke cover
	• Inadequate choke unloader adjustment	• Adjust choke unloader
	• Faulty ignition coil	• Test and replace as necessary
	• Improper spark plug gap	• Adjust gap
	• Incorrect ignition timing	• Adjust timing
	• Incorrect valve timing	• Check valve timing; repair as necessary
Rough idle or stalling	• Incorrect curb or fast idle speed	• Adjust curb or fast idle speed
	• Incorrect ignition timing	• Adjust timing to specification
	• Improper feedback system operation	• Refer to Chapter 4
	• Improper fast idle cam adjustment	• Adjust fast idle cam
	• Faulty EGR valve operation	• Test EGR system and replace as necessary
	• Faulty PCV valve air flow	• Test PCV valve and replace as necessary
	• Choke binding	• Locate and eliminate binding condition
	• Faulty TAC vacuum motor or valve	• Repair as necessary
	• Air leak into manifold vacuum	• Inspect manifold vacuum connections and repair as necessary
	• Improper fuel level	• Adjust fuel level
	• Faulty distributor rotor or cap	• Replace rotor or cap
	• Improperly seated valves	• Test cylinder compression, repair as necessary
	• Incorrect ignition wiring	• Inspect wiring and correct as necessary
	• Faulty ignition coil	• Test coil and replace as necessary
	• Restricted air vent or idle passages	• Clean passages
	• Restricted air cleaner	• Clean or replace air cleaner filler element
	• Faulty choke vacuum diaphragm	• Repair as necessary
Faulty low-speed operation	• Restricted idle transfer slots	• Clean transfer slots
	• Restricted idle air vents and passages	• Clean air vents and passages
	• Restricted air cleaner	• Clean or replace air cleaner filter element
	• Improper fuel level	• Adjust fuel level
	• Faulty spark plugs	• Clean or replace spark plugs
	• Dirty, corroded, or loose ignition secondary circuit wire connections	• Clean or tighten secondary circuit wire connections
	• Improper feedback system operation	• Refer to Chapter 4
	• Faulty ignition coil high voltage wire	• Replace ignition coil high voltage wire
	• Faulty distributor cap	• Replace cap
Faulty acceleration	• Improper accelerator pump stroke	• Adjust accelerator pump stroke
	• Incorrect ignition timing	• Adjust timing
	• Inoperative pump discharge check ball or needle	• Clean or replace as necessary
	• Worn or damaged pump diaphragm or piston	• Replace diaphragm or piston

Troubleshooting Engine Performance (cont.)

Problem	Cause	Solution
Faulty acceleration (cont.)	• Leaking carburetor main body cover gasket	• Replace gasket
	• Engine cold and choke set too lean	• Adjust choke cover
	• Improper metering rod adjustment (BBD Model carburetor)	• Adjust metering rod
	• Faulty spark plug(s)	• Clean or replace spark plug(s)
	• Improperly seated valves	• Test cylinder compression, repair as necessary
	• Faulty ignition coil	• Test coil and replace as necessary
	• Improper feedback system operation	• Refer to Chapter 4
Faulty high speed operation	• Incorrect ignition timing	• Adjust timing
	• Faulty distributor centrifugal advance mechanism	• Check centrifugal advance mechanism and repair as necessary
	• Faulty distributor vacuum advance mechanism	• Check vacuum advance mechanism and repair as necessary
	• Low fuel pump volume	• Replace fuel pump
	• Wrong spark plug air gap or wrong plug	• Adjust air gap or install correct plug
	• Faulty choke operation	• Adjust choke cover
	• Partially restricted exhaust manifold, exhaust pipe, catalytic converter, muffler, or tailpipe	• Eliminate restriction
	• Restricted vacuum passages	• Clean passages
	• Improper size or restricted main jet	• Clean or replace as necessary
	• Restricted air cleaner	• Clean or replace filter element as necessary
	• Faulty distributor rotor or cap	• Replace rotor or cap
	• Faulty ignition coil	• Test coil and replace as necessary
	• Improperly seated valve(s)	• Test cylinder compression, repair as necessary
	• Faulty valve spring(s)	• Inspect and test valve spring tension, replace as necessary
	• Incorrect valve timing	• Check valve timing and repair as necessary
	• Intake manifold restricted	• Remove restriction or replace manifold
	• Worn distributor shaft	• Replace shaft
	• Improper feedback system operation	• Refer to Chapter 4
Misfire at all speeds	• Faulty spark plug(s)	• Clean or replace spark plug(s)
	• Faulty spark plug wire(s)	• Replace as necessary
	• Faulty distributor cap or rotor	• Replace cap or rotor
	• Faulty ignition coil	• Test coil and replace as necessary
	• Primary ignition circuit shorted or open intermittently	• Troubleshoot primary circuit and repair as necessary
	• Improperly seated valve(s)	• Test cylinder compression, repair as necessary
	• Faulty hydraulic tappet(s)	• Clean or replace tappet(s)
	• Improper feedback system operation	• Refer to Chapter 4
	• Faulty valve spring(s)	• Inspect and test valve spring tension, repair as necessary
	• Worn camshaft lobes	• Replace camshaft
	• Air leak into manifold	• Check manifold vacuum and repair as necessary
	• Improper carburetor adjustment	• Adjust carburetor
	• Fuel pump volume or pressure low	• Replace fuel pump
	• Blown cylinder head gasket	• Replace gasket
	• Intake or exhaust manifold passage(s) restricted	• Pass chain through passage(s) and repair as necessary
	• Incorrect trigger wheel installed in distributor	• Install correct trigger wheel

Troubleshooting Engine Performance (cont.)

Problem	Cause	Solution
Power not up to normal	• Incorrect ignition timing	• Adjust timing
	• Faulty distributor rotor	• Replace rotor
	• Trigger wheel loose on shaft	• Reposition or replace trigger wheel
	• Incorrect spark plug gap	• Adjust gap
	• Faulty fuel pump	• Replace fuel pump
	• Incorrect valve timing	• Check valve timing and repair as necessary
	• Faulty ignition coil	• Test coil and replace as necessary
	• Faulty ignition wires	• Test wires and replace as necessary
	• Improperly seated valves	• Test cylinder compression and repair as necessary
	• Blown cylinder head gasket	• Replace gasket
	• Leaking piston rings	• Test compression and repair as necessary
	• Worn distributor shaft	• Replace shaft
	• Improper feedback system operation	• Refer to Chapter 4
Intake backfire	• Improper ignition timing	• Adjust timing
	• Faulty accelerator pump discharge	• Repair as necessary
	• Defective EGR CTO valve	• Replace EGR CTO valve
	• Defective TAC vacuum motor or valve	• Repair as necessary
	• Lean air/fuel mixture	• Check float level or manifold vacuum for air leak. Remove sediment from bowl
Exhaust backfire	• Air leak into manifold vacuum	• Check manifold vacuum and repair as necessary
	• Faulty air injection diverter valve	• Test diverter valve and replace as necessary
	• Exhaust leak	• Locate and eliminate leak
Ping or spark knock	• Incorrect ignition timing	• Adjust timing
	• Distributor centrifugal or vacuum advance malfunction	• Inspect advance mechanism and repair as necessary
	• Excessive combustion chamber deposits	• Remove with combustion chamber cleaner
	• Air leak into manifold vacuum	• Check manifold vacuum and repair as necessary
	• Excessively high compression	• Test compression and repair as necessary
	• Fuel octane rating excessively low	• Try alternate fuel source
	• Sharp edges in combustion chamber	• Grind smooth
	• EGR valve not functioning properly	• Test EGR system and replace as necessary
Surging (at cruising to top speeds)	• Low carburetor fuel level	• Adjust fuel level
	• Low fuel pump pressure or volume	• Replace fuel pump
	• Metering rod(s) not adjusted properly (BBD Model Carburetor)	• Adjust metering rod
	• Improper PCV valve air flow	• Test PCV valve and replace as necessary
	• Air leak into manifold vacuum	• Check manifold vacuum and repair as necessary
	• Incorrect spark advance	• Test and replace as necessary
	• Restricted main jet(s)	• Clean main jet(s)
	• Undersize main jet(s)	• Replace main jet(s)
	• Restricted air vents	• Clean air vents
	• Restricted fuel filter	• Replace fuel filter
	• Restricted air cleaner	• Clean or replace air cleaner filter element
	• EGR valve not functioning properly	• Test EGR system and replace as necessary
	• Improper feedback system operation	• Refer to Chapter 4

Gasoline Engine Tune-Up Specifications

Year	Engine Type	Spark Plugs Type	Gap (in.)	Distributor Point Dwell (deg)	Point Gap (in.)	Ignition Timing (deg) ▲ MT	AT	Compression Pressure (psi) @ 250 rpm **	Fuel Pump Pressure (psi)	Idle Speed (rpm) ▲ MT	AT	Valve Clearance (in.) ‡ Intake	Exhaust
1983–84	2S-E	BPR5EA-L11	0.043	Electronic	—	5B	5B	171	28–36	700	700	Hyd.	Hyd.
1985	2S-E	BPR5EA-11	0.043	Electronic	—	5B	5B	171	28–36	700 ⑤	750 ⑤	Hyd.	Hyd.
1986	2S-E	BPR5EA-11	0.043	Electronic	—	10B	10B	171	28–36	700	700	Hyd.	Hyd.

⑤ With cooling fan off, trans. in Neutral

Diesel Tune-Up Specifications

| Year | Engine | Valve Clearance (cold) | | Intake Valve Opens (deg.) | Injection Pump Setting (deg.) | Injection Nozzle Pressure (psi) | | Idle Speed (rpm) | Cranking Compression Pressure (psi) |
		Intake (in.)	Exhaust (in.)			New	Used		
1984–85	1C-TL	0.008–0.012	0.010–0.014	11B	25–30B	2062–2205	1920–2205	750	427
	1C-L, 1C-LC	0.008–0.012	0.010–0.014	11B	25–30B	2062–2205	1920–2205	700	427
1986	2C-T	0.008–0.012	0.010–0.014	11B	.028 in.①	2062–2205	1920–2205	750	427

① Figure represents injection pump plunger stroke at TDC. See text for measurement procedure.

thoroughly cleaned before installation. If the electrode ends of the plugs are not worn or damaged and if they are to be reused, wipe off the porcelain insulator on each plug and check for cracks of breaks. If either condition exists, the plug must be replaced.

If the plugs are judged reusable, have them cleaned on a plug cleaning machine (found in most service stations) or remove the deposits with a stiff wire brush.

Check the plug gap on both new and used plugs before installing them in the engine. The

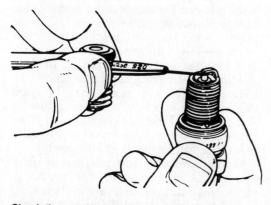

Check the spark plug gap with a wire gauge

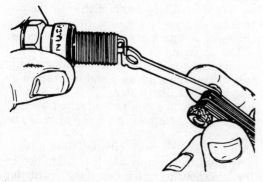

Adjust the spark plug gap with a bending tool

ground electrode must be parallel to the center electrode and the specified size wire gauge should pass through the opening with a slight drag.

NOTE: *Do not use a flat gauge; an inaccurate reading will result.*

If the center of ground electrode has worn unevenly, level them off with a file. If the air gap between the two electrodes is not correct, open or close the ground electrode, with the proper tool, to bring it to specifications. Such a tool is usually provided with a gap gauge.

Install the plugs, as follows:

1. Lightly oil the spark plug threads with engine oil.

2. Insert the plugs in the engine and hand tighten them. Do not cross-thread the plugs.

3. Torque the spark plugs to 11–14 ft.lb. Use caution when tightening the spark plugs, since Toyota engines have aluminum heads.

4. Install each wire on its respective plug, making sure that it is firmly connected.

SPARK PLUG HEAT RANGE

Spark plug heat range is the ability of the plug to dissipate heat. The longer the insulator (or the farther it extends into the engine), the hotter the plug will operate; the shorter the insulator the cooler it will operate. A plug that absorbs little heat and remains too cool will quickly accumulate deposits of oil and carbon since it is not hot enough to burn them off. This leads to plug fouling and consequently to misfiring. A plug that absorbs too much heat will have no deposits, but, due to the excessive heat, the electrodes will burn away quickly and in some instances, preignition may result. Preignition takes place when plug tips get so hot that they glow sufficiently to ignite the fuel/air mixture before the actual spark occurs. This early ignition will usually cause a pinging during low speeds and heavy loads.

The general rule of thumb for choosing the

correct heat range when picking a spark plug is: if most of your driving is long distance, high speed travel, use a colder plug; if most of your driving is stop and to, use a hotter plug. Original equipment plugs are compromise plugs, but most people never have occasion to change their plugs from the factory-recommended heat range.

CHECKING AND REPLACING SPARK PLUG CABLES

At every tune-up, visually inspect the spark plug cables for burns, cuts, or breaks in the insulation. Check the boots and the nipples on the distributor cap and coil. Replace any damaged wiring.

Every 36,000 miles or so, the resistance of the wires should be checked with an ohmmeter. Wires with excessive resistance will cause misfiring, and may make the engine difficult to start in damp weather. Generally, the useful life of the cables is 36,000–50,000 miles.

To check resistance, remove the distributor cap, leaving the wires attached. Connect one lead of an ohmmeter to an electrode within the cap. Connect the other lead to the corresponding spark plug terminal (remove it from the plug for this test). Replace any wire which shows a resistance over 50,000Ω. Generally speaking, however, resistance should not be over 30,000Ω, and 50,000Ω must be considered the outer limit of acceptability. Test the high tension lead from the coil by connecting the ohmmeter between the center contact in the distributor cap and either of the primary terminals of the coil. If resistance is more than 25,000Ω, remove the cable from the coil and check the resistance of the cable alone. Anything over 15,000Ω is cause for replacement. It should be remembered that resistance is also a function of length; the longer the cable, the greater the resistance. Thus, if the cables on your car are longer than the factory originals, resistance will be higher, quite possibly outside these limits.

When installing new cables, replace them one at a time to avoid mixups. Start by replacing the longest one first. Install the boot firmly over the spark plug. Route the wire over the same path as the original. Insert the nipple firmly into the tower on the cap or the coil.

Ignition Timing

Ignition timing is the measurement in degrees of crankshaft rotation of the instant the spark plugs in the cylinders fire, in relation to the location of the piston, while the piston is on its compression stroke.

Ignition timing is adjusted by loosening the

2S-E timing marks

distributor locking device and turning the distributor in the engine.

Ideally, the air/fuel mixture in the cylinder will be ignited (by the spark plug) and just beginning its rapid expansion as the piston passes top dead center (TDC) of the compression stroke. If this happens, the piston will be beginning the power stroke just as the compressed (by the movement of the piston) and ignited (by the spark plug) air/fuel mixture starts to expand. The expansion of the air/fuel mixture will then force the piston down on the power stroke and turn the crankshaft.

It takes a fraction of a second for the spark from the plug to completely ignite the mixture in the cylinder. Because of this, the spark plug must fire before the piston reaches TDC, if the mixture is to be completely ignited as the piston passes TDC. This measurement is given in degrees (of top dead center (BTDC). If the ignition timing setting for your engine is seven degrees (7°) BTDC, this means that the spark plug must fire at a time when the piston for that cylinder is 7° before top dead center of the compression stroke. However, this only holds true while your engine is at idle speed.

As you accelerate from idle, the speed of your engine (rpm) increases. The increase in rpm means that the pistons are now traveling up and down much faster. Because of this, the spark plugs will have to fire even sooner if the mixture is to be completely ignited as the piston passes TDC. To accomplish this, the distributor incorporates means to advance the timing of the spark as engine speed increases.

The distributor in your Toyota has two means of advancing the ignition timing. One is called centrifugal advance and is actuated by weights in the distributor. The other is called vacuum advance and is controlled by that large circular housing on the side of the distributor.

In addition, some distributors have a vacuum-retard mechanism which is contained in the same housing on the side of the distributor as the vacuum advance. The function of this mechanism is to retard the timing of the ignition spark under certain engine conditions. This causes more complete burning of the air/fuel mixture in the cylinder and consequently lowers exhaust emissions.

Because these mechanisms change ignition timing, it is necessary to disconnect and plug the one or two vacuum lines from the distributor when setting the basic ignition timing.

Because these mechanisms change ignition timing, it is necessary to disconnect and plug the one or two vacuum lines from the distributor when setting the basic ignition timing.

If ignition timing is set too far advanced (BTDC), the ignition and expansion of the air/fuel mixture in the cylinder will try to force the piston down the cylinder while it is still traveling upward. This causes engine ping, a sound which resembles marbles being dropped into an empty tin can. If the ignition timing is too far retarded (after, or ATDC), the piston will have already started down on the power stroke when the air/fuel mixture ignites and expands. This will cause the piston to be forced down only a portion of its travel and will result in poor engine performance and lack of power.

Ignition timing adjustment is checked with a timing light. This instrument is connected to the number one (No. 1) spark plug of the engine. The timing light flashes every time an electrical current is sent from the distributor, through the No. 1 spark plug wire, to the spark plug. The crankshaft pulley and the front cover of the engine are marked with a timing pointer and a timing scale. When the timing pointer is aligned with the 0 mark on the timing scale, the piston in No. 1 cylinder is at TDC of its compression stroke. With the engine running, and the timing light aimed at the timing pointer and timing scale, the stroboscopic flashes from the timing light will allow you to check the ignition timing setting of the engine. The timing light flashes every time the spark plug in the No. 1 cylinder of the engine fires. Since the flash from the timing light makes the crankshaft pulley seem stationary for a moment, you will be able to read the exact position of the piston in the No. 1 cylinder on the timing scale on the front of the engine.

ADJUSTMENT

1. Start the engine and allow it to reach normal operating temperature. Connect a tachometer and check that the idle speed is within specifications. Attach the tachometer to the negative (–) side of the ignition coil, not to the distributor primary lead. Damage to the ignition control unit will result from improper connections.

2. Connect a timing light to the engine ac-

cording to the manufacturer's instructions. If the timing marks are difficult to see, use chalk or a dab of paint to make them more visible.

3. Disconnect the vacuum line from the distributor vacuum advance and plug the line. If a vacuum advance/retard unit is used, disconnect and plug both hoses.

4. Start and run the engine at idle with the transmission in Neutral on manual models, or Drive on automatic models. Make sure the parking brake is securely set and the wheels are chocked before allowing the car to idle in gear.

5. Point the timing light at the timing marks. With the engine at idle, timing should be set at the specifications given in the tune-up chart at the beginning of this section, or according to the values listed on the underhood emission control sticker. If not, loosen the pinch bolt at the base of the distributor, then rotate the distributor to advance or retard the timing as required.

6. Stop the engine and tighten the pinch bolt. Start the engine and recheck the timing.

7. Stop the engine and disconnect the timing light and the tachometer. Reconnect the vacuum lines to the distributor advance unit.

Diesel Injection Timing
ADJUSTMENT

NOTE: *This procedure requires the use of a plunger stroke measuring tool and dial indicator.*

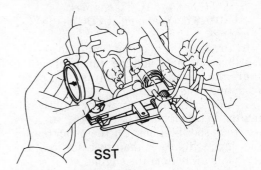

SST 09275-54010 installation

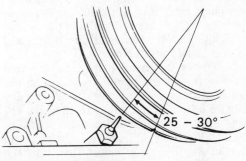

Measuring engine rotation

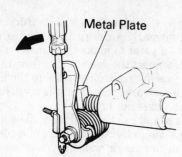

Positioning the metal plate

1. Remove the injection pump head bolt and install stroke measuring tool 09275-54010 or equivalent, along with the dial indicator.

2. Rotate the engine in the normal direction of rotation to set No. 1 cylinder to approximately 25–30°BTDC on the compression stroke.

3. Use a screwdriver to turn the cold start lever 20° counterclockwise, then place a metal plate 0.335–0.394 in. (8.5–10mm) thick between the cold start lever and thermo wax plunger.

4. Zero the dial indicator, then check to make sure the indicator remains at zero while rotating the crankshaft pulley slightly to the left and right.

5. Slowly rotate the crankshaft pulley until the No. 1 cylinder comes to TDC/compression, then measure the plunger stroke. It should read as follows on the dial indicator.

   a. 0.032 in. (0.80 mm) at TDC on the 1C-L, 1C-LC and the 1C-TL engines.

   b. 0.028 in. (0.70 mm) at TDC on the 2C-T engine.

6. To adjust the injection timing, loosen the four injection lines and the union bolt of the fuel inlet line. Loosen the injection pump mounting bolts and nuts.

7. Adjust the plunger stroke by slightly tilting the injection pump body. If the stroke is less than specifications, tilt the pump toward the engine. If greater than specifications, tilt the pump away from the engine.

8. Once the pump stroke is within specifications (as described in Step 5), tighten the injection pump mounting bolts and nuts. Torque the bolts to 34 ft. lbs. (47 Nm) and the nuts to 13 ft. lbs. (18 Nm). Torque all union nuts and bolts to 22 ft. lbs. (29 Nm).

9. Remove the metal plate from the cold start lever and the pump stroke measuring tool from the injection pump. Install the distributor head bolt and torque to 12 ft. lbs. (17 Nm). Replace the head bolt washer when installing. Bleed any air from the injection pump by cranking the starter motor, then start the engine and check for leaks.

Integrated Ignition Assembly (IIA) Inspection

PRIMARY COIL RESISTANCE

Using a suitable ohmmeter, measure the resistance between the positive and negative terminals. The primary coil resistance (cold) should be 0.3 to 0.5 ohms (USA) and 1.2 to 1.5 ohms (Canada).

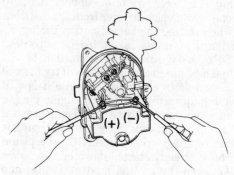

Primary coil resistance test

SECONDARY COIL RESISTANCE

Using a suitable ohmmeter, measure the resistance between the positive terminal and the high tension terminal. The secondary coil resistance (cold) should be 7.5 to 10.5 kilo-ohms.

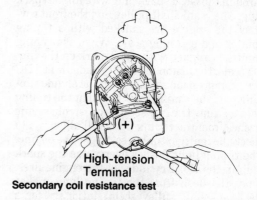

Secondary coil resistance test

IIA IGNITER INSPECTION

1. Turn the ignition switch to the on position. Using a suitable voltmeter, connect the positive probe to the ignition coil positive terminal and the negative probe to a suitable body ground. The voltage should be approximately 12 volts.

2. Inspect the power transistor in the igniter by using the following procedure:

   a. Connect the voltmeter positive probe to the ignition coil negative terminal and the negative probe to the body ground. The voltmeter should read approximately 12 volts.

Problem	Possible cause	Remedy
Engine will not start/ hard to start (cranks ok)	Incorrect ignition timing	Adjust timing
	IIA faulty	
	• Ignition coil faulty	Inspect ignition coil
	• Igniter faulty	Inspect igniter
	• Pickup coil faulty	Inspect pickup coil
	• Incorrect air gap	Adjust air gap
	• Cap or rotor dirty or cracked	Clean or replace
	High tension cord faulty	Inspect high tension cord
	Spark plugs faulty	Adjust plugs
	Ignition wiring disconnected or broken	Inspect wiring
Rough idle or stalls	Spark plugs faulty	Inspect plugs
	Ignition wiring faulty	Inspect wiring
	Incorrect ignition timing	Adjust timing
	IIA faulty	
	• Ignition coil faulty	Inspect ignition coil
	• Ignition faulty	Inspect igniter
	• Pickup coil faulty	Inspect pickup coil
	• Incorrect air gap	Adjust air gap
	• Cap or rotor dirty or cracked	Clean or replace
	• Governor faulty	Inspect governor
	• Vacuum advancer faulty	Inspect vacuum advancer
	High tension cord faulty	Inspect high tension cord
Engine hesitates/ poor acceleration	Spark plugs faulty	Inspect plugs
	Ignition wiring faulty	Inspect wiring
	Incorrect ignition timing	Adjust timing
	IIA faulty	
	• Incorrect air gap	Adjust air gap
	• Governor faulty	Inspect governor
	• Vacuum advancer faulty	Inspect vacuum advancer
	• Breaker plate faulty	Inspect breaker plate
Muffler explosion (after fire) all the time	Incorrect ignition timing	Adjust timing
	IIA faulty	
	• Governor faulty	Inspect goveror
	• Vacuum advancer faulty	Inspect vacuum advancer
	• Breaker plate faulty	Inspect breaker plate
Engine backfires	Incorrect ignition timing	Adjust timing
	IIA faulty	
	• Governor faulty	Inspect governor
	• Vacuum advancer faulty	Inspect vacuum advancer
	• Breaker plate faulty	Inspect breaker plate
Poor gasoline mileage	Spark plugs faulty	Inspect plugs
	Incorrect ignition timing	Adjust timing
	IIA faulty	
	• Governor faulty	Inspect governor
	• Vacuum advancer faulty	Inspect vacuum advancer
	• Breaker plate faulty	Inspect reaker plate
	• Incorrect air gap	Adjust air gap
Engine overheats	Incorrect ignition timing	Adjust timing
	IIA faulty	
	• Governor faulty	Inspect governor
	• Vacuum advancer faulty	Inspect vacuum advancer
	• Breaker plate faulty	Inspect breaker plate
	• Incorrect air gap	Adjust air gap

Troubleshooting

b. Using a dry cell (1.5V) battery, connect the positive terminal of the battery to the pink wire terminal and the negative terminal to the white terminal.

CAUTION: *Do not apply battery voltage for more than five seconds to avoid destroying the power transistor in the igniter.*

c. Using a voltmeter, connect the positive probe to the ignition coil negative terminal and the negative probe to a suitable body ground. Check the voltage reading, it should read 5 volts - less the battery voltage (USA) and 0 to 3 volts (Canada). If there is a problem with the igniter, replace it with a new one.

3. Turn off the ignition switch and remove the test equipment.

DISTRIBUTOR INSPECTION

1. Inspect the air gap, by using a feeler gauge. Measure the gap between the signal rotor and the pick-up coil projection. The air gap should be 0.008 to 0.0016 in.

2. Inspect the pick-up coil by, using an ohmmeter to check the resistance of the pick-up coil. The pick-up coil resistance should be 140 to 180 ohms. If the resistance is nor correct, replace the pick-up coil with the breaker assembly.

3. Inspect the vacuum advance by disconnecting the vacuum hose and connecting a vacuum pump to the diaphragms. Apply a vacuum and check that the vacuum advance moves freely. If the advance unit does not respond to the vacuum, replace it.

4. Inspect the governor advance by turning the rotor shaft counterclockwise, release it and check that the rotor returns slightly clockwise. Check that the rotor shaft is not excessively loose.

REMOVAL AND INSTALLATION

IIA Distributor and Ignitor

1. Remove the number one spark plug. Place a finger over the spark plug hole and rotate the crankshaft clockwise to top dead center. When there is pressure felt on the finger at the spark plug hole, this will be top dead center of the compression stroke on number one cylinder. If not, repeat the procedure. Install the number one spark plug.

2. Disconnect the negative battery cable. Disconnect and tag (if necessary) all ignition wires and vacuum hoses from the IIA distributor. Do not remove the high tension wire from the distributor cap.

3. Remove the IIA distributor hold down bolt and remove the distributor.

4. Remove the IIA distributor cap, gasket and rotor. Remove the igniter dust cover and remove the ignition coil dust cover.

5. Remove the ignition coil by, removing the nuts and disconnecting the wires from the terminals of the ignition coil. Remove the four ignition coil retaining screws and remove the coil.

6. Remove the IIA wire with the condenser.

7. Remove the igniter screws and nuts and disconnect the wires from the terminals of the

igniter. Remove the two igniter retaining screws and remove the igniter.

8. Installation is the reverse order of the removal procedure.

IIA Igniter Removal (Without Removing The Distributor)

1. Remove the distributor cap, rotor and dielectric insulator covers. Disconnect the red and yellow wires from the coil and the pink, white and black wires from the igniter.

2. Remove the igniter. It may be necessary to mark and rotate the distributor to gain access to the igniter retaining screws. The timing should be checked after the distributor is returned to the mark.

3. Install the new igniter using the to new retaining screws.

4. Twist the pick-up coil wires together, install the white wire first then pink and black wires to their original locations. Make sure the wires do not touch the housing generator or advance plate.

5. Route the red and yellow wires from the igniter so they do not contact moving parts. Connect the red wire to the right coil terminal (with the brown wire) and the yellow wire to the left terminal (with the blue wire). Replace the covers, rotor and cap. Make all necessary adjustments.

Valve Lash

ADJUSTMENT

Diesel Engines

1. Run the engine to normal operating temperature.

2. Remove the cylinder head cover.

3. With a wrench, turn the crankshaft pulley until the notch in the pulley aligns with the timing pointer on the front cover. The engine will now be at TDC #1 cylinder. The lifters on #1 cylinder should both be loose, and both those on #4 should be tight.

4. Using a flat feeler gauge measure the gap between the lifter and the camshaft lobe on each valve of the #1 cylinder. Then, check each valve shown in the "First Pass" illustration. If the clearance is not within specifications, note what it is.

5. Turn the crankshaft 360°, in the direction of normal rotation, and align the pointer and notch. Measure the clearance on the valves marked in the "Second Pass" illustration.

6. If all measurements were within specifications, you can stop here. If not, record the measurements and go on.

7. Turn the crankshaft so that the intake lobe of the camshaft on any cylinder in need of

SHIM SELECTION CHART

Intake

Installed Shim Thickness (mm)

Measured Clearance	2.200	2.225	2.250	2.275	2.300	2.325	2.350	2.375	2.400	2.425	2.450	2.475	2.500	2.525	2.550	2.575	2.600	2.625	2.650	2.675	2.700	2.725	2.750	2.775	2.800	2.825	2.850	2.875	2.900	2.925	2.950	2.975	3.000	3.025	3.050	3.075	3.100	3.125	3.150	3.175	3.200	3.225	3.250	3.275	3.300	3.325	3.350	3.375	3.400
0.000-0.025									01	01	01	03	03	05	05	07	07	09	09	11	11	13	13	15	15	17	17	19	19	21	21	23	23	25	25	27	27	29	29	31	31	33	33	35	35	37	37	39	39
0.026-0.050								01	01	01	03	03	05	05	07	07	09	09	11	11	13	13	15	15	17	17	19	19	21	21	23	23	25	25	27	27	29	29	31	31	33	33	35	35	37	37	39	39	41
0.051-0.075							01	01	01	03	03	05	05	07	07	09	09	11	11	13	13	15	15	17	17	19	19	21	21	23	23	25	25	27	27	29	29	31	31	33	33	35	35	37	37	39	39	41	41
0.076-0.100						01	01	01	03	03	05	05	07	07	09	09	11	11	13	13	15	15	17	17	19	19	21	21	23	23	25	25	27	27	29	29	31	31	33	33	35	35	37	37	39	39	41	41	43
0.101-0.125					01	01	01	03	03	05	05	07	07	09	09	11	11	13	13	15	15	17	17	19	19	21	21	23	23	25	25	27	27	29	29	31	31	33	33	35	35	37	37	39	39	41	41	43	43
0.126-0.150				01	01	01	03	03	05	05	07	07	09	09	11	11	13	13	15	15	17	17	19	19	21	21	23	23	25	25	27	27	29	29	31	31	33	33	35	35	37	37	39	39	41	41	43	43	45
0.151-0.175			01	01	01	03	03	05	05	07	07	09	09	11	11	13	13	15	15	17	17	19	19	21	21	23	23	25	25	27	27	29	29	31	31	33	33	35	35	37	37	39	39	41	41	43	43	45	45
0.176-0.199		01	01	01	03	03	05	05	07	07	09	09	11	11	13	13	15	15	17	17	19	19	21	21	23	23	25	25	27	27	29	29	31	31	33	33	35	35	37	37	39	39	41	41	43	43	45	45	47
0.200-0.300																																																	
0.301-0.325	03	05	05	07	07	09	09	11	11	13	13	15	15	17	17	19	19	21	21	23	23	25	25	27	27	29	29	31	31	33	33	35	35	37	37	39	39	41	41	43	43	45	45	47	47	49	49	49	
0.326-0.350	05	05	07	07	09	09	11	11	13	13	15	15	17	17	19	19	21	21	23	23	25	25	27	27	29	29	31	31	33	33	35	35	37	37	39	39	41	41	43	43	45	45	47	47	49	49	49		
0.351-0.375	05	07	07	09	09	11	11	13	13	15	15	17	17	19	19	21	21	23	23	25	25	27	27	29	29	31	31	33	33	35	35	37	37	39	39	41	41	43	43	45	45	47	47	49	49	49			
0.376-0.400	07	07	09	09	11	11	13	13	15	15	17	17	19	19	21	21	23	23	25	25	27	27	29	29	31	31	33	33	35	35	37	37	39	39	41	41	43	43	45	45	47	47	49	49	49				
0.401-0.425	07	09	09	11	11	13	13	15	15	17	17	19	19	21	21	23	23	25	25	27	27	29	29	31	31	33	33	35	35	37	37	39	39	41	41	43	43	45	45	47	47	49	49	49					
0.426-0.450	09	09	11	11	13	13	15	15	17	17	19	19	21	21	23	23	25	25	27	27	29	29	31	31	33	33	35	35	37	37	39	39	41	41	43	43	45	45	47	47	49	49	49						
0.451-0.475	09	11	11	13	13	15	15	17	17	19	19	21	21	23	23	25	25	27	27	29	29	31	31	33	33	35	35	37	37	39	39	41	41	43	43	45	45	47	47	49	49	49							
0.476-0.500	11	11	13	13	15	15	17	17	19	19	21	21	23	23	25	25	27	27	29	29	31	31	33	33	35	35	37	37	39	39	41	41	43	43	45	45	47	47	49	49	49								
0.501-0.525	11	13	13	15	15	17	17	19	19	21	21	23	23	25	25	27	27	29	29	31	31	33	33	35	35	37	37	39	39	41	41	43	43	45	45	47	47	49	49	49									
0.526-0.550	13	13	15	15	17	17	19	19	21	21	23	23	25	25	27	27	29	29	31	31	33	33	35	35	37	37	39	39	41	41	43	43	45	45	47	47	49	49	49										
0.551-0.575	13	15	15	17	17	19	19	21	21	23	23	25	25	27	27	29	29	31	31	33	33	35	35	37	37	39	39	41	41	43	43	45	45	47	47	49	49	49											
0.576-0.600	15	15	17	17	19	19	21	21	23	23	25	25	27	27	29	29	31	31	33	33	35	35	37	37	39	39	41	41	43	43	45	45	47	47	49	49	49												
0.601-0.625	15	17	17	19	19	21	21	23	23	25	25	27	27	29	29	31	31	33	33	35	35	37	37	39	39	41	41	43	43	45	45	47	47	49	49	49													
0.626-0.650	17	17	19	19	21	21	23	23	25	25	27	27	29	29	31	31	33	33	35	35	37	37	39	39	41	41	43	43	45	45	47	47	49	49	49														
0.651-0.675	17	19	19	21	21	23	23	25	25	27	27	29	29	31	31	33	33	35	35	37	37	39	39	41	41	43	43	45	45	47	47	49	49	49															
0.676-0.700	19	19	21	21	23	23	25	25	27	27	29	29	31	31	33	33	35	35	37	37	39	39	41	41	43	43	45	45	47	47	49	49	49																
0.701-0.725	19	21	21	23	23	25	25	27	27	29	29	31	31	33	33	35	35	37	37	39	39	41	41	43	43	45	45	47	47	49	49	49																	
0.726-0.750	21	21	23	23	25	25	27	27	29	29	31	31	33	33	35	35	37	37	39	39	41	41	43	43	45	45	47	47	49	49	49																		
0.751-0.775	21	23	23	25	25	27	27	29	29	31	31	33	33	35	35	37	37	39	39	41	41	43	43	45	45	47	47	49	49	49																			
0.776-0.800	23	23	25	25	27	27	29	29	31	31	33	33	35	35	37	37	39	39	41	41	43	43	45	45	47	47	49	49	49																				
0.801-0.825	23	25	25	27	27	29	29	31	31	33	33	35	35	37	37	39	39	41	41	43	43	45	45	47	47	49	49	49																					
0.826-0.850	25	25	27	27	29	29	31	31	33	33	35	35	37	37	39	39	41	41	43	43	45	45	47	47	49	49	49																						
0.851-0.875	25	27	27	29	29	31	31	33	33	35	35	37	37	39	39	41	41	43	43	45	45	47	47	49	49	49																							
0.876-0.900	27	27	29	29	31	31	33	33	35	35	37	37	39	39	41	41	43	43	45	45	47	47	49	49	49																								
0.901-0.925	27	29	29	31	31	33	33	35	35	37	37	39	39	41	41	43	43	45	45	47	47	49	49	49																									
0.926-0.950	29	29	31	31	33	33	35	35	37	37	39	39	41	41	43	43	45	45	47	47	49	49	49																										
0.951-0.975	29	31	31	33	33	35	35	37	37	39	39	41	41	43	43	45	45	47	47	49	49	49																											
0.976-1.000	31	31	33	33	35	35	37	37	39	39	41	41	43	43	45	45	47	47	49	49	49																												
1.001-1.025	31	33	33	35	35	37	37	39	39	41	41	43	43	45	45	47	47	49	49	49																													
1.026-1.050	33	33	35	35	37	37	39	39	41	41	43	43	45	45	47	47	49	49	49																														
1.051-1.075	33	35	35	37	37	39	39	41	41	43	43	45	45	47	47	49	49	49																															
1.076-1.100	35	35	37	37	39	39	41	41	43	43	45	45	47	47	49	49	49																																
1.101-1.125	35	37	37	39	39	41	41	43	43	45	45	47	47	49	49	49																																	
1.126-1.150	37	37	39	39	41	41	43	43	45	45	47	47	49	49	49																																		
1.151-1.175	37	39	39	41	41	43	43	45	45	47	47	49	49	49																																			
1.176-1.200	39	39	41	41	43	43	45	45	47	47	49	49	49																																				
1.201-1.225	39	41	41	43	43	45	45	47	47	49	49	49																																					
1.226-1.250	41	41	43	43	45	45	47	47	49	49	49																																						
1.251-1.275	41	43	43	45	45	47	47	49	49	49																																							
1.276-1.300	43	43	45	45	47	47	49	49	49																																								
1.301-1.325	43	45	45	47	47	49	49	49																																									
1.326-1.350	45	45	47	47	49	49	49																																										
1.351-1.375	45	47	47	49	49	49																																											
1.376-1.400	47	47	49	49	49																																												
1.401-1.425	47	49	49	49																																													
1.426-1.450	49	49	49																																														
1.451-1.475	49	49																																															
1.476-1.500	49																																																

Intake valve clearance (cold) :
0.20 – 0.30 mm (0.08 – 0.012 in.)
Example : 2.700 mm (0.1063 in.) shim installed
Measured clearance is 0.350 mm (0.0138 in.)
Replace 2.700 mm (0.1063 in.) shim with shim No. 25.

Shim Thickness

Shim No.	Thickness mm (in.)	Shim No.	Thickness mm (in.)
01	2.20 (0.0866)	27	2.85 (0.1122)
03	2.25 (0.0886)	29	2.90 (0.1142)
05	2.30 (0.0906)	31	2.95 (0.1161)
07	2.35 (0.0925)	33	3.00 (0.1181)
09	2.40 (0.0945)	35	3.05 (0.1201)
11	2.45 (0.0965)	37	3.10 (0.1220)
13	2.50 (0.0984)	39	3.15 (0.1240)
15	2.55 (0.1004)	41	3.20 (0.1260)
17	2.60 (0.1024)	43	3.25 (0.1280)
19	2.65 (0.1043)	45	3.30 (0.1299)
21	2.70 (0.1063)	47	3.35 (0.1319)
23	2.75 (0.1083)	49	3.40 (0.1339)
25	2.80 (0.1102)		

SHIM SELECTION CHART

Exhaust

Installed Shim Thickness (mm)

Measured Clearance	2.200	2.225	2.250	2.275	2.300	2.325	2.350	2.375	2.400	2.425	2.450	2.475	2.500	2.525	2.550	2.575	2.600	2.625	2.650	2.675	2.700	2.725	2.750	2.775	2.800	2.825	2.850	2.875	2.900	2.925	2.950	2.975	3.000	3.025	3.050	3.075	3.100	3.125	3.150	3.175	3.200	3.225	3.250	3.275	3.300	3.325	3.350	3.375	3.400
0.000–0.025											01	01	01	03	03	05	05	07	07	09	09	11	11	13	13	15	15	17	17	19	19	21	21	23	23	25	25	27	27	29	29	31	31	33	33	35	35	37	37
0.026–0.050										01	01	01	03	03	05	05	07	07	09	09	11	11	13	13	15	15	17	17	19	19	21	21	23	23	25	25	27	27	29	29	31	31	33	33	35	35	37	37	39
0.051–0.075									01	01	01	03	03	05	05	07	07	09	09	11	11	13	13	15	15	17	17	19	19	21	21	23	23	25	25	27	27	29	29	31	31	33	33	35	35	37	37	39	39
0.076–0.100								01	01	01	03	03	05	05	07	07	09	09	11	11	13	13	15	15	17	17	19	19	21	21	23	23	25	25	27	27	29	29	31	31	33	33	35	35	37	37	39	39	41
0.101–0.125							01	01	01	03	03	05	05	07	07	09	09	11	11	13	13	15	15	17	17	19	19	21	21	23	23	25	25	27	27	29	29	31	31	33	33	35	35	37	37	39	39	41	41
0.126–0.150						01	01	01	03	03	05	05	07	07	09	09	11	11	13	13	15	15	17	17	19	19	21	21	23	23	25	25	27	27	29	29	31	31	33	33	35	35	37	37	39	39	41	41	43
0.151–0.175					01	01	01	03	03	05	05	07	07	09	09	11	11	13	13	15	15	17	17	19	19	21	21	23	23	25	25	27	27	29	29	31	31	33	33	35	35	37	37	39	39	41	41	43	43
0.176–0.200				01	01	01	03	03	05	05	07	07	09	09	11	11	13	13	15	15	17	17	19	19	21	21	23	23	25	25	27	27	29	29	31	31	33	33	35	35	37	37	39	39	41	41	43	43	43
0.201–0.225			01	01	01	03	03	05	05	07	07	09	09	11	11	13	13	15	15	17	17	19	19	21	21	23	23	25	25	27	27	29	29	31	31	33	33	35	35	37	37	39	39	41	41	43	43	43	45
0.226–0.249		01	01	01	03	03	05	05	07	07	09	09	11	11	13	13	15	15	17	17	19	19	21	21	23	23	25	25	27	27	29	29	31	31	33	33	35	35	37	37	39	39	41	41	43	43	45	45	47
0.250–0.350																																																	
0.351–0.375	03	05	05	07	07	09	09	11	11	13	13	15	15	17	17	19	19	21	21	23	23	25	25	27	27	29	29	31	31	33	33	35	35	37	37	39	39	41	41	43	43	45	45	47	47	49	49	49	
0.376–0.400	05	05	07	07	09	09	11	11	13	13	15	15	17	17	19	19	21	21	23	23	25	25	27	27	29	29	31	31	33	33	35	35	37	37	39	39	41	41	43	43	45	45	47	47	49	49	49		
0.401–0.425	05	07	07	09	09	11	11	13	13	15	15	17	17	19	19	21	21	23	23	25	25	27	27	29	29	31	31	33	33	35	35	37	37	39	39	41	41	43	43	45	45	47	47	49	49	49			
0.426–0.450	07	07	09	09	11	11	13	13	15	15	17	17	19	19	21	21	23	23	25	25	27	27	29	29	31	31	33	33	35	35	37	37	39	39	41	41	43	43	45	45	47	47	49	49	49				
0.451–0.475	07	09	09	11	11	13	13	15	15	17	17	19	19	21	21	23	23	25	25	27	27	29	29	31	31	33	33	35	35	37	37	39	39	41	41	43	43	45	45	47	47	49	49	49					
0.476–0.500	09	09	11	11	13	13	15	15	17	17	19	19	21	21	23	23	25	25	27	27	29	29	31	31	33	33	35	35	37	37	39	39	41	41	43	43	45	45	47	47	49	49	49						
0.501–0.525	09	11	11	13	13	15	15	17	17	19	19	21	21	23	23	25	25	27	27	29	29	31	31	33	33	35	35	37	37	39	39	41	41	43	43	45	45	47	47	49	49	49							
0.526–0.550	11	11	13	13	15	15	17	17	19	19	21	21	23	23	25	25	27	27	29	29	31	31	33	33	35	35	37	37	39	39	41	41	43	43	45	45	47	47	49	49	49								
0.551–0.575	11	13	13	15	15	17	17	19	19	21	21	23	23	25	25	27	27	29	29	31	31	33	33	35	35	37	37	39	39	41	41	43	43	45	45	47	47	49	49	49									
0.576–0.600	13	13	15	15	17	17	19	19	21	21	23	23	25	25	27	27	29	29	31	31	33	33	35	35	37	37	39	39	41	41	43	43	45	45	47	47	49	49	49										
0.601–0.625	13	15	15	17	17	19	19	21	21	23	23	25	25	27	27	29	29	31	31	33	33	35	35	37	37	39	39	41	41	43	43	45	45	47	47	49	49	49											
0.626–0.650	15	15	17	17	19	19	21	21	23	23	25	25	27	27	29	29	31	31	33	33	35	35	37	37	39	39	41	41	43	43	45	45	47	47	49	49	49												
0.651–0.675	15	17	17	19	19	21	21	23	23	25	25	27	27	29	29	31	31	33	33	35	35	37	37	39	39	41	41	43	43	45	45	47	47	49	49	49													
0.676–0.700	17	17	19	19	21	21	23	23	25	25	27	27	29	29	31	31	33	33	35	35	37	37	39	39	41	41	43	43	45	45	47	47	49	49	49														
0.701–0.725	17	19	19	21	21	23	23	25	25	27	27	29	29	31	31	33	33	35	35	37	37	39	39	41	41	43	43	45	45	47	47	49	49	49															
0.726–0.750	19	19	21	21	23	23	25	25	27	27	29	29	31	31	33	33	35	35	37	37	39	39	41	41	43	43	45	45	47	47	49	49	49																
0.751–0.775	19	21	21	23	23	25	25	27	27	29	29	31	31	33	33	35	35	37	37	39	39	41	41	43	43	45	45	47	47	49	49	49																	
0.776–0.800	21	21	23	23	25	25	27	27	29	29	31	31	33	33	35	35	37	37	39	39	41	41	43	43	45	45	47	47	49	49	49																		
0.801–0.825	21	23	23	25	25	27	27	29	29	31	31	33	33	35	35	37	37	39	39	41	41	43	43	45	45	47	47	49	49	49																			
0.826–0.850	23	23	25	25	27	27	29	29	31	31	33	33	35	35	37	37	39	39	41	41	43	43	45	45	47	47	49	49	49																				
0.851–0.875	23	25	25	27	27	29	29	31	31	33	33	35	35	37	37	39	39	41	41	43	43	45	45	47	47	49	49	49																					
0.876–0.900	25	25	27	27	29	29	31	31	33	33	35	35	37	37	39	39	41	41	43	43	45	45	47	47	49	49	49																						
0.901–0.925	25	27	27	29	29	31	31	33	33	35	35	37	37	39	39	41	41	43	43	45	45	47	47	49	49	49																							
0.926–0.950	27	27	29	29	31	31	33	33	35	35	37	37	39	39	41	41	43	43	45	45	47	47	49	49	49																								
0.951–0.975	27	29	29	31	31	33	33	35	35	37	37	39	39	41	41	43	43	45	45	47	47	49	49	49																									
0.976–1.000	29	29	31	31	33	33	35	35	37	37	39	39	41	41	43	43	45	45	47	47	49	49	49																										
1.001–1.025	29	31	31	33	33	35	35	37	37	39	39	41	41	43	43	45	45	47	47	49	49	49																											
1.026–1.050	31	31	33	33	35	35	37	37	39	39	41	41	43	43	45	45	47	47	49	49	49																												
1.051–1.075	31	33	33	35	35	37	37	39	39	41	41	43	43	45	45	47	47	49	49	49																													
1.076–1.100	33	33	35	35	37	37	39	39	41	41	43	43	45	45	47	47	49	49	49																														
1.101–1.125	33	35	35	37	37	39	39	41	41	43	43	45	45	47	47	49	49	49																															
1.126–1.150	35	35	37	37	39	39	41	41	43	43	45	45	47	47	49	49	49																																
1.151–1.175	35	37	37	39	39	41	41	43	43	45	45	47	47	49	49	49																																	
1.176–1.200	37	37	39	39	41	41	43	43	45	45	47	47	49	49	49																																		
1.201–1.225	37	39	39	41	41	43	43	45	45	47	47	49	49	49																																			
1.226–1.250	39	39	41	41	43	43	45	45	47	47	49	49	49																																				
1.251–1.275	39	41	41	43	43	45	45	47	47	49	49	49																																					
1.276–1.300	41	41	43	43	45	45	47	47	49	49	49																																						
1.301–1.325	41	43	43	45	45	47	47	49	49	49																																							
1.326–1.350	43	43	45	45	47	47	49	49	49																																								
1.351–1.375	43	45	45	47	47	49	49	49																																									
1.376–1.400	45	45	47	47	49	49	49																																										
1.401–1.425	45	47	47	49	49	49																																											
1.426–1.450	47	47	49	49	49																																												
1.451–1.475	47	49	49	49																																													
1.476–1.500	49	49	49																																														
1.501–1.525	49	49																																															
1.526–1.550	49																																																

Exhaust valve clearance (cold) :
0.25 – 0.35 mm (0.010 – 0.014 in.)
Example : 2.700 mm (0.1063 in.) shim installed
Measure clearance is 0.450 mm (0.0177 in.)
Replace 2.700 mm (0.1063 in.) shim with shim No. 27.

Shim Thickness

Shim No.	Thickness mm (in.)	Shim No.	Thickness mm (in.)
01	2.20 (0.0866)	27	2.85 (0.1122)
03	2.25 (0.0886)	29	2.90 (0.1142)
05	2.30 (0.0906)	31	2.95 (0.1161)
07	2.35 (0.0925)	33	3.00 (0.1181)
09	2.40 (0.0945)	35	3.05 (0.1201)
11	2.45 (0.0965)	37	3.10 (0.1220)
13	2.30 (0.0984)	39	3.15 (0.1240)
15	2.55 (0.1004)	41	3.20 (0.1260)
17	2.60 (0.1024)	43	3.25 (0.1280)
19	2.65 (0.1043)	45	3.30 (0.1299)
21	2.70 (0.1063)	47	3.35 (0.1319)
23	2.75 (0.1083)	49	3.40 (0.1339)
25	2.80 (0.1102)		

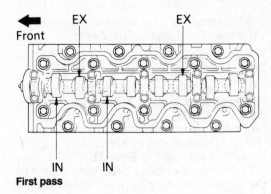

First pass

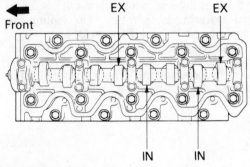

Second pass

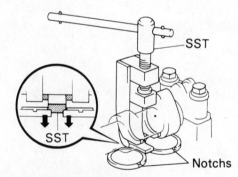

Service tool installation

Intake side:
New shim thickness
= T + [A − 0.25 mm
(0.010 in.)]

Exhaust side:
New shim thickness
= T + [A − 0.30 mm
(0.012 in.)]

Shim determination formulae

adjustment, is pounting straight up. Both valves on that cylinder may now be adjusted.

8. Using a small screwdriver, turn the lifter so that the notch is easily accessible.

9. Install SST #09248-64010 between the two lobes and turn the handle so that the tool presses down both lifters evenly.

10. Using a small screwdriver and magnet, remove the shims.

11. Using the accompanying thickness chart, measure the thickness of the old shims and locate the previosuly recorded gap measurement in the chart. Index the two columns to determine the new shim thickness.

12. Install the new shims and remove the tool. Recheck the gaps.

13. Repeat this procedure for each affected valve.

Idle Speed and Mixture

ADJUSTMENT

Gasoline Engine

1. Leave the air cleaner installed and all the air pipes and hoses of the air intake system connected. Leave all vacuum lines connected to the ESA and EGR systems, etc.

2. Make sure that the Electronic Fuel Injection wiring connectors are fully plugged in. Apply the emergency brake and block the wheels. Start the engine and let it run until it reaches normal operating temperature.

3. Turn all the accessories off and place the transmission in the neutral range. Remove the rubber cap on the distributor and connect the tachometer positive terminal to the check connector at the distributor.

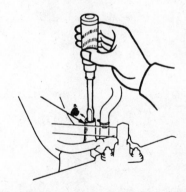

Idle speed adjustment for fuel injected models

CAUTION: *Never allow the tachometer terminal; to touch the ground as it could result in damage to the ignition igniter and/or the ignition coil. There are some tachometers that are not compatible with this ignition system, and it is recommended that the tachometer to be used is compatible with this ignition system.*

4. Race the engine at 2,500 rpm for approximately two minutes. Return the engine to idle and disconnect the vacuum switching valve for the idle speed control.

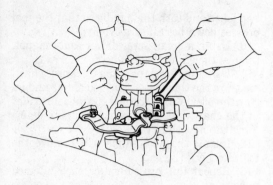

Diesel idle speed adjustment

5. Set the idle speed by turning the idle speed adjusting screw. The idle speed should be as follows:

    a. 700 rpm for A/T & M/T USA models.
    b. 700 rpm for M/T Canada models.
    c. 750 rpm for A/T Canada models.

6. After setting the idle speed, shut off the engine, remove the tachometer and re-install the rubber cover on the distributor.

Diesel Engines

1. This adjustment should be made with the engine at normal operating temperature under the following conditions:

    a. Air cleaner installed.
    b. All accessories switched off.
    c. Transmission in Neutral.

2. Connect a suitable diesel tachometer to the engine according to the manufacturer's instructions.

3. Start the engine and allow it to reach normal operating temperature. The cooling fan should be off for all adjustments.

4. Check the idle speed with the tachometer. It should be 700 rpm. If not, adjust the idle speed by loosening the locknut and turning the idle speed adjusting screw located on the injection pump.

Troubleshooting the Fully Transistorized Ignition System

Troubleshooting the fully transistorized ignition system is easy, but you must have an accurate ohmmeter and voltmeter and take certain precautions as follows.

IGNITION SYSTEM PRECAUTIONS

1. Do not allow the ignition switch to be ON for more than 10 minutes if the engine will not start.

2. Some tachometers are not compatible with the fully transistorized system. Check the tach's instruction sheet or its manufacturer if there is any doubt in your mind about compatibility.

3. When connecting a tachometer: On USA models, connect the tachometer (plus) terminal to the ignition coil (minus) terminal. On some Canadian models a service wiring connector (covered with a rubber boot) is provided for tachometer connection.

4. Never allow the ignition coil terminals to touch ground. Damage to the ignitor or coil could result if the terminals are grounded.

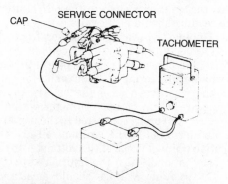

Tachometer hook-up—1986 and later 2S-E

5. Do not disconnect the battery when the engine is running.

6. Make sure that the ignitor is properly grounded to the body.

TESTING

Before testing the signal generator and the ignitor, several other ignition system components should be checked.

1. Connect a timing light to each plug wire in turn. Crank the engine, if the light flashes it can be assumed that voltage is reaching the plugs. If there is no flash from the timing light; (See Step 2).

2. Inspect the spark plug wires. Carefully remove the wires from the spark plugs by twisting the boots. Do not pull or bend the wire, damage to the inside conductor will occur. Inspect the terminals for dirt, looseness and corrosion. If the outside insulation is cracked or broken, replace the wire. Check the resistance of the wire with an ohmmeter. Do not disconnect the wire from the distributor cap. Remove the distributor cap, connect one lead of the ohmmeter to the distributor cap contact and the other to the terminal of the connected plug wire. Replace any wires with excessive resistance, over 8000Ω per foot of cable length (more than 25kΩ), or any that have no continuity. Inspect the distributor cap and ignition rotor for cracks, damage or carbon tracking. Replace as necessary.

3. Remove the spark plugs and check for electrode wear, carbon deposits, thread damage and insulator damage. If any problem is found, replace the plugs. If the old plugs are to be reused, clean them with a wire brush or have them cleaned in a spark plug cleaner. (Check your local gas station). After cleaning the plugs, check the gap (see Chapter two) and reinstall.

NOTE: *If the engine still will not start, or the*

timing light test shows no spark, check the ignition coil resistances.

IGNITION COIL TESTS

Primary Resistance

With an ohmmeter, check between the positive (plus) and negative (minus) terminals of the ignition coil. With the coil cold, the resistances should be:

USA: $0.8-1.0\Omega$
Canada: $0.4-0.5\Omega$

Secondary Resistance

With an ohmmeter, check between the positive (plus) coil terminal and the high tension (coil wire) terminal. Clean the coil wire terminal with a wire brush before testing. The resistance on all except Canadian models should be; $11.5-15.5k\Omega$. Canadian models should be $8.5-11.5k\Omega$.

BALLAST RESISTOR/RESISTOR WIRE TEST

On models with a coil mounted resistor, connect the ohmmeter leads to the end terminals of the resistor. Resistance should measure $1.2-1.4\Omega$. On models with a resistor wire, disconnect the plastic connector at the igniter. Connect one ohmmeter lead to the yellow wire and the other to the brown wire. Resistance should measure $1.2-1.4\Omega$.

NOTE: *If the tests on the coil or the resistor show values far from the standard, replace the part or wire, perform the timing light test or attempt to start the engine.*

CHECKING THE AIR GAP

Remove the distributor cap and ignition rotor. Check the air gap between the timing rotor spoke and the pick up coil. When aligned, the air gap should be 0.2-0.4mm. You will probably have to bump the engine around with the starter to line up the timing rotor. Refer to air gap adjustment in Chapter 2 for adjustment procedure.

SIGNAL GENERATOR TEST (PICKUP COIL)

Check the resistance of the signal generator. Unplug the connector to the distributor. Connect one lead of the ohmmeter to the white wire, the other lead to the pink wire. Resistance should be $130-190\Omega$. If resistance is not correct, replace the signal generator.

REPLACING THE SIGNAL GENERATOR (PICKUP COIL)

Remove the distributor cap and ignition rotor. Disconnect the distributor wiring connector. Remove the two screws that mount the signal generator (pickup coil). Install the new signal generator with the two mounting screws, do not completely tighten the screws until you have adjusted the air gap. (See air gap adjustment, Chapter 2). Reconnect the wiring harness, install the rotor and distributor cap. Check for engine starting. If the engine will not start, check the ignitor.

TESTING THE IGNITOR

Canadian Models

1. Connect the negative (minus) probe of the voltmeter to the negative (minus) terminal of the ignition coil and the positive (plus) probe of the voltmeter to the yellow resistor wire at the connector unplugged from the ignitor. With the ignition switch ON (not start) the voltage should read 12 volts.

2. Check the voltage between the negative (minus) coil terminal and the yellow resistor wire again, but this time use the ohmmeter as resistance. Connect the positive (plus) ohmmeter lead to the pink wire in the plug connector. Connect the negative (minus) ohmmeter lead to the white wire in the connector.

CAUTION: *Do not reverse the connection of the ohmmeter.*

Select either the 1Ω or 10Ω range on the ohmmeter. With the voltmeter connected as in Step one and the ignition switch turned ON, the voltage should measure nearly zero. If a problem is found, replace the ignitor.

U.S.A. Models

1. Connect the positive (plus) probe of the voltmeter to the positive (plus) terminal of the ignition coil. Connect the negative (minus) probe of the voltmeter to the car body ground. Turn the ignition switch to the ON position. The voltage should read 12 volts.

2. To check the power transistor in the ignitor; connect the positive (plus) probe of the voltmeter to the negative (minus) terminal of the ignition coil and the negative (minus) probe of the voltmeter to the car body ground. Turn the ignition switch to the ON position. The reading should be 12 volts.

3. Unplug the wiring connector from the distributor. With a 1.5 volt dry cell battery in circuit, i.e. connect the positive pole of the battery to the pink terminal of the connector plug, and the negative pole of the battery to the white wire. Connect the voltmeter with the positive (plus) probe connected to the negative (minus) terminal of the ignition coil and the negative (minus) probe of the voltmeter to the car body ground. Turn the ignition switch to the ON position. Voltage should measure 5 volts, less than battery voltage.

CAUTION: *Do not apply voltage for more than five seconds or the power transistor will be destroyed.*

If a problem is found, replace the ignitor.

Distributor

REMOVAL

1983

1. Unfasten the retaining clips and lift the distributor cap straight up. It will be easier to install the distributor if the wiring is left connected to the cap. If the wires must be removed from the cap, mark their positions to aid in installation.

2. Remove the dust cover and mark the position of the rotor relative to the distributor body; then mark the position of the body relative to the block.

3. Disconnect the coil primary wire and the vacuum line(s). If the distributor vacuum unit has two vacuum lines, mark which is which for installation.

4. Remove the retaining bolt and lift the distributor straight up, away from the engine. The rotor and body are marked so that they can be returned to the position from which they were removed. Do not turn or disturb the engine (unless absolutely necessary, such as for engine rebuilding), after the distributor has been removed.

1984 and Later

1. Disconnect the battery ground, disconnect the electrical leads, vacuum hoses and spark plug wires from the distributor.

2. Remove the holddown bolts, and pull the distributor from the engine.

INSTALLATION – CAMSHAFT OR CRANK-SHAFT NOT ROTATED

1983

1. Insert the distributor in the block and align the matchmarks made during removal.

2. Engage the distributor driven gear with the distributor drive.

3. Install the distributor clamp and secure it with the pinch bolt.

4. Install the cap, primary wire, and vacuum line(s).

5. Install the spark plug leads. Consult the marks made during removal to be sure that the proper lead goes to each plug. Install the high tension wire if it was removed.

6. Start the engine. Check the timing and adjust it as outlined in Chapter 2.

INSTALLATION – CAMSHAFT OR CRANK-SHAFT ROTATED

1983

If the engine has been cranked, dismantled, or the timing otherwise lost, proceed as follows:

1. Determine top dead center (TDC) of the No. 1 cylinder's compression stroke by removing the spark plug from the No. 1 cylinder and placing a screwdriver handle or a vacuum gauge over the vacuum gauge over the spark plug hole. This is important because the timing marks will also line up with the last cylinder in the firing order in its exhaust stroke. Crank the engine until compression pressure starts to build up. Continue cranking the engine until the timing marks indicate TDC (or 0).

2. Next, align the timing marks to the specifications given in the Ignition Timing column of the Tune-Up Specifications chart at the beginning of Chapter 2.

3. Temporarily install the rotor in the distributor without the dust cover. Turn the distributor shaft so that the rotor is pointing toward the No. 1 terminal in the distributor cap.

4. Use a small screwdriver to align the slot on the distributor drive (oil pump driveshaft) with the key on the bottom of the distributor shaft.

5. Align the matchmarks on the distributor body and the blocks which were made during the removal. Install the distributor in the block by rotating it slightly (no more than one gear tooth in either direction) until the driven gear meshes with the drive.

NOTE: *Oil the distributor spiral gear and the oil pump driveshaft end before distributor installation.*

6. Rotate the distributor, once it is installed, so that the projection on the pickup coil is almost opposite the signal rotor tooth. Temporarily tighten the pinch bolt.

7. Remove the rotor and install the dust cover. Replace the rotor and the distributor cap.

8. Install the primary wire and the vacuum line(s).

9. Install the No. 1 spark plug. Connect the cables to the spark plugs in the proper order by using the marks made during removal. Install the high tension lead if it was removed.

10. Start the engine.

1984 and Later

1. Set the engine at TDC of #1 cylinder's firing stroke. This can be accomplished by removing #1 spark plug and turn the engine by hand with your thumb over the spark plug hole. As #1 is coming up on its firing stroke, you'll feel

the pressure against your thumb. Make sure the timing marks are set at 0.

2. Remove the right front wheel and fender apron seal, remove the hole plug of the #2 timing belt cover, and, using a mirror, align the mark on the oil seal retainer with the center of the small hole on the camshaft timing pulley by turning the crankshaft pulley clockwise. Install the plug, fender apron and seal, and the wheel. Coat the spiral gear with clean engine oil, align the protrusion on the housing with the mark on the spiral gear and insert the distributor, aligning the center of the flange with the bolt hole on the head. Tighten the bolts.

Alternator

OPERATION

An alternator differs from a conventional DC shunt generator in that the armature is stationary, and is called the stator, while the field rotates and is called the rotor. The higher current values in the alternator's stator are conducted to the external circuit through fixed leads and connections, rather than through a rotating commutator and brushes as in a DC generator. This eliminates a major point of maintenance.

The alternator employs a 3-phase stator winding. The rotor consists of a field coil encased between 6-poled, interleaved sections, producing a 12-pole magnetic field with alternating north and south poles. By rotating the rotor inside the stator, and alternating current is induced in the stator windings. This alternating current is changed to direct current by diodes and is routed out of the alternator through the output terminal. Diode rectifiers act as one way electrical valves. Half of the diodes have a negative polarity and are grounded. The other half of the diodes have a positive polarity and are connected to the output terminal.

Since the diodes have a high resistance to the flow of current in one direction, and a low resistance in the opposite direction, they are connected in a manner which allows current to flow from the alternator to the battery in the low resistance direction.

The high resistance in the other direction prevents the flow of current from the battery to the alternator. Because of this feature, there is no need for a circuit breaker between the alternator and the battery.

Residual magnetism in the rotor field poles is minimal. The starting field current must, therefore, be supplied by the battery. It is connected to the field winding through the ignition switch and the charge indicator lamp or ammeter.

As in the DC shunt generator, the alternator voltage is regulated by varying the field current. This is accomplished electronically in the transistorized voltage regulator. No current regulator is required because all alternators have self limiting current characteristics.

An alternator is better that a conventional,

Troubleshooting Basic Charging System Problems

Problem	Cause	Solution
Noisy alternator	• Loose mountings • Loose drive pulley • Worn bearings • Brush noise • Internal circuits shorted (High pitched whine)	• Tighten mounting bolts • Tighten pulley • Replace alternator • Replace alternator • Replace alternator
Squeal when starting engine or accelerating	• Glazed or loose belt	• Replace or adjust belt
Indicator light remains on or ammeter indicates discharge (engine running)	• Broken fan belt • Broken or disconnected wires • Internal alternator problems • Defective voltage regulator	• Install belt • Repair or connect wiring • Replace alternator • Replace voltage regulator
Car light bulbs continually burn out—battery needs water continually	• Alternator/regulator overcharging	• Replace voltage regulator/alternator
Car lights flare on acceleration	• Battery low • Internal alternator/regulator problems	• Charge or replace battery • Replace alternator/regulator
Low voltage output (alternator light flickers continually or ammeter needle wanders)	• Loose or worn belt • Dirty or corroded connections • Internal alternator/regulator problems	• Replace or adjust belt • Clean or replace connections • Replace alternator or regulator

DC shunt generator because it is lighter and more compact, because it is designed to supply the battery and accessory circuits through a wide range of engine speeds, and because it eliminates the necessary maintenance of replacing brushes and servicing commutators.

The transistorized voltage regulator is an electronic switching device. It senses the voltage at the auxiliary terminal of the alternator and supplies the necessary field current for maintaining the system voltage at the output terminal. The output current is determined by the battery electrical load, such as operating headlights or heater blower.

The transistorized voltage regulator is a sealed unit that has no adjustments and must be replaced as a complete unit when it ceases to operate.

ALTERNATOR PRECAUTIONS

1. Always observe proper polarity of the battery connections; be especially careful when jump-starting the car.

2. Never ground or short out any alternator or alternator regulator terminals.

3. Never operate the alternator with any of its or the battery's leads disconnected.

4. Always remove the battery or disconnect both cables (ground cable first) before charging.

5. Always disconnect the ground cable when replacing any electrical components.

6. Never subject the alternator to excessive heat or dampness if the engine is being steam-cleaned.

7. Never use arc welding equipment with the alternator connected.

REMOVAL AND INSTALLATION

1. Disconnect the battery ground (negative) cable. Unfasten the starter-to-battery cable at the battery end.

2. Remove the air cleaner, if necessary, to gain access to the alternator.

3. Unfasten the bolts which attach the adjusting link to the alternator. Remove the alternator drive belt.

4. Unfasten the alternator wiring connections.

5. Remove the alternator attaching bolt and then withdraw the alternator from its bracket.

6. Installation is performed in the reverse order of removal. After installing the alternator, adjust the belt tension as detailed in Chapter 1.

BELT TENSION ADJUSTMENT

The fan belt drives the generator/alternator and the water pump. If it is too loose, it will slip and the generator/alternator will not be able to produce the rated current. if the belt is too loose, the water pump would not be driven and the engine could overheat. Check the tension of the fan belt by pushing your thumb down on the longest span of belt midway between the pulleys. If the belt flexes more than ½" (12.7mm), it should be tightened. Loosen the bolt on the adjusting bracket and pivot bolt and move the alternator or generator away from the engine to tighten the belt. Do not apply pressure to the rear of the case aluminum housing of an alternator; it might break. Tighten the adjusting bolts when the proper tension is reached.

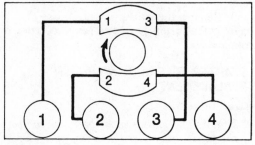

2S-E

Alternator and Regulator Specifications

| Engine Type | Alternator | | Regulator | | | | | | |
| | | | | Field Relay | | | Regulator | | |
	Manufacturer	Output (amps)	Manufacturer	Contact Spring Deflection (in.)	Point Gap (in.)	Volts to Close	Air Gap (in.)	Point Gap (in.)	Volts
2S-E	Nippon Denso	70	Nippon Denso	————————Not Adjustable————————					13.5–15.1
1C-TL, 2C-T	Nippon Denso	55, 60	Nippon Denso	————————Not Adjustable————————					13.8–14.4

IC Regulator

The IC regulator is mounted on the alternator housing, is transistorized and is non-adjustable.

REMOVAL AND INSTALLATION

1. Disconnect the negative (ground) battery cable from the battery.
2. Remove the end cover of the regulator.
3. Remove the three screws that go through the terminals.
4. Remove the (two) top mounting screws that mount the regulator to the alternator. Remove the regulator.
5. To install the new IC regulator. Place the regulator in position on the alternator. Install and secure the (two) top mounting screws. Install the (three) terminal screws. Install the end cover.
6. Reconnect the battery ground cable.

TESTING THE IC REGULATOR

To test the IC regulator you will need a voltmeter and an ammeter.

1. Disconnect the wire connected to the B terminal of the alternator. Connect the wire (that you disconnected) to the negative (minus) terminal of the ammeter.
2. Connect the test lead from the positive (plus) terminal of the ammeter to the B terminal of the alternator.
3. Connect the positive (plus) lead of the voltmeter to the B terminal of the alternator.
4. Connect the negative (minus) lead of the voltmeter to ground.
5. Start the engine and run at about 2000 rpm. Check the reading on the ammeter and voltmeter. Standard amperage should be less than 10 amps. Standard voltage should be from 14 to 14.7 volts (Temperature 77°F).
6. If the voltage is greater than 15 volts, replace the IC regulator.
7. If the voltage reading is less than 13.5 volts, check the regulator and alternator as follows; shut off engine.
8. Turn the ignition switch to ON. Check the voltage at the IG terminal of the alternator. If no voltage, check the ENGINE fuse and/or the ignition switch. No problems found, go to next step.
9. Remove the end cover from the IC regulator. Check the voltage reading at the regulator L terminal. If the voltage reading is zero to 2 volts, suspect the alternator.
10. If the voltage is the same as battery voltage, turn off the ignition switch (OFF position) and check for continuity between the regulator L and F terminals.
11. If there is no continuity, suspect the al-

Remove direct-drive starter solenoid in direction of arrow

ternator. If there is continuity (approx. 4Ω) replace the IC regulator.

Starter

REMOVAL AND INSTALLATION

1. Disconnect the negative (ground) cable from the battery.
2. Disconnect the wires/cables connected to the starter motor.
3. On some models it may be necessary to remove the air cleaner, splash shields or linkage that is in the way of easy access to the starter motor.
4. Loosen and remove the starter motor mounting nuts/bolts while supporting the motor.
5. Remove the starter motor.
6. Installation is in the reverse order of removal.

STARTER SOLENOID AND BRUSH REPLACEMENT

Direct Drive Type

NOTE: *The starter must be removed from the car in order to perform this operation.*

1. Disconnect the field coil lead from the solenoid terminal.
2. Unfasten the solenoid retaining screws. Remove the solenoid by tilting it upward and withdrawing it.
3. Unfasten the end frame bearing cover screws and remove the cover.
4. Unfasten and withdraw the thru-bolts. Remove the commutator endframe.
5. Withdraw the brushes from their holder it they are to be replaced.
6. Check the brush length against the specification in the Battery and Starter Specifications chart. Replace the brushes with new ones if required.

Troubleshooting Basic Starting System Problems

Problem	Cause	Solution
Starter motor rotates engine slowly	• Battery charge low or battery defective	• Charge or replace battery
	• Defective circuit between battery and starter motor	• Clean and tighten, or replace cables
	• Low load current	• Bench-test starter motor. Inspect for worn brushes and weak brush springs.
	• High load current	• Bench-test starter motor. Check engine for friction, drag or coolant in cylinders. Check ring gear-to-pinion gear clearance.
Starter motor will not rotate engine	• Battery charge low or battery defective	• Charge or replace battery
	• Faulty solenoid	• Check solenoid ground. Repair or replace as necessary.
	• Damage drive pinion gear or ring gear	• Replace damaged gear(s)
	• Starter motor engagement weak	• Bench-test starter motor
	• Starter motor rotates slowly with high load current	• Inspect drive yoke pull-down and point gap, check for worn end bushings, check ring gear clearance
	• Engine seized	• Repair engine
Starter motor drive will not engage (solenoid known to be good)	• Defective contact point assembly	• Repair or replace contact point assembly
	• Inadequate contact point assembly ground	• Repair connection at ground screw
	• Defective hold-in coil	• Replace field winding assembly
Starter motor drive will not disengage	• Starter motor loose on flywheel housing	• Tighten mounting bolts
	• Worn drive end busing	• Replace bushing
	• Damaged ring gear teeth	• Replace ring gear or driveplate
	• Drive yoke return spring broken or missing	• Replace spring
Starter motor drive disengages prematurely	• Weak drive assembly thrust spring	• Replace drive mechanism
	• Hold-in coil defective	• Replace field winding assembly
Low load current	• Worn brushes	• Replace brushes
	• Weak brush springs	• Replace springs

7. Dress the new brushes with emery cloth so that they will make proper contact.

8. Use a spring scale to check the brush spring tensions against the specification in the chart. Replace the springs if they do not meet specification.

9. Assembly is the reverse order of disassembly. Remember to pack the end bearing cover with multipurpose grease before installing it.

Gear Reduction Type

NOTE: *The starter must be removed from the car in order to perform this operation.*

1. Disconnect the solenoid lead terminal.

2. Loosen the two bolts on the starter housing and separate the field frame from the solenoid. Remove the O-ring and felt dust seal.

3. Unfasten the two screws and separate the starter drive from the solenoid.

4. Withdraw the clutch and gears. Remove the ball from the clutch shaft bore or solenoid.

5. Remove the brushes from the holder.

6. Measure the brush length and compare it to the figure in the Battery and Starter Specifications chart. Replace the brushes with new ones if they are too short.

7. Replace any worn or chipped gears.

8. Assembly is performed in the reverse order of disassembly. Lubricate all gears and bearings with high temperature grease. Grease the ball before inserting it in the clutch shaft bore. Align the tab on the brush holder with the notch on the field frame. Check the positive (+) brush leads to ensure that they aren't grounded. Align the solenoid marks with the field frame bolt anchors.

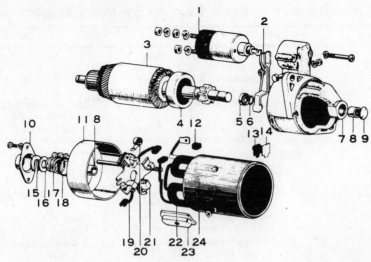

1. Solenoid	9. Bearing cover	17. Brake spring
2. Engagement lever	10. Bearing cover	18. Gasket
3. Armature	11. Commutator end frame	19. Brush
4. Overrunning clutch	12. Rubber bushing	20. Brush spring
5. Clutch stop	13. Rubber grommet	21. Brush holder
6. Snap-ring	14. Plate	22. Field coil
7. Drive housing	15. Lockplate	23. Pole shoes
8. Bushing	16. Washer	24. Field yoke

Components of the direct-drive starter motor

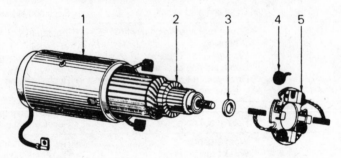

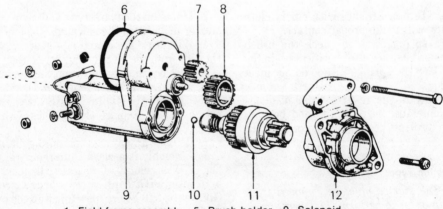

1. Field frame assembly	5. Brush holder	9. Solenoid
2. Armature	6. O-ring	10. Steel ball
3. Felt seal	7. Pinion gear	11. Clutch assembly
4. Brush spring	8. Idler gear	12. Starter housing

Components of the gear reduction starter motor

STARTER DRIVE REPLACEMENT

Direct Drive Starter

NOTE: *The starter must be removed from car.*

1. Loosen the locknut or bolt and remove the connection going to the terminal of the solenoid. Remove the securing screws and remove the solenoid.
2. Remove the front dust cover, E-ring, thrust washers, and the two screws retaining the brush holder assembly. Remove the brush cover thru-bolts and remove the cover assembly.
3. Lift the brushes to free them from the commutator and remove the brush holder.
4. Tap the yoke assembly lightly with a wooden hammer and remove it from the field and case.
5. Remove the nut and bolt which serve as a pin for the shift lever, carefully retaining the associated washers.
6. Remove the armature assembly and shift lever.
7. Push the stop ring (located at the end of the armature shaft) toward the clutch and remove the snapring. Remove the stop ring.
8. Remove the clutch assembly from the armature shaft.

To install the drive:

1. Install the clutch assembly onto the armature shaft.
2. Put the stop ring on and hold it toward the clutch while installing the snapring.
3. Install the armature assembly and shift lever into the yoke.
4. Install the washers, nut and bolt which serve as a shift lever pivot pin.
5. Install the field back onto the yoke assembly.
6. Lift the brushes and install the brush holder. Install the brush cover and thru-bolts.
7. Replace the brush holder set screws, the thrust washers, E-ring, and the dust cover.
8. Install the solenoid. Reconnect the wire to the terminal of the solenoid.

Gear Reduction Type

1. Remove the starter.
2. Remove the solenoid and the shift lever.
3. Remove the bolts securing the center housing to the front cover and separate the parts.
4. Remove the gears and the starter drive.
CAUTION: *Be careful not to lose the steel ball installed in the drive. Remember to reinstall when replacing the drive.*
5. Installation is the reverse.

Battery

Refer to Chapter 1 for details on battery maintenance.

REMOVAL AND INSTALLATION

1. Disconnect the negative (ground) cable from the terminal, and then the positive cable. Special pullers are available to remove the cable clamps.
NOTE: *To avoid sparks, always disconnect the ground cable first, and connect it last.*
2. Remove the battery holddown clamp.
3. Remove the battery, being careful not to spill the acid.
NOTE: *Spilled acid can be neutralized with a baking soda/water solution. If you somehow get acid into your eyes, flush it out with lots of water and get to a doctor.*
4. Clean the battery posts thoroughly before reinstalling, or when installing a new battery.
5. Clean the cable clamps, using a wire brush, both inside and out.
6. Install the battery and the holddown clamp or strap. Connect the positive, then the negative cable. Do not hammer them in place. The terminals should be coated lightly (externally) with grease to prevent corrosion. There are also felt washers impregnated with an anti-corrosion substance which are slipped over the battery posts before installing the cables; these are available in auto parts stores.
CAUTION: *Make absolutely sure that the battery is connected properly before you turn on the ignition switch. Reversed polarity can burn out your alternator and regulator within a matter of seconds.*

ENGINE MECHANICAL

Engine Overhaul Tips

Most engine overhaul procedures are fairly standard. In addition to specific parts replacement procedures and complete specifications for your individual engine, this chapter also is a guide to accept rebuilding procedures. Examples of standard rebuilding practice are shown and should be used along with specific details concerning your particular engine.

Competent and accurate machine shop services will ensure maximum performance, reliability and engine life.

In most instances it is more profitable for the do-it-yourself mechanic to remove, clean and inspect the component, buy the necessary parts and deliver these to a shop for actual machine work.

On the other hand, much of the rebuilding work (crankshaft, block, bearings, piston rods,

and other components) is well within the scope of the do-it-yourself mechanic.

TOOLS

The tools required for an engine overhaul or parts replacement will depend on the depth of your involvement. With a few exceptions, they will be the tools found in a mechanic's tool kit (see Chapter 1). More in-depth work will require any or all of the following:
• A dial indicator (reading in thousandths) mounted on a universal base
• Micrometers and telescope gauges
• Jaw and screw-type pullers
• Scraper
• Valve spring compressor
• Ring groove cleaner
• Piston ring expander and compressor
• Ridge reamer
• Cylinder hone or glaze breaker
• Plastigage®
• Engine stand

The use of most of these tools is illustrated in this chapter. Many can be rented for a one-time use from a local parts jobber or tool supply house specializing in automotive work.

Occasionally, the use of special tools is called for. See the information on Special Tools and Safety Notice in the front of this book before substituting another tool.

INSPECTION TECHNIQUES

Procedures and specifications are given in this chapter for inspecting, cleaning and assessing the wear limits of most major components. Other procedures such as Magnaflux® and Zyglo® can be used to locate material flaws and stress cracks. Magnaflux® is a magnetic process applicable only to ferrous materials. The Zyglo® process coats the material with a fluorescent dye penetrant and can be used on any material Check for suspected surface cracks can be more readily made using spot check dye. The dye is sprayed onto the suspected area, wiped off and the area sprayed with a developer. Cracks will show up brightly.

OVERHAUL TIPS

Aluminum has become extremely popular for use in engines, due to its low weight. Observe the following precautions when handling aluminum parts:
• Never hot tank aluminum parts (the caustic hot tank solution will eat the aluminum.
• Remove all aluminum parts (identification tag, etc.) from engine parts prior to the tanking.
• Always coat threads lightly with engine oil or anti-seize compounds before installation, to prevent seizure.

• Never over-torque bolts or spark plugs especially in aluminum threads.
Stripped threads in any component can be repaired using any of several commercial repair kits (Heli-Coil®, Microdot®, Keenserts®, etc.).

When assembling the engine, any parts that will be frictional contact must be prelubed to provide lubrication at initial start-up. Any product specifically formulated for this purpose can be used, but engine oil is not recommended as a prelube.

When semi-permanent (locked, but removable) installation of bolts or nuts is desired, threads should be cleaned and coated with Loctite® or other similar, commercial non-hardening sealant.

REPAIRING DAMAGED THREADS

Several methods of repairing damaged threads are available. Heli-Coil® (shown here), Keenserts® and Microdot® are among the most widely used. All involve basically the same principle—drilling out stripped threads, tapping the hole and installing a prewound insert—making welding, plugging and oversize fasteners unnecessary.

Two types of thread repair inserts are usually supplied: a standard type for most Inch Coarse, Inch Fine, Metric Course and Metric Fine thread sizes and a spark lug type to fit most spark plug port sizes. Consult the individual manufacturer's catalog to determine exact applications. Typical thread repair kits will contain a selection of prewound threaded inserts, a tap (corresponding to the outside diameter threads of the insert) and an installation tool. Spark plug inserts usually differ because they require a tap equipped with pilot threads and a combined reamer/tap section. Most manufacturers also supply blister-packed thread repair inserts separately in addition to a master kit containing a variety of taps and inserts plus installation tools.

Before effecting a repair to a threaded hole, remove any snapped, broken or damaged bolts or studs. Penetrating oil can be used to free frozen threads; the offending item can be removed with locking pliers or with a screw or stud extractor. After the hole is clear, the thread can be repaired, as follows:

Checking Engine Compression

A noticeable lack of engine power, excessive oil consumption and/or poor fuel mileage measured over an extended period are all indicators of internal engine war. Worn piston rings, scored or worn cylinder bores, blown head gaskets, sticking or burnt valves and worn valve seats are all possible culprits here. A check of

each cylinder's compression will help you locate the problems.

As mentioned in the Tools and Equipment section of Chapter 1, a screw-in type compression gauge is more accurate that the type you simply hold against the spark plug hole, although it takes slightly longer to use. It's worth it to obtain a more accurate reading. Follow the procedures below for gasoline and diesel engined trucks.

GASOLINE ENGINES

1. Warm up the engine to normal operating temperature.
2. Remove all spark plugs.
3. Disconnect the high tension lead from the ignition coil.
4. On fully open the throttle either by operating the carburetor throttle linkage by hand or by having an assistant floor the accelerator pedal.
5. Screw the compression gauge into the no.1 spark plug hole until the fitting is snug.
NOTE: *Be careful not to crossthread the plug hole. On aluminum cylinder heads use extra care, as the threads in these heads are easily ruined.*
6. Ask an assistant to depress the accelerator pedal fully on both carbureted and fuel injected trucks. Then, while you read the compression gauge, ask the assistant to crank the engine two or three times in short bursts using the ignition switch.
7. Read the compression gauge at the end of each series of cranks, and record the highest of these readings. Repeat this procedure for each of the engine's cylinders. Compare the highest reading of each cylinder to the compression pressure specification in the Tune-Up Specifications chart in Chapter 2. The specs in this chart are maximum values.

A cylinder's compression pressure is usually acceptable if it is not less than 80% of maximum. The difference between each cylinder should be no more than 12–14 pounds.
8. If a cylinder is unusually low, pour a tablespoon of clean engine oil into the cylinder through the spark plug hole and repeat the compression test. If the compression comes up after adding the oil, it appears that the cylinder's piston rings or bore are damaged or worn. If the pressure remains low, the valves may not be seating properly (a valve job is needed), or the head gasket may be blown near that cylinder. If compression in any two adjacent cylinders is low, and if the addition of oil doesn't help the compression, there is leakage past the head gasket. Oil and coolant water in the combustion chamber can result from this problem.

There may be evidence of water droplets on the engine dipstick when a head gasket has blown.

DIESEL ENGINES

Checking cylinder compression on diesel engines is basically the same procedure as on gasoline engines except for the following:
1. A special compression gauge adaptor suitable for diesel engines (because these engines have much greater compression pressures) must be used.
2. Remove the injector tubes and remove the injectors from each cylinder.
NOTE: *Don't forget to remove the washer underneath each injector; otherwise, it may get lost when the engine is cranked.*
3. When fitting the compression gauge adaptor to the cylinder head, make sure the bleeder of the gauge (if equipped) is closed.
4. When reinstalling the injector assemblies, install new washers underneath each injector.

Engine
REMOVAL AND INSTALLATION

1. Drain the engine coolant.
CAUTION: *When draining the coolant, keep in mind that cats and dogs are attracted by the ethylene glycol antifreeze, and are quite likely to drink any that is left in an uncovered container or in puddles on the ground. This will prove fatal in sufficient quantity. Always drain the coolant into a sealable container. Coolant should be reused unless it is contaminated or several years old.*
2. Remove the hood.
3. Remove the battery.
4. Disconnect and tag all cables attached to various engine parts.
5. Disconnect and tag all electrical wires attached to various engine parts.
6. Disconnect and tag all vacuum lines connected to various engine parts.
7. Remove the cruise control actuator and bracket. On the diesel, disconnect the accelerator cable at the injection pump.
8. Disconnect the radiator and heater hoses.
9. Disconnect the automatic transmission cooler lines at the radiator.
10. Unbolt the two radiator supports and lift out the radiator.
11. Remove the air cleaner assembly and air flow meter.
12. Disconnect all wiring and linkage at the transmission.
13. Pull out the fuel injection system wiring harness and secure to the right side fender apron.

Troubleshooting Engine Mechanical Problems

Problem	Cause	Solution
External oil leaks	• Fuel pump gasket broken or improperly seated	• Replace gasket
	• Cylinder head cover RTV sealant broken or improperly seated	• Replace sealant; inspect cylinder head cover sealant flange and cylinder head sealant surface for distortion and cracks
	• Oil filler cap leaking or missing	• Replace cap
	• Oil filter gasket broken or improperly seated	• Replace oil filter
	• Oil pan side gasket broken, improperly seated or opening in RTV sealant	• Replace gasket or repair opening in sealant; inspect oil pan gasket flange for distortion
	• Oil pan front oil seal broken or improperly seated	• Replace seal; inspect timing case cover and oil pan seal flange for distortion
	• Oil pan rear oil seal broken or improperly seated	• Replace seal; inspect oil pan rear oil seal flange; inspect rear main bearing cap for cracks, plugged oil return channels, or distortion in seal groove
	• Timing case cover oil seal broken or improperly seated	• Replace seal
	• Excess oil pressure because of restricted PCV valve	• Replace PCV valve
	• Oil pan drain plug loose or has stripped threads	• Repair as necessary and tighten
	• Rear oil gallery plug loose	• Use appropriate sealant on gallery plug and tighten
	• Rear camshaft plug loose or improperly seated	• Seat camshaft plug or replace and seal, as necessary
	• Distributor base gasket damaged	• Replace gasket
Excessive oil consumption	• Oil level too high	• Drain oil to specified level
	• Oil with wrong viscosity being used	• Replace with specified oil
	• PCV valve stuck closed	• Replace PCV valve
	• Valve stem oil deflectors (or seals) are damaged, missing, or incorrect type	• Replace valve stem oil deflectors
	• Valve stems or valve guides worn	• Measure stem-to-guide clearance and repair as necessary
	• Poorly fitted or missing valve cover baffles	• Replace valve cover
	• Piston rings broken or missing	• Replace broken or missing rings
	• Scuffed piston	• Replace piston
	• Incorrect piston ring gap	• Measure ring gap, repair as necessary
	• Piston rings sticking or excessively loose in grooves	• Measure ring side clearance, repair as necessary
	• Compression rings installed upside down	• Repair as necessary
	• Cylinder walls worn, scored, or glazed	• Repair as necessary
	• Piston ring gaps not properly staggered	• Repair as necessary
	• Excessive main or connecting rod bearing clearance	• Measure bearing clearance, repair as necessary
No oil pressure	• Low oil level	• Add oil to correct level
	• Oil pressure gauge, warning lamp or sending unit inaccurate	• Replace oil pressure gauge or warning lamp
	• Oil pump malfunction	• Replace oil pump
	• Oil pressure relief valve sticking	• Remove and inspect oil pressure relief valve assembly
	• Oil passages on pressure side of pump obstructed	• Inspect oil passages for obstruction

Troubleshooting Engine Mechanical Problems (cont.)

Problem	Cause	Solution
No oil pressure (cont.)	• Oil pickup screen or tube obstructed • Loose oil inlet tube	• Inspect oil pickup for obstruction • Tighten or seal inlet tube
Low oil pressure	• Low oil level • Inaccurate gauge, warning lamp or sending unit • Oil excessively thin because of dilution, poor quality, or improper grade • Excessive oil temperature • Oil pressure relief spring weak or sticking • Oil inlet tube and screen assembly has restriction or air leak • Excessive oil pump clearance • Excessive main, rod, or camshaft bearing clearance	• Add oil to correct level • Replace oil pressure gauge or warning lamp • Drain and refill crankcase with recommended oil • Correct cause of overheating engine • Remove and inspect oil pressure relief valve assembly • Remove and inspect oil inlet tube and screen assembly. (Fill inlet tube with lacquer thinner to locate leaks.) • Measure clearances • Measure bearing clearances, repair as necessary
High oil pressure	• Improper oil viscosity • Oil pressure gauge or sending unit inaccurate • Oil pressure relief valve sticking closed	• Drain and refill crankcase with correct viscosity oil • Replace oil pressure gauge • Remove and inspect oil pressure relief valve assembly
Main bearing noise	• Insufficient oil supply • Main bearing clearance excessive • Bearing insert missing • Crankshaft end play excessive • Improperly tightened main bearing cap bolts • Loose flywheel or drive plate • Loose or damaged vibration damper	• Inspect for low oil level and low oil pressure • Measure main bearing clearance, repair as necessary • Replace missing insert • Measure end play, repair as necessary • Tighten bolts with specified torque • Tighten flywheel or drive plate attaching bolts • Repair as necessary
Connecting rod bearing noise	• Insufficient oil supply • Carbon build-up on piston • Bearing clearance excessive or bearing missing • Crankshaft connecting rod journal out-of-round • Misaligned connecting rod or cap • Connecting rod bolts tightened improperly	• Inspect for low oil level and low oil pressure • Remove carbon from piston crown • Measure clearance, repair as necessary • Measure journal dimensions, repair or replace as necessary • Repair as necessary • Tighten bolts with specified torque
Piston noise	• Piston-to-cylinder wall clearance excessive (scuffed piston) • Cylinder walls excessively tapered or out-of-round • Piston ring broken • Loose or seized piston pin • Connecting rods misaligned • Piston ring side clearance excessively loose or tight • Carbon build-up on piston is excessive	• Measure clearance and examine piston • Measure cylinder wall dimensions, rebore cylinder • Replace all rings on piston • Measure piston-to-pin clearance, repair as necessary • Measure rod alignment, straighten or replace • Measure ring side clearance, repair as necessary • Remove carbon from piston

Troubleshooting Engine Mechanical Problems (cont.)

Problem	Cause	Solution

Valve actuating component noise	• Insufficient oil supply	• Check for:
		  (a) Low oil level
		  (b) Low oil pressure
		  (c) Plugged push rods
		  (d) Wrong hydraulic tappets
		  (e) Restricted oil gallery
		  (f) Excessive tappet to bore clearance

	• Push rods worn or bent • Rocker arms or pivots worn	• Replace worn or bent push rods • Replace worn rocker arms or pivots
	• Foreign objects or chips in hydraulic tappets	• Clean tappets
	• Excessive tappet leak-down • Tappet face worn	• Replace valve tappet • Replace tappet; inspect corresponding cam lobe for wear
	• Broken or cocked valve springs	• Properly seat cocked springs; replace broken springs
	• Stem-to-guide clearance excessive	• Measure stem-to-guide clearance, repair as required
	• Valve bent • Loose rocker arms • Valve seat runout excessive • Missing valve lock • Push rod rubbing or contacting cylinder head • Excessive engine oil (four-cylinder engine)	• Replace valve • Tighten bolts with specified torque • Regrind valve seat/valves • Install valve lock • Remove cylinder head and remove obstruction in head • Correct oil level

Troubleshooting the Cooling System

Problem	Cause	Solution
High temperature gauge indication—overheating	• Coolant level low • Fan belt loose • Radiator hose(s) collapsed • Radiator airflow blocked	• Replenish coolant • Adjust fan belt tension • Replace hose(s) • Remove restriction (bug screen, fog lamps, etc.)
	• Faulty radiator cap • Ignition timing incorrect • Idle speed low • Air trapped in cooling system • Heavy traffic driving	• Replace radiator cap • Adjust ignition timing • Adjust idle speed • Purge air • Operate at fast idle in neutral intermittently to cool engine
	• Incorrect cooling system component(s) installed • Faulty thermostat • Water pump shaft broken or impeller loose • Radiator tubes clogged • Cooling system clogged • Casting flash in cooling passages	• Install proper component(s) • Replace thermostat • Replace water pump • Flush radiator • Flush system • Repair or replace as necessary. Flash may be visible by removing cooling system components or removing core plugs.
	• Brakes dragging • Excessive engine friction • Antifreeze concentration over 68%	• Repair brakes • Repair engine • Lower antifreeze concentration percentage

Troubleshooting the Cooling System (cont.)

Problem	Cause	Solution
High temperature gauge indication—overheating (cont.)	• Missing air seals • Faulty gauge or sending unit • Loss of coolant flow caused by leakage or foaming • Viscous fan drive failed	• Replace air seals • Repair or replace faulty component • Repair or replace leaking component, replace coolant • Replace unit
Low temperature indication—undercooling	• Thermostat stuck open • Faulty gauge or sending unit	• Replace thermostat • Repair or replace faulty component
Coolant loss—boilover	• Overfilled cooling system • Quick shutdown after hard (hot) run • Air in system resulting in occasional "burping" of coolant • Insufficient antifreeze allowing coolant boiling point to be too low • Antifreeze deteriorated because of age or contamination • Leaks due to loose hose clamps, loose nuts, bolts, drain plugs, faulty hoses, or defective radiator • Faulty head gasket • Cracked head, manifold, or block • Faulty radiator cap	• Reduce coolant level to proper specification • Allow engine to run at fast idle prior to shutdown • Purge system • Add antifreeze to raise boiling point • Replace coolant • Pressure test system to locate source of leak(s) then repair as necessary • Replace head gasket • Replace as necessary • Replace cap
Coolant entry into crankcase or cylinder(s)	• Faulty head gasket • Crack in head, manifold or block	• Replace head gasket • Replace as necessary
Coolant recovery system inoperative	• Coolant level low • Leak in system • Pressure cap not tight or seal missing, or leaking • Pressure cap defective • Overflow tube clogged or leaking • Recovery bottle vent restricted	• Replenish coolant to FULL mark • Pressure test to isolate leak and repair as necessary • Repair as necessary • Replace cap • Repair as necessary • Remove restriction
Noise	• Fan contacting shroud • Loose water pump impeller • Glazed fan belt • Loose fan belt • Rough surface on drive pulley • Water pump bearing worn • Belt alignment	• Reposition shroud and inspect engine mounts • Replace pump • Apply silicone or replace belt • Adjust fan belt tension • Replace pulley • Remove belt to isolate. Replace pump. • Check pulley alignment. Repair as necessary.
No coolant flow through heater core	• Restricted return inlet in water pump • Heater hose collapsed or restricted • Restricted heater core • Restricted outlet in thermostat housing • Intake manifold bypass hole in cylinder head restricted • Faulty heater control valve • Intake manifold coolant passage restricted	• Remove restriction • Remove restriction or replace hose • Remove restriction or replace core • Remove flash or restriction • Remove restriction • Replace valve • Remove restriction or replace intake manifold

NOTE: *Immediately after shutdown, the engine enters a condition known as heat soak. This is caused by the cooling system being inoperative while engine temperature is still high. If coolant temperature rises above boiling point, expansion and pressure may push some coolant out of the radiator overflow tube. If this does not occur frequently it is considered normal.*

Troubleshooting the Serpentine Drive Belt

Problem	Cause	Solution
Tension sheeting fabric failure (woven fabric on outside circumference of belt has cracked or separated from body of belt)	• Grooved or backside idler pulley diameters are less than minimum recommended • Tension sheeting contacting (rubbing) stationary object • Excessive heat causing woven fabric to age • Tension sheeting splice has fractured	• Replace pulley(s) not conforming to specification • Correct rubbing condition • Replace belt • Replace belt
Noise (objectional squeal, squeak, or rumble is heard or felt while drive belt is in operation)	• Belt slippage • Bearing noise • Belt misalignment • Belt-to-pulley mismatch • Driven component inducing vibration • System resonant frequency inducing vibration	• Adjust belt • Locate and repair • Align belt/pulley(s) • Install correct belt • Locate defective driven component and repair • Vary belt tension within specifications. Replace belt.
Rib chunking (one or more ribs has separated from belt body)	• Foreign objects imbedded in pulley grooves • Installation damage • Drive loads in excess of design specifications • Insufficient internal belt adhesion	• Remove foreign objects from pulley grooves • Replace belt • Adjust belt tension • Replace belt
Rib or belt wear (belt ribs contact bottom of pulley grooves)	• Pulley(s) misaligned • Mismatch of belt and pulley groove widths • Abrasive environment • Rusted pulley(s) • Sharp or jagged pulley groove tips • Rubber deteriorated	• Align pulley(s) • Replace belt • Replace belt • Clean rust from pulley(s) • Replace pulley • Replace belt
Longitudinal belt cracking (cracks between two ribs)	• Belt has mistracked from pulley groove • Pulley groove tip has worn away rubber-to-tensile member	• Replace belt • Replace belt
Belt slips	• Belt slipping because of insufficient tension • Belt or pulley subjected to substance (belt dressing, oil, ethylene glycol) that has reduced friction • Driven component bearing failure • Belt glazed and hardened from heat and excessive slippage	• Adjust tension • Replace belt and clean pulleys • Replace faulty component bearing • Replace belt
"Groove jumping" (belt does not maintain correct position on pulley, or turns over and/or runs off pulleys)	• Insufficient belt tension • Pulley(s) not within design tolerance • Foreign object(s) in grooves • Excessive belt speed • Pulley misalignment • Belt-to-pulley profile mismatched • Belt cordline is distorted	• Adjust belt tension • Replace pulley(s) • Remove foreign objects from grooves • Avoid excessive engine acceleration • Align pulley(s) • Install correct belt • Replace belt
Belt broken (Note: identify and correct problem before replacement belt is installed)	• Excessive tension • Tensile members damaged during belt installation • Belt turnover • Severe pulley misalignment • Bracket, pulley, or bearing failure	• Replace belt and adjust tension to specification • Replace belt • Replace belt • Align pulley(s) • Replace defective component and belt

Troubleshooting the Serpentine Drive Belt (cont.)

Problem	Cause	Solution
Cord edge failure (tensile member exposed at edges of belt or separated from belt body)	• Excessive tension • Drive pulley misalignment • Belt contacting stationary object • Pulley irregularities • Improper pulley construction • Insufficient adhesion between tensile member and rubber matrix	• Adjust belt tension • Align pulley • Correct as necessary • Replace pulley • Replace pulley • Replace belt and adjust tension to specifications
Sporadic rib cracking (multiple cracks in belt ribs at random intervals)	• Ribbed pulley(s) diameter less than minimum specification • Backside bend flat pulley(s) diameter less than minimum • Excessive heat condition causing rubber to harden • Excessive belt thickness • Belt overcured • Excessive tension	• Replace pulley(s) • Replace pulley(s) • Correct heat condition as necessary • Replace belt • Replace belt • Adjust belt tension

1. The basic troubleshooting procedures for the diesel engine itself (valve clearance, compression, bearings, valves, pistons, etc.) are the same checks you would make for a gasoline engine.
2. The repair of the injection pump requires considerable skill and use of a special test bench.

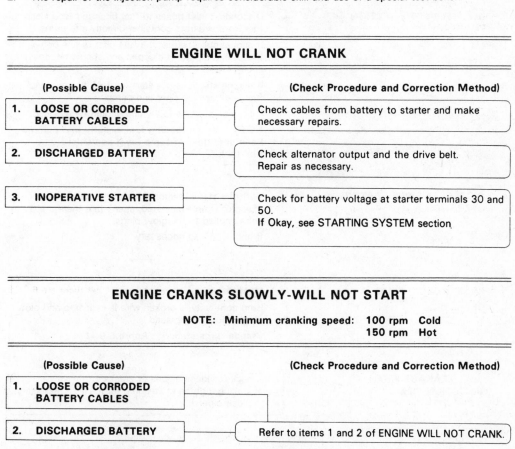

ENGINE WILL NOT CRANK

(Possible Cause)	(Check Procedure and Correction Method)
1. LOOSE OR CORRODED BATTERY CABLES	Check cables from battery to starter and make necessary repairs.
2. DISCHARGED BATTERY	Check alternator output and the drive belt. Repair as necessary.
3. INOPERATIVE STARTER	Check for battery voltage at starter terminals 30 and 50. If Okay, see STARTING SYSTEM section.

ENGINE CRANKS SLOWLY-WILL NOT START

NOTE: Minimum cranking speed: 100 rpm Cold
                                 150 rpm Hot

(Possible Cause)	(Check Procedure and Correction Method)
1. LOOSE OR CORRODED BATTERY CABLES	
2. DISCHARGED BATTERY	Refer to items 1 and 2 of ENGINE WILL NOT CRANK.
3. IMPROPER ENGINE OIL	Check engine oil. If improper viscosity, drain and refill with oil of viscosity recommended by manufacturer.

ENGINE CRANKS NORMALLY BUT WILL NOT START

(Possible Cause)	(Check Procedure and Correction Method)
1. NO FUEL TO NOZZLE	Loosen any one injection pipe union nut from its nozzle holder. Crank the engine for about 5 seconds while confirming that fuel is being discharged from the pipe. If fuel is coming out, begin diagnosis from item 4. If not, begin from item 2.
2. NO FUEL CUT SOLENOID OPERATION	With starter switch turned ON, check for fuel cut solenoid operation noise (clicking sound) while repeatedly connecting and disconnecting fuel cut solenoid. If no noise, check if there is battery voltage to the solenoid when the starter switch is ON. If battery voltage is confirmed, fuel cut solenoid is faulty and should be replaced. If no voltage, make necessary repairs.
3. NO FUEL INTO INJECTION PUMP	Disconnect inlet hoses to fuel filter and feed clean fuel from separate container directly into pump. If engine starts, either the fuel filter or line between fuel tank and filter is clogged and should be repaired accordingly. If engine still does not start (no fuel intake), check fuel line between filter and pump. If normal, pump is faulty and should be replaced. **NOTE: When feeding fuel directly into pump, keep container at same level as vehicle fuel tank.**
4. INOPERATIVE PRE-HEATING OPERATION	With the starter switch ON and the glow plug indicator lamp illuminated, check that there are 6 volts applied to the glow plugs. If not, repair as necessary.
5. FAULTY GLOW PLUG OPERATION	Measure glow plug resistance. If no continuity, a broken wire is indicated and glow plug should be replaced. **Standard resistance: Approx. 0 Ω**
6. FUEL LEAKAGE FROM INJECTION PIPE	Check for loose unions or cracks. If leaking, tighten to standard torque or, if necessary, replace pipe(s).

7. IMPROPER INJECTION TIMING

Turn crankshaft pulley clockwise to where either No.1 or No. 4 piston is at top dead center and, after releasing cold start advance system, check plunger stroke with SST.

If not at the standard indicated below, injection pump is maladjusted.
Change pump installation position and readjust.
Standard: 0.80 mm (0.032 in.) at TDC
NOTE: If injection timing is off more than 10°, it could indicate a jumped timing belt.

8. IMPROPER COLD START ADVANCE AND FAST IDLE

Measure timer piston stroke and fast idle lever opening angle with injection pump tester when cold start advance is operated.

9. FAULTY NOZZLE OR NOZZLE HOLDER

Check injection pressure with nozzle tester.

If not within standard indicated below, nozzle adjustment is improper and pressure should be readjusted.

Standard pressure: 135 − 155 kg/cm^2
(1,920 − 2,205 psi)
(13,239 − 15,200 kPa)
If pressure cannot be adjusted to standard, replace nozzle holder assembly.

ROUGH IDLE WITH WARM ENGINE

(Possible Cause)   **(Check Procedure and Correction Method)**

1. IMPROPER ADJUSTMENT OF ACCELERATOR CABLE

With accelerator pedal released, check that adjusting lever is in contact with idle screw. Also check if accelerator cable is catching on something.

If necessary, adjust so lever is in contact with screw, or make other required repairs.

2. IDLE SPEED TOO LOW

Check if idle rpm is at standard indicated below.

If not adjust with idle adjusting screw.

Standard idle speed: 700 rpm
NOTE: If less than standard, idling would normally be rough.

3. FUEL LEAKAGE

Check for leaks at the pump connections, pump distributor head bolts, nozzle holder and delivery valve.
Tighten any loose connections to specified torque or replace parts as necessary.

4. IMPROPER INJECTION TIMING

Refer to item 7 of ENGINE CRANKS NORMALLY BUT WILL NOT START, above.

5.	IMPROPER OPERATION OF NOZZLE OR DELIVERY VALVE	With engine idling, loosen the injection pipe to each cylinder in order, and check if the idle speed changes.

With engine idling, loosen the injection pipe to each cylinder in order, and check if the idle speed changes.

If no change, a faulty cylinder is indicated.
Check according to following procedure.
Faulty Nozzle or Nozzle Holder
Check injection pressure with nozzle tester.

If pressure is not within standard indicated below, nozzle is faulty and injection pressure should be readjusted.

Standard pressure: 135 − 155 kg/cm^2
(1,920 − 2,205 psi)
(13,239 − 15,200 kPa)

Faulty Delivery Valve
If injection pressure is within standard, delivery valve is defective and should be replaced.

ENGINE SUDDENLY STOPS

(Possible Cause)	(Check Procedure and Correction Method)
1. **ENGINE WILL NOT RE-START**	Check to see if engine re-starts according to prescribed procedure. If not, refer to ENGINE CRANKS NORMALLY BUT WILL NOT START, above, and repair as necessary.
2. **ROUGH IDLE**	If idle is not stable, refer to ROUGH IDLE and repair accordingly.
3. **MALFUNCTION OF FUEL CUT SOLENOID**	Refer to ENGINE CRANKS NORMALLY BUT WILL NOT START, above, and check accordingly. **NOTE:** No operation noise from the fuel cut solenoid may be due to loose electrical connections, so check connectors before proceeding with further repairs.
4. **NO FUEL INTO INJECTION PUMP**	Refer to item 3 of ENGINE CRANKS NORMALLY BUT WILL NOT START, above.

LACK OF POWER

NOTE:
1. First confirm that the air cleaner is not clogged or the engine overheating.
2. Not applicable if the customer desires an output power higher than specified for that vehicle. For accuracy, adjust with a chassis dynamo.

(Possible Cause)	(Check Procedure and Correction Method)
1. **IMPROPER ACCELERATOR CABLE ADJUSTMENT**	With accelerator fully depressed, check that adjusting lever is in contact with maximum speed set screw. If not, adjust accordingly.

2.   **INSUFFICIENT NO-LOAD MAXIMUM SPEED**

Start engine, depress accelerator pedal to floor and check that no-load max. speed is within standard.

If not, adjust with maximum speed adjusting screw.

3.   **INTERCHANGED OVERFLOW SCREW (OUT) AND INLET (NO MARK) FITTING**

NOTE: Overflow screw is marked "OUT" and has an inner jet. Although both fittings are same size, they must not be interchanged.

4.   **FUEL LEAKAGE**

Refer to item 3 of ROUGH IDLE WITH WARM ENGINE.

5.   **CLOGGED FUEL FILTER**

Disconnect inlet hose to fuel filter and feed clean fuel directly into the pump.

If engine condition improves, fuel filter is clogged and should be replaced.

NOTE: When feeding fuel directly into pump, keep container at same level as vehicle fuel tank.

If no increase in engine condition after replacing fuel filter, check priming pump or perform other necessary repairs.

6.   **IMPROPER INJECTION TIMING**

Refer to item 7 of ENGINE CRANKS NORMALLY BUT WILL NOT START.

7.   **FAULTY NOZZLE OR NOZZLE HOLDER**

Refer to item 9 of ENGINE CRANKS NORMALLY BUT WILL NOT START.

EXCESSIVE EXHAUST SMOKE

NOTE:
1. Confirm that the air cleaner is not clogged.
2. Confirm with the customer whether or not oil consumption has been excessive.

(Possible Cause)   **(Check Procedure and Correction Method)**

1. '   **IMPROPER INJECTION TIMING**

Refer to item 7 of ENGINE CRANKS NORMALLY BUT WILL NOT START.

NOTE: Black smoke indicates advanced timing while white smoke indicates retarded timing. Adjustments should be made accordingly.

2.   **CLOGGED FUEL FILTER**

Refer to item 5 of LACK OF POWER.

NOTE: At high speed (2,000 – 3,000 rpm), a clogged filter tends to make the exhaust smoke white.

3.   **FAULTY NOZZLE OR NOZZLE HOLDER**

Refer to item 9 of ENGINE CRANKS NORMALLY BUT WILL NOT START.

NOTE: Excessive exhaust smoke is often caused by nozzle pressure being too low.

EXCESSIVE FUEL CONSUMPTION

NOTE: Confirm whether clutch slipping, brakes grabbing, tires wrong size or air filter clogged.

(Possible Cause)	(Check Procedure and Correction Method)
1. FUEL LEAKAGE	Refer to item 3 of ROUGH IDLE WITH WARM ENGINE.
2. IDLE SPEED TOO HIGH	After sufficiently warming up engine, check that idle speed is as specified below. If not, adjust with idle adjusting screw. **Idle speed: 700 rpm**
3. NO-LOAD MAXIMUM SPEED TOO HIGH	Start engine, depress accelerator pedal to floor and check that no-load maximum speed is within standard. If not, adjust with maximum speed adjusting screw. **No-load max. speed: 5,100 rpm**
4. IMPROPER INJECTION TIMING	Refer to item 7 of ENGINE CRANKS NORMALLY BUT WILL NOT START.
5. FAULTY NOZZLE OR NOZZLE HOLDER	Refer to item 9 of ENGINE CRANKS NORMALLY BUT WILL NOT START.

ENGINE NOISE WHEN WARM

(Clanking Noise with Excessive Vibration)

(Possible Cause)	(Check Procedure and Correction Method)
1. COOLANT TEMPERATURE TOO LOW	Check coolant temperature with coolant temperature gauge. If not sufficiently warm, thermostat is faulty and should be replaced.
2. IMPROPER INJECTION TIMING	Refer to item 7 of ENGINE CRANKS NORMALLY BUT WILL NOT START.
3. FAULTY NOZZLE OR NOZZLE HOLDER	Refer to item 9 of ENGINE CRANKS NORMALLY BUT WILL NOT START.

ENGINE WILL NOT RETURN TO IDLE

(Possible Cause)	(Check Procedure and Correction Method)
BINDING ACCELERATOR CABLE	Operate adjusting lever on top of injection pump and check if engine returns to idle. If so, accelerator cable is binding or improperly adjusted and should be repaired accordingly. If engine does not return to idle, injection pump is faulty and should be replaced.

ENGINE WILL NOT SHUT OFF WITH KEY

(Possible Cause)

(Check Procedure and Correction Method)

IMPROPER FUEL CUT SOLENOID OPERATION

Disconnect connector on top of fuel cut solenoid and check if engine stops.

If so, starter switch is faulty and should be repaired as necessary or replaced.

If engine does not stop, either fuel cut solenoid if faulty or there is interference by foreign particles. Repair as necessary.

ELECTRICAL SYSTEM DIAGNOSIS

ENGINE DOES NOT START COLD

- NOTE: 1. Battery voltage at least 12 volts — starter switch OFF.
  2. Engine cranks normally.
  3. Fusible link okay.
  4. Check the voltage marked with an asterisk (*) jsut as the starter switch is placed at ON because the voltage will change with elapse of time.

1. Super Glow System

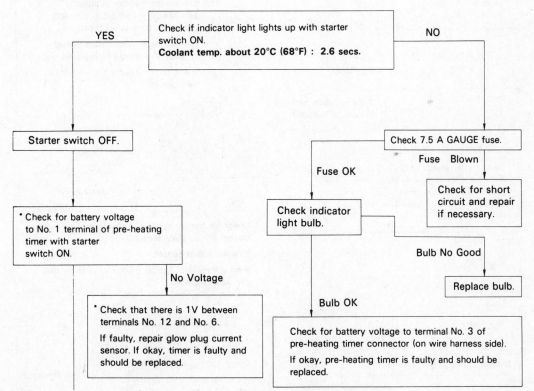

Check if indicator light lights up with starter switch ON.
Coolant temp. about 20°C (68°F) : 2.6 secs.

YES

Starter switch OFF.

* Check for battery voltage to No. 1 terminal of pre-heating timer with starter switch ON.

No Voltage

* Check that there is 1V between terminals No. 12 and No. 6.

If faulty, repair glow plug current sensor. If okay, timer is faulty and should be replaced.

NO

Check 7.5 A GAUGE fuse.

Fuse OK

Fuse Blown

Check for short circuit and repair if necessary.

Check indicator light bulb.

Bulb No Good

Replace bulb.

Bulb OK

Check for battery voltage to terminal No. 3 of pre-heating timer connector (on wire harness side).

If okay, pre-heating timer is faulty and should be replaced.

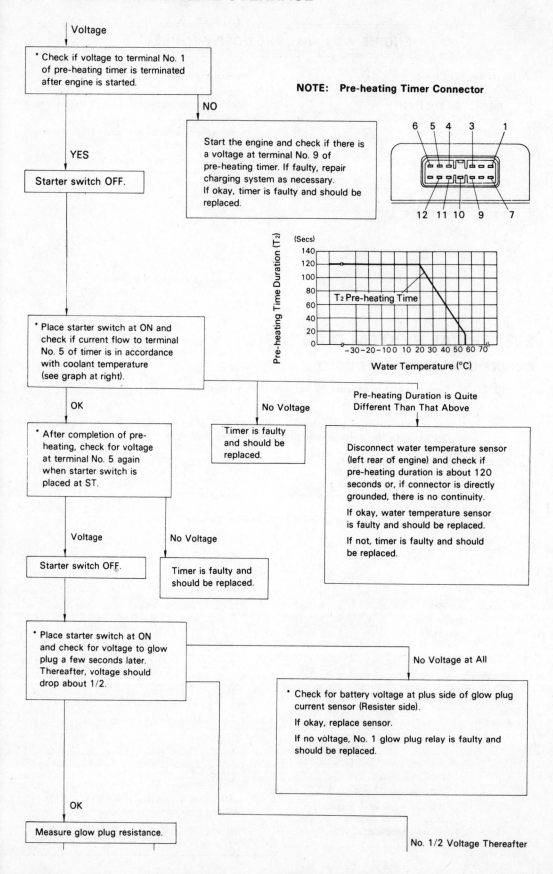

Voltage

* Check if voltage to terminal No. 1 of pre-heating timer is terminated after engine is started.

NO

NOTE: Pre-heating Timer Connector

Start the engine and check if there is a voltage at terminal No. 9 of pre-heating timer. If faulty, repair charging system as necessary. If okay, timer is faulty and should be replaced.

YES

Starter switch OFF.

6 5 4 3 1

12 11 10 9 7

Pre-heating Time Duration (T₂)

(Secs)
140
120
100
80
60
40
20
0

T_2 Pre-heating Time

−30 −20 −10 0 10 20 30 40 50 60 70

Water Temperature (°C)

* Place starter switch at ON and check if current flow to terminal No. 5 of timer is in accordance with coolant temperature (see graph at right).

OK

No Voltage

Timer is faulty and should be replaced.

Pre-heating Duration is Quite Different Than That Above

Disconnect water temperature sensor (left rear of engine) and check if pre-heating duration is about 120 seconds or, if connector is directly grounded, there is no continuity.

If okay, water temperature sensor is faulty and should be replaced.

If not, timer is faulty and should be replaced.

* After completion of pre-heating, check for voltage at terminal No. 5 again when starter switch is placed at ST.

Voltage

No Voltage

Starter switch OFF.

Timer is faulty and should be replaced.

* Place starter switch at ON and check for voltage to glow plug a few seconds later. Thereafter, voltage should drop about 1/2.

No Voltage at All

* Check for battery voltage at plus side of glow plug current sensor (Resister side).

If okay, replace sensor.

If no voltage, No. 1 glow plug relay is faulty and should be replaced.

OK

Measure glow plug resistance.

No. 1/2 Voltage Thereafter

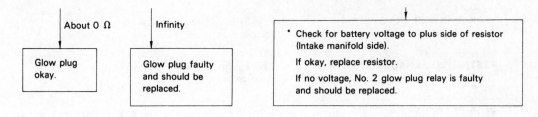

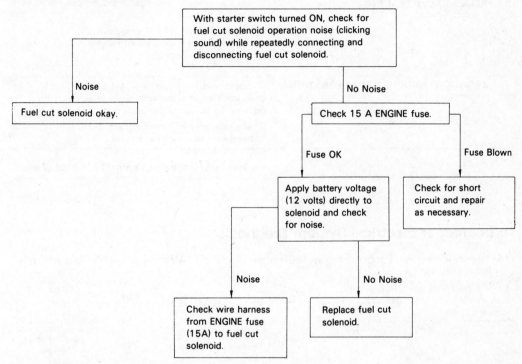

2. Fuel Cut Solenoid

TURBOCHARGER DIAGNOSIS

INSUFFICIENT ACCELERATION, LACK OF POWER OR EXCESSIVE FUEL CONSUMPTION

NOTE: Before troubleshooting the turbocharger, first check the valve clearance, injection timing, etc.

(Possible Cause)	(Check Procedure and Correction Method)
1. INSUFFICIENT TURBOCHARGING PRESSURE	Check turbocharging pressure If not within the standard shown below, begin diagnosis from Item 2. **Standard pressure: 0.54 − 0.68 kg/cm^2** **(7.7 − 9.7 psi, 53 − 67 kPa)**
2. RESTRICTED INTAKE AIR SYSTEM	Check intake air system, and repair or replace parts as necessary

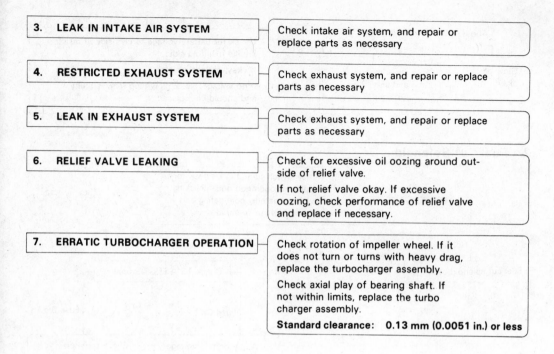

3.   **LEAK IN INTAKE AIR SYSTEM**

Check intake air system, and repair or replace parts as necessary

4.   **RESTRICTED EXHAUST SYSTEM**

Check exhaust system, and repair or replace parts as necessary

5.   **LEAK IN EXHAUST SYSTEM**

Check exhaust system, and repair or replace parts as necessary

6.   **RELIEF VALVE LEAKING**

Check for excessive oil oozing around outside of relief valve.

If not, relief valve okay. If excessive oozing, check performance of relief valve and replace if necessary.

7.   **ERRATIC TURBOCHARGER OPERATION**

Check rotation of impeller wheel. If it does not turn or turns with heavy drag, replace the turbocharger assembly.

Check axial play of bearing shaft. If not within limits, replace the turbo charger assembly.

Standard clearance: 0.13 mm (0.0051 in.) or less

Turbocharger Electrical System Diagnosis

Troubleshooting of Turbocharger Indicator Light and Warning Light Operation

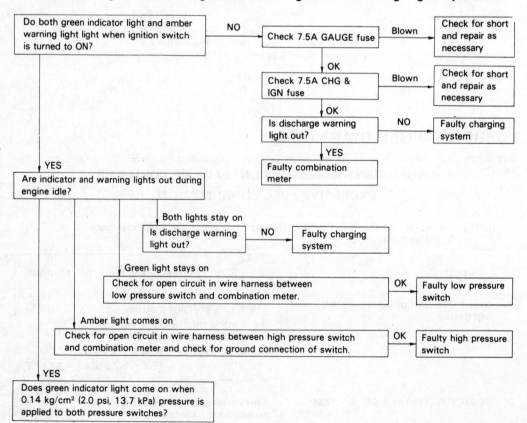

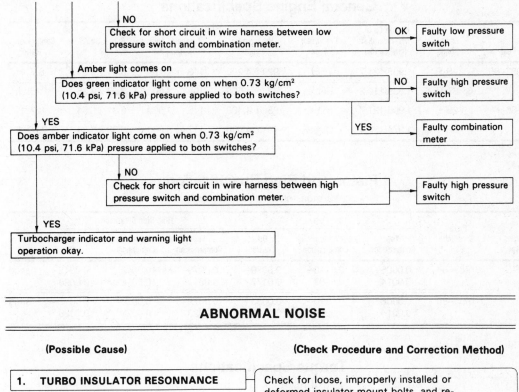

ABNORMAL NOISE

(Possible Cause)	(Check Procedure and Correction Method)
1. TURBO INSULATOR RESONNANCE	Check for loose, improperly installed or deformed insulator mount bolts, and repair or replace as necessary.
2. EXHAUST PIPE LEAKING OR VIBRATING	Check for deformed exhaust pipe, loose mount bolts or damaged gasket, and repair or replace as necessary.
3. ERRATIC TURBOCHARGER OPERATION	Refer to Item 7 of INSUFFICIENT ACCELERATION, LACK OF POWER OR EXCESSIVE FUEL CONSUMPTION.

EXCESSIVE OIL CONSUMPTION OR WHITE EXHAUST

(Possible Cause)	(Check Procedure and Correction Method)
Faulty turbocharger seal	Check for oil leakage in exhaust system. ● Remove the turbine elbow from the turbo charger and check for excessive carbon deposits on the turbine wheel. Excessive carbon deposits would indicate a faulty turbocharger. Check for oil leakage in intake air system. ● Check for axial play in impeller wheel, and replace the turbocharger if necessary. **CAUTION: There is some oil mist from the PCV in the blowby gas so care must be taken not to diagnosis this as an oil leakage from the turbocharger.**

General Engine Specifications

Year	Engine Type	Engine Cu In. Displacement (cm³/cu in.)	Carburetor Type	Horsepower @ rpm ①	Torque @ rpm (ft. lbs.) ①	Bore x Stroke (in.)	Compression Ratio
1983–85	2S-E	1,995/121.7	EFI	92 @ 4,200	113 @ 2,400	3.31 x 3.54	8.7:1
	1C-TL	1,839/112.2	Diesel	72 @ 4,500	104 @ 3,000	3.27 x 3.35	22.5:1
1986	2S-E	1,995/121.7	EFI	95 @ 4,400	116 @ 4,000	3.31 x 3.54	8.7:1
	2C-T	1,974/120.4	Diesel	79 @ 4,500	117 @ 3,000	3.39 x 3.39	23.0:1

Piston and Ring Specifications

(All measurements in inches)

Engine Type	Piston Clearance 68°F	Ring Gap			Ring Side Clearance			
		Top Compression	Bottom Compression	Oil Control	Top Compression	Bottom Compression	Control Oil	
2S-E	1983–84	0.0006–0.0014	0.0110–0.0197	0.0079–0.0177	0.0079–0.0311	0.0012–0.0028	0.0012–0.0028	snug
	1985–86	0.0006–0.0014	0.0110–0.0209	0.0083–0.0189	0.0079–0.0323	0.0012–0.0028	0.0012–0.0028	snug

Torque Specifications

(All readings in ft. lbs.)

Engine Type	Cylinder Head Bolts	Rod Bearing Bolts	Main Bearing bolts	Crankshaft Pulley Bolt	Flywheel to Crankshaft Bolts	Manifold	
						Intake	Exhaust
2S-E	45–50	33–38	40–45	78–82	70–75	30–33	30–33
1C-TL, 2C-T	60–65 ①	45–50	75–78	70–75	63–68	10–15	32–36

① See text for proper torquing procedure

14. Disconnect the fuel lines at the fuel filter and return pipes.

15. Disconnect the speedometer cable at the transmission.

16. Remove the clutch release cylinder without disconnect the fluid line.

17. Unbolt the air conditioning compressor and secure it out of the way.

18. Raise and support the car on jackstands.

19. Drain the transaxle fluid.

20. While someone holds the brake pedal depressed, unbolt both axle shafts. It's a good idea to wrap the boots with shop towels to prevent grease loss.

21. Unbolt the power steering pump and secure it out of the way.

22. Disconnect the exhaust pipe from the manifold or turbocharger outlet.

23. Disconnect the front and rear engine mounts at the frame member.

24. Lower the vehicle.

25. Attach an engine crane at the lifting eyes.

26. Take up the engine weight with the crane and remove the right and left side engine mounts.

27. Slowly and carefully, remove the engine and transaxle assembly.

28. Installation is the reverse of removal. Torque the engine mount bolts to 29 ft.lb. Torque the axle shaft bolts to 27 ft.lb. Torque the fuel line connectors to 22 ft.lb.

Compressor

Removal and Installation

1. Run the engine at idle with the A/C on for approximately ten minutes.

2. Disconnect the negative battery cable. Discharge the air conditioning system.

2. Remove any necessary components in order to gain access to the compressor. These may include the power steering pump and/or the alternator.

3. Tag and disconnect the electrical connections from the compressor.

Valve Specifications

Engine Type	Seat Angle (deg)	Face Angle (deg)	Spring Test Pressure (lbs.)		Spring Installed Height (in.)		Stem to Guide Clearance (in.) ▲		Stem Diameter (in.)	
			Inner	Outer	Inner	Outer	Intake	Exhaust	Intake	Exhaust
2S-E	45.5	45.5	—	68.0 ①	—	1.555	0.0010–0.0024	0.0012–0.0026	0.3138–0.3144	0.3136–0.3142
1C-L, 1C-LC, 1C-TL, 2C-T	45	44.5	—	53.0	—	1.587	0.0008–0.0022	0.0014–0.0028	0.3140–0.3146	0.3134–0.3140

① 1986: 0.0024–0.0031

Crankshaft and Connecting Rod Specifications
(All measurements are given in inches)

Engine Type	Crankshaft				Connecting Rod		
	Main Brg Journal Dia	Main Brg Oil Clearance	Shaft End-Play	Thrust on No.	Journal Diameter	Oil Clearance	Side Clearance
2S-E	2.1648–2.1654	0.0008–0.0019 ①	0.0008–0.0087	3	1.8892–1.8898	0.0009–0.0022	0.0063–0.0083 ⑦
1C-L, 1C-TL, 2C-T	2.2435–2.2441	0.0013–0.0026	0.0016–0.0094 ②	3	1.9877–1.9882	0.0014–0.0025 ③	0.0031–0.0118

① No. 3: 0.0012–0.0022
② 3S-GE: 0.0063–0.0124
③ 2C-T: 0.0017–0.0028

4. Remove the air conditioning hoses from the compressor. Note their position on the compressor.

5. Loosen the compressor mounting bolts. Remove the compressor drive belt.

6. Remove the compressor mounting bolts. Remove the compressor from the vehicle.

7. Installation is the reverse of the removal procedure. Charge the A/C system. Check for proper operation and leak.

Cylinder Head
REMOVAL AND INSTALLATION
2S-E

1. Disconnect the battery ground.
2. Drain the coolant.
CAUTION: *When draining the coolant, keep in mind that cats and dogs are attracted by the ethylene glycol antifreeze, and are quite likely to drink any that is left in an uncovered*

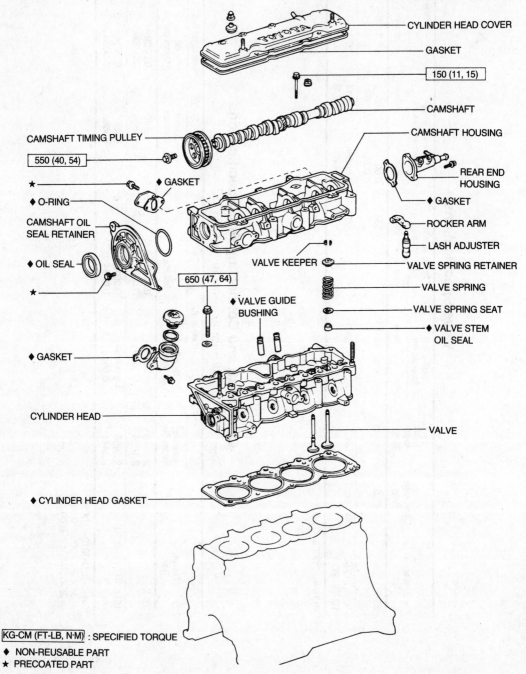

CYLINDER HEAD COVER

GASKET

150 (11, 15)

CAMSHAFT

CAMSHAFT HOUSING

CAMSHAFT TIMING PULLEY

550 (40, 54)

★

◆ GASKET

◆ O-RING

CAMSHAFT OIL SEAL RETAINER

◆ OIL SEAL

★

REAR END HOUSING

◆ GASKET

ROCKER ARM

LASH ADJUSTER

VALVE KEEPER

VALVE SPRING RETAINER

VALVE SPRING

650 (47, 64)

◆ VALVE GUIDE BUSHING

VALVE SPRING SEAT

◆ VALVE STEM OIL SEAL

◆ GASKET

CYLINDER HEAD

VALVE

◆ CYLINDER HEAD GASKET

KG-CM (FT-LB, N·M) : SPECIFIED TORQUE

◆ NON-REUSABLE PART
★ PRECOATED PART

Exploded view of the cylinder head—2S-E

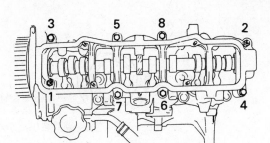

2S-E Cam housing bolt loosening sequence

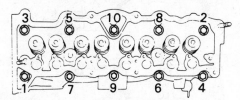

2S-E Head bolt loosening sequence

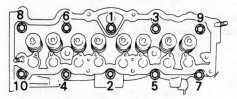

2S-E Head bolt tightening sequence

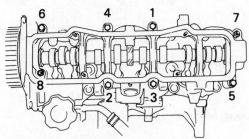

2S-E Cam housing tightening sequence

11. Remove the upper radiator hose and by-pass hose.

12. Unbolt and remove the water outlet housing.

13. Disconnect the heater hoses.

14. Disconnect the two air hoses from the fuel injection air valve.

15. Unbolt and remove the rear end housing.

16. Remove the heater pipe.

17. Disconnect the fuel line at the filter and the fuel return line at the return pipe.

18. Raise and support the car on jackstands.

19. Drain the oil.

20. Disconnect the exhaust pipe at the manifold.

21. Disconnect the power steering pump hoses.

22. Remove the intake manifold stay.

23. Lower the car.

24. Remove the timing belt.

25. Remove the #1 idler pulley and tension spring.

26. Remove the throttle body.

27. Remove the valve cover.

28. Unbolt and remove the camshaft housing. Loosen the bolts gradually in the order shown.

29. Remove the rocker arms and lash adjusters.

30. Loosen and remove the head bolts, in three passes, in the order shown. Lift the head from the engine and place it on wood blocks in a clean work area.

31. Installation is the reverse of removal. Note the following points:

   a. Always use a new head gasket.

   b. Tighten the head bolts, in three passes, in the order shown, to 47 ft.lb.

   c. When installing the camshaft housing, note that RTV silicone gasket compound is used in place of a gasket. Run a 2mm bear of compound around the sealing surface of the housing. Torque the housing bolts, in three passes, in the order shown, to 11 ft.lb.

   d. Torque the fuel line connections to 22 ft.lb.

   e. Road test the car.

Diesel

1. Disconnect the battery ground.

2. Drain the coolant.

CAUTION: *When draining the coolant, keep in mind that cats and dogs are attracted by the ethylene glycol antifreeze, and are quite likely to drink any that is left in an uncovered container or in puddles on the ground. This will prove fatal in sufficient quantity. Always drain the coolant into a sealable container.*

container or in puddles on the ground. This will prove fatal in sufficient quantity. Always drain the coolant into a sealable container. Coolant should be reused unless it is contaminated or several years old.

3. Disconnect the throttle cable.

4. Remove the air cleaner assembly.

5. Disconnect and tag all wires connected to or running across the head.

6. Disconnect and tag all vacuum hoses connected to or running across the head.

7. Remove the vacuum pipe from the head cover.

8. Disconnect and tag any remaining cables.

9. Remove the alternator.

10. Remove the distributor.

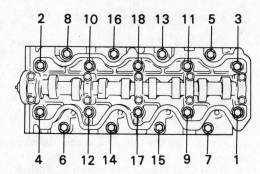

Diesel head bolt loosening sequence

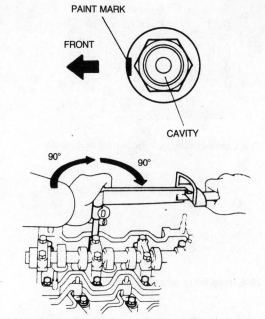

Mark each cylinder head bolt with a dab of paint prior to angle-torquing—2C-T

Coolant should be reused unless it is contaminated or several years old.

3. Remove the cruise control actuator.

4. Disconnect and tag all wires connected to or running across the head.

5. Disconnect and tag all vacuum hoses connected to or running across the head.

6. Disconnect and tag all cables and linkage rods connected to or running across the head.

7. Raise and support the car on jackstands.

8. Drain the oil.

9. Disconnect the exhaust pipe from the turbocharger or manifold.

10. Lower the car.

11. Remove the turbocharger.

12. Remove the water outlet and pipe.

13. Remove the heater hoses.

14. Remove the heater pipe.

15. Remove the bypass hoses.

16. Remove the glow plugs.

17. Remove the injector nozzles.

18. Remove the level gauge guide support mounting bolt.

19. Remove the number 2 timing cover.

20. Turn the engine so that #1 cylinder is at TDC of the firing stroke. Make sure that the line mark on the camshaft pulley is aligned with the top surface of the head.

21. Remove the timing belt and camshaft pulley.

22. Remove the belt tension spring.

23. Remove the #1 idler pulley. Remove the camshaft #3 cover.

24. Remove the valve cover.

25. Remove the front head lifting eye.

26. Loosen the head bolts gradually, in three passes, in the order shown. Lift off the head. If the head is difficult to break loose, there is a recess at the front end in which you may pry with a suitable tool.

27. Installation is the reverse of removal. Note the following points:

a. Always use a new head gasket.

b. Make sure that all sealing surfaces are absolutely clean.

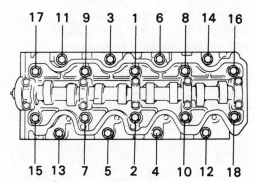

Diesel head bolt tightening sequence

c. Coat all bolt threads with clean engine oil, lightly.

d. On the 1C-TL, tighten the head bolts, in three passes, in the order shown, to 62 ft.lb. On the 2C-T, tighten the head bolts in three stages, to 33 ft.lb. Matchmark one point on each bolt and the head, and torque each bolt, in sequence, an additional 90° from that point. When all bolts are torqued, tighten each an additional 90° turn, in sequence.

e. When installing the valve cover, note that RTV silicone gasket compound is used in place of a gasket.

f. Torque the valve cover bolts to 65 in.lb.

g. Torque the camshaft pulley bolt to 72 ft.lb. on the 1C-TL or 65 ft.lb. on the 2C-T.

h. Make sure that the timing marks align

by rotating the engine 2 full revolutions and rechecking the alignment.

i. Torque the #1 idler pulley bolt to 27 ft.lb.

j. Road test the car.

Valve Guide
REPLACEMENT

1. Heat the cylinder head to 176–212°F, evenly, before beginning the replacement procedure.

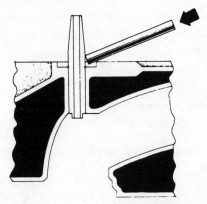

Use a brass drift to break the top off of the valve guide

2. Use a brass rod to break the valve guide off above its snapring. (See the illustration).

3. Drive out the valve guide, toward the combustion chamber. Use a tool fabricated as described in the Engine Rebuilding section.

4. Install a snapring on the new valve guide. Apply liquid sealer. Drive in the valve guide until the snapring contacts the head. Use the tool previously described.

5. Measure the guide bore; if the stem-to-guide clearance is below specification, ream it out, using a valve guide reamer.

Turbocharger
REMOVAL AND INSTALLATION

1. Remove the air cleaner.

2. Disconnect and tag all wiring and hoses in the way of turbocharger removal.

3. Remove the compressor elbow and relief hose.

4. Remove the heat shields.

5. Disconnect the exhaust pipe from the turbine elbow.

6. Disconnect the turbocharger oil pipes.

7. Unbolt and remove the turbocharger.

8. Installation is the reverse of removal. Torque the turbocharger mounting nuts to 38 ft.lb.

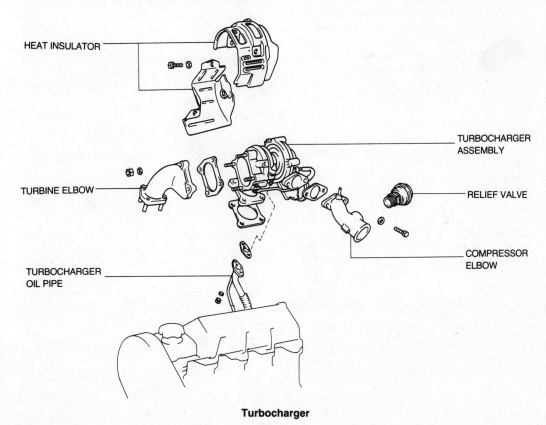

HEAT INSULATOR

TURBINE ELBOW

TURBOCHARGER OIL PIPE

TURBOCHARGER ASSEMBLY

RELIEF VALVE

COMPRESSOR ELBOW

Turbocharger

Intake Manifold
REMOVAL AND INSTALLATION
1C-TL, 2C-T

1. Disconnect the battery ground.
2. Drain the coolant.
CAUTION: *When draining the coolant, keep in mind that cats and dogs are attracted by the ethylene glycol antifreeze, and are quite likely to drink any that is left in an uncovered container or in puddles on the ground. This will prove fatal in sufficient quantity. Always drain the coolant into a sealable container. Coolant should be reused unless it is contaminated or several years old.*
3. Remove the air cleaner.
4. Disconnect and tag any wire, hose or cable in the way of manifold removal.
5. Remove the turbocharger as described later.
6. Remove the coolant by-pass pipe.
7. Unbolt and remove the manifold.
8. Installation is the reverse of removal.

2S-E

1. Disconnect the battery ground.
2. Drain the coolant.
CAUTION: *When draining the coolant, keep in mind that cats and dogs are attracted by the ethylene glycol antifreeze, and are quite likely to drink any that is left in an uncovered container or in puddles on the ground. This will prove fatal in sufficient quantity. Always drain the coolant into a sealable container. Coolant should be reused unless it is contaminated or several years old.*
3. Disconnect and tag any wires, hoses or cable in the way of manifold removal.
4. Remove the throttle body.
5. Unbolt and remove the manifold.
6. Installation is the reverse of removal.

Exhaust Manifold
REMOVAL AND INSTALLATION

CAUTION: *Do not perform this operation on a warm or hot engine.*
1. Raise the front and the rear of the car and support it with jackstands.
CAUTION: *Be sure that the car is securely supported.*
2. Remove the right hand gravel shield from beneath the engine.
3. Remove the downpipe support bracket.
4. Unfasten the bolts from the flange and detach the downpipe from the manifold. It may be necessary to remove the outer heat shield first.
5. Remove the automatic choke and air cleaner stove hoses from the exhaust manifold.

6. Remove or move aside, any of the air injection system components which may be in the way when removing the manifold. Unfasten the EGR valve and pipes.
7. In order to remove the manifold, unfasten the manifold retaining bolts.
CAUTION: *Remove and tighten the bolts in two or three stages and, starting from the inside, working out.*
8. Installation is performed in the reverse order of removal. Always use a new gasket. Tighten the retaining bolts to the specifications given in two or three stages.

Timing Gear Cover
REMOVAL AND INSTALLATION

1. Remove the right front wheel.
2. Remove the fender liner.
3. Remove the alternator belt.
4. Remove the cruise control actuator and bracket.
5. Remove the power steering reservoir and belt.
6. Using a wood block on the jack, raise the engine slightly.
7. Remove the right engine mount.
8. Remove the timing covers.
9. Installation is the reverse of removal.

Timing Chain Cover Oil Seal
REPLACEMENT
All Engines

1. Remove the timing chain cover, as previously detailed in the appropriate section.
2. Inspect the oil seal for signs of wear, leakage, or damage.
3. If worn, pry the old oil seal out, using a small pry bar. Remove it toward the front of the cover.
NOTE: *Once the oil seal has been removed, it must be replaced with a new one.*
4. Use a socket, pipe, or block of wood and a hammer to drift the oil seal into place. Work from the front of the cover.

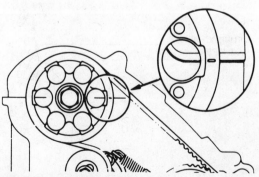

Diesel valve timing mark alignment

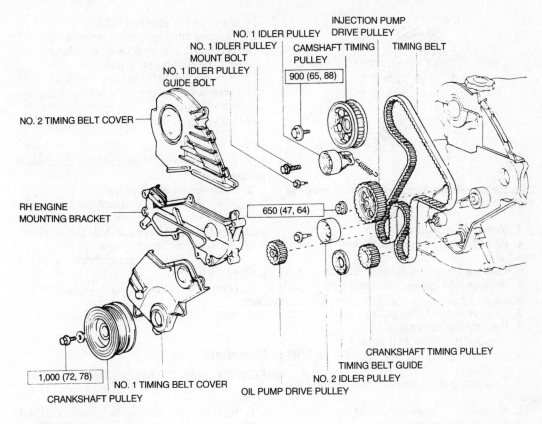

Front cover and related components—diesel engines

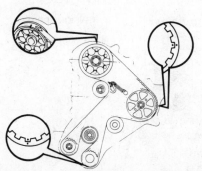

When planning to reuse the timing belt on diesel engines, matchmark the belt to the timing pulleys as shown

CAUTION: *Be extremely careful not to damage the seal or else it will leak.*

5. Install the timing chain cover as previously outlined.

Timing Chain and Tensioner
REMOVAL AND INSTALLATION
DIESEL

1. Disconnect the battery ground.
2. Remove the right front wheel.

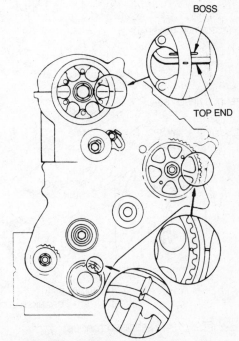

Timing pulley alignment on the diesel engine

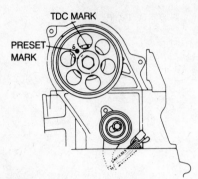

2S-E Timing belt installation showing alignment of timing marks

3. Remove the fender liner.
4. Remove the washer bottle and radiator overflow.
5. Remove the cruise control actuator.
6. Remove the power steering pump and bracket.
7. Remove the AC idler pulleys and bracket.
8. Remove the alternator.
9. Remove the lower belt cover.
10. Turn the engine to #1 cylinder at TDC compression.
11. Using a puller, remove the crankshaft pulley.
12. Remove the upper belt cover.
13. Remove the belt guide.

14. Jack up the engine slightly.
15. Remove the right side engine mount.
16. If the belt is to be reused, matchmark the belt and the pulleys with paint.
17. Remove the belt tensioner spring.
18. Loosen the idler pulley bolt and remove the belt.
19. Installation is the reverse of removal.

2S-E

1. Follow steps 1 through 9 of the Diesel procedure.
2. Remove the spark plugs.
3. Align the oil seal retainer mark with the center of the small hole on the camshaft timing pulley by turning the crankshaft pulley clockwise. This will set #1 piston at BTDC.
4. If reusing the belt, matchmark it and the pulleys with paint.
5. Loosen the idler pulley and remove the belt.
6. Installation is the reverse of removal.

Camshaft
REMOVAL AND INSTALLATION
2S-E

1. Remove the timing belt as described above.

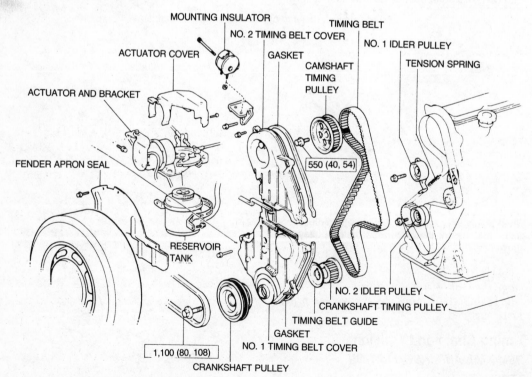

Front cover and related components—2SE

USA   "E" MARK

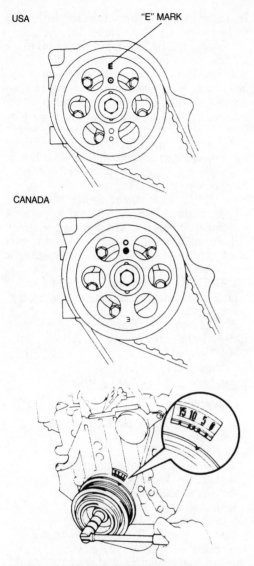

"E" MARK

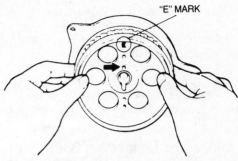

Align the knock pin with the pin hole on the timing pulley "E" mark side—U.S. 2S-E

CANADA

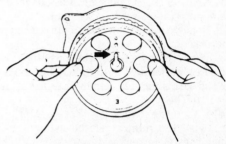

Align the knock pin with the pin hold on the timing pulley—Canada 2S-E

Align the camshaft knock pin with the matchmark on the camshaft oil seal retainer—2S-E

2. Remove the camshaft housing as described in Cylinder Head Removal.
3. Remove the camshaft pulley.
4. Remove the cam bearing caps.

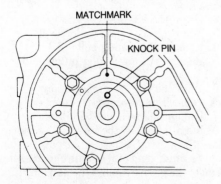

MATCHMARK

KNOCK PIN

5. Turning the camshaft slowly, slide it from the housing.
6. Installation is the reverse of removal. Always use new oil seals.
7. Installation is the reverse of removal. See the Cylinder Head Installation procedure.

Diesel

1. Remove the cylinder head.
2. Remove the camshaft pulley.
3. Remove the thrust plate.
4. Unbolt and remove the cam bearing caps.
5. Turning the camshaft slowly, slide the camshaft from the head.
6. Installation is the reverse of removal.

CAMSHAFT INSPECTION

Prior to removal of the camshaft, measure the end play with a feeler gauge. Refer to the Specifications Chart, if the end play is beyond specs, it may be necessary to replace the cylinder head or camshaft.

Measure the bearing oil clearance by placing a piece of Plastigage® on each bearing journal. Replace the bearing caps and tighten the bolts to 13–16 ft.lb.

NOTE: *Do not turn the camshaft.*

Remove the caps and measure each piece of Plastigage®. If the clearance is greater than the values on the Specifications Chart, replace the bearings, head or cam; depending on which engine you are working on.

Place the camshaft in V-block supports and measure its run-out at the center bearing journal with a dial indicator. If the run-out exceeds specs, replace the cam.

Use a micrometer and measure the bearing journals and the cam lobe heights. If the bearing journals are not within specs, or the lobes differ greatly in size from wear, replace the camshaft.

Pistons and Connecting Rods
REMOVAL AND INSTALLATION
All Engines

1. Remove the cylinder head as outlined in the appropriate preceding section.
2. Remove the oil pan and pump; see Engine Lubrication.
3. Ream the ridges from the top of the cylinder bores, as detailed in Engine Rebuilding, at the end of this chapter. Remove the oil strainer if it is in the way.
4. Unbolt the connecting rod caps. Mark the caps with the number of the cylinder from which they were removed.
5. Remove the connecting rod and piston through the top of the cylinder bore.
CAUTION: *Use care not to scratch the journals or the cylinder walls.*
6. Mark the pistons and connecting rods with the numbers of the cylinders from which they were removed.

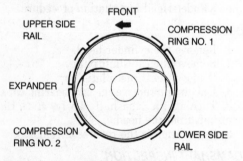

Piston ring gap positioning—2S-E

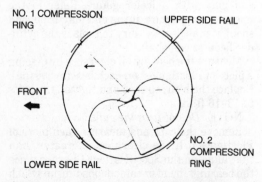

Piston ring gap positioning—diesel engines

Installation is performed in the following order:

1. Apply a light coating of engine oil to the pistons, rings, and wrist pins.
2. Examine the piston to ensure that it has been assembled with its parts positioned correctly. (See the illustrations.) Be sure that the ring gaps are not pointed toward the thrust face of the piston and that they do not overlap.
3. Install the pistons, using a ring compressor, into the cylinder bore. Be sure that the appropriate marks on the piston are facing the front of the cylinder.
CAUTION: *It is important that the pistons, rods, bearings, etc., be returned to the same cylinder bore from which they were removed.*
4. Install the connecting rod bearing caps and tighten them to the torque figures given in the Torque Specifications chart.
CAUTION: *Be sure that the mating marks on the connecting rods and rod bearing caps are aligned.*
5. The rest of the removal procedure is performed in the reverse order of installation.

Oil Pan
REMOVAL AND INSTALLATION
Gasoline Engine

1. Raise the support the front end on jackstands.
2. Drain the oil.
3. Remove the engine undercover.
4. Remove the dipstick.
5. Unbolt and remove the oil pan.
6. Installation is the reverse of removal. Clean the gasket mating surfaces. Always use a new pan gasket. Some engines were assembled using RTV gasket material in place of a conventional gasket. In that case, apply a thin (5mm) bead of RTV material to the groove around the pan mating surface. Assemble the pan within 15 min. Torque pan bolts to 48 in.lb.

Diesel Engine

1. Raise and support the front end on jackstands.
2. Drain the oil.
3. Remove the engine undercovers.
4. Remove the timing belt.
5. Remove the lower idler pulley and crankshaft pulley.
6. With the engine supported by a hoist or jack, remove the center crossmember.
7. Unbolt and remove the oil pan.
8. Installation is the reverse of removal. Clean the mating surface of the pan and block. Apply a 5mm bead of RTV silicone gasket material to the groove around the pan mating sur-

face. Install the pan within 15 min. Torque the pan bolts to 48 in.lb.

Rear Main Oil Seal
REPLACEMENT
All Engines

1. Remove the transmission as detailed in Chapter 6.
2. Remove the clutch cover assembly and flywheel. See Chapter 6 also.
3. Remove the oil seal retaining plate, complete with the oil seal.
4. Use a screwdriver to pry the oil seal from the retaining plate. Be careful not to damage the plate.
5. Install the new seal, carefully, by using a block of wood to drift it into place.
CAUTION: *Do not damage the seal; a leak will result.*
6. Lubricate the lips of the seal with multipurpose grease.
7. Installation is performed in the reverse order from removal.

Oil Pump
REMOVAL AND INSTALLATION
2S-E

1. Remove the oil pan, as outlined in the appropriate preceding section.
2. Remove the crankshaft pulley and timing belt.
3. Remove the oil lever gauge guide, then remove the gauge.
4. Unbolt the oil pump securing bolts and remove it as an assembly. It may be necessary to break it loose with a rubber mallet.
3. Installation is the reverse of removal. Make sure that the drive teeth engage the driven teeth.

Diesel

1. Remove the hood.
2. Remove the oil pan.
3. Remove the engine undershield.
4. Disconnect the center engine mount.
5. Attach a shop crane to the lifting eyes and suspend the engine.
6. Remove all the drive belts, the water pump pulley, the air conditioner idler puley and the crankshaft pulley.
7. Remove the timing belt.
8. Remove the oil lever gauge guide, then remove the gauge.
9. Unbolt the oil pump securing bolts and remove it as an assembly. It may be necessary to break it loose with a rubber mallet.
10. Installation is the reverse of removal.

Make sure that the drive teeth engage the driven teeth.

Radiator
REMOVAL AND INSTALLATION

1. Drain the cooling system.
CAUTION: *When draining the coolant, keep in mind that cats and dogs are attracted by the ethylene glycol antifreeze, and are quite likely to drink any that is left in an uncovered container or in puddles on the ground. This will prove fatal in sufficient quantity. Always drain the coolant into a sealable container. Coolant should be reused unless it is contaminated or several years old.*

Removing the radiator

2. Unfasten the clamps and remove the radiator upper and lower hoses. If equipped with an automatic transmission, remove the oil cooler lines.
3. Detach the hood lock cable and remove the hood lock from the radiator upper support.
NOTE: *It may be necessary to remove the grille in order to gain access to the hood lock/radiator support assembly.*
4. Remove the fan shroud, if so equipped.
5. On models equipped with a coolant recovery system, disconnect the hose from the thermal expansion tank and remove the tank from its bracket.
6. Unbolt and remove the radiator upper support.
7. Unfasten the bolts and remove the radiator.
CAUTION: *Use care not to damage the radiator fins on the cooling fan.*
8. Installation is performed in the reverse order of removal. Remember to check the transmission fluid level on cars with automatic transmissions. Fill the radiator to the specified level, as detailed under Fluid Level Checks, in Chapter 1. Remember to check for leaks after installation is completed.

Water Pump

REMOVAL AND INSTALLATION

1. Drain the cooling system.

CAUTION: *When draining the coolant, keep in mind that cats and dogs are attracted by the ethylene glycol antifreeze, and are quite likely to drink any that is left in an uncovered container or in puddles on the ground. This will prove fatal in sufficient quantity. Always drain the coolant into a sealable container. Coolant should be reused unless it is contaminated or several years old.*

2. Unfasten the fan shroud securing bolts and remove the fan shroud, if so equipped.

3. Loosen the alternator adjusting link bolt and remove the drive belt.

4. Repeat Step 3 for the air and/or power steering pump drive belt, if so equipped.

5. With the 2S-E engine, remove the timing covers. On the diesels, remove the timing covers and injection pump pulley.

6. Detach the by-pass hose from the water pump.

7. Unfasten the water pump retaining bolts and remove the water pump and fan assembly, using care not to damage the radiator with the fan.

CAUTION: *If the fan is equipped with a flu-id coupling, do not tip the fan/pump assembly on its side, as the fluid will run out.*

8. Installation is performed in the reverse order of removal. Always use a new gasket between the pump body and its mounting.

Thermostat

REMOVAL AND INSTALLATION

1. Drain the cooling system.

CAUTION: *When draining the coolant, keep in mind that cats and dogs are attracted by the ethylene glycol antifreeze, and are quite likely to drink any that is left in an uncovered container or in puddles on the ground. This will prove fatal in sufficient quantity. Always drain the coolant into a sealable container. Coolant should be reused unless it is contaminated or several years old.*

2. Unfasten the clamp and remove the supper radiator hose from the water outlet elbow.

3. Unbolt and remove the water outlet (thermostat housing).

4. Withdraw the thermostat.

5. Installation is performed in the reverse order of the removal procedure. Use a new gasket on the water outlet.

CAUTION: *Be sure that the thermostat is installed with the spring pointing down.*

SPARK PLUG DIAGNOSIS

Normal

APPEARANCE: This plug is typical of one operating normally. The insulator nose varies from a light tan to grayish color with slight electrode wear. The presence of slight deposits is normal on used plugs and will have no adverse effect on engine performance. The spark plug heat range is correct for the engine and the engine is running normally.

CAUSE: Properly running engine.

RECOMMENDATION: Before reinstalling this plug, the electrodes should be cleaned and filed square. Set the gap to specifications. If the plug has been in service for more than 10-12,000 miles, the entire set should probably be replaced with a fresh set of the same heat range.

Oil Deposits

APPEARANCE: The firing end of the plug is covered with a wet, oily coating.

CAUSE: The problem is poor oil control. On high mileage engines, oil is leaking past the rings or valve guides into the combustion chamber. A common cause is also a plugged PCV valve, and a ruptured fuel pump diaphragm can also cause this condition. Oil fouled plugs such as these are often found in new or recently overhauled engines, before normal oil control is achieved, and can be cleaned and reinstalled.

RECOMMENDATION: A hotter spark plug may temporarily relieve the problem, but the engine is probably in need of work.

Incorrect Heat Range

APPEARANCE: The effects of high temperature on a spark plug are indicated by clean white, often blistered insulator. This can also be accompanied by excessive wear of the electrode, and the absence of deposits.

CAUSE: Check for the correct spark plug heat range. A plug which is too hot for the engine can result in overheating. A car operated mostly at high speeds can require a colder plug. Also check ignition timing, cooling system level, fuel mixture and leaking intake manifold.

RECOMMENDATION: If all ignition and engine adjustments are known to be correct, and no other malfunction exists, install spark plugs one heat range colder.

Photos Courtesy Fram Corporation

Carbon Deposits

APPEARANCE: Carbon fouling is easily identified by the presence of dry, soft, black, sooty deposits.

CAUSE: Changing the heat range can often lead to carbon fouling, as can prolonged slow, stop-and-start driving. If the heat range is correct, carbon fouling can be attributed to a rich fuel mixture, sticking choke, clogged air cleaner, worn breaker points, retarded timing or low compression. If only one or two plugs are carbon fouled, check for corroded or cracked wires on the affected plugs. Also look for cracks in the distributor cap between the towers of affected cylinders.

RECOMMENDATION: After the problem is corrected, these plugs can be cleaned and reinstalled if not worn severely.

veyed over 6,000 cars nationwide, they found that a tune-up, on cars that needed one, increased fuel economy over 11%. Replacing worn plugs alone, accounted for a 3% increase. The same test also revealed that 8 out of every 10 vehicles will have some maintenance deficiency that will directly affect fuel economy, emissions or performance. Most of this mileage-robbing neglect could be prevented with regular maintenance.

Modern engines require that all of the functioning systems operate properly for maximum efficiency. A malfunction anywhere wastes fuel. You can keep your vehicle running as efficiently and economically as possible, by being aware of your vehicle's operating and performance characteristics. If your vehicle suddenly develops performance or fuel economy problems it could be due to one or more of the following:

PROBLEM	POSSIBLE CAUSE
Engine Idles Rough	Ignition timing, idle mixture, vacuum leak or something amiss in the emission control system.
Hesitates on Acceleration	Dirty carburetor or fuel filter, improper accelerator pump setting, ignition timing or fouled spark plugs.
Starts Hard or Fails to Start	Worn spark plugs, improperly set automatic choke, ice (or water) in fuel system.
Stalls Frequently	Automatic choke improperly adjusted and possible dirty air filter or fuel filter.
Performs Sluggishly	Worn spark plugs, dirty fuel or air filter, ignition timing or automatic choke out of adjustment.

Check spark plug wires on conventional point type ignition for cracks by bending them in a loop around your finger.

Be sure that spark plug wires leading to adjacent cylinders do not run too close together. (Photo courtesy Champion Spark Plug Co.)

7. If your vehicle does not have electronic ignition, check the points, rotor and cap as specified.

8. Check the spark plug wires (used with conventional point-type ignitions) for cracks and burned or broken insulation by bending them in a loop around your finger. Cracked wires decrease fuel efficiency by failing to deliver full voltage to the spark plugs. One misfiring spark plug can cost you as much as 2 mpg.

9. Check the routing of the plug wires. Misfiring can be the result of spark plug leads to adjacent cylinders running parallel to each other and too close together. One wire tends to pick up voltage from the other causing it to fire "out of time".

10. Check all electrical and ignition circuits for voltage drop and resistance.

11. Check the distributor mechanical and/or vacuum advance mechanisms for proper functioning. The vacuum advance can be checked by twisting the distributor plate in the opposite direction of rotation. It should spring back when released.

12. Check and adjust the valve clearance on engines with mechanical lifters. The clearance should be slightly loose rather than too tight.

CHILTON'S FUEL ECONOMY & TUNE-UP TIPS

Fuel economy is important to everyone, no matter what kind of vehicle you drive. The maintenance-minded motorist can save both money and fuel using these tips and the periodic maintenance and tune-up procedures in this Repair and Tune-Up Guide.

There are more than 130,000,000 cars and trucks registered for private use in the United States. Each travels an average of 10-12,000 miles per year, and, and in total they consume close to 70 billion gallons of fuel each year. This represents nearly 2/3 of the oil imported by the United States each year. The Federal government's goal is to reduce consumption 10% by 1985. A variety of methods are either already in use or under serious consideration, and they all affect you driving and the cars you will drive. In addition to "down-sizing", the auto industry is using or investigating the use of electronic fuel delivery, electronic engine controls and alternative engines for use in smaller and lighter vehicles, among other alternatives to meet the federally mandated Corporate Average Fuel Economy (CAFE) of 27.5 mpg by 1985. The government, for its part, is considering rationing, mandatory driving curtailments and tax increases on motor vehicle fuel in an effort to reduce consumption. The government's goal of a 10% reduction could be realized — and further government regulation avoided — if every private vehicle could use just 1 less gallon of fuel per week.

How Much Can You Save?

Tests have proven that almost anyone can make at least a 10% reduction in fuel consumption through regular maintenance and tune-ups. When a major manufacturer of spark plugs sur-

TUNE-UP

1. Check the cylinder compression to be sure the engine will really benefit from a tune-up and that it is capable of producing good fuel economy. A tune-up will be wasted on an engine in poor mechanical condition.

2. Replace spark plugs regularly. New spark plugs alone can increase fuel economy 3%.

3. Be sure the spark plugs are the correct type (heat range) for your vehicle. See the Tune-Up Specifications.

Heat range refers to the spark plug's ability to conduct heat away from the firing end. It must conduct the heat away in an even pattern to avoid becoming a source of pre-ignition, yet it must also operate hot enough to burn off conductive deposits that could cause misfiring.

The heat range is usually indicated by a number on the spark plug, part of the manufacturer's designation for each individual spark plug. The numbers in bold-face indicate the heat range in each manufacturer's identification system.

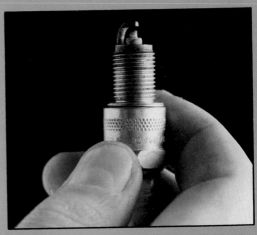

Periodically, check the spark plugs to be sure they are firing efficiently. They are excellent indicators of the internal condition of your engine.

Manufacturer	Typical Designation
AC	R **45** TS
Bosch (old)	WA **145** T30
Bosch (new)	HR **8** Y
Champion	RBL **15** Y
Fram/Autolite	**415**
Mopar	P-**62** PR
Motorcraft	BRF-**42**
NGK	BP **5** ES-15
Nippondenso	W **16** EP
Prestolite	14GR **5** 2A

On AC, Bosch (new), Champion, Fram/Autolite, Mopar, Motorcraft and Prestolite, a higher number indicates a hotter plug. On Bosch (old), NGK and Nippondenso, a higher number indicates a colder plug.

4. Make sure the spark plugs are properly gapped. See the Tune-Up Specifications in this book.

5. Be sure the spark plugs are firing efficiently. The illustrations on the next 2 pages show you how to "read" the firing end of the spark plug.

6. Check the ignition timing and set it to specifications. Tests show that almost all cars have incorrect ignition timing by more than 2°.

CHILTON'S
FUEL ECONOMY
& TUNE-UP TIPS

Tune-up • Spark Plug Diagnosis • Emission Controls

Fuel System • Cooling System • Tires and Wheels

General Maintenance

MMT Fouled

APPEARANCE: Spark plugs fouled by MMT (Methycyclopentadienyl Maganese Tricarbonyl) have reddish, rusty appearance on the insulator and side electrode.

CAUSE: MMT is an anti-knock additive in gasoline used to replace lead. During the combustion process, the MMT leaves a reddish deposit on the insulator and side electrode.

RECOMMENDATION: No engine malfunction is indicated and the deposits will not affect plug performance any more than lead deposits (see Ash Deposits). MMT fouled plugs can be cleaned, regapped and reinstalled.

High Speed Glazing

APPEARANCE: Glazing appears as shiny coating on the plug, either yellow or tan in color.

CAUSE: During hard, fast acceleration, plug temperatures rise suddenly. Deposits from normal combustion have no chance to fluff-off; instead, they melt on the insulator forming an electrically conductive coating which causes misfiring.

RECOMMENDATION: Glazed plugs are not easily cleaned. They should be replaced with a fresh set of plugs of the correct heat range. If the condition recurs, using plugs with a heat range one step colder may cure the problem.

Ash (Lead) Deposits

APPEARANCE: Ash deposits are characterized by light brown or white colored deposits crusted on the side or center electrodes. In some cases it may give the plug a rusty appearance.

CAUSE: Ash deposits are normally derived from oil or fuel additives burned during normal combustion. Normally they are harmless, though excessive amounts can cause misfiring. If deposits are excessive in short mileage, the valve guides may be worn.

RECOMMENDATION: Ash-fouled plugs can be cleaned, gapped and reinstalled.

Detonation

APPEARANCE: Detonation is usually characterized by a broken plug insulator.

CAUSE: A portion of the fuel charge will begin to burn spontaneously, from the increased heat following ignition. The explosion that results applies extreme pressure to engine components, frequently damaging spark plugs and pistons.

Detonation can result by over-advanced ignition timing, inferior gasoline (low octane) lean air/fuel mixture, poor carburetion, engine lugging or an increase in compression ratio due to combustion chamber deposits or engine modification.

RECOMMENDATION: Replace the plugs after correcting the problem.

Photos Courtesy Champion Spark Plug Co.

EMISSION CONTROLS

13. Be aware of the general condition of the emission control system. It contributes to reduced pollution and should be serviced regularly to maintain efficient engine operation.

14. Check all vacuum lines for dried, cracked or brittle conditions. Something as simple as a leaking vacuum hose can cause poor performance and loss of economy.

15. Avoid tampering with the emission control system. Attempting to improve fuel econ-

FUEL SYSTEM

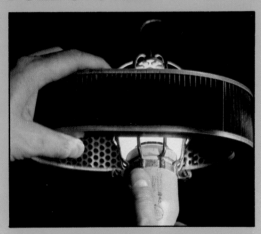

Check the air filter with a light behind it. If you can see light through the filter it can be reused.

Extremely clogged filters should be discarded and replaced with a new one.

18. Replace the air filter regularly. A dirty air filter richens the air/fuel mixture and can increase fuel consumption as much as 10%. Tests show that ⅓ of all vehicles have air filters in need of replacement.

19. Replace the fuel filter at least as often as recommended.

20. Set the idle speed and carburetor mixture to specifications.

21. Check the automatic choke. A sticking or malfunctioning choke wastes gas.

22. During the summer months, adjust the automatic choke for a leaner mixture which will produce faster engine warm-ups.

COOLING SYSTEM

29. Be sure all accessory drive belts are in good condition. Check for cracks or wear.

30. Adjust all accessory drive belts to proper tension.

31. Check all hoses for swollen areas, worn spots, or loose clamps.

32. Check coolant level in the radiator or expansion tank.

33. Be sure the thermostat is operating properly. A stuck thermostat delays engine warm-up and a cold engine uses nearly twice as much fuel as a warm engine.

34. Drain and replace the engine coolant at least as often as recommended. Rust and scale

TIRES & WHEELS

38. Check the tire pressure often with a pencil type gauge. Tests by a major tire manufacturer show that 90% of all vehicles have at least 1 tire improperly inflated. Better mileage can be achieved by over-inflating tires, but never exceed the maximum inflation pressure on the side of the tire.

39. If possible, install radial tires. Radial tires deliver as much as ½ mpg more than bias belted tires.

40. Avoid installing super-wide tires. They only create extra rolling resistance and decrease fuel mileage. Stick to the manufacturer's recommendations.

41. Have the wheels properly balanced.

omy by tampering with emission controls is more likely to worsen fuel economy than improve it. Emission control changes on modern engines are not readily reversible.

16. Clean (or replace) the EGR valve and lines as recommended.

17. Be sure that all vacuum lines and hoses are reconnected properly after working under the hood. An unconnected or misrouted vacuum line can wreak havoc with engine performance.

---

23. Check for fuel leaks at the carburetor, fuel pump, fuel lines and fuel tank. Be sure all lines and connections are tight.

24. Periodically check the tightness of the carburetor and intake manifold attaching nuts and bolts. These are a common place for vacuum leaks to occur.

25. Clean the carburetor periodically and lubricate the linkage.

26. The condition of the tailpipe can be an excellent indicator of proper engine combustion. After a long drive at highway speeds, the inside of the tailpipe should be a light grey in color. Black or soot on the insides indicates an overly rich mixture.

27. Check the fuel pump pressure. The fuel pump may be supplying more fuel than the engine needs.

28. Use the proper grade of gasoline for your engine. Don't try to compensate for knocking or "pinging" by advancing the ignition timing. This practice will only increase plug temperature and the chances of detonation or pre-ignition with relatively little performance gain.

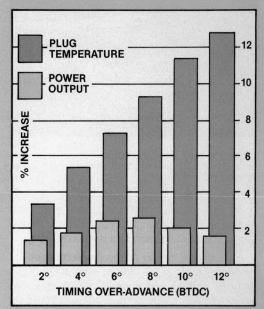

Increasing ignition timing past the specified setting results in a drastic increase in spark plug temperature with increased chance of detonation or preignition. Performance increase is considerably less. (Photo courtesy Champion Spark Plug Co.)

---

that form in the engine should be flushed out to allow the engine to operate at peak efficiency.

35. Clean the radiator of debris that can decrease cooling efficiency.

36. Install a flex-type or electric cooling fan, if you don't have a clutch type fan. Flex fans use curved plastic blades to push more air at low speeds when more cooling is needed; at high speeds the blades flatten out for less resistance. Electric fans only run when the engine temperature reaches a predetermined level.

37. Check the radiator cap for a worn or cracked gasket. If the cap does not seal properly, the cooling system will not function properly.

---

42. Be sure the front end is correctly aligned. A misaligned front end actually has wheels going in differed directions. The increased drag can reduce fuel economy by .3 mpg.

43. Correctly adjust the wheel bearings. Wheel bearings that are adjusted too tight increase rolling resistance.

Check tire pressures regularly with a reliable pocket type gauge. Be sure to check the pressure on a cold tire.

GENERAL MAINTENANCE

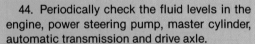

Check the fluid levels (particularly engine oil) on a regular basis. Be sure to check the oil for grit, water or other contamination.

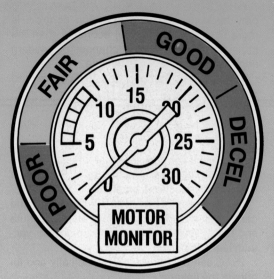

A vacuum gauge is another excellent indicator of internal engine condition and can also be installed in the dash as a mileage indicator.

44. Periodically check the fluid levels in the engine, power steering pump, master cylinder, automatic transmission and drive axle.

45. Change the oil at the recommended interval and change the filter at every oil change. Dirty oil is thick and causes extra friction between moving parts, cutting efficiency and increasing wear. A worn engine requires more frequent tune-ups and gets progressively worse fuel economy. In general, use the lightest viscosity oil for the driving conditions you will encounter.

46. Use the recommended viscosity fluids in the transmission and axle.

47. Be sure the battery is fully charged for fast starts. A slow starting engine wastes fuel.

48. Be sure battery terminals are clean and tight.

49. Check the battery electrolyte level and add distilled water if necessary.

50. Check the exhaust system for crushed pipes, blockages and leaks.

51. Adjust the brakes. Dragging brakes or brakes that are not releasing create increased drag on the engine.

52. Install a vacuum gauge or miles-per-gallon gauge. These gauges visually indicate engine vacuum in the intake manifold. High vacuum = good mileage and low vacuum = poorer mileage. The gauge can also be an excellent indicator of internal engine conditions.

53. Be sure the clutch is properly adjusted. A slipping clutch wastes fuel.

54. Check and periodically lubricate the heat control valve in the exhaust manifold. A sticking or inoperative valve prevents engine warm-up and wastes gas.

55. Keep accurate records to check fuel economy over a period of time. A sudden drop in fuel economy may signal a need for tune-up or other maintenance.

Emission Controls and Fuel System

4

EMISSION CONTROL SYSTEMS

Emission Systems Used

GASOLINE ENGINES

- Air Flow Controlled Fuel Injection (AFC)
- Catalytic Converter (CAT)
- Electronic Control Unit (ECU)
- Exhaust Gas Recirculation (EGR)
- Fuel Evaporation System (FEC)
- Oxygen Sensor (OS)
- Positive Crankcase Ventilation (PCV)

DIESEL ENGINES

- High Altitude Compensator (HAC)
- Positive Crankcase Ventilation (PCV)

Required Emission Control Maintenance

NOTE: *In addition to the services listed below, Toyota recommends an oil and filter change every 10,000 miles and an air filter replacement every 30,000 miles. Cut the mileage intervals in half if the vehicle is driven daily in heavy traffic, under dusty conditions or is used to tow a trailer. Valve and Idle Speed/Mixture adjustments are also considered part of emission maintenance.*

PCV SYSTEM

Check operation and replace the PCV valve (carbureted engine), or clean any gum deposits from the orifices (fuel injected engine) every 30,000 miles. Inspect all hoses for leaks or deterioration and replace as necessary.

FUEL EVAPORATION EMISSION CONTROL (EVAP) SYSTEM

Inspect the system for proper operation every 30,000 miles. Check all hose connections and hoses for leaks or deterioration and replace as necessary. Check the charcoal canister for raw gas contamination or damage and replace if necessary.

EXHAUST GAS RECIRCULATION (EGR) SYSTEM

Inspect the system for proper operation every 30,000 miles. Check the EGR valve operation and inspect all hoses and connections for leaks or deterioration and replace as necessary.

OXYGEN SENSOR (OXS) SYSTEM

Although no replacement interval is specified by the manufacturer, the oxygen sensor should be checked for proper operation every 30,000 miles and replaced every 60,000 miles. Any oxygen sensor found to be malfunctioning should be replaced.

Positive Crankcase Ventilation

A positive crankcase ventilation (PCV) system is used on all Toyotas sold in the United States. Blow-by gases are routed from the crankcase to the manifold, where they are combined with the fuel/air mixture and burned during combustion.

A valve (PCV) is used in the line to prevent the gases in the crankcase from being ignited in case of a backfire. The amount of blow-by gases entering the mixture is also regulated by the PCV Valve, which is spring-loaded and has a variable orifice.

On Toyotas, the valve is either mounted on the valve cover or in the line which runs from the intake manifold to the crankcase.

The valve should be replaced at the following intervals:
- Except Calif. — 30,000mi/24mo
- Calif. — 69,000 mi/48mo

REMOVAL AND INSTALLATION

Remove the PCV valve from the cylinder head cover or from the manifold-to-crankcase hose.

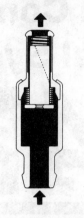
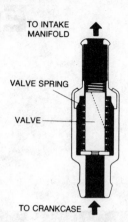

IDLE SPEED OR DECELERATION
(HIGH MANIFOLD VACUUM)

NOT RUNNING
OR BACKFIRE

PCV valve operation

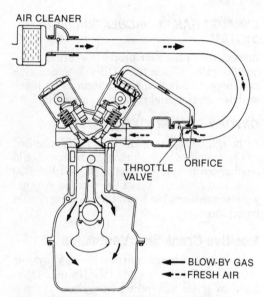

Typical PCV system on fuel injected engine

Check the attaching hoses for cracks or clogs. Install a new PCV valve into the hoses, or reinstall in the cylinder head cover.

TESTING

Check the PCV system hoses and connections, to ensure that there are no leaks, then replace or tighten, as necessary.

To check the valve, remove it and blow through both of its ends. When blowing from the side which goes toward the intake manifold, very little air should pass through. When blowing from the crankcase (valve cover) side, air should pass through freely.

Replace the valve with a new one, if the valve fails to function as outlined.

NOTE: *Do not attempt to clean or adjust the valve. Replace it with a new one.*

Air Injection System

A belt-driven pump supplies air to an injection manifold which has nozzles in each exhaust port. Injection of air at this point causes combustion of unburned hydrocarbons in the exhaust manifold rather than allowing them to escape into the atmosphere. An anti-backfire valve controls the flow of air from the pump to prevent backfiring which results from an overly rich mixture under closed throttle conditions.

A check valve prevents hot exhaust gas backflow into the pump and hoses, in case of a pump failure, or when the antibackfire valve is not working.

In addition, all engines have an air switching valve (ASV). On engines without catalytic converters, the ASV is used to stop air injection under a constant heavy engine load condition.

On engines with catalytic converters, the ASV is also used to protect the catalyst from overheating, by blocking the injector air necessary for the operation of the converter.

The pump relief valve is built into the ASV.

REMOVAL AND INSTALLATION

Air Pump

1. Disconnect the air hoses from the pump.
2. Loosen the bolt on the adjusting link and remove the drive belt.
3. Remove the mounting bolts and withdraw the pump.
CAUTION: *Do not pry on the pump housing. It may be distorted.*
4. Installation is in the reverse order of removal. Adjust the drive belt tension after installation. Belt deflection should be ½–¾" with 22 lbs. pressure.

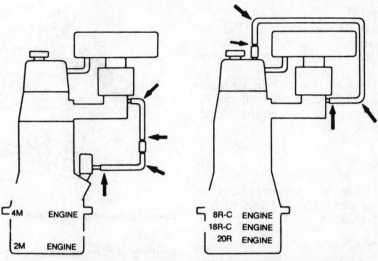

| 4M | ENGINE |
| 2M | ENGINE |

8R-C	ENGINE
18R-C	ENGINE
20R	ENGINE

Hose routing for PCV system—arrows indicate inspection points

Anti-backfire Valve and Air Switching Valve

1. Detach the air hoses from the valve, and electrical leads (if equipped).
2. Remove the valve securing bolt.
3. Withdraw the valve.
4. Installation is performed in the reverse order of removal.

Check Valve

1. Detach the intake hose from the valve.
2. Use an open-end wrench to remove the valve from its mounting.
3. Installation is the reverse of removal.

Relief Valve

NOTE: *On models with ASV-mounted relief valves, replace the entire ASV/relief valve as an assembly.*

1. Remove the air pump from the car.
2. Support the pump so that it cannot rotate.

Removing the check valve

Removing the pump-mounted relief valve

CAUTION: *Never clamp the pump in a vise. The aluminum case will be distorted.*

3. Use a bridge to remove the relief valve from the top of the pump.
4. Position the new relief valve over the opening in the pump.

NOTE: *The air outlet should be pointing toward the left.*

5. Gently tap the relief valve home, using a block of wood and a hammer.
6. Install the pump on the engine, as outlined above.

Air Injection Manifold

1. Remove the check valve, as previously outlined.
2. Loosen the air injection manifold attachment nuts and withdraw the manifold.

NOTE: *On some engines it may be necessary to remove the exhaust manifold first.*

3. Installation is in the reverse order of removal.

Air Injection Nozzles

1. Remove the air injection manifold as previously outlined.
2. Remove the cylinder head, as detailed in Chapter 3.
3. Place a new nozzle on the cylinder head.
4. Install the air injection manifold over it.
5. Install the cylinder head on the engine block.

TESTING

Air Pump

CAUTION: *Do not hammer, pry, or bend the pump housing while tightening the drive belt or testing the pump.*

BELT TENSION AND AIR LEAKS

1. Before proceeding with the tests, check the pump drive belt tension to ensure that it is within specifications.
2. Turn the engine. If the pump has seized, the belt will slip, making a noise. Disregard any chirping, squealing, or rolling sounds from inside the pump. These are normal when it is turned by hand.
3. Check the hoses and connections for leaks. Hissing or a blast of air indicates a leak. Soapy water, applied lightly around the area in question, is a good method for detecting leaks.

AIR OUTPUT

1. Disconnect the air supply hose at the antibackfire valve.
2. Connect a vacuum gauge, using a suitable adaptor, to the air supply hose.
NOTE: *If there are two hoses, plug the second one.*
3. With the engine at normal operating temperature, increase the idle speed and watch the vacuum gauge.
4. The airflow from the pump should be steady (between 2 and 6 psi). If it is unsteady or falls below specs, the pump is defective and must be replaced.

PUMP NOISE DIAGNOSIS

The air pump is normally noisy. As engine speed increases, the noise of the pump will rise in pitch. The rolling sound the pump bearings make is normal. But if this sound becomes objectionable at certain speeds, the pump is defective and will have to be replaced.

A continual hissing sound from the air pump pressure relief valve at idle, indicates a defective valve. Replace the relief valve.

If the pump rear bearing fails, a continual knocking sound will be heard. Since the rear

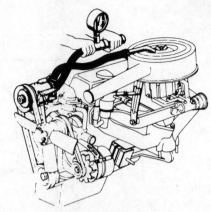

Checking the air pump output

bearing is not separately replaceable, the pump will have to be replaced as an assembly.

Anti-backfire Valve Tests

There are two different types of anti-backfire valve used with air injection systems. A bypass valve is used on all engines. Test procedures are given below.

GULP VALVE

1. Detach the air supply hose which runs between the pump and the gulp valve.
2. Connect a tachometer and run the engine to 1,500–2,000 rpm.
3. Allow the throttle to snap shut. This should produce a loud sucking sound from the gulp valve.
4. Repeat this operation several times. If no sound is present, the valve is not working or else the vacuum connections are loose.
5. Check the vacuum connections. If they are secure, replace the gulp valve.

BY-PASS VALVE

1. Detach the hose, which runs from the bypass valve to the check valve, at the by-pass valve hose connection.
2. Connect a tachometer to the engine. With the engine running at normal idle speed, check to see that air is flowing from the by-pass valve hose connection.
3. Speed up the engine so that it is running at 1,500–2,000 rpm. Allow the throttle to snap shut. The flow of air from the by-pass valve at the check valve hose connection should stop momentarily and air should then flow from the exhaust port on the valve body or the silencer assembly.
4. Repeat Step 3 several times. If the flow of air is not diverted into the atmosphere from the valve exhaust port or if it fails to stop flowing from the hose connection, check the vacuum lines and connections. If these are tight,

Air Injection System Diagnosis Chart

Problem	Cause	Cure
1. Noisy drive belt	Loose belt	Tighten belt
	Seized pump	Replace
2. Noisy pump	Leaking hose	Trace and fix leak
	Loose hose	Tighten hose clamp
	Hose contacting other parts	Reposition hose
	Diverter or check valve failure	Replace
	Pump mounting loose	Tighten securing bolts
	Defective pump	Replace
3. No air supply	Loose belt	Tighten belt
	Leak in hose or at fitting	Trace and fix leak
	Defective antibackfire valve	Replace
	Defective check valve	Replace
	Defective pump	Replace
	Defective ASV	Replace
4. Exhaust backfire	Vacuum or air leaks	Trace and fix leak
	Defective antibackfire valve	Replace
	Sticking choke	Service choke
	Choke setting rich	Adjust choke

the valve is defective and requires replacement.

5. A leaking diaphragm will cause the air to flow out both the hose connection and the exhaust port at the same time. If this happens, replace the valve.

Check Valve Test

1. Before starting the test, check all of the hoses and connections for leaks.

2. Insert a suitable probe into the check valve and depress the plate. Release it. The plate should return to its original position

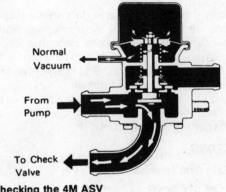

Checking the 4M ASV

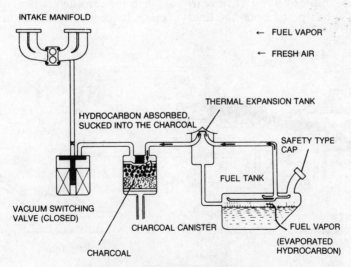

Typical canister vapor storage system

against the valve seat. If binding is evident, re-place the valve.

3. With the engine running at normal oper-ating temperature, gradually increase its speed to 1,500 rpm. Check for exhaust gas leakage. If any is present, replace the valve assembly.

NOTE: *Vibration and flutter of the check valve at idle speed is a normal condition and does not mean that the valve should be replaced.*

Evaporative Emission Control System

To prevent hydrocarbon emissions from enter-ing the atmosphere, Toyota vehicles use evapo-rative emission control (EEC) systems.

Fuel vapors are stored in a canister filled with activated charcoal. A vaccuum switching valve is used to purge the system. The air filter is an integral part of the charcoal canister.

REMOVAL AND INSTALLATION

Removal and installation of the various evapo-rative emission control system components consists of unfastening hoses, loosening secur-ing screws, and removing the part which is to be replaced from its mounting bracket. Instal-lation is the reverse of removal.

NOTE: *When replacing any EEC system hoses, always use hoses that are fuel-resis-tant or are marked 'EVAP'.*

TESTING

EEC System Troubleshooting

There are several things which may be checked if a malfunction of the evaporative emission control system is suspected.

1. Leaks may be traced by using a hydrocar-bon tests. Run the test probe along the lines

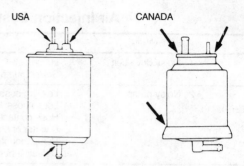

Inspection of a typical charcoal canister

and connections. The meter will indicate the presence of a leak by a high hydrocarbon (HC) reading. This method is much more accurate than visual inspection which would only indi-cate the presence of a leak large enough to pass liquid.

2. Leaks may be caused by any of the following:

    a. Defective or worn hoses.

    b. Disconnected or pinched hoses.

3. Detach the vacuum line from the posi-tioner diaphragm unit and plug the line up.

4. Accelerate the engine slightly to set the throttle positioner in place.

5. Check the engine speed with a tachome-ter when the throttle positioner is set.

6. If necessary, adjust the engine speed, with the throttle positioner adjusting screw, to the specifications given in the Throttle Posi-tioner Settings chart at the end of this section.

7. Connect the vacuum hose to the position-er diaphragm.

8. The throttle lever should be freed form the positioner as soon as the vacuum hose is connected. Engine idle should return to normal.

9. If the throttle positioner fails to function properly, check its linkage, and vacuum dia-

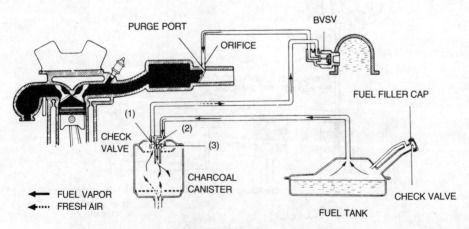

Typical EVAP system on fuel injected engine

phragm. If there are no defects in either of these, the fault probably lies in the vacuum switching valve or the speed marker unit.

NOTE: *Due to the complexity of these two components, and also because they require special test equipment, their service is best left to an authorized facility.*

Mixture Control Valve

The mixture control valve, used on some models with manual transmissions, aids in combustion of unburned fuel during periods of deceleration. The mixture control valve is operated by the vacuum switching valve during periods of deceleration to admit additional fresh air into the intake manifold. The extra air allows more complete combustion of the fuel, thus reducing hydrocarbon emissions.

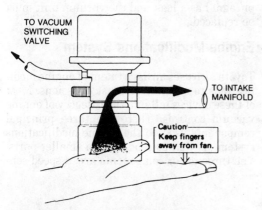

TO VACUUM
SWITCHING
VALVE

TO INTAKE
MANIFOLD

Caution:
Keep fingers
away from fan.

Testing the mixture control valve

REMOVAL AND INSTALLATION

1. Unfasten the vacuum switching valve line from the mixture control valve.
2. Remove the intake manifold hose from the valve.
3. Remove the valve from its engine mounting.
4. Installation is performed in the reverse order of removal.

TESTING

1. Start the engine and allow it to idle (warmed up).
2. Place your hand over the air intake at the bottom of the valve.
    CAUTION: *Keep your fingers clear of the engine fan.*
3. Increase the engine speed and then release the throttle.
4. Suction should be felt at the air intake only while the engine is decelerating. Once the

engine has returned to idle, no suction should be felt.

If the above test indicates a malfunction, proceed with the next step. If not, the mixture control valve is functioning properly and requires no further adjustment.

5. Disconnect the vacuum line from the mixture control valve. If suction can be felt underneath the valve with the engine at idle, the valve seat is defective and must be replaced.
6. Reconnect the vacuum line to the valve. Disconnect the other end of the line from the vacuum switching valve and place it in your mouth.
7. With the engine idling, suck on the end of the vacuum line to duplicate the action of the vacuum switching valve.
8. Suction at the valve air intake should only be felt for an instant. If air cannot be drawn into the valve at all, or if it is continually drawn in, replace the mixture control valve.

If the mixture control valve is functioning properly, and all of the hose and connections are in good working order, the vacuum switching valve is probably at fault.

Spark Delay Valve

The spark delay valve (SDV) is located in the distributor vacuum line. The valve has a small orifice in it, which slows down the vacuum flow to the vacuum advance unit on the distributor. By delaying the vacuum to the distributor, a reduction in HC and CO emissions is possible.

When the coolant temperature is below 95°F, a coolant temperature operated vacuum control valve is opened, allowing the distributor to receive undelayed, ported vacuum through a separate vacuum line. Above 95°F, this line is blocked and all ported vacuum must go through the spark delay valve.

TESTING

1. Allow the engine to cool, so that the coolant temperature is below 95°F.
2. Disconnect the vacuum line which runs from the coolant temperature operated vacuum valve to the vacuum advance unit at the advance unit end. Connect a vacuum gauge to this line.
3. Start the engine. Increase the engine speed. The gauge should indicate a vacuum.
4. Allow the engine to warm-up to normal operating temperature. Increase the engine speed. This time the vacuum gauge should read zero.
5. Replace the coolant temperature operated vacuum valve, if it fails either of these tests. Disconnect the vacuum gauge and reconnect the vacuum lines.

6. Remove the spark delay valve from the vacuum line, noting which side faces the distributor.

7. Connect a hand-operated vacuum pump which has a built-in vacuum gauge to the manifold side of the spark delay valve.

8. Connect a vacuum gauge to the distributor side of the valve.

9. Operate the hand pump to create a vacuum. The vacuum gauge on the distributor side should show a hesitation before registering.

10. The gauge reading on the pump side should drop slightly, taking several seconds for it to balance with the reading on the other gauge.

11. If Steps 9 and 10 are negative, replace the spark delay valve.

12. Remove the vacuum gauge from the distributor side of the valve. Cover the distributor side of the valve with your finger and operate the pump to create a vacuum of 15 in. Hg.

13. The reading on the pump gauge should remain steady. If the gauge reading drops, replace the valve.

14. Remove your finger. The reading of the gauge should drop slowly. If the reading goes to zero rapidly, replace the valve.

Dual Diaphragm Distributor

Some Toyota models are equipped with a dual diaphragm distributor unit. This distributor has a retard diaphragm, as well as a diaphragm for advance.

TESTING

1. Connect a timing light to the engine. Check the ignition timing.

NOTE: *Before proceeding with the tests, disconnect any spark control devices, distributor vacuum valves, etc. If these are left connected, inaccurate results may be obtained.*

2. Remove the retard hose from the distributor and plug it. Increase the engine speed. The timing should advance. If it fails to do so, then the vacuum unit is faulty and must be replaced.

3. Check the timing with the engine at normal idle speed. Unplug the retard hose and connect it to the vacuum unit. The timing should instantly be retarded from 4 to 10 degrees. If this does not occur, the retard diaphragm has a leak and the vacuum unit must be replaced.

Engine Modifications System

Toyota also uses an assortment of engine modifications to regulate exhaust emissions. Most of these devices fall into the category of engine vacuum controls. There are three principal components used on the engine modifications system, as well as a number of smaller parts. The three major components are: a speed sen-

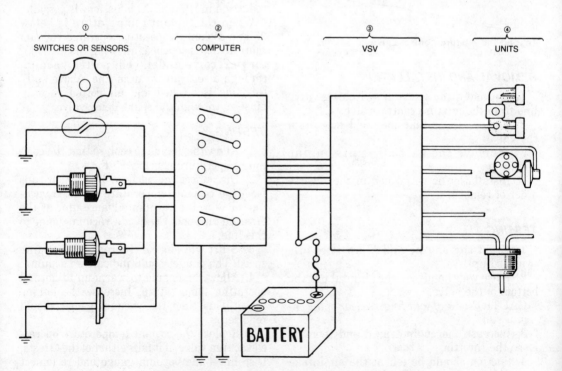

Block diagram of a typical engine modification system

sor, a computer (speed marker), and a vacuum switching valve.

The vacuum switching valve and computer circuit operates most of the emission control components. Depending upon year and engine usage, the vacuum switching valve and computer may operate the pure control for the evaporative emission control system, the transmission controlled spark (TCS) or speed controlled spark (SCS), the dual diaphragm distributor, the throttle positioner systems, the EGR system, the catalyst protection system, etc.

The functions of the evaporative emission control system, the throttle positioner, and the dual diaphragm distributor are described in detail in the preceding sections. However, a word is necessary about the functions of the TCS and SCS systems before discussing the operation of the vacuum switching valve/computer circuit.

The major difference between the transmission controlled spark and speed controlled spark systems is the manner in which system operation is determined. Toyota TCS systems use a speed sensor built into the speedometer cable.

Below a predetermined speed, or any gear other than Fourth, the vacuum advance unit on the distributor is rendered inoperative or the timing retarded. By changing the distributor advance curve in this manner, it is possible to reduce emissions of oxides of nitrogen NOx).

NOTE: *Some engines are equipped with a thermo-sensor so that the TCS or SCS system only operates when the coolant temperature is 140°–212°F.*

Aside from determining the preceding conditions, the vacuum switching valve computer circuit operates other devices in the emission control system (EGR, Catalytic converter, etc.)

The computer acts as a speed marker, At certain speeds it sends a signal to the vacuum switching valve which acts as a gate, opening and closing the emission control system vacuum circuits.

The vacuum switching valve contains several solenoid and valve assemblies so that different combinations of opened and closed vacuum ports are possible. This allows greater flexibility of operation for the emission control system.

SYSTEM CHECKS

Due to the complexity of the components involved, about the only engine modification system checks which can be made, are the following:

1. Examine the vacuum lines to ensure that they are not clogged, pinched, or loose.

2. Check the electrical connections for tightness and corrosion.

3. Be sure that the vacuum sources for the vacuum switching valve are not plugged.

4. On models equipped with speed controlled spark, a broken speedometer cable could also render the system inoperative.

Beyond these checks, servicing the engine modifications system is best left to an authorized service facility.

NOTE: *A faulty vacuum switching valve or computer could cause more than one of the emission control systems to fail. Therefore, if several systems are out, these two units (and the speedometer cable) would be the first things to check.*

High Altitude Compensation System

For all engines to be sold in areas over 4000 ft. in altitude, a system has been installed to automatically lean out the fuel mixture by supplying additional air. This also results in lower emissions.

Low atmospheric pressure allows the bellows in the system to expand the close a port, allowing more air to enter from different sources.

All parts in this system must be replaced. The only adjustment available is in the timing.

Bi-Metal Vacuum Switching Valve
TESTING

1. Drain the engine coolant.
2. Remove the vacuum hoses and remove the BVSV.
3. Cool the BVSV to 86°F.
4. Blow air through the valve. At this time the valve should be closed and not allow air to pass.
5. Heat the valve to 111°F. The valve should open and allow air to pass through.
6. Repeat Step 4.
7. If the valve is inoperative it must be replaced.
8. Apply a liquid sealer to the threads and replace the valve.
9. Reconnect the vacuum lines.
10. Refill the coolant.

Exhaust Gas Recirculation (EGR)

In all cases, the EGR valve is controlled by the same computer and vacuum switching valve which is used to operate other emission control system components.

The EGR valve is operated by vacuum supplied from a port above the throttle blades and fed through the vacuum switching valve.

There are several conditions, determined by

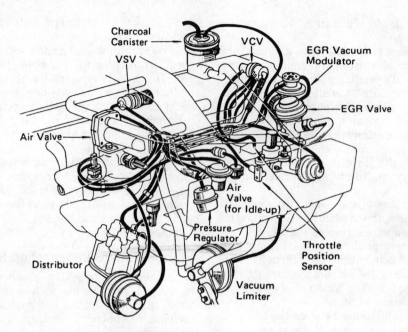

Vacuum limiter and other controls—EFI

the computer and vacuum switching valve, which permit exhaust gas recirculation to take place:

1. Vehicle speed.
2. Engine coolant temperature.
3. EGR valve temperature.
4. Manifold flange temperature.

EGR VALVE CHECKS

1. Allow the engine to warm up and remove the top from the air cleaner.

NOTE: *Do not remove the entire air cleaner assembly.*

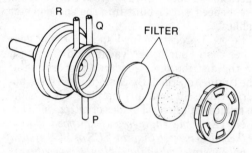

Typical EGR vacuum modulator showing port locations and filter

To reduce NOx emission, part of the exhaust gases are recirculated through the EGR valve to the intake manifold to lower the maximum combustion temperature.							
Coolant Temp.	BVSV	Throttle Valve Opening Angle	Pressure in the EGR Valve Pressure Chamber		EGR Vacuum Modulator	EGR Valve	Exhaust Gas
Below 45°C (113°F)	CLOSED	—	—		—	CLOSED	Not recirculated
Above 66°C (151°F)	OPEN	Positioned below EGR port	—		—	CLOSED	Not recirculated
		Positioned between EGR port and R port	(1) LOW	*Pressure constantly alternating between low and high	OPENS passage to atmosphere	CLOSED	Not recirculated
			(2) HIGH		CLOSES passage to atmosphere	OPEN	Recirculated
		Positioned above R port	(3) HIGH	**	CLOSES passage to atmosphere	OPEN	Recirculated (increase)

Remarks: *Pressure increase → Modulator closes → EGR valve opens → Pressure drops
                  └─ EGR valve closes ← Modulator opens ◄─┘
              **When the throttle valve is positioned above the R port, the EGR vacuum modulator will
              close the atmosphere passage and open the EGR valve to increase the EGR gas, even if the
              exhaust pressure is insufficiently low.

Typical EGR operations

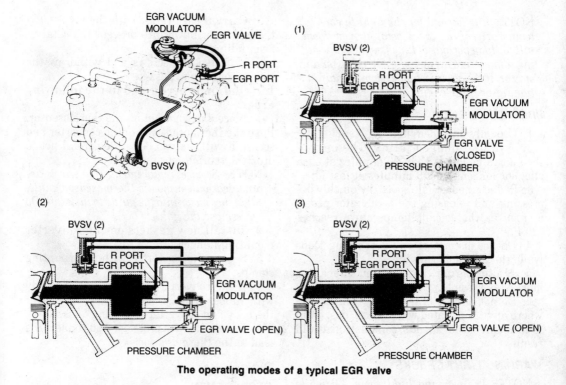

The operating modes of a typical EGR valve

2. Disconnect the hose (white tape coded), which runs from the vacuum switching valve to the EGR valve, at its EGR valve end.

3. Remove the intake manifold hose (red coded) from the vacuum switching valve and connect it to the EGR valve. When the engine is at idle, a hollow sound should be heard coming from the air cleaner.

4. Disconnect the hose from the EGR valve. The hollow sound should disappear.

5. If the sound doesn't vary, the EGR valve is defective and must be replaced.

6. Reconnect the vacuum hoses as they were originally found. Install the top on the air cleaner.

SYSTEM CHECKS

If, after having completed the above tests, the EGR system still doesn't work right and everything else checks out OK, the fault probably lies in the computer or the vacuum switching valve systems. If this is the case, it is best to have the car checked out by test facility which has the necessary Toyota emission system test equipment.

NOTE: *A good indication that the fault doesn't lie in the EGR system, but rather in the vacuum supply system, would be if several emission control systems were not working properly.*

Catalytic Converters

A three-way (TWC) catalytic converter is used by itself or with an oxidation converter. The TWC acts on all three major pollutants. Hydrocarbons and carbon monoxide are oxidized in the usual manner (into carbon dioxide and water) and the oxides of nitrogen are reduced to free oxygen and nitrogen.

An air pump is used to supply air to the exhaust system to aid in the reaction. A thermosensor, inserted into the converter, shuts off the air supply if the catalyst temperature becomes excessive.

The same sensor circuit also causes a dash warning light labeled EXH TEMP to come one when the catalyst temperature gets too high.

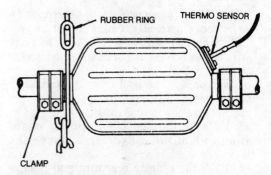

Catalytic converter installation

NOTE: *It is normal for the light to come on temporarily if the car is being driven downhill for long periods of time (such as descending a mountain). The light will come on and stay on if the air injection system is malfunctioning or if the engine is misfiring.*

PRECAUTIONS

1. Use only unleaded fuel.
2. Avoid prolonged idling. The engine should run no longer than 20 minutes at curb idle, nor longer than 10 minutes at fast idle.
3. Reduce the fast idle speed, by quickly depressing and releasing the accelerator pedal, as soon as the coolant temperature reaches 120°F.
4. Do not disconnect any spark plug leads while the engine is running.
5. Make engine compression checks as quickly as possible.
6. Do not dispose of the catalyst in a place where anything coated with grease, gas, or oil is present. Spontaneous combustion could result.

WARNING LIGHT CHECKS

NOTE: *The warning light comes on while the engine is being cranked, to test its operation, just like any of the other warning lights.*
1. If the warning light comes on and stays on, check the components of the air injection system as previously outlined. If these are not defective, check the ignition system for faulty leads, plugs, points, or control box.
2. If no problems can be found in Step 1, check the wiring for the light for shorts or opened circuits.
3. If nothing else can be found wrong in Steps 1 and 2, check the operation of the emission control system vacuum switching valve or computer, either by substitution of a new unit, or by taking it to a service facility which has Toyota's special emission control system checker.

CONVERTER REMOVAL AND INSTALLATION

CAUTION: *Do not perform this operation on a hot (or even warm) engine. Catalyst temperatures may go as high as 1,700°F, so that any contact with the catalyst could cause severe burns.*
1. Disconnect the lead from the converter thermosensor.
2. Remove the wiring shield.
3. Unfasten the pipe clamp securing bolts at either end of the converter. Remove the clamps.
4. Push the tailpipe rearward and remove the converter, complete with thermosensor.

5. Carry the converter with the thermosensor upward to prevent the catalyst from falling out.
6. Unfasten the screws and withdraw the thermosensor and gasket.

Installation is performed in the following order:
1. Place a new gasket on the thermosensor. Push the thermosensor into the converter and secure it with its two bolts. Be careful not to drop the thermosensor.
NOTE: *Service replacement converters are provided with a plastic thermosensor guide. Slide the sensor into the guide to install it. Do not remove the guide.*
2. Install new gaskets on the converter mounting flanges.
3. Secure the converter with its mounting clamps.
4. If the converter is attached to the body with rubber O-rings, install the O-rings over the body and converter mounting hooks.
5. Install the wire protector and connect the lead to the thermosensor.

Oxygen Sensor
REPLACEMENT

1. Disconnect the battery ground.
2. Unplug the connector at the sensor. Be careful to not bend the hose.
3. Remove the two attaching nuts and remove the sensor.
4. Installation is the reverse of removal. Use a new gasket, and torque the nuts to 13–16 ft.lb.

OXYGEN SENSOR WARNING LIGHT

The light is hooked into an elapsed mileage counter which is designed to go off every 30,000 miles, indicating sensor replacement. After the sensor is replaced, the counter must be reset:
1. Locate the counter, under the left side of the instrument panel, on the brake pedal bracket.

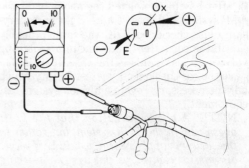

Testing oxygen sensor

WITH VOLTMETER

1. Warm up the engine.
2. Connect SST to the 4-terminal connector. (SST 09842-14010)
3. Using a voltmeter connect the positive probe to the red wire of the SST and negative testing probe to the black wire.
4. Warm up the oxygen sensor with the engine at 2,500 rpm for about 120 seconds.

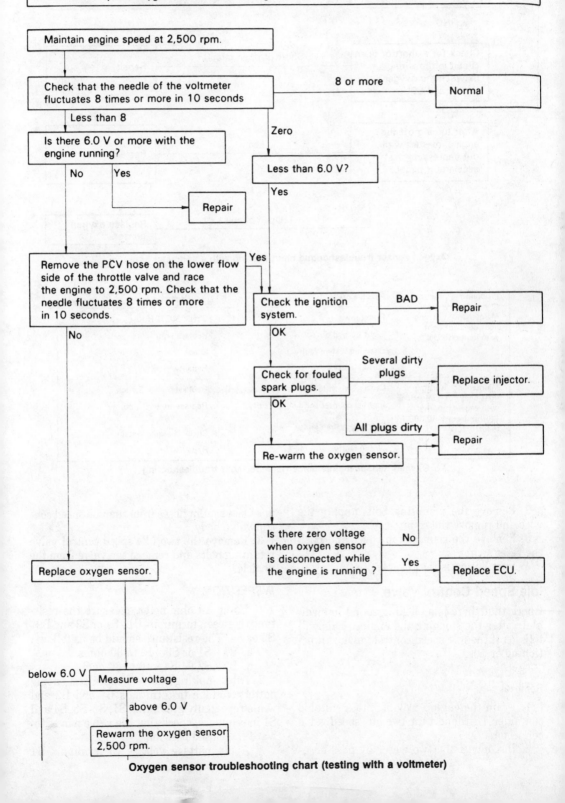

Oxygen sensor troubleshooting chart (testing with a voltmeter)

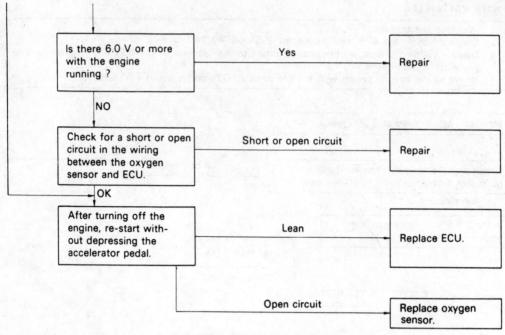

Oxygen sensor troubleshooting chart (testing with a voltmeter cont.)

Problem	Possible cause	Remedy
Maintenance warning light does not light with ignition "ON"	Fuse blown	Check METER fuse
	Light burned out	Replace light
	Charging system faulty	Check charging system
	Wiring faulty	Repair wiring
Maintenance warning light does not go out with engine running (Without every 30,000 miles)	Cancel Switch faulty	Replace Cancel Switch
	Interval counter and switch faulty	Replace Interval Counter
	Charging system faulty	Check charging system
	Wiring faulty	Repair wiring

Oxygen sensor maintenance reminder light troubleshooting

2. Remove the mounting bolt, unplug the wire and remove the counter.

3. Remove the counter top cover and push the reset switch.

4. Installation is the reverse of removal.

Idle Speed Control Valve

Check that there is a clicking sound immediately after the stopping the engine. This will tell you if the idle speed control valve is functioning or not.

Removal

1. Drain the engine coolant into a suitable container. Disconnect the two idle speed valve connectors.

2. Disconnect the two water by pass hoses and the vacuum hoses from the idle speed control valve body.

3. Remove the two idle speed control valve retaining bolts and remove the valve from the vehicle.

INSPECTION

1. Using an ohmmeter. measure the resistance between terminals B1 - S1 or S3 and B2 - S2 or S4. The resistance should be as follows:

   a. B1 - S1 or S3 - 10 to 30 ohms.

   b. B2 - S2 04 S4 - 10 to 30 ohms.

2. After making the resistance test, apply battery voltage to terminals B1 and B2 and while repeatedly grounding S1, S2, S3, S4 and S1 in sequence, check that the valve moves toward the closed position.

3. Apply battery voltage to terminals B1

WITH EFI CHECKER

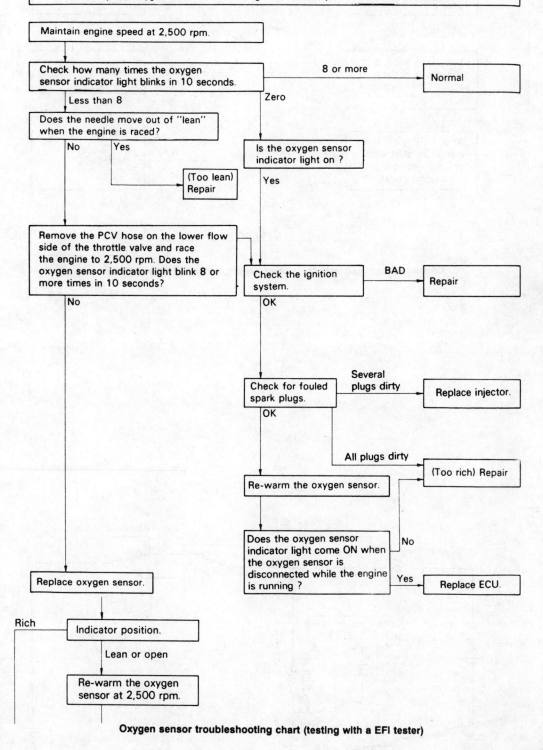

1. Warm up the engine.
2. Connect SST to the EFI service connector. (SST 09991-00100)
3. Warm up the oxygen sensor with the engine at 2,500 rpm for about 120 seconds.

Maintain engine speed at 2,500 rpm.

Check how many times the oxygen sensor indicator light blinks in 10 seconds.

8 or more → Normal

Less than 8

Zero

Does the needle move out of "lean" when the engine is raced?

No   Yes

(Too lean) Repair

Is the oxygen sensor indicator light on ?

Yes

Remove the PCV hose on the lower flow side of the throttle valve and race the engine to 2,500 rpm. Does the oxygen sensor indicator light blink 8 or more times in 10 seconds?

No

Check the ignition system.

BAD → Repair

OK

Check for fouled spark plugs.

Several plugs dirty → Replace injector.

OK

All plugs dirty → (Too rich) Repair

Re-warm the oxygen sensor.

Does the oxygen sensor indicator light come ON when the oxygen sensor is disconnected while the engine is running ?

No

Yes → Replace ECU.

Replace oxygen sensor.

Rich

Indicator position.

Lean or open

Re-warm the oxygen sensor at 2,500 rpm.

Oxygen sensor troubleshooting chart (testing with a EFI tester)

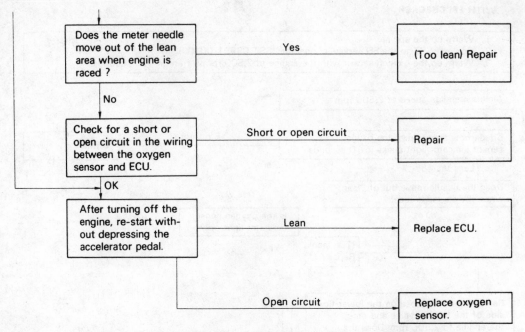

Oxygen sensor troubleshooting chart (testing with a EFI tester cont.)

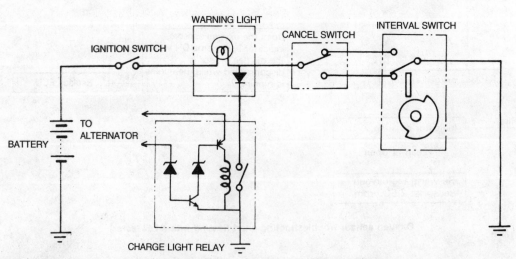

Oxygen sensor maintenance reminder light wiring diagram

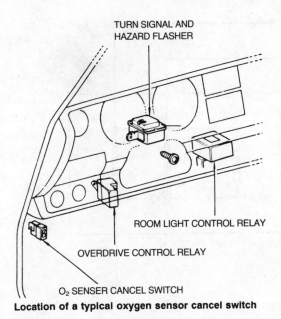

Location of a typical oxygen sensor cancel switch

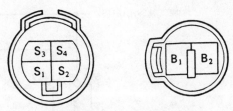

Checking the resistance of the idle speed control valve

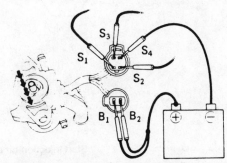

Checking the ISC valve in the open position

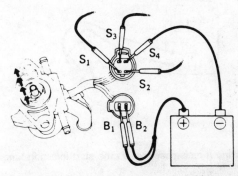

Checking the ISC valve in the closed position

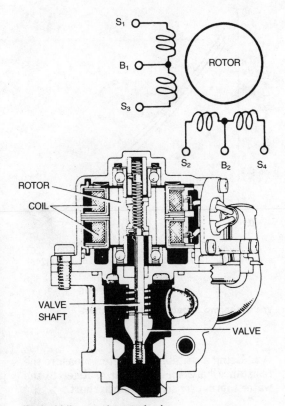

Typical idle speed control valve

and B2 and while repeatedly grounding S4 - S3 - S2 - S1- and in sequence, check that the valve moves toward the open position.

4. If the idle speed control valve fails any of this inspection, replace it with a new one.

INSTALLATION

1. Install the valve onto the vehicle and install two idle speed control valve retaining bolts.

2. Re-connect the two water by pass hoses and the vacuum hoses to the idle speed control valve body.

3. Re-connect the two idle speed valve connectors and refill the engine coolant.

Start Injector Time Switch (EFI)
INSPECTION

1. Disconnect the start injector time switch electrical connector.

2. Using a suitable ohmmeter, measure the resistance between each terminal. The ohmmeter reading should read as follows:

    a. Between STA - STJ terminals - 24 to 40 ohms with the coolant temperature below

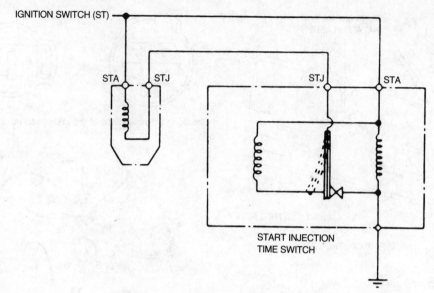

Start injection time switch wiring schematic

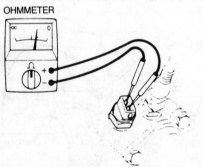

Making a resistance test on the start injection time switch

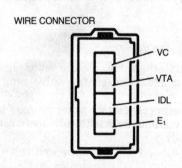

Terminal location on the wire connector

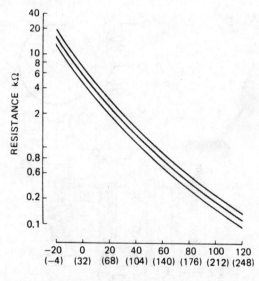

Water thermo sensor resistance chart

86°F. 40 to 60 ohms with the coolant temperature above 104°F.

b. STA - Ground terminals - 20 to 80.

Water Thermo Sensor

INSPECTION

1. Disconnect the electrical connector to the water thermo sensor.

2. Using a suitable ohmmeter, measure the resistance between both charts. Refer to the water thermo sensor resistance chart.

ELECTRONIC FUEL INJECTION (EFI) SYSTEM

This system is broken down into three major systems. The Fuel System, Air Induction System and Electronic Control System.

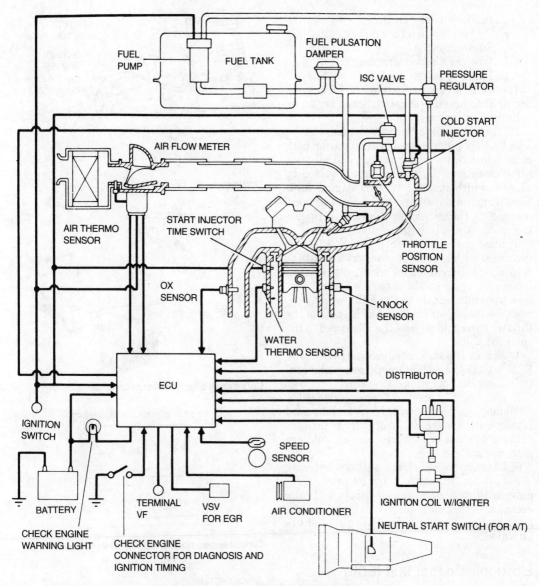

Exploded view of a typical Toyota EFI system

Fuel System

An electric fuel pump supplies sufficient fuel, under a constant pressure, to the EFI injectors. These injectors inject a metered quantity of fuel into the intake manifold in accordance with signals from the EFI computer. Each injector injects at the same time, one half of the fuel required for ideal combustion with each engine revolution.

Air Induction System

The air induction system provides sufficient air for the engine operation.

Electronic Control System

The engine is equipped with a Toyota Computer Control System (TCCS) which centrally controls the electronic fuel injection, electronic spark advance and the exhaust gas recirculation valve. The systems can be diagnosed by means of an Electronic Control Unit (ECU) which employs a microcomputer. The ECU and the TCCS control the following functions:

1. Electronic Fuel Injection (EFI). The ECU receives signals from the various sensors indicating changing engine operations conditions such as:

a. Intake air volume.

b. Intake air temperature.

c. Coolant temperature sensor.

e. Engine rpm.

f. Acceleration/deceleration.

g. Exhaust oxygen content.

These signals are utilized by the ECU to determine the injection duration necessary for an optimum air-fuel ratio.

2. The Electronic Spark Advance (ESA). The ECU is programmed with data for optimum ignition timing during any and all operating conditions. Using the data provided by sensors which monitor various engine functions (rpm, intake air volume, coolant temperature, etc.), the microcomputer (ECU) triggers the spark at precisely the right moment.

3. Idle Speed Control (ISC). The ECU is programmed with specific engine speed values to respond to different engine conditions (coolant temperature, air conditioner on/off, etc.). Sensors transmit signals to the ECU which controls the flow of air through the by-pass of the throttle valve and adjusts the idle speed to the specified value.

4. Exhaust Gas Recirculation (EGR). The ECU detects the coolant temperature and controls the EGR operations accordingly.

5. Electronic Controlled Transmission (ECT - automatic transmission only). A serial signal is transmitted to the ECT computer to prevent shift up to third or overdrive during cold engine operation.

6. Diagnostics, which are outlined below.

7. Fail-Safe Function. In the event of a computer malfunction, a backup circuit will take over to provide minimal driveability. Simultaneously, the "Check Engine" warning light is activated.

Electronic Control Unit (ECU)

DIAGNOSIS

The ECU contains a built in self diagnosis system by which troubles with the engine signal the engine signal network are detected and a "Check Engine" warning light on the instrument panel flashes code numbers 12, 13, 14, 21, 22, 31, 32, 42, 52 and 53. The "Check Engine" light on the instrument panel informs the driver that a malfunction has been detected. The light goes out automatically when the malfunction has been cleared.

The diagnostic code can be read by the number of blinks of the "Check Engine" warning light when the proper terminals of the check connector are short-circuited. If the vehicle is equipped with a supper monitor display, the diagnostic code is indicated on the display screen.

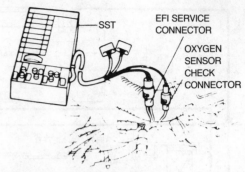

Connecting the EFI tester

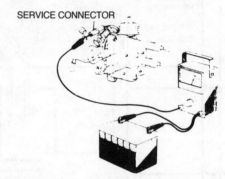

Connecting a tachometer to an IIA distributor

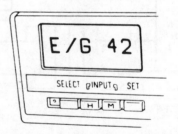

Typical super monitor display of trouble codes

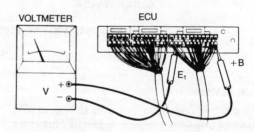

Measuring voltage at the ECU connectors

Check Engine Warning Light

1. The "Check Engine" warning light will come on when the ignition switch is placed On and the engine is not running.

2. When the engine is started, the "Check Engine" warning light should go out.

3. If the light remains on, the diagnosis system has detected a malfunction in the system.

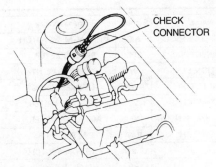

Short circuiting the check connector

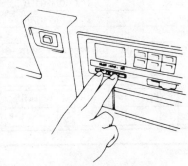

Holding in the SELECT AND INPUT buttons

Output Of Diagnostic Codes

1. The battery voltage should be above 11 volts. Throttle valve fully closed (throttle position sensor IDL points closed).

2. Place the transmission in "P" or "N" range. Turn the A/C switch Off. Start the engine and let it run to reach its normal operating temperature.

WITHOUT SUPER MONITOR DISPLAY

1. Turn the ignition switch to the On position. Do not start the engine. Use a suitable jumper wire and short the terminals of the check connector.

2. Read the diagnostic code as indicated by the number of flashes of the "Check Engine" warning light.

3. If the system is operating normally (no malfunction), the light will blink once every 0.25 seconds.

4. In the event of a malfunction, the light will blink once every 0.5 seconds. the first number of blinks will equal the first digit of a two digit diagnostic code. After a 1.5 second pause, the second number of blinks will equal the second number of a 2 digit diagnostic code. If there are two or more codes, there will be a 2.5 second pause between each.

NOTE: *In event of a number of trouble codes, indication will begin from the smaller value and continue to the larger in order.*

5. After the diagnosis check, remove the jumper wire from the check connector.

WITH SUPER MONITOR DISPLAY

1. Turn the ignition switch to the On position. Do not start the engine.

2. Simultaneously push and hold in the SELECT and INPUT M keys for at least three seconds. The letters DIAG will appear on the screen.

3. After a short pause, hold the SET key in for at least three seconds. If the system is normal (no malfunctions), E/G OK will appear on the screen.

4. If there is a malfunction, the code number for it will appear on the screen. In the event of two or more numbers, there will be a three second pause between each (Eample E/G 42).

5. After confirmation of the diagnostic code, either turn off the ignition switch or push the super monitor display key on so the time appears.

Cancelling Out The Diagnostic Code

1. After repairing the trouble area, the diagnostic code that is retained in the ECU memory must be cancelled out by removing the EFI (15A) fuse for thirty seconds or more, depending on the ambient temperature (the lower temperature, the longer the fuse must be left out with the ignition switch off).

NOTE: *Cancellation can also be done by removing the battery negative terminal, but keep in mind when removing the negative battery cable, the other memory systems (radio, ETR, clock, etc.) will also be cancelled out.*

If the diagnostic code is not cancelled out, it will be retained by the ECU and appear along with a new code in event of future trouble. If it is necessary to work on engine components requiring removal of the battery terminal, a check must first be made to see if a diagnostic code is detected.

2. After cancellation, perform a road test, if necessary, confirm that a normal code is now read on the "Check Engine" warning light or super monitor display.

3. If the same diagnostic code is still indicated, it indicates that the trouble area has not been repaired throughly.

Diagnosis Indication

1. Including "Normal", the ECU is programmed with sixteen diagnostic codes.

2. When two or more codes are indicated, the lowest number code will appear first. However, no other code will appear along with code number eleven.

3. All dectected diagnostic codes, except fif-

Symbol	Terminal Name	Symbol	Terminal Name	Symbol	Terminal Name
E$_{01}$	ENGINE GROUND	G$\ominus$	ENGINE REVOLUTION SENSOR	A/C	A/C MAGNET SWITCH
E$_{02}$	ENGINE GROUND	V$_F$	CHECK CONNECTOR	SPD	SPEEDOMETER
No. 10	INJECTOR	G	ENGINE REVOLUTION SENSOR	W	WARNING LIGHT
No. 20	INJECTOR	T	CHECK CONNECTOR	THA	AIR TEMP. SENSOR
STA	STARTER SWITCH	VTA	THROTTLE SWITCH	Vs	AIR FLOW METER
IG$_t$	IGNITER	Ne	ENGINE REVOLUTION SENSOR	Vc	AIR FLOW METER
EGR	EGR VSV	IDL	THROTTLE SWITCH	BAT	BATTERY +B
E$_1$	ENGINE GROUND	KNK	KNOCK SENSOR	IG S/W	IGNITION SWITCH
N/C	NEUTRAL START SWITCH (A/T)	IG$_f$	IGNITER	+B	MAIN RELAY
N/C	CLUTCH SWITCH (M/T)	Ox	Ox SENSOR	TCD	ECT COMPUTER
ISC$_1$	ISC MOTOR NO. 1 COIL	THW	WATER TEMP. SENSOR	L$_1$	ECT COMPUTER
ISC$_2$	ISC MOTOR NO. 2 COIL	E$_2$	SENSOR EARTH	L$_2$	ECT COMPUTER
ISC$_3$	ISC MOTOR NO. 3 COIL	E$_1$	ENGINE GROUND	L$_3$	ECT COMPUTER
ISC$_4$	ISC MOTOR NO. 4 COIL	M-REL	MAIN RELAY COIL	OIL	OIL PRESSURE SWITCH

E$_{01}$	No. 10	STA	EGR	N/C		ISC 1	ISC 2	G$\ominus$		G		Ne		IG$_f$	THW		L$_1$	L$_2$	L$_3$	M-REL		SPD		THA	Vs	Vc	BAT	IG S/W
E$_{02}$	No. 20	IG$_t$	E$_1$			ISC 3	ISC 4	V$_F$		T	VTA	IDL	KNK	Ox	E$_2$		E$_2$	E$_1$	TCD		A/C	W	OIL					+B	+B

ECU connector identifications

ty one and fifty three, will be retained in memory by the ECU from the time of detection until cancelled out.

4. Once the malfunction is cleared, the "Check Engine" warning light on the instrument panel will go out but the diagnostic code(s) remain stored in the ECU memory (except for code 51).

ECU Connectors Voltage Inspection

The EFI circuit can be checked by measuring the resistance and the voltage at the wiring connectors of the ECU. The following list should be followed before making the ECU inspection:

1. Perform all voltage measurements with the connectors connected.

Code No.	Light Pattern	Code No.	Light Pattern
–	ON / OFF	31	
11		32	
12		41	
13		42	
14		43	
21		51	
22		52	
23		53	

Exploded view of the diagnostic trouble code flashes

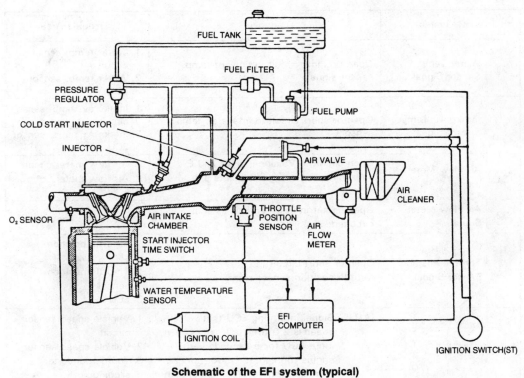

Schematic of the EFI system (typical)

2. Verify that the battery voltage is 11 volts or more when the ignition switch is turned off.

3. The testing probes must not make contact with the ECU Ox and Vf terminals.

4. Remove the glove box turn the ignition switch to the on position and measure the voltage at each terminal.

ECU Connectors Resistance Inspection

Be sure not to touch the ECU terminals. The tester probe should be inserted into the wiring connector from the wiring side.

1. Remove the glove box. Unplug the wiring connectors from the ECU.

Code No.	System	Diagnosis	Trouble Area
	Normal	This appears when none of the other codes (11 thru 51) are identified.	
11	ECU (+B)	Wire severence, however slight, in + B (ECU).	1. Main relay circuit 2. Main relay 3. ECU
12	RPM Signal	No Ne, G signal to ECU within several seconds after engine is cranked.	1. Distributor circuit 2. Distributor 3. Starter signal circuit 4. ECU
13	RPM Signal	No Ne signal to ECU within several seconds after engine reaches 1,000 rpm.	Same as 12, above.
14	Ignition Signal	No signal from igniter six times in succession	1. Igniter circuit (+B, IGt, IGf) 2. Igniter 3. ECU
21	Oxygen Sensor Signal	Oxygen sensor gives a lean signal for several seconds even when coolant temperature is above 50°C (122°F) and engine is running under high load conditions above 1,500 rpm.	1. Oxygen sensor circuit 2. Oxygen sensor 3. ECU

Diagnostic trouble codes

Code No.	System	Diagnosis	Trouble Area
22	Water Temp. Sensor Signal	Open or short circuit in coolant temp. sensor signal.	1. Water temp. sensor circuit 2. Water temp. sensor 3. ECU
23	Intake Air Temp. Sensor Signal	Open or short circuit in intake air temp. sensor.	1. Intake air temp. sensor circuit 2. Intake air temp. sensor 3. ECU
31	Air Flow Meter Signal	Open circuit in V_c signal or V_s and E_2 short circuited when idle points are closed.	1. Air flow meter circuit 2. Air flow meter 3. ECU
32	Air Flow Meter Signal	Open circuit in E_2 or V_c and V_s short circuited.	Same as 31, above.
41	Throttle Position Sensor Signal	Open or short circuit in throttle position sensor signal.	1. Throttle position sensor circuit 2. Throttle position sensor 3. ECU
42	Vehile Speed Sensor Signal	(A/T): Signal informing ECU that vehicle speed is 2.0 km/h or less has been input ECU for 5 seconds with engine running at 2,500 rpm or more and shift lever is in other than N or P range. (M/T): Signal informing ECU that vehicle speed is 2.0 km/h or less has been input ECU for 5 seconds with engine running at 2,500 rpm or more.	1. Vehicle speed sensor circuit 2. Vehicle speed sensor 3. Torque converter slipping 4. ECU
43	Starter Signal (+ B)	No STA signal to ECU when engine is running over 800 rpm.	1. Main relay circuit 2. IG switch circuit (starter) 3. IG switch 4. ECU
51	Switch Signal	Neutral start switch OFF or air conditioner switch ON during diagnostic check.	1. Neutral start S/W 2. Air con. S/W 3. ECU
52	Knock Sensor Signal	Open or short circuit in knock sensor.	1. Knock sensor citcuit 2. Knock sensor 3. ECU
53	Knock Sensor Signal	Faulty ECU. (KNOCK CPU)	ECU

Diagnostic trouble codes (cont.)

2. Measure the resistance between each terminal of the wiring connector.

GENERAL FUEL SYSTEM COMPONENTS

Fuel Filter

REPLACEMENT

1. Unbolt the retaining screws and remove the protective shield for the fuel filter.

2. Place a pan under the delivery pipe (large connection) to catch the dripping fuel and SLOWLY loosen the union bolt to bleed off the fuel pressure.

3. Remove the union bolt and drain the remaining fuel.

4. Disconnect and plug the inlet line.

5. Unbolt and remove the fuel filter.

NOTE: *When tightening the fuel line bolts to the fuel filter, you must use a torque wrench. The tightening torque is very important, as under or over tightening may cause fuel leakage. Insure that there is no fuel line interference and that there is sufficient clearance between it and any other parts.*

6. Coat the flare nut, union nut and bolt threads with engine oil.

7. Hand tighten the inlet line to the fuel filter.

8. Install the fuel filter and then tighten the inlet bolt to 23–33 ft.lb.

9. Reconnect the delivery pipe using new gaskets and then tighten the union bolt to 18–25 ft.lb.

10. Run the engine for a few minutes and check for any fuel leaks.

11. Install the protective shield.

Terminals	STD Voltage	Condition	
BAT — E_1		—	
+B — E_1	10 — 14	IG S/W ON	
IG S/W — E_1			
M-REL — E_1			
IDL — E_2	4 — 6	IG S/W ON	Throttle valve open
VTA — E_2	0.1 — 1.0		Throttle valve fully closed
	4 — 5		Throttle valve fully opened
Vc — E_2	4 — 6		—
Vs — E_2	4 — 5	IG S/W ON	Measuring plate fully closed
	0.02 — 0.08		Measuring plate fully open
	2 — 4		Idling
	0.3 — 1.0		3,000 rpm
THA — E_2	1 — 2	IG S/W ON	Intake air temperature 20°C (68°F)
THW — E_1	0.1 — 0.5	IG S/W ON	Coolant temperature 80°C (176°F)
STA — E_1	6 — 12	IG S/W ST position	
No. 10 No. 20 — E_1	9 — 14	IG S/W ON	
IGt — E_1	0.7 — 1.0	Idling	
ISC_1 { ISC_4 — E_1	9 — 14	IG S/W ON	
	9 — 14	2 — 3 secs, after engine off	
+B — EGR	10 — 13	IG S/W ON	
	0	Start engine and warm up Ox sensor	
N/C — E_1	0	IG S/W ON	Shift position P or N range (for A/T)
	10 — 14		Ex. P or N range (for A/T)
	0		Clutch pedal not depressed (for M/T)
	10 — 14		Clutch pedal depressed (for M/T)
	9 — 11	Cranking	

ECU connectors voltage specifications

	4 – 6		Check connector T₁ – E₁ not short
T – E₁	0	IG S/W ON	Check connector T₁ – E₂ short
OIL – E₁	4 – 6		IG S/W ON (Warning light on)
	0		Start engine (Warning light out)
A/C – E₁	10 – 13	IG S/W ON	A/C S/W ON
	0		A/C S/W OFF
Vғ – E₁	0 – 5		Start engine (Throttle valve open)
W – E₁	0		IG S/W ON
	10 – 13		Start engine
TCD – E₁	2 – 3	IG S/W ON	Coolant temp. Less than 35°C (95°F)
	0		Coolant temp. 35 – 60°C (95 – 140°F)
	4 – 6		Coolant temp. More than 60°C (140°F)

ECU connectors voltage specifications (cont.)

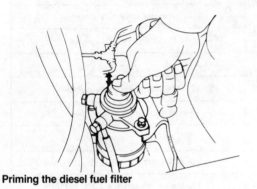

Priming the diesel fuel filter

Electrical Fuel Pump
REMOVAL AND INSTALLATION

The pump used on these models is removed by simply disconnecting the fuel lines and electrical connector from the pump and dismounting the pump.

TESTING

1. Turn the ignition switch to the ON position, but don't start the engine.
2. Remove the rubber cap from the fuel

Terminals	Condition	Resistance (Ω)
IDL – E₂	Throttle valve open	∞
	Throttle valve fully closed	0
VTA – E₂	Throttle valve fully opened	3,300 – 10,000
	Throttle valve fully closed	200 – 800
Vc – E₂	Disconnect air flow meter connector	3,000 – 7,000
	Disconnect throttle position sensor connector	200 – 400
Vs – E₂	Measuring plate fully closed	20 – 400
	Measuring plate fully open	20 – 1000
THA – E₂	Intake air temperature 20°C (68°F)	2,000 – 3,000
G – G ⊖	—	140 – 180
Ne – G ⊖	—	
ISC₁, ISC₂, ISC₃, ISC₄ – +B	—	10 – 30

ECU wiring connectors resistance specifications

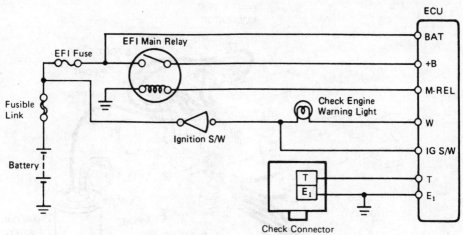

Inspecting the diagnostic circuit

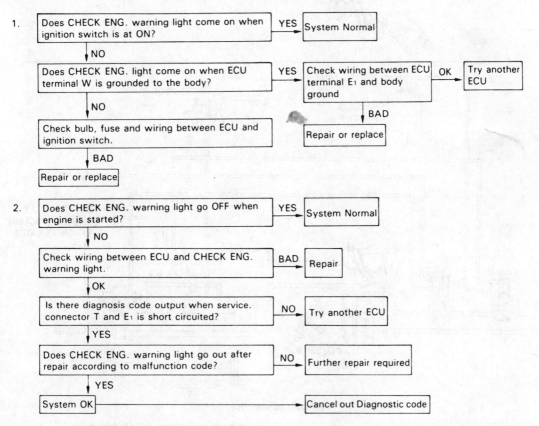

pump check connector and short both terminals.

3. Check that there is pressure in the hose to the cold start injector.

NOTE: *At this time you should be able to hear the fuel return noise from the pressure regulator.*

4. If no pressure can be felt in the line, check the fuses and all other related electrical connections. If everything is all right, the fuel pump will probably require replacement.

5. Remove the service wire, reinstall the rubber cap and turn off the ignition switch.

Fuel Tank

REMOVAL AND INSTALLATION

1. Reduce the fuel pressure to zero. See Chapter one under fuel filters for correct procedure.

2. Disconnect the fuel outlet hose from the

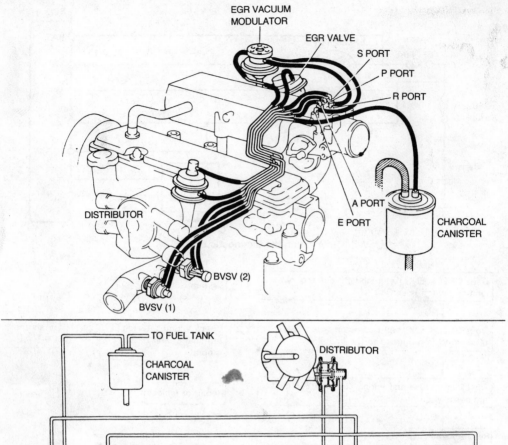

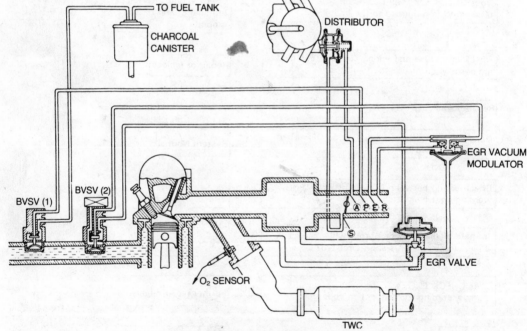

Vacuum schematics

fuel pipe and drain the tank if no drain plug is provided.

3. Remove the luggage compartment mat. Remove the cover over the tank sending unit and hose connections. Disconnect the gauge electrical harness and the ventilation, fuel feed and fuel return hoses.

4. Remove the nut and the fuel tank retaining straps. Remove the tank.

5. Installation is the reverse of removal. Be careful not to twist or kink any of the hoses.

GASOLINE FUEL INJECTION SYSTEM COMPONENTS

The EFI system precisely controls fuel injection to match engine requirements, reducing emissions and increasing driveability.

The electric fuel pump pumps fuel through a damper and filter to the pressure regulator. The six fuel injectors are electric solenoid valves which open and close by signals from the control unit.

The EFI computer receives input from various sensors to determine engine operating condition.

1. Air flow meter – measures the amount of intake air.

2. Ignition coil – engine RPM.

3. Throttle valve switch – amount of throttle opening.

4. Water temperature sensor or cylinder head temperature sensor – temperature of coolant or engine.

5. Air temperature sensor – temperature of intake air (ambient temperature).

6. Thermotime switch – signal used to control cold start valve fuel enrichment when the engine is cold.

7. Starting switch – signals that the starter is operating.

8. Altitude switch used to signal changes in atmospheric pressure.

9. Exhaust gas sensor used to measure the oxygen content of the exhaust gas.

The sensors provide the input to the control unit, which determines the amount of fuel to be injected by its preset program.

The fuel injection system is a highly complex unit. All repair or adjustment should be left to an expert Toyota technician.

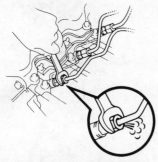

Bleeding the fuel lines on a diesel engine

DIESEL FUEL SYSTEM COMPONENTS

Injection Nozzle
REMOVAL AND INSTALLATION

1. Loosen the clamps and remove the injection hoses from between the injection pump and pipe.

2. Disconnect both ends of the injection pipes from the pump and nozzle holders.

3. Disconnect the fuel cut off wire from the connector clamp.

4. Remove the nut, connector clamp and bond cable.

5. Unbolt and remove the injector pipes.

6. Disconnect the fuel hoses from the leakage pipes.

7. Remove the four nuts, leakage pipe and four washers.

8. Unscrew and remove the nozzles.

9. Installation is the reverse of removal. Torque the nozzles to 47 ft.lb. Always use new nozzle seat gaskets and seats. Bleed the system by loosening the pipes at the nozzles and

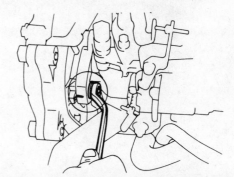

Matchmark the index mark on the injection pump flange to the cylinder block—diesel engines

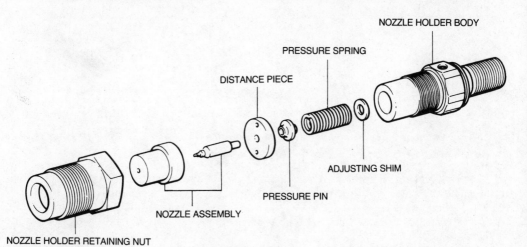

Diesel injector

cranking the engine until all air is expelled and fuel sprays.

Injection Pump
REMOVAL AND INSTALLATION

1. Drain the cooling system.
2. Disconnect the accelerator and cruise control cables from the pump.
3. Disconnect the fuel cut off wire at the pump.

4. Disconnect the fuel inlet and outlet hoses, the water by-pass hoses, the boost compensator hoses, the A/C or heater idle-up vacuum hoses and the heater hose.
5. Remove the injector pipes at the pump.
6. Remove the pump pulley.
7. Matchmark the raised timing mark on the pump flange with the block. Unbolt and remove the pump.
8. Installation is the reverse of removal. There must be no clearance between the pump bracket and stay.

Chassis Electrical

5

HEATER

On some models the air conditioner, if so equipped, is integral with the heater, and therefore, heater removal may differ from the procedures detailed below.

Blower

REMOVAL AND INSTALLATION

1. Remove the parcel tray located under the dash.
2. Remove the two discharge duct bracket mounting screens, and then remove the two brackets and the duct.
3. Remove the mounting screw, and remove the right side forward console cover.
4. Unscrew the mounting screw and remove the relay bracket located under the motor.
5. Remove the three mounting screws, and remove the motor, gasket, and blower assembly. If necessary, remove the blower mounting nut and washers, and remove the blower from the shaft.
6. Install in reverse order.

Core

REMOVAL AND INSTALLATION

1. Disconnect the battery ground and drain the radiator. Remove parts as described in steps 1–4 in the blower motor removal procedure above.
2. Remove the console.
3. Remove the two remaining air ducts.
4. Remove:
   a. Right and left side cowl trim panels.
   b. Fuse box and steering column covers.
   c. Glove box.
   d. Radio (see below).

Troubleshooting the Heater

Problem	Cause	Solution
Blower motor will not turn at any speed	• Blown fuse • Loose connection • Defective ground • Faulty switch • Faulty motor • Faulty resistor	• Replace fuse • Inspect and tighten • Clean and tighten • Replace switch • Replace motor • Replace resistor
Blower motor turns at one speed only	• Faulty switch • Faulty resistor	• Replace switch • Replace resistor
Blower motor turns but does not circulate air	• Intake blocked • Fan not secured to the motor shaft	• Clean intake • Tighten security
Heater will not heat	• Coolant does not reach proper temperature • Heater core blocked internally • Heater core air-bound • Blend-air door not in proper position	• Check and replace thermostat if necessary • Flush or replace core if necessary • Purge air from core • Adjust cable
Heater will not defrost	• Control cable adjustment incorrect • Defroster hose damaged	• Adjust control cable • Replace defroster hose

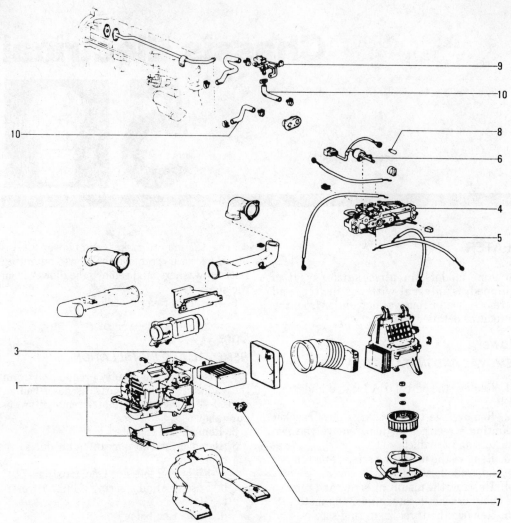

Typical heater assembly removal and installation illustation

5. Remove the center air discharge panel.

6. Remove the instrument cluster.

7. Disengage damper operating cables and spring.

8. Remove the lower duct plenum by lifting it up at the rear.

9. Remove the heater valve and disconnect the two core hoses.

10. Remove the two heater unit retaining bolts and the mounting nuts, and pull the unit out on the passenger's side. Pull the heater core upward out of the unit.

11. Installation is the reverse of removal.

Heater Main Relay

Relay Continuity Inspection

1. Using a suitable ohmmeter, check that here is continuity between terminals 1 and 3.

2. Check that there is continuity between terminals 2 and 4.

3. Check that there is continuity between terminals 4 and 5.

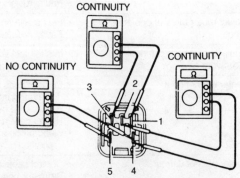

Inspection of the heater main relay—all models

Troubleshooting Basic Turn Signal and Flasher Problems

Most problems in the turn signals or flasher system, can be reduced to defective flashers or bulbs, which are easily replaced. Occasionally, problems in the turn signals are traced to the switch in the steering column, which will require professional service.

F = Front   R = Rear   ● = Lights off   o = Lights on

Problem		Solution
Turn signals light, but do not flash		• Replace the flasher
No turn signals light on either side		• Check the fuse. Replace if defective. • Check the flasher by substitution • Check for open circuit, short circuit or poor ground
Both turn signals on one side don't work		• Check for bad bulbs • Check for bad ground in both housings
One turn signal light on one side doesn't work		• Check and/or replace bulb • Check for corrosion in socket. Clean contacts. • Check for poor ground at socket
Turn signal flashes too fast or too slow		• Check any bulb on the side flashing too fast. A heavy-duty bulb is probably installed in place of a regular bulb. • Check the bulb flashing too slow. A standard bulb was probably installed in place of a heavy-duty bulb. • Check for loose connections or corrosion at the bulb socket
Indicator lights don't work in either direction		• Check if the turn signals are working • Check the dash indicator lights • Check the flasher by substitution

One indicator light doesn't light		• On systems with 1 dash indicator: See if the lights work on the same side. Often the filaments have been reversed in systems combining stoplights with taillights and turn signals.
		    Check the flasher by substitution
		• On systems with 2 indicators:
		    Check the bulbs on the same side
		    Check the indicator light bulb
		    Check the flasher by substitution

Troubleshooting Basic Lighting Problems

Problem	Cause	Solution
Lights		
One or more lights don't work, but others do	• Defective bulb(s) • Blown fuse(s) • Dirty fuse clips or light sockets • Poor ground circuit	• Replace bulb(s) • Replace fuse(s) • Clean connections • Run ground wire from light socket housing to car frame
Lights burn out quickly	• Incorrect voltage regulator setting or defective regulator • Poor battery/alternator connections	• Replace voltage regulator • Check battery/alternator connections
Lights go dim	• Low/discharged battery • Alternator not charging • Corroded sockets or connections • Low voltage output	• Check battery • Check drive belt tension; repair or replace alternator • Clean bulb and socket contacts and connections • Replace voltage regulator
Lights flicker	• Loose connection • Poor ground • Circuit breaker operating (short circuit)	• Tighten all connections • Run ground wire from light housing to car frame • Check connections and look for bare wires
Lights "flare"—Some flare is normal on acceleration—if excessive, see "Lights Burn Out Quickly"	• High voltage setting	• Replace voltage regulator
Lights glare—approaching drivers are blinded	• Lights adjusted too high • Rear springs or shocks sagging • Rear tires soft	• Have headlights aimed • Check rear springs/shocks • Check/correct rear tire pressure
Turn Signals		
Turn signals don't work in either direction	• Blown fuse • Defective flasher • Loose connection	• Replace fuse • Replace flasher • Check/tighten all connections
Right (or left) turn signal only won't work	• Bulb burned out • Right (or left) indicator bulb burned out • Short circuit	• Replace bulb • Check/replace indicator bulb • Check/repair wiring
Flasher rate too slow or too fast	• Incorrect wattage bulb • Incorrect flasher	• Flasher bulb • Replace flasher (use a variable load flasher if you pull a trailer)
Indicator lights do not flash (burn steadily)	• Burned out bulb • Defective flasher	• Replace bulb • Replace flasher
Indicator lights do not light at all	• Burned out indicator bulb • Defective flasher	• Replace indicator bulb • Replace flasher

4. If there is no continuity at the specified terminals, replace the relay.

Relay Operations Inspection

1. Apply battery voltage across terminals 1 and 3 of the relay connector.

2. Using a suitable ohmmeter, check that there is continuity between terminals 4 and 5.

3. Check that there is no continuity between terminals 2 and 4.

4. If the operation of the relay is not as just described, replace the relay.

Inspection of The Heater Blower Resistor Continuity

1. Remove the heater blower resistor connector.

2. Using a suitable ohmmeter, check that there is continuity between terminals 1 and 3 of the resistor connector.

Troubleshooting Basic Dash Gauge Problems

Problem	Cause	Solution
Coolant Temperature Gauge		
Gauge reads erratically or not at all	• Loose or dirty connections • Defective sending unit	• Clean/tighten connections • Bi-metal gauge: remove the wire from the sending unit. Ground the wire for an instant. If the gauge registers, replace the sending unit.
	• Defective gauge	• Magnetic gauge: disconnect the wire at the sending unit. With ignition ON gauge should register COLD. Ground the wire; gauge should register HOT.
Ammeter Gauge—Turn Headlights ON (do not start engine). Note reaction		
Ammeter shows charge Ammeter shows discharge Ammeter does not move	• Connections reversed on gauge • Ammeter is OK • Loose connections or faulty wiring • Defective gauge	• Reinstall connections • Nothing • Check/correct wiring • Replace gauge
Oil Pressure Gauge		
Gauge does not register or is inaccurate	• On mechanical gauge, Bourdon tube may be bent or kinked	• Check tube for kinks or bends preventing oil from reaching the gauge
	• Low oil pressure	• Remove sending unit. Idle the engine briefly. If no oil flows from sending unit hole, problem is in engine.
	• Defective gauge	• Remove the wire from the sending unit and ground it for an instant with the ignition ON. A good gauge will go to the top of the scale.
	• Defective wiring	• Check the wiring to the gauge. If it's OK and the gauge doesn't register when grounded, replace the gauge.
	• Defective sending unit	• If the wiring is OK and the gauge functions when grounded, replace the sending unit
All Gauges		
All gauges do not operate	• Blown fuse • Defective instrument regulator	• Replace fuse • Replace instrument voltage regulator
All gauges read low or erratically	• Defective or dirty instrument voltage regulator	• Clean contacts or replace
All gauges pegged	• Loss of ground between instrument voltage regulator and car • Defective instrument regulator	• Check ground • Replace regulator
Warning Lights		
Light(s) do not come on when ignition is ON, but engine is not started	• Defective bulb • Defective wire	• Replace bulb • Check wire from light to sending unit
	• Defective sending unit	• Disconnect the wire from the sending unit and ground it. Replace the sending unit if the light comes on with the ignition ON.
Light comes on with engine running	• Problem in individual system • Defective sending unit	• Check system • Check sending unit (see above)

Troubleshooting Basic Windshield Wiper Problems

Problem	Cause	Solution
Electric Wipers		
Wipers do not operate— Wiper motor heats up or hums	• Internal motor defect • Bent or damaged linkage • Arms improperly installed on linking pivots	• Replace motor • Repair or replace linkage • Position linkage in park and reinstall wiper arms
Wipers do not operate— No current to motor	• Fuse or circuit breaker blown • Loose, open or broken wiring • Defective switch • Defective or corroded terminals • No ground circuit for motor or switch	• Replace fuse or circuit breaker • Repair wiring and connections • Replace switch • Replace or clean terminals • Repair ground circuits
Wipers do not operate— Motor runs	• Linkage disconnected or broken	• Connect wiper linkage or replace broken linkage
Vacuum Wipers		
Wipers do not operate	• Control switch or cable inoperative • Loss of engine vacuum to wiper motor (broken hoses, low engine vacuum, defective vacuum/fuel pump) • Linkage broken or disconnected • Defective wiper motor	• Repair or replace switch or cable • Check vacuum lines, engine vacuum and fuel pump • Repair linkage • Replace wiper motor
Wipers stop on engine acceleration	• Leaking vacuum hoses • Dry windshield • Oversize wiper blades • Defective vacuum/fuel pump	• Repair or replace hoses • Wet windshield with washers • Replace with proper size wiper blades • Replace pump

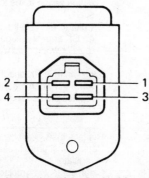

Continuity inspection of the heater blower resistor— all models

Setting the heater control cable to the "Fresh" position

3. If there is no continuity, replace the resistor.

HEATER CONTROL CABLE

Adjustment

1. Set the air inlet damper and control lever to the "Fresh" position.

2. Set the mode selector damper and control lever to the "Vent" position.

3. Set the air mix damper and control lever to the "Cool" position.

4. Set the water valve and control lever to the "Cool" position.

NOTE: *Place the water valve lever on the "Cool" position and while pushing the outer*

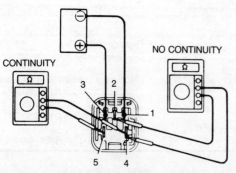

Inspection of the heater main relay operations—all models

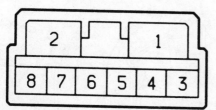

Typical heater blower switch connector terminal location

	Terminal	2	3	5	6	1	7 •	8 •
Switch position								
OFF							o—o	
LO		o—o					o—o	
•		o—o—o				o—o		
•		o—o	o			o—o		
HI		o—o		o		o—o		

Heater blower switch continuity check chart—all models

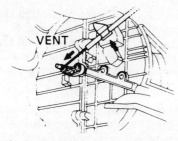

Setting the heater control cable to the "Vent" position

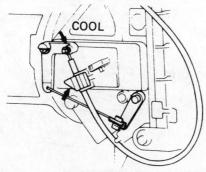

Setting the heater control cable to the "Cool" position

cable in the direction of "Cool" position, clamp the outer cable to the water valve bracket.

5. Move the control levers left and right and check for stiffness or binding through the full range of the levers.

ELECTRIC COOLING FAN

On Vehicle Inspection (temperature below 181°F.)

1. Turn the ignition switch to the "ON" position. If the fan runs, then check the fan relay

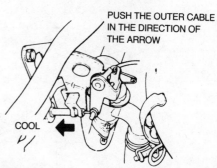

PUSH THE OUTER CABLE IN THE DIRECTION OF THE ARROW

COOL

Setting the water valve and control lever to the "Cool" position

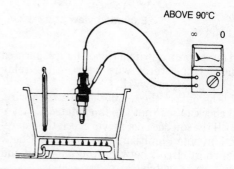

ABOVE 90°C

Testing the temperature switch

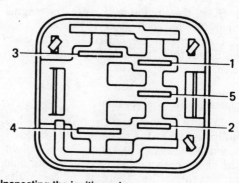

Inspecting the ignition relay

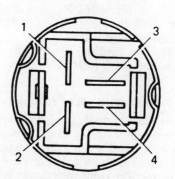

Inspecting the fan motor relay

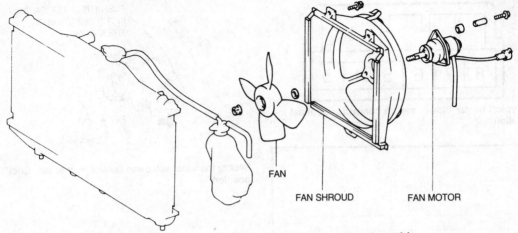

Exploded view of a typical electrical cooling fan assembly

and temperature switch. Check for a separated connector or severed wire between the relay and temperature switch.

2. Disconnect the temperature switch wire, and check to see that the fan rotates.

3. If the fan does not move, check the fan relay, fan motor, ignition relay and fuse. Check for a short circuit between the fan relay and temperature switch.

On Vehicle Inspection (temperature above 194°F.)

1. Start the engine and raise the engine temperature to reach above 194°F.

2. Confirm that the fan rotates, if the fan does not rotate, replace the temperature switch.

Temperature Switch Inspection

1. Remove the temperature switch (which is usually located at the radiator lower tank).

2. Place the switch in a container of coolant which is at or above 194°F. Using a suitable ohmeter, check that there is no continuity when the coolant is above 194°F.

3. Place the switch in a container of coolant which is at or below 181°F. Using a suitable ohmeter, check that there is continuity when the coolant is below 181°F.

4. If the temperature switch fails any of these test, replace it with a new switch.

Ignition Relay Inspection (if so equipped)

1. This relay is usually located in the engine compartment in the relay box.

2. Using a suitable ohmmeter, measure the resistance between terminals 1 and 2 of the relay connector. The resistance should be 50–80 ohms.

3. Connect a 12 volt battery across terminals 1 and 2.

4. Using the ohmmeter, check that there is continuity between terminals 3 and 4.

5. Using the ohmmeter, check that there is no continuity between terminals 4 and 5.

6. If any of the above checks are not as specified, replace the ignition relay.

Fan Motor Relay Inspection

1. This relay is usually located in the engine compartment in the relay box.

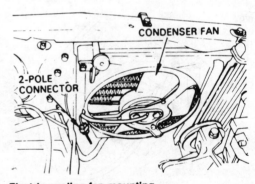

Electric cooling fan mounting

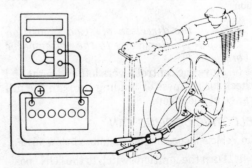

Inspecting the fan motor

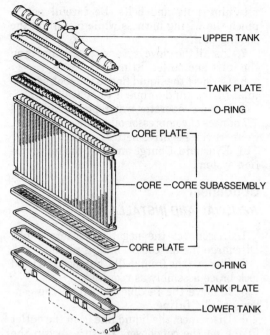

UPPER TANK

TANK PLATE

O-RING

CORE PLATE

CORE — CORE SUBASSEMBLY

CORE PLATE

O-RING

TANK PLATE

LOWER TANK

Typical radiator-exploded view (© Toyota Motor Sales)

2. Using a suitable ohmmeter, measure the resistance between terminals 1 and 2 of the relay connector. The resistance should be 50–80 ohms.

3. Connect a 12 volt battery across terminals 1 and 2.

4. Using the ohmmeter, check that there is continuity between terminals 3 and 4.

5. If any of the above checks are not as specified, replace the fan motor relay.

Fan Motor Inspection

1. Connect the battery and the ammeter to the fan motor connector.

2. Check to see that the motor rotates smoothly and current is 3.1–4.3 amps.

3. If any of the above checks are not as specified, replace the fan motor.

ELECTRIC COOLING FAN

Removal and Installation

1. Disconnect the negative battery cable. Disconnect the fan motor electrical connector.

2. Remove the front grill assembly. Remove the fan motor assembly retaining bolts and remove the fan motor assembly.

3. Remove the fan, spacer and nut. Remove the fan motor, bushings and screws from the fan motor assembly.

4. Installation is the reverse order of the removal procedure.

AIR CONDITIONING

Blower Motor

NOTE: *For information on the blower motor refer to the Heater portion of this section.*

Expansion Valve

Removal

NOTE: *The expansion valve is attached to the evaporator core. In order to service the expansion valve the evaporator core must be removed first.*

1. Disconnect the negative battery cable. Discharge the refrigerant system.

2. Disconnect the suction flexible hose from the cooling unit outlet fitting.

3. Disconnect the liquid line from the cooling unit inlet fitting. Cap the open fittings immediately to keep the moisture out of the system.

4. Remove the grommets from the inlet and outlet fittings.

5. Remove the glove box with the under cover. Disconnect all necessary connectors, such as the pressure switch connector and the A/C harness.

6. Remove the cooling unit attaching nuts and bolts. Remove the cooling unit from the vehicle.

7. Place the cooling unit on a suitable work

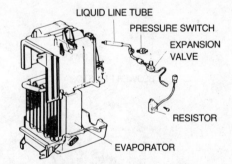

LIQUID LINE TUBE

PRESSURE SWITCH

EXPANSION VALVE

RESISTOR

EVAPORATOR

Expansion valve-exploded view

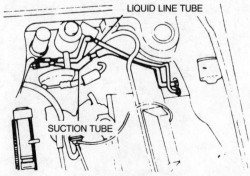

LIQUID LINE TUBE

SUCTION TUBE

Location of the liquid line and suction line—typical

bench and unscrew the thermister, if so equipped.

8. Using suitable tools, remove the lower cooling unit case clamps and retaining screws.

9. Remove the upper cooling unit case retainer screws and remove the upper case from the evaporator.

10. Remove the heat insulator and the clamp from the outlet tube. Disconnect the liquid line from the inlet fitting of the expansion valve.

11. Disconnect the expansion valve from the inlet fitting of the evaporator. Remove the pressure switch (if so equipped) if required.

Installation

1. Connect the expansion valve to the inlet fitting of the evaporator and torque it to 17 ft. lbs. Be sure that the O-ring is positioned on the tube fitting.

2. Connect the liquid line tube to the inlet fitting on the expansion valve. Torque the nut to 10 ft. lbs.

3. Install the pressure switch, if removed. Torque it to 10 ft. lbs. Install the clamp and heat insulator to the outlet tube.

4. Install the uper and lower cases on the evaporator. Install the thermistor.

5. Install the A/C wiring harness to the cooling unit and all other necessary components.

6. Install the cooling unit assembly and its retaining nuts and bolts. Be careful not to pinch the wiring harness while installing the cooling unit.

7. Install the glove box and the grommets on the inlet and outlet fittings.

8. Connect the liquid line to the cooling unit inlet fittings and torque it to 10 ft. lbs.

9. If the evaporator was replaced, add 1.4–1.7 ounces of compressor oil to the compressor. Connect the negative battery cable.

10. Evacuate, Charge and Test the refrigeration system.

Condenser
REMOVAL AND INSTALLATION

1. Disconnect the negative battery cable. Discharge the air conditioning system.

2. Remove the front grille, bumper and hood lock brace assembly as required.

3. Remove the flexible hose from the condenser inlet fitting.

4. Disconnect the liquid line from the outlet fitting on the condenser. Be sure to cap the openings immediately to keep the moisture out of the system.

5. Remove the condenser retaining bolts. Remove the condenser.

6. Installation is the reverse of the removal procedure. Install the condenser making cer-

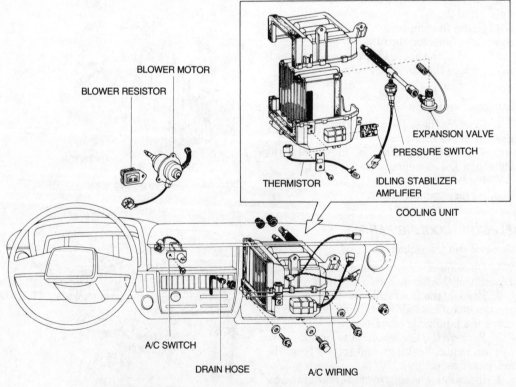

Air conditioning system components location with underdash exploded view

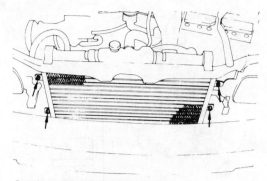
Condenser retaining bolts location

tain that the rubber cushion fit properly on the mounting flanges. Torque the liquid line to 10 ft. lbs. and the discharge flexible line to 16 ft. lbs.

NOTE: *When installing a new condenser in the vehicle, add 1.4–1.7 ounces of compressor oil to the compressor.*

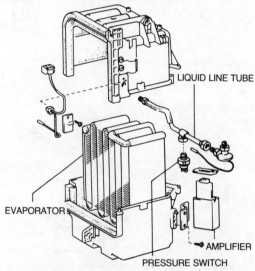
Pressure switch location

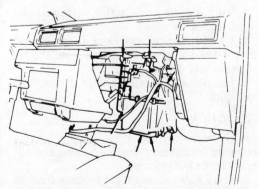
Typical cooling unit assembly removal and installation

Evaporator
REMOVAL

1. Disconnect the negative battery cable. Discharge the refrigerant system.
2. Disconnect the suction flexible hose from the cooling unit outlet fitting.
3. Disconnect the liquid line from the cooling unit inlet fitting. Cap the open fittings immediately to keep the moisture out of the system.
4. Remove the grommets from the inlet and outlet fitings.
5. Remove the glove box with the under cover. Disconnect all necessary connectors, such as the pressure switch connector and the A/C harness.

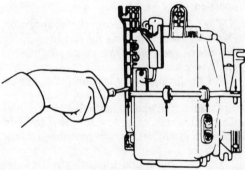
Removing the lower cooling unit case

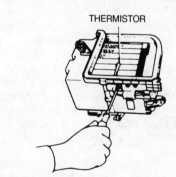
Removing the thermistor

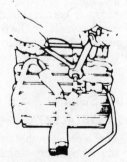
Removing the expansion valve

6. Remove the cooling unit attaching nuts and bolts. Remove the cooling unit from the vehicle.

7. Place the cooling unit on a suitable work bench and unscrew the thermister, if so equipped.

8. Using suitable tools, remove the lower cooling unit case clamps and retaining screws.

9. Remove the upper cooling unit case retainer screws and remove the upper case from the evaporator.

10. Remove the heat insulator and the clamp from the outlet tube. Disconnect the liquid line from the inlet fitting of the expansion valve.

11. Disconnect the expansion valve from the inlet fitting of the evaporator. Remove the pressure switch (if so equipped) if required and remove the evaporator from the cooling unit.

Installation

NOTE: *Before installing the evaporator, check the evaporator fins for blockage. If the fins are clogged, clean them with compressed air. Never use water to clean the evaporator. Check the fittings for cracks and or scratches and repair as necessary.*

1. Connect the expansion valve to the inlet fitting of the evaporator and torque it to 17 ft. lbs. Be sure that the O-ring is positioned on the tube fitting.

2. Connect the liquid line tube to the inlet fitting on the expansion valve. Torque the nut to 10 ft. lbs.

3. Install the pressure switch, if removed. Torque it to 10 ft. lbs. Install the clamp and heat insulator to the outlet tube.

4. Install the upper and lower cases on the evaporator. Install the thermistor.

5. Install the A/C wiring harness to the cooling unit and all other necessary components.

6. Install the cooling unit assembly and its retaining nuts and bolts. Be careful not to pinch the wiring harness while installing the cooling unit.

7. Install the glove box and the grommets on the inlet and outlet fittings.

8. Connect the liquid line to the cooling unit inlet fittings and torque it to 10 ft. lbs.

9. If the evaporator was replaced, add 1.4–1.7 ounces of compressor oil to the compressor. Connect the negative battery cable.

10. Evacuate, Charge and Test the refrigeration system.

Low Pressure Switch

REMOVAL AND INSTALLATION

1. Disconnect the negative battery cable.

2. Remove the evaporator assembly as previously outlined.

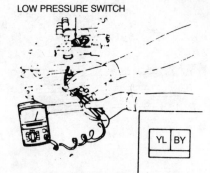

LOW PRESSURE SWITCH

YL | BY

Testing the low pressure switch

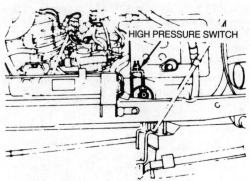

HIGH PRESSURE SWITCH

Location of the high pressure switch

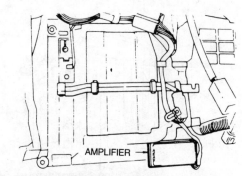

AMPLIFIER

Typical air conditioning amplifier

3. Tag and disconnect the wiring at the round topped terminal.

4. Using a spanner wrench or its equivalent, remove the low pressure switch form the refrigerant piping.

5. Installation is the reverse of the removal procedure.

INSPECTION

1. Connect the hoses of the manifold gauge set to the compressor service valves and observe the gauge reading.

2. The gauge reading must be more than 30 psi. when the ambient temperature is higher than 32°F.

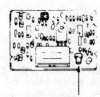

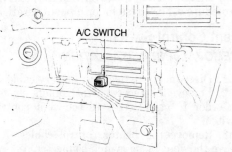

COMPRESSOR CUT-OFF RPM ADJUSTING KNOB

Location of the compressor cut-off rpm adjusting knob

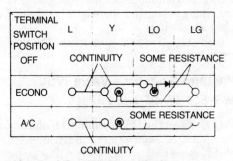

Air conditioning switch location on dash assembly

Checking the A/C switch for continuity

3. If the pressure is less than 30 psi., charge the system with refrigerant.

4. Remove the glove box and under cover. Disconnect the lead wires of the low pressure switch at the A/C harness.

5. Using a suitable ohmmeter, check the continuity between the two terminals of the low pressure switch.

6. The ohmmeter must indicate zero ohms, if it does not, replace the low pressure switch.

High Pressure Switch
INSPECTION

1. Connect the hoses of the manifold gauge set to the compressor service valves and observe the gauge reading.

2. The gauge reading must be less than 256 psi., when the ambient temperature is higher than 32°F.

3. If the pressure is less than 256 psi., charge the system with refrigerant.

4. Disconnect the lead wires for the high pressure switch at the A/C harness.

5. Using a suitable ohmmeter, check the continuity between the two terminals of the high pressure switch.

6. The ohmmeter must indicate zero ohms, if it does not, replace the high pressure switch.

Thermistor
REMOVAL

1. Disconnect the negative battery cable and remove the glove box and undercover.

2. With the thermistor still install, use an ohmmeter and measure the resistance at the connector (resistance 1,500 ohms at 77° F.)

3. Disconnect the thermistor connector and remove the thermistor securing screws along with the thermistor.

INSPECTION

1. Place the thermistor in cold water and while varying the temperature of the water, measure the resistance at the connector with a ohmmeter, and at the same time measure the temperature of the water with a thermometer.

2. Compare the two reading on the chart below.

Resistance and Temperature Chart

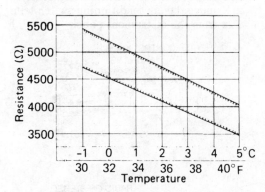

NOTE: *If the intersection is not between the two lines, replace the thermistor.*

INSTALLATION

1. Place the thermistor in position and install the thermistor securing screws.

2. Connect the electrical connector and install the glove box and undercover.

3. Connect the negative batter cable.

Air Condtioning Amplifier
REMOVAL AND INSTALLATION

1. Disconnect the negative battery cable.

2. Remove the glove box and the glove box undercover.

3. Remove the electrical connectors to the amplifier and remove the securing screws.

4. Remove the idling stabilizer amplifier.

5. Installation is the reverse order of the removal procedure.

TESTING

Testing the engine speed detection circuit:

1. Start the engine with the air conditioning system operating.

2. Inspect to verify that the magnetic clutch is disengages at the specified engine rpm.

1982 Models: 700–800 rpm.

1983 and Later: 600–700rpm

3. If the cut off rpm is too high, adjust the rpm setting register, located on the amplifier, to the specified rpm setting. If the cut-off rpm is too low, turn the rpm knob counterclockwise. If the cut-off rpm is too high, turn the rpm knob clockwise.

Heater Core

NOTE: *For more information on heater core removal, refer to the heater portion of this section.*

Air Conditioning Control Switch

REMOVAL AND INSTALLATION

1. Disconnect the negative battery cable.

2. Remove the air conditioning switch trim cluster from the instrument panel.

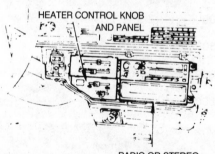

Removing the instrument cluster in order to gain access to the vent mode switch

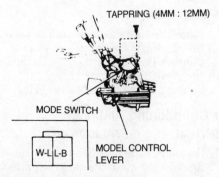

Testing the vent mode switch

3. Remove the air conditioning switch retaining screws as required.

4. Tag and disconnect the electrical connection from the rear of the switch assembly.

5. Remove the switch from the vehicle.

6. Using a suitable ohmmeter, check the continuity between the terminals for each switch position (as shown in the illustration). If there is no continuity, replace the A/C switch.

7. Installation is the reverse of the removal procedure. Check system for proper operation.

Vent Control Switch

REMOVAL AND INSTALLATION

1. Disconnect the negative battery cable.

2. Remove the necessary instrument cluster in order to gain access to the vent control switch.

3. Remove the heater control cables. Remove the vent mode switch connector.

4. Check the continuity between the terminal at the vent mode position using an ohmmeter. In the event that there is no continuity, replace the switch.

5. Installation is the reverse of the removal procedure.

Vacuum Switching Valve (VSV)

INSPECTION OF THE VSV

1. Connect the VSV terminals to the battery terminals (as shown in the illustration). Blow air into pipe F (the lower port on the two ported valve) and check to see that air comes out of the top pipe E (the upper port on the two ported valve).

2. Disconnect the battery. Blow air into pipe F (the lower port on the two ported valve) and see if air comes out of pipe G (the long single port in the rear of the VSV).

3. If the VSV fails any of these test, replace it.

4. Using a suitable ohmmeter, check that there is no continuity between each terminal and the VSV body.

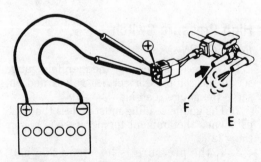

Applying battery voltage to the VSV terminals

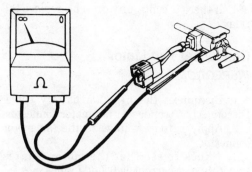

Testing the VSV for a short circuit

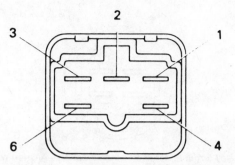

Relay terminal connector identification—A/C fan relay No. 2

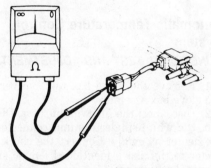

Checking the VSV for an open circuit

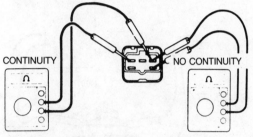

Testing the A/C fan relay No. 2 for continuity

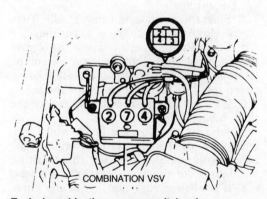

COMBINATION VSV

Typical combination vacuum switch valve

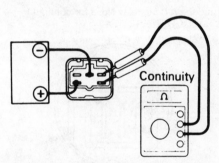

Applying battery voltage to terminals 6 and 2 (relay No. 2)

5. If there is continuity present, replace the VSV.

6. Using a suitable ohmmeter, measure the resistance between the two terminals. The resistance should be 34–44 ohms at 68°F.

7. If the resistance is not within specifications, replace the VSV.

A/C Fan Relay Number Two
INSPECTION

1. Check the power source line between terminal number 6 of the wiring connector and the body ground, and between terminal number 2 and the body ground.

2. Check the ground connection between terminal number 3 of the wiring connector and the body ground.

3. Check that there is continuity between terminals 1 and 3. Check to see than there is no continuity between terminals 1 and 4.

4. Check that there is continuity between terminals 1 and 4, with battery voltage applied between terminals 6 and 2.

5. If there is continuity present, replace the relay.

A/C Fan Relay Number Three and Idle-Up Relay
INSPECTION

1. Check the power source line between terminal number 1 of the wiring connector and the body ground, and between terminal number 2 and the body ground.

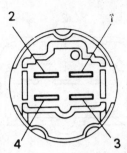

Relay terminal connector identification—A/C fan relay No. 3

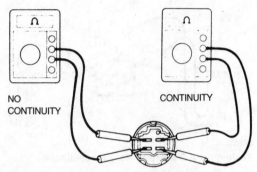

NO CONTINUITY

CONTINUITY

Testing the A/C fan relay No. 3 for continuity

Relay terminal connector identification—A/C cut relay

2. Check that there is continuity between terminals 1 and 3. Check to see than there is no continuity between terminals 2 and 4.

3. Check that there is continuity between terminals 2 and 4, with battery voltage applied between terminals 1 and 3.

4. If there is continuity present, replace the relay.

A/C Cut Relay
INSPECTION

1. Check that there is continuity between terminals number 3 and 4.

2. Check that there is no continuity between terminals 3 and 4, with battery voltage applied between terminals 1 and 2.

3. Check that there is continuity between terminals 2 and 4. Check to see that there is no continuity between terminals 1 and 3.

4. If there is continuity present, replace the relay.

Condenser Fan Motor
INSPECTION

1. Disconnect the negative battery cable. Disconnect the condenser fan motor connector.

2. Apply battery voltage to the fan motor connector.

3. Check to see that the motor rotates smoothly and current is 6.7–0.7 amps.

4. If any of the above checks are not as specified, replace the condenser fan motor.

Automatic Temperature Control System
FUNCTIONAL TEST AND ADJUSTMENTS

1. Remove the glove box under cover and the glove box assembly.

2. Disconnect the A/C wire harness. Disconnect the white single terminal connectors at the heater assembly. Connect the check connector to the above mentioned female single terminal connector.

3. Place the temperature control lever at (77°F.) position.

4. Start the engine and run it at idle. Turn on the blower switch to the auto position.

5. Check the automatic temperature control system, by verifying that the lower edge of the guide plate on the servo motor is positioned between the lines on the servo motor shaft.

6. If the left edge position is not between the lines, adjust as follows.

7. Adjust the automatic temperature control system, by changing the connections of the adjusting terminals. Normally the adjusting terminal is the number 10 terminal position.

8. If the lower edge position of the guide plate is over the "R" area, install the adjusting terminal into the number 9 position.

9. If the lower edge position of the guide

CHECK CONNECTOR (GREEN-BLACK)

Automatic temperature control testing terminals

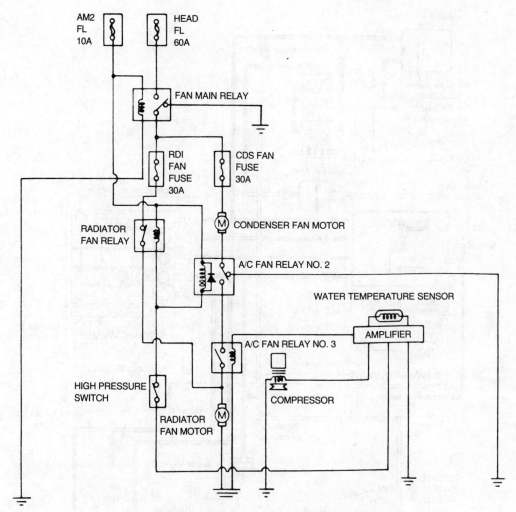

Typical condenser fan motor wiring schematic

Item		Conditions						
A/C Switch	ON				○	○	○	○
	OFF	○	○	○				
Water temperature Switch	Below 90°C (194°F)	○	○		○	○		
	Above 90°C (194°F)			○			○	○
A/C high pressure Switch	Below 18 kg/cm² (25 psi, 1,765 kPa)	—	—	—	○		○	
	Above 18 kg/cm² (25 psi, 1,765 kPa)	—	•○	—		○		○
Condenser fan motor and radiator fan motor speed		OFF	Hi	Hi	Lo	Hi	Hi	Hi

* When the high pressure S/W connector is disconnected, both fans should operate at high speed.

Radiator and condenser fan motor operations

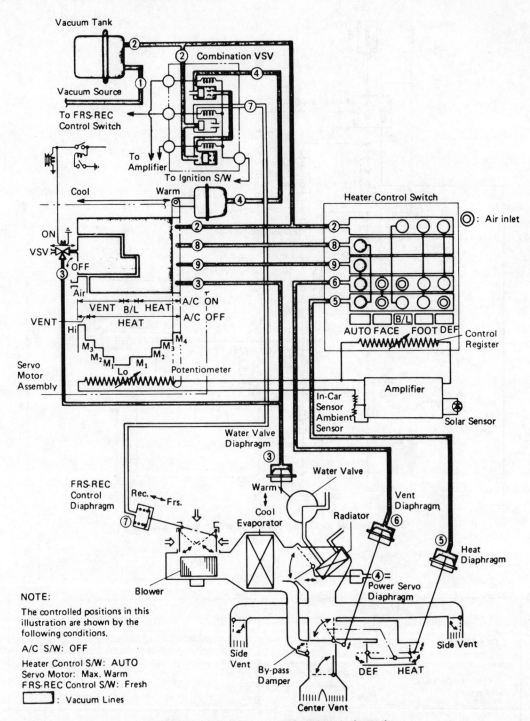

Automatic temperature control vacuum schematic

plate is over the "W" area, install the adjusting terminal into the number 2 position.

10. Reconnect the A/C wire harness, disconnect the check connector from the A/C wire harness. Reconnect the white connectors and re-install the glove box assembly with under covers.

IN-CAR SENSOR

Test and Inspection

1. On all models, check the sensor resistance (use the chart provided to check the resistance specifications). If there is an open circuit in the sensor, the system will operate at

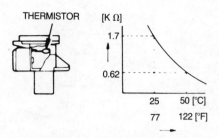

IN-Car sensor resistance graph chart

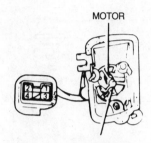

Testing the in-car sensor assembly

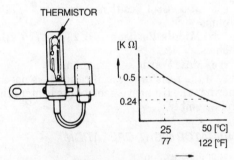

Ambient sensor resistance graph chart

Terminal Position of mode control lever	1 – 4	2 – 5
FOOT	NO CONTINUITY	NO CONTINUITY
VENT, BI-LEVEL or DEF	CONTINUITY	CONTINUITY

Heater mode switch terminals – continuity check

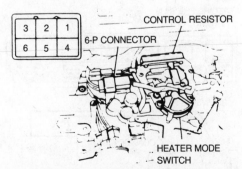

Control resistor connector and terminal locations

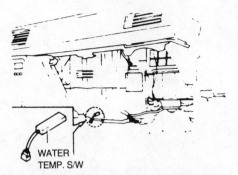

Typical location of the water temperature switch

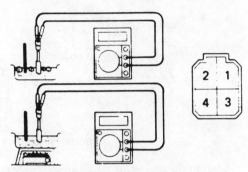

Testing the Water temperature switch

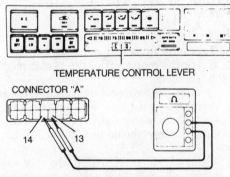

Checking the heater control assembly resistance

maximum heating. Conversely, if there is a short in the system, it will operate at maximum cooling.

2. Disconnect the in-car sensor connector. Apply battery voltage between terminals number 3 and 4 of the in-car sensor connector.

3. If the motor operates smoothly then the sensor is good, if the motor does not operate properly, replace the in-car sensor assembly.

NOTE: *To test the ambient sensor, use the graph chart provided to check the resistance of the ambient sensor. The ambient sensor is usually located near the A/C condenser.*

The solar sensor is located on safety pad of the passenger's side. This sensor can be check by using a suitable ohmmeter and

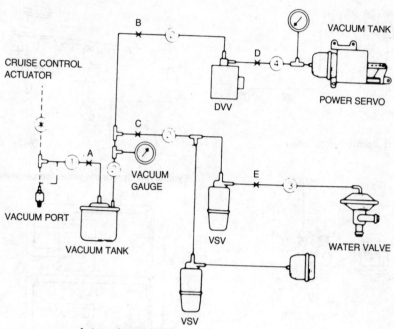

Automatic temperature control vacuum schematic

checking the sensor for continuity. If there is no continuity present, replace the sensor.

CONTROL RESISTOR HEATER MODE SWITCH

Test and Inspection

1. Take out the control assembly loosely.
2. Check the continuity of the heater mode switch terminals.
3. Position the temperature control lever at 25. Verify the resistance between terminals number 3 and 6 of the control resistor connector, the resistance should be 1.275–1.725 kilo ohms.
4. If there is an open circuit in the rheostat, the system will operate at maximum cooling. Conversely, if there is a short in the system, it will operate at maximum heating.

WATER TEMPERATURE SWITCH

Test and Inspection

The water temperature switch is usually located under the heater radiator. Inspect the switch continuity between each terminal at each water temperature.

NOTE: When checking the switch on the vehicle, the coolant temperature must be higher than that of the contact point on the switch.

HEATER CONTROL ASSEMBLY (PUSH TYPE)

Test and Inspection

1. Measure the resistance between terminals A13 and A14 for each lever position. The resistance specifications are as follows:

a. Max. Cool Position — Infinity (x) kilo ohms.
b. Middle Position — 1.275–1.725 kilo ohms.
c. Max. Warm — 0 kilo ohms.
2. If the resistance specifications are not as shown in the list above, replace the heater control assembly.

INDICATOR LIGHT OPERATION

Test and Inspection

1. Using a suitable pair of jumper wires, connect the positive lead of the battery to terminal A7 and the negative lead of the battery to terminal A3.
2. With the blower button pushed in, check that the indicator light is lit (the indicator light will not go on when the blower button is on the off position).
3. With the Recirc/Fresh control button

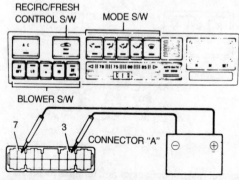

Inspecting the indicator light operation

pushed in, check that the Recirc indicator light is lit. This check should be done in the DEF mode.

4. Press the Recirc/Fresh button in again (Fresh) and check that the indicator light goes off.

5. Press each of the mode buttons in and check that their indicator lights go on.

6. With the Recirc/Fresh control set at Recirc, press the DEF mode button in and check that the Recirc/Fresh control indicator light goes off. Check that when one of the mode buttons other than DEF is pushed in, the Recirc indicator light goes off.

7. Connect the positve battery lead to terminal B5 and the negative battery lead to terminal B2. With the A/C button pushed in, check that the indicator light is lit. If the operation is not as specified, replace the heater control.

8. Check that the illumination lights come on when the positive battery lead is connected to terminal A4 and the negative battery lead is connected to terminal A5. If the operation is not as specified, inspect the bulbs.

RECIRC/FRESH CONTROL SWITCH OPERATION

Test and Inspection

1. Using a suitable pair of jumper wires, connect the positive lead of the battery to terminal A7 and the negative lead of the battery to terminal A11, check that the Recirc indicator light comes on.

2. With the Recirc/Fresh control button pushed in (Fresh) and any mode except DEF on, check that there is continuity between terminals A3 and A12.

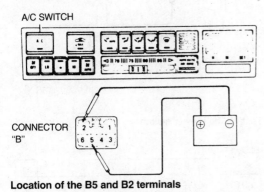

Location of the B5 and B2 terminals

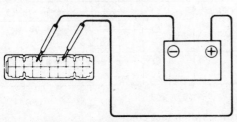

Location of the A4 and A5 terminals

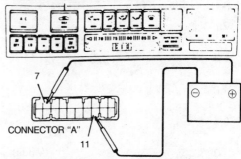

RECIRC/FRESH CONTROL SWITCH

Inspecting the Recirc/Fresh control switch

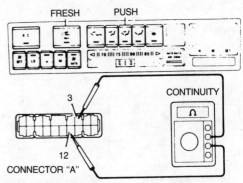

FRESH   PUSH

CONTINUITY

Inspecting the Recirc/Fresh control switch

3. If the operation is not as specified, replace the heater control.

AIR MIX CONTROL SERVO MOTOR (PUSH TYPE)

Servo Motor Inspection

1. Using a suitable pair of jumper wires, connect the positive lead of the battery to terminal 8 and the negative lead of the battery to terminal 2, check that the lever moves smoothly from Warm to Cool.

NOTE: *This check should not be performed if the wire harness or any of the seven pole connectors are corroded or damaged in any way.*

2. Using a suitable pair of jumper wires, connect the positive lead of the battery to terminal 2 and the negative lead of the battery to

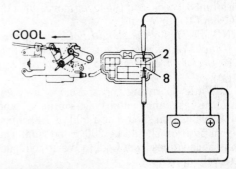

COOL

Testing the servo motor

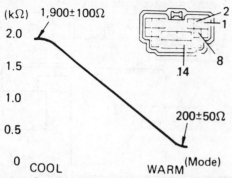

Servo motor connector terminal location and graph chart

CIRCUIT

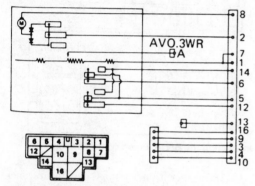

Servo motor wiring schematic

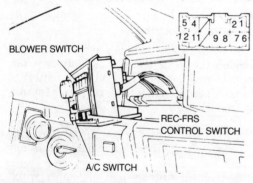

Removing the satellite switch

terminal 8, check that the lever moves smoothly from Cool to Warm.

NOTE: *This check should not be performed if the wire harness or any of the seven pole connectors are corroded or damaged in any way.*

3. While operating the servo motor, measure the resistance values of terminals 1 and 14. Cool position should be 1,900 ± 100 ohms, Warm position should be 200 ± 50 rpm. The resistance values from Cool to Warm will successively decrease.

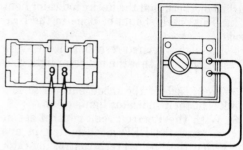

Testing the A/C switch

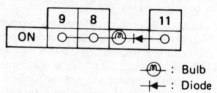

	9	8		11
ON	○	○	ⓜ◀	○

ⓜ : Bulb
◀ : Diode

A/C switch test chart

NOTE: *This check should not be performed if the wire harness or any of the seven pole connectors are corroded or damaged in any way.*

4. If operation is not as specified, replace the servo motor.

SUB-HEATER CONTROL SWITCH

Test and Inspection

1. Remove the satellite switch.
2. Check for continuity between each termi-

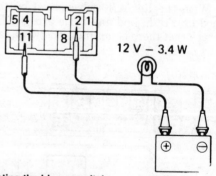

Testing the blower switch

BLOWER SWITCH

	1	2	4	5	8		11
AUTO	○	○			○	⊕◀	○
OFF		○			○	⊕◀	○
LO		○	○	○		⊕◀	○
HI		○	○	○		⊕◀	○

⊕ : LED

Blower switch test chart

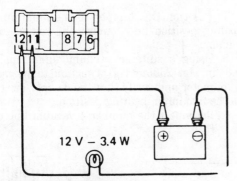

12 V – 3.4 W

Testing the Control switch

REC-FRS CONTROL SWITCH

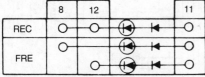

	8	12			11
REC	○	○	⊕◁	◁	○
FRE		○	◁⊕	◁	○
		○	⊕◁	◁	○

Control switch test chart

nal, and that each light emitting diode (LED) lights according to the following procedure:

a. When checking the LED, use a battery and small bulbs (12V–3.4W).

b. Connect the positive battery terminal to the number 11 position and the negative battery terminal to the position being check.

Automatic Temperature Control System

VACUUM CIRCUITS

Functional Test and Adjustments

1. Remove the under cover panel from the lower dash panel.

2. Disconnect the A/C wire harness. Disconnect the white (normal) single terminal connectors at the heater assembly. Connect the check connector (blue) to the A/C amplifier.

3. Place the temperature control lever at (77°F.) position. Remove the center cluster.

4. Run the engine and observe the movement of the power servo stem visually for one minute or more. The stem must be stable. If the stem moves, check the vacuum circuits for leaks.

5. Reconnect the A/C wire harness, disconnect the check connector from the A/C amplifier. Reconnect the white connectors and re-install the under covers and center cluster.

POWER SERVO UNIT OPERATION

Test and Inspection

1. Remove the under cover panel from the lower dash panel.

2. Disconnect the A/C wire harness. Disconnect the white (normal) single terminal connectors at the heater assembly. Connect the check connector (blue) to the A/C amplifier.

3. Place the blower control lever at Auto, the air flow control lever at Vent and place the temperature control lever at (77°F.) position. Remove the center cluster.

4. CVheck the blower speed control by, sliding the lever to 70, the blower speed will change in five steps. When sliding the lever to 85, the blower speed will change in four steps.

5. Check the water valve operation by, placing the lever at the left side fully, this should close the water valve. When placing the lever at 75 or more, the water valve should open.

6. Check the power servo stem for a smooth operation by sliding the temperature control lever.

7. If any item listed in this test fails to operate as specified, replace or repair the defective unit.

8. Reconnect the A/C wire harness, disconnect the check connector from the A/C amplifier. Reconnect the white connectors and re-install the under covers and center cluster.

AUTOMATIC TEMPERATURE CONTROL SYSTEM

On Vehicle Inspection

1. Remove the under cover panel from the lower dash panel.

2. Disconnect the A/C wire harness. Disconnect the white (normal) single terminal connectors at the heater assembly. Connect the check connector (blue) to the A/C amplifier.

3. Place the temperature control lever at (77°F.) position. Remove the center cluster.

4. Run the engine at idle. Verify that the white line marked on the stem of the servo motor, is positioned within the orange area on the power servo unit. If the white line positions are not in the orange area adjust as follows:

a. Normally the orange adjusting terminal is connected. If the white line on the stem is in the red area, change the connections to the red adjusting terminal.

b. If the white line is within the white area, change the connections to the white adjusting terminal.

5. Reconnect the A/C wire harness, disconnect the check connector from the A/C amplifier. Reconnect the white connectors and re-install the under covers and center cluster.

AIR MIX DAMPER LINKAGE

Adjustment

1. Remove the under cover panel from the lower dash panel. Remove the center cluster.

2. Disconnect the rod from the clamp. Disconnect the number 4 vacuum line from the double vacuum valve (DVV) and the vacuum motor in the power servo unit will release the vacuum pressure in the vacuum motor.

3. The stem of the power servo should extend fully to the full maximum cooling position.

4. Position the damper to the maximum cooling position and connect the rod to the clamp.

5. Using a suitable vacuum pump, apply 9.84 in. Hg. (250mm Hg) of vacuum to the vacuum motor and verify that the damper moves to the maximum heating position.

6. Reconnect the number 4 vacuum line to

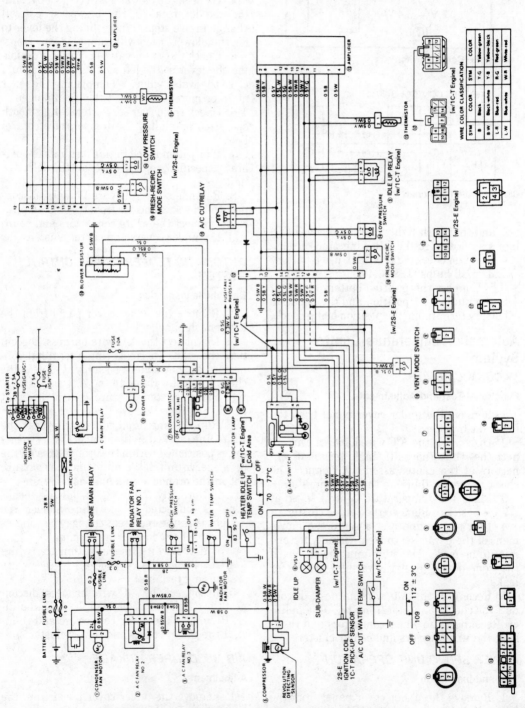

1983 and later Camry A/C and heater electrical schmatic (© Toyota Motor Sales)

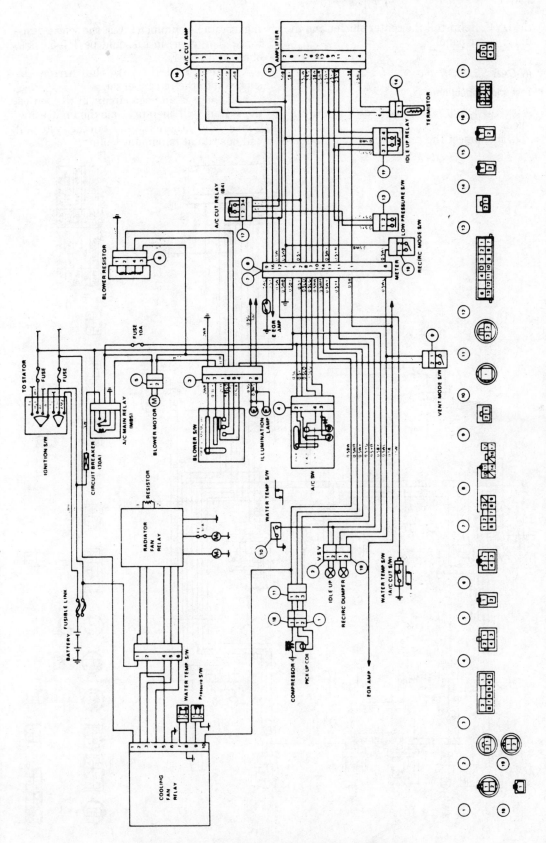

1985 and later Camry A/C wiring schematic—2C-T engine

the DVV. Re-install the center cluster and the under cover panel.

IN-CAR SENSOR

Test and Inspection

1. This sensor is usually located in the console box.

2. Disconnect the sensor connector and us- ing a suitable ohmmeter, test the sensor resistance. The resistance should be 1.7–5.6 kilo ohms at 32–77°F.

3. Check to make sure that air can be sucked into the in-car sensor.

4. If there is an open circuit in the sensor, the system will operate at maximum heating. Conversely, if there is a short in the system, it will operate at maximum cooling.

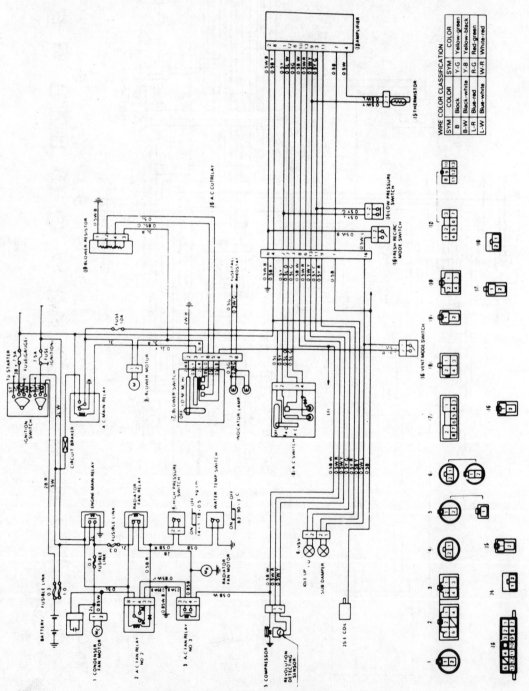

1985 and later Camry A/C wiring schematic—2S-E engine

NOTE: *To test the ambient sensor, use a suitable ohmmeter to check the resistance of the ambient sensor. The resistance should be 0.4–0.6 kilo ohms at 32–77°F. The ambient sensor is usually located on the A/C condenser.*

The solar sensor is usually located on safety pad of the passenger's side or on the passenger's side defroster nozzle. This sensor can be check by using a suitable voltmeter and checking the sensor voltage. The voltage should be 0.3–0.5 volts (in the daylight).

INSTRUMENT PANEL

Cluster

REMOVAL AND INSTALLATION

1. Disconnect the negative battery cable at the battery.
2. Remove the fuse box cover from under the left side of the instrument panel.
3. Remove the heater control knobs.
4. Using a screwdriver, carefully pry off the heater control panel.
5. Unscrew the cluster finish panel retaining screws and pull out the bottom of the panel.
6. Unplug the two electrical connectors and unhook the speedometer cable.
7. Remove the instrument cluster.
8. Installation is performed in the reverse of the previous steps.

Radio

REMOVAL AND INSTALLATION

1. Remove the knobs.
2. Remove the nuts from the control shafts.
3. Disconnect the antenna lead from the radio.
4. Remove the cowl air intake duct.
5. Unplug the wiring from the radio.
6. Remove the radio support nuts and bolts.
7. Lower the radio from under the instrument panel.
8. Installation is the reverse of removal.

WINDSHIELD WIPERS

Motor

REMOVAL AND INSTALLATION

1. Remove the access hole cover.
2. Carefully pry the wiper link and motor apart.
3. Remove the left and right cowl ventilators.
4. Remove the wiper arms and the linkage mounting nuts.

5. Push the pivots into the ventilators.
6. Loosen the wiper link connector ends and remove them along with the linkage.
7. Operate the wiper motor and turn off the ignition key when the crank is at the position illustrated.
8. Unplug the wiring connector from the motor.
9. Remove the mounting bolts and lift out the motor.
10. Installation is the reverse of removal. Make sure that you return the motor crank to the PARK position before connecting the linkage.

LIGHTS

Headlights

REMOVAL AND INSTALLATION

1. Remove the headlight bezel and/or radiator grille, as necessary.
2. Remove the trim ring and remove the headlight mounting screws.

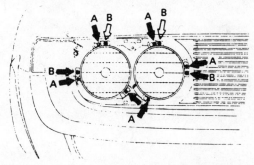

To remove the headlights, remove the retaining screws "A"; but do not loosen adjusting screws "B"

3. Pull the headlight out and unplug the connector.
NOTE: *On some models, the headlight retainer must be rotated clockwise in order to remove the headlight unit.*
4. Installation is performed in the reverse order of removal.
CAUTION: *Do not interchange inner and outer headlight units.*

Turn Signals and Flashers

These models' turn signals and hazard warning flashers are combined in a single unit. It is located on the left hand side, underneath the dashboard, next to the fuse block.

NOTE: *On some models it may be necessary to remove the fuse block bracket in order to gain access to the flasher.*

FUSES AND FUSIBLE LINK

A single fuse block unit is located under the hood (driver's side) on these models.

WIRING DIAGRAMS

Wiring diagrams have been left out of this book. As cars have become more complex, and available with longer and longer option lists, wiring diagrams have grown in size and complexity also. It has become virtually impossible to provide a readable reproduction in a reasonable number of pages. Information on ordering wiring diagrams from the vehicle manufacturer can be found in the owners manual.

6

MANUAL TRANSAXLE

Understanding the Manual Transmission and Clutch

Because of the way an internal combustion engine breathes, it can produce torque, or twisting force, only within a narrow speed range. Most modern engines must turn at about 2,500 rpm to produce their peak torque. By 4,500 rpm they are producing so little torque that continued increases in engine speed produce no power increases.

The transmission and clutch are employed to vary the relationship between engine speed and the speed of the wheels so that adequate engine power can be produced under all circumstances. The clutch allows engine torque to be applied to the transmission input shaft gradually, due to mechanical slippage. The car can, consequently, be started smoothly from a full stop.

The transmission changes the ratio between the rotating speeds of the engine and the wheels by the use of gears. Three-speed or four-speed transmissions are most common. The lower gears allow full engine power to be applied to the rear wheels during acceleration at low speeds.

The clutch drive plate is a thin disc, the center of which is splined to the transmission input shaft. Both sides of the disc are covered with a layer of material which is similar to brake lining and which is capable of allowing slippage without roughness or excessive noise.

The clutch cover is bolted to the engine flywheel and incorporates a diaphragm spring which provides the pressure to engage the clutch. The cover also houses the pressure plate. The driven disc is sandwiched between the pressure plate and the smooth surface of the flywheel when the clutch pedal is released,

thus forcing it to turn at the same speed as the engine crankshaft.

The transmission contains a mainshaft which passes all the way through the transmission, from the clutch to the driveshaft. This shaft is separated at one point, so that front and rear portions can turn at different speeds.

Power is transmitted by a countershaft in the lower gears and reverse. The gears of the countershaft mesh with gears on the mainshaft, allowing power to be carried from one to the other. All the countershaft gears are integral with that shaft, while several of the mainshaft gears can either rotate independently of the shaft or be locked to it. Shifting from one gear to the next causes one of the gears to be freed from rotating with the shaft and locks another to it. Gears are locked and unlocked by internal dog clutches which slide between the center of the gear and the shaft. The forward gears usually employ synchronizers, friction members which smoothly bring gear and shaft to the same speed before the toothed dog clutches are engaged.

The clutch is operating properly if:

1. It will stall the engine when released with the vehicle held stationary.

2. The shift lever can be moved freely between first and reverse gears when the vehicle is stationary and the clutch disengaged.

A clutch pedal free play adjustment is incorporated in the linkage. If there is about 25–50mm of motion before the pedal begins to release the clutch, it is adjusted properly. Inadequate free play wears all parts of the clutch releasing mechanisms and may cause slippage. Excessive free play may cause inadequate release and hard shifting of gears.

Some clutches use a hydraulic system in place of mechanical linkage. If the clutch fails to release, fill the clutch master cylinder with fluid to the proper level and pump the clutch pedal to fill the system with fluid. Bleed the system in the same way as a brake system. If leaks are located, tighten loose connections or overhaul the master or slave cylinder as necessary.

LINKAGE ADJUSTMENT

No external adjustments are needed or possible.

REMOVAL AND INSTALLATION

The transaxle must be removed along with the engine. See Engine Removal and Installation earlier in this section. Once the whole unit is out of the car, unbolt the transaxle from the engine.

CLUTCH

The clutch is a single plate, dry disc type, with a diaphragm spring pressure plate. Clutch release bearings are sealed ball bearing units which need no lubrication and should never be washed in any kind of solvent.

Pedal Height Specifications

Year	Height (in.)	Measure Between:
1983–85	7.6–8.0	Pedal pad and kickpanel
1986	8.0–8.4	Pedal pad and kickpanel

PEDAL HEIGHT ADJUSTMENT

Adjust the pedal height to the 191–201mm for 1983–85 models, or to the specification given in the following chart, by rotating the pedal stop (nut).

FREE PLAY ADJUSTMENT

Measure the clutch pedal free play. It should be ½–1½mm. If it fails to fall within specifications, loosen the pushrod locknut and rotate the pushrod while depressing the clutch pedal lightly with your finger.

Troubleshooting Basic Clutch Problems

Problem	Cause
Excessive clutch noise	Throwout bearing noises are more audible at the lower end of pedal travel. The usual causes are: • Riding the clutch • Too little pedal free-play • Lack of bearing lubrication A bad clutch shaft pilot bearing will make a high pitched squeal, when the clutch is disengaged and the transmission is in gear or within the first 2″ of pedal travel. The bearing must be replaced. Noise from the clutch linkage is a clicking or snapping that can be heard or felt as the pedal is moved completely up or down. This usually requires lubrication. Transmitted engine noises are amplified by the clutch housing and heard in the passenger compartment. They are usually the result of insufficient pedal free-play and can be changed by manipulating the clutch pedal.
Clutch slips (the car does not move as it should when the clutch is engaged)	This is usually most noticeable when pulling away from a standing start. A severe test is to start the engine, apply the brakes, shift into high gear and SLOWLY release the clutch pedal. A healthy clutch will stall the engine. If it slips it may be due to: • A worn pressure plate or clutch plate • Oil soaked clutch plate • Insufficient pedal free-play
Clutch drags or fails to release	The clutch disc and some transmission gears spin briefly after clutch disengagement. Under normal conditions in average temperatures, 3 seconds is maximum spin-time. Failure to release properly can be caused by: • Too light transmission lubricant or low lubricant level • Improperly adjusted clutch linkage
Low clutch life	Low clutch life is usually a result of poor driving habits or heavy duty use. Riding the clutch, pulling heavy loads, holding the car on a grade with the clutch instead of the brakes and rapid clutch engagement all contribute to low clutch life.

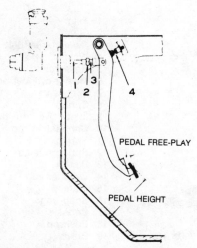

1. Master cylinder pushrod   3. Clevis
2. Pushrod locknut   4. Pedal stop (bolt)

Clutch pedal adjustment

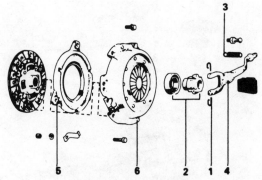

1. Release bearing hub clips
2. Release bearing hub
   w/bearing
3. Tension spring
4. Release fork
5. Clutch pressure plate
6. Clutch cover w/spring

Clutch components

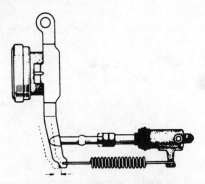

Release cylinder free-play is the distance between the arrows

REMOVAL AND INSTALLATION

CAUTION: *Do not allow grease or oil to get on any of the disc, pressure plate, or flywheel surfaces.*

1. Remove the transmission from the car as previously detailed.

2. Remove the clutch cover and disc from the bellhousing.

3. Unfasten the release fork bearing clips. Withdraw the release bearing hub, complete with the release bearing.

4. Remove the tension spring from the clutch linkage.

5. Remove the release fork and support.

6. Punch matchmarks on the clutch cover and the pressure plate so that the pressure plate can be returned to its original position during installation.

7. Slowly unfasten the screws which attach the retracting springs.

NOTE: *If the screws are released too fast, the clutch assembly will fly apart, causing possible injury or loss of parts.*

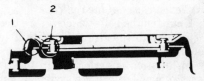

Lightly apply multipurpose grease to points "1" and "2"

8. Separate the pressure plate from the clutch cover/spring assembly.

9. Inspect the parts for wear or deterioration. Replace parts as required.

10. Installation is performed in the reverse order of removal. Several points should be noted, however:

   a. Be sure to align the matchmarks on the clutch cover and pressure plate which were made during disassembly.

   b. Apply a thin coating of multipurpose grease to the release bearing hub and release fork contact points. Also, pack the groove inside the clutch hub with multipurpose grease.

   c. Center the clutch disc by using a clutch pilot tool or an old input shaft. Insert the pilot into the end of the input shaft front bearing and bolt the clutch to the flywheel.

NOTE: *Bolt the clutch assembly to the flywheel in two or three stages, evenly and to the torque specified in the chart below.*

   d. Adjust the clutch as outlined below.

Master Cylinder
REMOVAL AND INSTALLATION

1. Remove the clevis pin.
2. Detach the hydraulic line from the tube.

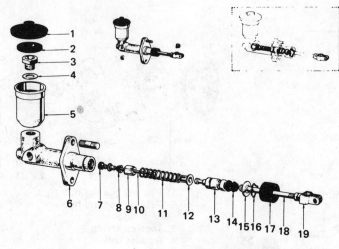

1. Filler cap
2. Float
3. Reservoir setbolt
4. Washer
5. Reservoir
6. Master cylinder body
7. Inlet valve
8. Spring
9. Inlet valve housing
10. Connecting rod
11. Spring
12. Spring retainer
13. Piston
14. Cylinder cup
15. Plate
16. Snap-ring
17. Boot
18. Pushrod
19. Clevis

Clutch master cylinder components

CAUTION: *Do not spill brake fluid on the painted surfaces of the vehicle.*

3. Unfasten the bolts which secure the master cylinder to the firewall. Withdraw the assembly.

4. Installation is performed in the reverse order of removal. Blend the system as detailed following. Adjust the clutch pedal height and free play as previously detailed.

OVERHAUL

1. Clamp the master cylinder body in a vise with soft jaws.

2. Separate the reservoir assembly from the master cylinder.

3. Remove the snapring and remove the pushrod/piston assembly.

4. Inspect all of the parts and replace any which are worn or defective.

NOTE: *Honing of the cylinder may be necessary to smooth pitting.*

Assembly is performed in the following order:

1. Coat all parts with clean brake fluid, prior to assembly.

2. Install the piston assembly in the cylinder bore.

3. Fit the pushrod over the washer and secure them with the snapring.

4. Install the reservoir.

Clutch Hydraulic System

BLEEDING

1. Fill the master cylinder reservoir with brake fluid.

CAUTION: *Do not spill brake fluid on the painted surfaces of the system.*

2. Remove the cap and loosen the bleeder plug. Block the outlet hole with your finger.

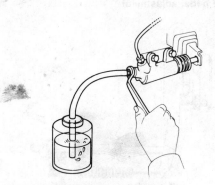

Bleeding the clutch hydraulic system

3. Pump the clutch pedal several times, then take your finger from the hole while depressing the clutch pedal. Allow the air to flow out. Place your finger back over the hole and release the pedal.

4. After fluid pressure can be felt (with your finger), tighten the bleeder plug.

5. Fit a bleeder tube over the plug and place the other end into a clean jar half filled with brake fluid.

6. Depress the clutch pedal, loosen the bleeder plug with a wrench, and allow the fluid to flow into the jar.

7. Tighten the plug and then release the clutch pedal.

8. Repeat Steps 6–7 until no air bubbles are visible in the bleeder tube.

9. When there are no more air bubbles, tighten the plug while keeping the clutch pedal fully depressed. Replace the cap.

10. Fill the master cylinder to the specified level. (See Chapter 1).

11. Check the system for leaks.

AUTOMATIC TRANSAXLE

Understanding Automatic Transaxles

The automatic transmission allows engine torque and power to be transmitted to the rear wheels within a narrow range of engine operating speeds. The transmission will allow the engine to turn fast enough to produce plenty of power and torque at very low speeds, while keeping it at a sensible rpm at high vehicle speeds. The transmission performs this job entirely without driver assistance. The transmission uses a light fluid as the medium for the transmission of power. This fluid also works in the operation of various hydraulic control circuits and as a lubricant. Because the transmission fluid performs all of these three functions, trouble within the unit can easily travel from one part to another. For this reason, and because of the complexity and unusual operating principles of the transmission, a very sound understanding of the basic principles of operation will simplify troubleshooting.

THE TORQUE CONVERTER

The torque converter replaces the conventional clutch. It has three functions:

1. It allows the engine to idle with the vehicle at a standstill even with the transmission in gear.

2. It allows the transmission to shift from range to range smoothly, without requiring that the driver close the throttle during the shift.

3. It multiplies engine torque to an increasing extent as vehicle speed drops and throttle opening is increased. This has the effect of making the transmission more responsive and reduces the amount of shifting required.

The torque converter is a metal case which is shaped like a sphere that has been flattened on

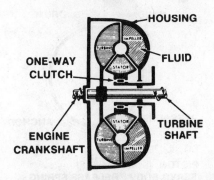

The torque converter housing is roated by the engine's crankshaft, and turns the impeller. The impeller spins the turbine, which gives motion to the turbine shaft, driving the gears

opposite sides. It is bolted to the rear end of the engine's crankshaft. Generally, the entire metal case rotates at engine speed and serves as the engine's flywheel.

The case contains three sets of blades. One set is attached directly to the case. This set forms the torus or pump. Another set is directly connected to the output shaft, and forms the turbine. The third set is mounted on a hub which, in turn, is mounted on a stationary shaft through a one-way clutch. This third set is known as the stator.

A pump, which is driven by the converter hub at engine speed, keeps the torque converter full of transmission fluid at all times. Fluid flows continuously through the unit to provide cooling.

Under low speed acceleration, the torque converter functions as follows: The torus is turning faster than the turbine. It picks up fluid at the center of the converter and, through centrifugal force, slings it outward. Since the outer edge of the converter moves faster than the portions at the center, the fluid picks up speed.

The fluid then enters the outer edge of the turbine blades. It then travels back toward the center of the converter case along the turbine blades. In impinging upon the turbine blades, the fluid loses the energy picked up in the torus.

If the fluid were now to immediately be returned directly into the torus, both halves of the converter would have to turn at approximately the same speed at all times, and torque input and output would both be the same.

In flowing through the torus and turbine, the fluid picks up two types of flow, or flow in two separate directions. It flows through the turbine blades, and it spins with the engine. The stator, whose blades are stationary when the vehicle is being accelerated at low speeds, converts one type of flow into another. Instead of allowing the fluid to flow straight back into the torus, the stator's curved blades turn the fluid almost 90 degrees toward the direction of rotation of the engine. Thus the fluid does not flow as fast toward the torus, but is already spinning when the torus picks it up. This has the effect of allowing the torus to turn much faster than the turbine. This difference in speed may be compared to the difference in speed between the smaller and larger gears in any gear train. The result is that engine power output is higher, and engine torque is multiplied.

As the speed of the turbine increases, the fluid spins faster and faster in the direction of engine rotation. As a result, the ability of the stator to redirect the fluid flow is reduced. Under cruising conditions, the stator is eventually forced to rotate on its one-way clutch in the direction of engine rotation. Under these conditions, the torque converter begins to behave almost like a solid shaft, with the torus and turbine speeds being almost equal.

THE PLANETARY GEARBOX

The ability of the torque converter to multiply engine torque is limited. Also, the unit tends to be more efficient when the turbine is rotating at relatively high speeds. Therefore, a planetary gearbox is used to carry the power output of the turbine to the driveshaft.

Planetary gears function very similarly to conventional transmission gears. However, their construction is different in that three elements make up one gear system, and in that all three elements are different from one another. The three elements are: an outer gear that is shaped like a hoop, with teeth cut into the inner surface. A sun gear, mounted on a

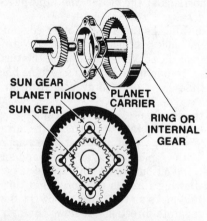

SUN GEAR
PLANET PINIONS
SUN GEAR
PLANET CARRIER
RING OR INTERNAL GEAR

Planetary gears are similar to manual transmission gears but are composed of three parts

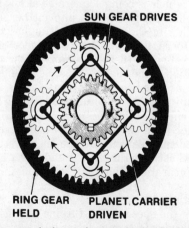

SUN GEAR DRIVES

RING GEAR HELD
PLANET CARRIER DRIVEN

Planetary gears in the maximum reduction (low) range. The ring gear is held and a lower gear ration is obtained

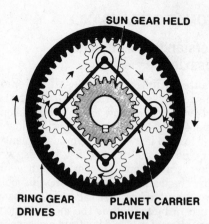

SUN GEAR HELD

RING GEAR DRIVES
PLANET CARRIER DRIVEN

Planetary gears in the minimum reduction (drive) range. The ring gear is allowed to revolve, providing a higher gear ratio

shaft and located at the very center of the outer gear, and a set of three planet gears, held by pins in a ring-like planet carrier and meshing with both the sun gear and the outer gear. Either the outer gear or the sun gear may be held stationary, providing more than one possible torque multiplication factor for each set of gears. Also, if all three gears are forced to rotate at the same speed, the gearset forms, in effect, a solid shaft.

Most modern automatics use the planetary gears to provide either a single reduction ratio of about 1.8:1, or two reduction gears: a low of about 2.5:1, and an intermediate of about 1.5:1. Bands and clutches are used to hold various portions of the gearsets to the transmission case or to the shaft on which they are mounted. Shifting is accomplished, then, by changing the portion of each planetary gearset which is held to the transmission case or to the shaft.

THE SERVOS AND ACCUMULATORS

The servos are hydraulic pistons and cylinders. They resemble the hydraulic actuators used on

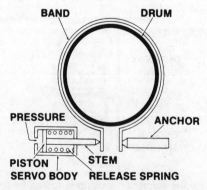

BAND   DRUM

PRESSURE   ANCHOR
PISTON   STEM
SERVO BODY   RELEASE SPRING

Servos, operated by pressure, are used to apply or release the bands, to either hold the ring gear or allow it to rotate

many familiar machines, such as bulldozers. Hydraulic fluid enters the cylinder, under pressure, and forces the piston to move to engage the band or clutches.

The accumulators are used to cushion the engagement of the servos. The transmission fluid must pass through the accumulator on the way to the servo. The accumulator housing contains a thin piston which is sprung away from the discharge passage of the accumulator. When fluid passes through the accumulator on the way to the servo, it must move the piston against spring pressure, and this action smooths out the action of the servo.

THE HYDRAULIC CONTROL SYSTEM

The hydraulic pressure used to operate the servos comes from the main transmission oil pump. This fluid is channeled to the various servos through the shift valves. There is generally a manual shift valve which is operated by the transmission selector lever and an automatic shift valve for each automatic upshift the transmission provides: i.e., two-speed automatics have a low-high shift valve, while three-speeds have a 1–2 valve, and a 2–3 valve.

There are two pressures which effect the operation of these valves. One is the governor pressure which is affected by vehicle speed. The other is the modulator pressure which is affected by intake manifold vacuum or throttle position. Governor pressure rises with an increase in vehicle speed, and modulator pressure rises as the throttle is opened wider. By responding to these two pressures, the shift valves cause the upshift points to be delayed with increased throttle opening to make the best use of the engine's power output.

Most transmissions also make use of an auxiliary circuit for downshifting. This circuit may be actuated by the throttle linkage or the vacuum line which actuates the modulator, or by a cable or solenoid. It applies pressure to a special downshift surface on the shift valve or valves.

The transmission modulator also governs the line pressure, used to actuate the servos. In

Troubleshooting Basic Automatic Transmission Problems

Problem	Cause	Solution
Fluid leakage	• Defective pan gasket	• Replace gasket or tighten pan bolts
	• Loose filler tube	• Tighten tube nut
	• Loose extension housing to transmission case	• Tighten bolts
	• Converter housing area leakage	• Have transmission checked professionally
Fluid flows out the oil filler tube	• High fluid level	• Check and correct fluid level
	• Breather vent clogged	• Open breather vent
	• Clogged oil filter or screen	• Replace filter or clean screen (change fluid also)
	• Internal fluid leakage	• Have transmission checked professionally
Transmission overheats (this is usually accompanied by a strong burned odor to the fluid)	• Low fluid level	• Check and correct fluid level
	• Fluid cooler lines clogged	• Drain and refill transmission. If this doesn't cure the problem, have cooler lines cleared or replaced.
	• Heavy pulling or hauling with insufficient cooling	• Install a transmission oil cooler
	• Faulty oil pump, internal slippage	• Have transmission checked professionally
Buzzing or whining noise	• Low fluid level	• Check and correct fluid level
	• Defective torque converter, scored gears	• Have transmission checked professionally
No forward or reverse gears or slippage in one or more gears	• Low fluid level	• Check and correct fluid level
	• Defective vacuum or linkage controls, internal clutch or band failure	• Have unit checked professionally
Delayed or erratic shift	• Low fluid level	• Check and correct fluid level
	• Broken vacuum lines	• Repair or replace lines
	• Internal malfunction	• Have transmission checked professionally

Lockup Torque Converter Service Diagnosis

Problem	Cause	Solution

No lockup	• Faulty oil pump
	• Sticking governor valve
	• Valve body malfunction
	  (a) Stuck switch valve
	  (b) Stuck lockup valve
	  (c) Stuck fail-safe valve
	• Failed locking clutch
	• Leaking turbine hub seal
	• Faulty input shaft or seal ring
		• Replace oil pump
		• Repair or replace as necessary
		• Repair or replace valve body or its internal components as necessary
		
		• Replace torque converter
		• Replace torque converter
		• Repair or replace as necessary

Will not unlock	• Sticking governor valve
	• Valve body malfunction
	  (a) Stuck switch valve
	  (b) Stuck lockup valve
	  (c) Stuck fail-safe valve
		• Repair or replace as necessary
		• Repair or replace valve body or its internal components as necessary

Stays locked up at too low a speed in direct	• Sticking governor valve
	• Valve body malfunction
	  (a) Stuck switch valve
	  (b) Stuck lockup valve
	  (c) Stuck fail-safe valve
		• Repair or replace as necessary
		• Repair or replace valve body or its internal components as necessary

Locks up or drags in low or second	• Faulty oil pump
	• Valve body malfunction
	  (a) Stuck switch valve
	  (b) Stuck fail-safe valve
		• Replace oil pump
		• Repair or replace valve body or its internal components as necessary

Sluggish or stalls in reverse	• Faulty oil pump
	• Plugged cooler, cooler lines or fittings
	• Valve body malfunction
	  (a) Stuck switch valve
	  (b) Faulty input shaft or seal ring
		• Replace oil pump as necessary
		• Flush or replace cooler and flush lines and fittings
		• Repair or replace valve body or its internal components as necessary

Loud chatter during lockup engagement (cold)	• Faulty torque converter • Failed locking clutch • Leaking turbine hub seal	• Replace torque converter • Replace torque converter • Replace torque converter
Vibration or shudder during lockup engagement	• Faulty oil pump • Valve body malfunction • Faulty torque converter • Engine needs tune-up	• Repair or replace oil pump as necessary • Repair or replace valve body or its internal components as necessary • Replace torque converter • Tune engine
Vibration after lockup engagement	• Faulty torque converter • Exhaust system strikes underbody • Engine needs tune-up • Throttle linkage misadjusted	• Replace torque converter • Align exhaust system • Tune engine • Adjust throttle linkage
Vibration when revved in neutral Overheating: oil blows out of dip stick tube or pump seal	• Torque converter out of balance • Plugged cooler, cooler lines or fittings • Stuck switch valve	• Replace torque converter • Flush or replace cooler and flush lines and fittings • Repair switch valve in valve body or replace valve body
Shudder after lockup engagement	• Faulty oil pump • Plugged cooler, cooler lines or fittings • Valve body malfunction • Faulty torque converter • Fail locking clutch • Exhaust system strikes underbody • Engine needs tune-up • Throttle linkage misadjusted	• Replace oil pump • Flush or replace cooler and flush lines and fittings • Repair or replace valve body or its internal components as necessary • Replace torque converter • Replace torque converter • Align exhaust system • Tune engine • Adjust throttle linkage

Transmission Fluid Indications

The appearance and odor of the transmission fluid can give valuable clues to the overall condition of the transmission. Always note the appearance of the fluid when you check the fluid level or change the fluid. Rub a small amount of fluid between your fingers to feel for grit and smell the fluid on the dipstick.

If the fluid appears:	It indicates:
Clear and red colored	• Normal operation
Discolored (extremely dark red or brownish) or smells burned	• Band or clutch pack failure, usually caused by an overheated transmission. Hauling very heavy loads with insufficient power or failure to change the fluid, often result in overheating. Do not confuse this appearance with newer fluids that have a darker red color and a strong odor (though not a burned odor).
Foamy or aerated (light in color and full of bubbles)	• The level is too high (gear train is churning oil) • An internal air leak (air is mixing with the fluid). Have the transmission checked professionally.
Solid residue in the fluid	• Defective bands, clutch pack or bearings. Bits of band material or metal abrasives are clinging to the dipstick. Have the transmission checked professionally.
Varnish coating on the dipstick	• The transmission fluid is overheating

this way, the clutches and bands will be actuated with a force matching the torque output of the engine.

Transaxle

REMOVAL AND INSTALLATION

The engine must be removed with the transaxle. See Engine Removal and Installation. Once the assembly is out, Unbolt and separate the transaxle from the engine. When assembling note the following torques:
• Transaxle-to-engine: 12mm 47 ft.lb.
• Torque converter: 13 ft.lb.

PAN REMOVAL

1. Unfasten the oil plug and drain the fluid from the transaxle.
2. Unfasten the pan securing bolts.
3. Withdraw the pan.
4. Installation is performed in the reverse order of removal. Torque the pan securing bolts to 4–6 ft.lb. Refill the transaxle with fluid as outlined in Chapter 1.

BAND ADJUSTMENTS

The transaxle has no band adjustments.

NEUTRAL SAFETY SWITCH ADJUSTMENT

The neutral safety switch is on the linkage located beneath the console.
To adjust it, proceed in the following manner:

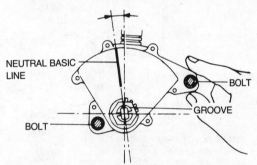

Neutral safety switch adjustment—most late models similar

1. Remove the screws securing the center console.
2. Unfasten the console multiconnector, if so equipped, and completely remove the console.
3. Adjust the switch in the manner outlined in the preceding column selector section.
4. Install the console in the reverse order of removal after completion of the switch adjustment.

SHIFT LINKAGE ADJUSTMENT

1. Loosen the swivel nut on the lever.
2. Push the lever to the right as far as it will go.
3. Bring the lever back two notches to Neutral.
4. Place the shifter in Neutral.
5. Hold the lever, lightly, toward the engine and tighten the nut.

DRIVELINE

Halfshafts

REMOVAL AND INSTALLATION

1. Raise and support the front end on jackstands.

2. Remove the cotter pin, locknut cap and locknut from the hub.

3. Remove the six nuts attaching the halfshaft to the transaxle.

4. Remove the caliper and support it out of the way with a wire.

5. Remove the rotor.

6. Remove the left side case shield.

7. Remove the axle hub from the shaft with a puller.

8. Unbolt the right side intermediate shaft from the block bracket. Remove the intermediate shaft from the U-joint.

9. With a slide hammer, pull the U-joint from the case.

10. Installation is the reverse of removal. Torque the intermediate shaft bracket bolts to 40 ft.lb.; the caliper bolts to 65 ft.lb.; the hub bearing nut to 137 ft.lb.; the driveshaft-to-intermediate shaft nuts to 27 ft.lb.

Front Hub and Bearing

REMOVAL, PACKING AND INSTALLATION

1. Raise and support the front end on jackstands.

2. Remove the cotter pin and axle bearing locknut cap.

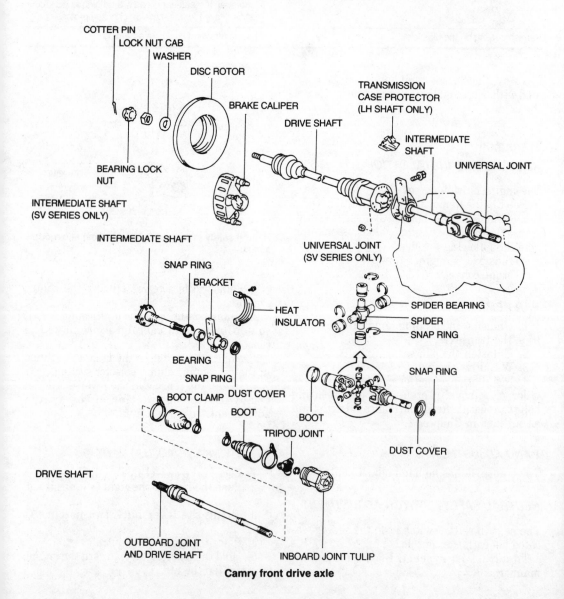

Camry front drive axle

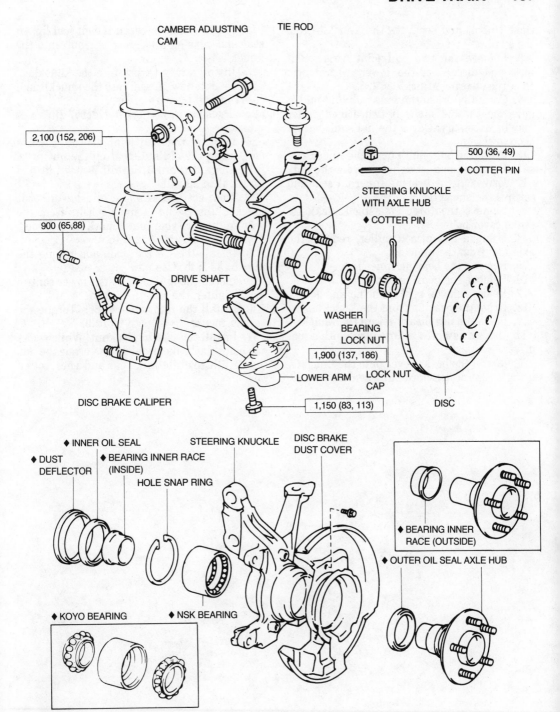

CAMBER ADJUSTING CAM

TIE ROD

2,100 (152, 206)

STEERING KNUCKLE WITH AXLE HUB

500 (36, 49)

◆ COTTER PIN

◆ COTTER PIN

900 (65,88)

DRIVE SHAFT

WASHER
BEARING
LOCK NUT

1,900 (137, 186)

LOCK NUT CAP

LOWER ARM

DISC BRAKE CALIPER

1,150 (83, 113)

DISC

◆ INNER OIL SEAL

STEERING KNUCKLE

DISC BRAKE DUST COVER

◆ DUST DEFLECTOR

◆ BEARING INNER RACE (INSIDE)

HOLE SNAP RING

◆ BEARING INNER RACE (OUTSIDE)

◆ OUTER OIL SEAL AXLE HUB

◆ KOYO BEARING

◆ NSK BEARING

KG-CM (FT-LB, N·M) : TIGHTENING TORQUE

◆ : NON-REUSABLE PART

Front axle hub and steering knuckle assembly—front wheel drive models

3. With a helper depressing the brake pedal, loosen the axleshaft locknut.

4. Dismount the caliper and suspend it out of the way.

5. Remove the rotor.

6. Remove the cotter pin and nut from the tie rod end, and, using a separator tool, disconnect the tie rod.

7. Matchmark the shock absorber lower mounting bracket and the camber adjustment

cam. Unbolt and separate the knuckle from the strut.

8. Remove the two ball joint attachment nuts and disconnect the lower control arm from the steering knuckle.

9. Carefully grasp the axle hub and pull it out from the halfshaft. A two armed puller may be necessary. Cover the halfshaft with a shop towel.

10. Press the ball joint out of the knuckle.

11. Remove the dust deflector from the hub.

12. Drive out the bearing inner oil seal and remove the snapring.

13. Remove the three steering knuckle-to-brake cover bolts.

14. Using a two armed puller, remove the axle hub from the knuckle.

15. Remove the bearing inner race.

16. Remove the bearing outer race.

17. Remove the oil seal from the knuckle.

18. Drive the bearing from the knuckle.

19. Press the new bearing into the knuckle.

20. Drive a new oil seal into place with a seal driver.

21. Install the brake cover onto the knuckle, using a coat of non-hardening sealer.

22. Apply grease between the oil seal lip, oil seal and bearing and press the hub into the knuckle.

23. Install a new snapring in the knuckle.

24. Press a new oil seal into the knuckle and coat the seal lip with grease.

25. Press a new dust deflector into the knuckle.

26. Position the ball joint on the knuckle and, using the old nut, tighten the nut to 14 ft.lb. Discard the nut, install a new nut and torque it to 82 ft.lb.

27. Connect the knuckle and lower strut bracket. Insert the mounting bolts from the rear. Make sure your matchmarks are aligned. Tighten the nuts to 152 ft.lb.

28. Install the tie rod ends and torque the nuts to 36 ft.lb. Use new cotter pins.

29. Install the ball joint on the lower control arm. Tighten the bolt to 47 ft.lb.

30. Install the rotor and caliper. Torque the caliper mounting bolts to 65 ft.lb.

31. Install the bearing locknut. While someone holds the brake pedal down, torque the nut to 137 ft.lb. Install the nut cap and a new cotter pin.

FRONT SUSPENSION

MacPherson Struts

REMOVAL AND INSTALLATION

1. Raise and support the front end on jackstands placed under the frame pads.
2. Remove the wheels.

3. Disconnect the brake tube and flexible hose from the clamp.
4. Dismount the caliper and support it out of the way, without disconnecting the brake line.
5. Remove the three nuts and lockwashers from the top of the strut inside the engine compartment.
6. Remove the two bolts and lockwashers at-

Troubleshooting Basic Steering and Suspension Problems

Problem	Cause	Solution
Hard steering (steering wheel is hard to turn)	• Low or uneven tire pressure • Loose power steering pump drive belt • Low or incorrect power steering fluid • Incorrect front end alignment • Defective power steering pump • Bent or poorly lubricated front end parts	• Inflate tires to correct pressure • Adjust belt • Add fluid as necessary • Have front end alignment checked/adjusted • Check pump • Lubricate and/or replace defective parts
Loose steering (too much play in the steering wheel)	• Loose wheel bearings • Loose or worn steering linkage • Faulty shocks • Worn ball joints	• Adjust wheel bearings • Replace worn parts • Replace shocks • Replace ball joints
Car veers or wanders (car pulls to one side with hands off the steering wheel)	• Incorrect tire pressure • Improper front end alignment • Loose wheel bearings • Loose or bent front end components • Faulty shocks	• Inflate tires to correct pressure • Have front end alignment checked/adjusted • Adjust wheel bearings • Replace worn components • Replace shocks
Wheel oscillation or vibration transmitted through steering wheel	• Improper tire pressures • Tires out of balance • Loose wheel bearings • Improper front end alignment • Worn or bent front end components	• Inflate tires to correct pressure • Have tires balanced • Adjust wheel bearings • Have front end alignment checked/adjusted • Replace worn parts
Uneven tire wear	• Incorrect tire pressure • Front end out of alignment • Tires out of balance	• Inflate tires to correct pressure • Have front end alignment checked/adjusted • Have tires balanced

Noise Diagnosis

The Noise Is	Most Probably Produced By
· Identical under Drive or Coast	· Road surface, tires or front wheel bearings
· Different depending on road surface	· Road surface or tires
· Lower as the car speed is lowered	· Tires
· Similar with car standing or moving	· Engine or transmission
· A vibration	· Unbalanced tires, rear wheel bearing, unbalanced driveshaft or worn U-joint
· A knock or click about every 2 tire revolutions	· Rear wheel bearing
· Most pronounced on turns	· Damaged differential gears
· A steady low-pitched whirring or scraping, starting at low speeds	· Damaged or worn pinion bearing
· A chattering vibration on turns	· Wrong differential lubricant or worn clutch plates (limited slip rear axle)
· Noticed only in Drive, Coast or Float conditions	· Worn ring gear and/or pinion gear

Troubleshooting the Steering Column

Problem	Cause	Solution
Will not lock	· Lockbolt spring broken or defective	· Replace lock bolt spring
High effort (required to turn ignition key and lock cylinder)	· Lock cylinder defective	· Replace lock cylinder
	· Ignition switch defective	· Replace ignition switch
	· Rack preload spring broken or deformed	· Replace preload spring
	· Burr on lock sector, lock rack, housing, support or remote rod coupling	· Remove burr
	· Bent sector shaft	· Replace shaft
	· Defective lock rack	· Replace lock rack
	· Remote rod bent, deformed	· Replace rod
	· Ignition switch mounting bracket bent	· Straighten or replace
	· Distorted coupling slot in lock rack (tilt column)	· Replace lock rack
Will stick in "start"	· Remote rod deformed	· Straighten or replace
	· Ignition switch mounting bracket bent	· Straighten or replace
Key cannot be removed in "off-lock"	· Ignition switch is not adjusted correctly	· Adjust switch
	· Defective lock cylinder	· Replace lock cylinder
Lock cylinder can be removed without depressing retainer	· Lock cylinder with defective retainer	· Replace lock cylinder
	· Burr over retainer slot in housing cover or on cylinder retainer	· Remove burr
High effort on lock cylinder between "off" and "off-lock"	· Distorted lock rack	· Replace lock rack
	· Burr on tang of shift gate (automatic column)	· Remove burr
	· Gearshift linkage not adjusted	· Adjust linkage
Noise in column	· One click when in "off-lock" position and the steering wheel is moved (all except automatic column)	· Normal—lock bolt is seating
	· Coupling bolts not tightened	· Tighten pinch bolts
	· Lack of grease on bearings or bearing surfaces	· Lubricate with chassis grease
	· Upper shaft bearing worn or broken	· Replace bearing assembly
	· Lower shaft bearing worn or broken	· Replace bearing. Check shaft and replace if scored.
	· Column not correctly aligned	· Align column
	· Coupling pulled apart	· Replace coupling

Troubleshooting the Steering Column (cont.)

Problem	Cause	Solution
Noise in column (cont.)	• Broken coupling lower joint	• Repair or replace joint and align column
	• Steering shaft snap ring not seated	• Replace ring. Check for proper seating in groove.
	• Shroud loose on shift bowl. Housing loose on jacket—will be noticed with ignition in "off-lock" and when torque is applied to steering wheel.	• Position shroud over lugs on shift bowl. Tighten mounting screws.
High steering shaft effort	• Column misaligned	• Align column
	• Defective upper or lower bearing	• Replace as required
	• Tight steering shaft universal joint	• Repair or replace
	• Flash on I.D. of shift tube at plastic joint (tilt column only)	• Replace shift tube
	• Upper or lower bearing seized	• Replace bearings
Lash in mounted column assembly	• Column mounting bracket bolts loose	• Tighten bolts
	• Broken weld nuts on column jacket	• Replace column jacket
	• Column capsule bracket sheared	• Replace bracket assembly
Lash in mounted column assembly (cont.)	• Column bracket to column jacket mounting bolts loose	• Tighten to specified torque
	• Loose lock shoes in housing (tilt column only)	• Replace shoes
	• Loose pivot pins (tilt column only)	• Replace pivot pins and support
	• Loose lock shoe pin (tilt column only)	• Replace pin and housing
	• Loose support screws (tilt column only)	• Tighten screws
Housing loose (tilt column only)	• Excessive clearance between holes in support or housing and pivot pin diameters	• Replace pivot pins and support
	• Housing support-screws loose	• Tighten screws
Steering wheel loose—every other tilt position (tilt column only)	• Loose fit between lock shoe and lock shoe pivot pin	• Replace lock shoes and pivot pin
Steering column not locking in any tilt position (tilt column only)	• Lock shoe seized on pivot pin	• Replace lock shoes and pin
	• Lock shoe grooves have burrs or are filled with foreign material	• Clean or replace lock shoes
	• Lock shoe springs weak or broken	• Replace springs
Noise when tilting column (tilt column only)	• Upper tilt bumpers worn	• Replace tilt bumper
	• Tilt spring rubbing in housing	• Lubricate with chassis grease
One click when in "off-lock" position and the steering wheel is moved	• Seating of lock bolt	• None. Click is normal characteristic sound produced by lock bolt as it seats.
High shift effort (automatic and tilt column only)	• Column not correctly aligned	• Align column
	• Lower bearing not aligned correctly	• Assemble correctly
	• Lack of grease on seal or lower bearing areas	• Lubricate with chassis grease
Improper transmission shifting—automatic and tilt column only	• Sheared shift tube joint	• Replace shift tube
	• Improper transmission gearshift linkage adjustment	• Adjust linkage
	• Loose lower shift lever	• Replace shift tube

taching the MacPherson strut to the lower control arm. Push the arm downward slightly, and then remove the strut assembly.

7. The strut must be mounted in a vise for further disassembly. It must not be mounted by the shock absorber shell as this part is ma-chined perfectly round and can easily be distorted. A special tool is available from Toyota for this purpose, or you can make some sort of flange that will bolt to the bottom (where the control arm attaches).

8. Using a special tool designed for this pur-

Troubleshooting the Turn Signal Switch

Problem	Cause	Solution
Turn signal will not cancel	• Loose switch mounting screws • Switch or anchor bosses broken • Broken, missing or out of position detent, or cancelling spring	• Tighten screws • Replace switch • Reposition springs or replace switch as required
Turn signal difficult to operate	• Turn signal lever loose • Switch yoke broken or distorted • Loose or misplaced springs • Foreign parts and/or materials in switch • Switch mounted loosely	• Tighten mounting screws • Replace switch • Reposition springs or replace switch • Remove foreign parts and/or material • Tighten mounting screws
Turn signal will not indicate lane change	• Broken lane change pressure pad or spring hanger • Broken, missing or misplaced lane change spring • Jammed wires	• Replace switch • Replace or reposition as required • Loosen mounting screws, reposition wires and retighten screws
Turn signal will not stay in turn position	• Foreign material or loose parts impeding movement of switch yoke • Defective switch	• Remove material and/or parts • Replace switch
Hazard switch cannot be pulled out	• Foreign material between hazard support cancelling leg and yoke	• Remove foreign material. No foreign material impeding function of hazard switch—replace turn signal switch.
No turn signal lights	• Inoperative turn signal flasher • Defective or blown fuse • Loose chassis to column harness connector • Disconnect column to chassis connector. Connect new switch to chassis and operate switch by hand. If vehicle lights now operate normally, signal switch is inoperative • If vehicle lights do not operate, check chassis wiring for opens, grounds, etc.	• Replace turn signal flasher • Replace fuse • Connect securely • Replace signal switch • Repair chassis wiring as required
Instrument panel turn indicator lights on but not flashing	• Burned out or damaged front or rear turn signal bulb • If vehicle lights do not operate, check light sockets for high resistance connections, the chassis wiring for opens, grounds, etc. • Inoperative flasher • Loose chassis to column harness connection • Inoperative turn signal switch • To determine if turn signal switch is defective, substitute new switch into circuit and operate switch by hand. If the vehicle's lights operate normally, signal switch is inoperative.	• Replace bulb • Repair chassis wiring as required • Replace flasher • Connect securely • Replace turn signal switch • Replace turn signal switch
Stop light not on when turn indicated	• Loose column to chassis connection • Disconnect column to chassis connector. Connect new switch into system without removing old.	• Connect securely • Replace signal switch

Troubleshooting the Turn Signal Switch (cont.)

Problem	Cause	Solution
Stop light not on when turn indicated (cont.)	Operate switch by hand. If brake lights work with switch in the turn position, signal switch is defective. • If brake lights do not work, check connector to stop light sockets for grounds, opens, etc.	• Repair connector to stop light circuits using service manual as guide
Turn indicator panel lights not flashing	• Burned out bulbs • High resistance to ground at bulb socket • Opens, ground in wiring harness from front turn signal bulb socket to indicator lights	• Replace bulbs • Replace socket • Locate and repair as required
Turn signal lights flash very slowly	• High resistance ground at light sockets • Incorrect capacity turn signal flasher or bulb • If flashing rate is still extremely slow, check chassis wiring harness from the connector to light sockets for high resistance • Loose chassis to column harness connection • Disconnect column to chassis connector. Connect new switch into system without removing old. Operate switch by hand. If flashing occurs at normal rate, the signal switch is defective.	• Repair high resistance grounds at light sockets • Replace turn signal flasher or bulb • Locate and repair as required • Connect securely • Replace turn signal switch
Hazard signal lights will not flash—turn signal functions normally	• Blow fuse • Inoperative hazard warning flasher • Loose chassis-to-column harness connection • Disconnect column to chassis connector. Connect new switch into system without removing old. Depress the hazard warning lights. If they now work normally, turn signal switch is defective. • If lights do not flash, check wiring harness "K" lead for open between hazard flasher and connector. If open, fuse block is defective	• Replace fuse • Replace hazard warning flasher in fuse panel • Conect securely • Replace turn signal switch • Repair or replace brown wire or connector as required

Troubleshooting the Ignition Switch

Problem	Cause	Solution
Ignition switch electrically inoperative	• Loose or defective switch connector • Feed wire open (fusible link) • Defective ignition switch	• Tighten or replace connector • Repair or replace • Replace ignition switch
Engine will not crank	• Ignition switch not adjusted properly	• Adjust switch
Ignition switch wil not actuate mechanically	• Defective ignition switch • Defective lock sector • Defective remote rod	• Replace switch • Replace lock sector • Replace remote rod
Ignition switch cannot be adjusted correctly	• Remote rod deformed	• Repair, straighten or replace

Troubleshooting the Manual Steering Gear

Problem	Cause	Solution
Hard or erratic steering	• Incorrect tire pressure	• Inflate tires to recommended pressures
	• Insufficient or incorrect lubrication	• Lubricate as required (refer to Maintenance Section)
	• Suspension, or steering linkage parts damaged or misaligned	• Repair or replace parts as necessary
	• Improper front wheel alignment	• Adjust incorrect wheel alignment angles
	• Incorrect steering gear adjustment	• Adjust steering gear
	• Sagging springs	• Replace springs
Play or looseness in steering	• Steering wheel loose	• Inspect shaft spines and repair as necessary. Tighten attaching nut and stake in place.
	• Steering linkage or attaching parts loose or worn	• Tighten, adjust, or replace faulty components
	• Pitman arm loose	• Inspect shaft splines and repair as necessary. Tighten attaching nut and stake in place
	• Steering gear attaching bolts loose	• Tighten bolts
	• Loose or worn wheel bearings	• Adjust or replace bearings
	• Steering gear adjustment incorrect or parts badly worn	• Adjust gear or replace defective parts
Wheel shimmy or tramp	• Improper tire pressure	• Inflate tires to recommended pressures
	• Wheels, tires, or brake rotors out-of-balance or out-of-round	• Inspect and replace or balance parts
	• Inoperative, worn, or loose shock absorbers or mounting parts	• Repair or replace shocks or mountings
	• Loose or worn steering or suspension parts	• Tighten or replace as necessary
	• Loose or worn wheel bearings	• Adjust or replace bearings
	• Incorrect steering gear adjustments	• Adjust steering gear
	• Incorrect front wheel alignment	• Correct front wheel alignment
Tire wear	• Improper tire pressure	• Inflate tires to recommended pressures
	• Failure to rotate tires	• Rotate tires
	• Brakes grabbing	• Adjust or repair brakes
	• Incorrect front wheel alignment	• Align incorrect angles
	• Broken or damaged steering and suspension parts	• Repair or replace defective parts
	• Wheel runout	• Replace faulty wheel
	• Excessive speed on turns	• Make driver aware of conditions
Vehicle leads to one side	• Improper tire pressures	• Inflate tires to recommended pressures
	• Front tires with uneven tread depth, wear pattern, or different cord design (i.e., one bias ply and one belted or radial tire on front wheels)	• Install tires of same cord construction and reasonably even tread depth, design, and wear pattern
	• Incorrect front wheel alignment	• Align incorrect angles
	• Brakes dragging	• Adjust or repair brakes
	• Pulling due to uneven tire construction	• Replace faulty tire

pose, the spring must be compressed to there is no tension on the upper seat.

NOTE: *Failure to fully compress the spring and hold it securely before performing the next step is extremely hazardous.*

9. Hold the shock absorber seat (at top) with a large spanner wrench, and remove the nut from the top of the shock absorber.

10. Remove upper support, upper seat, dust cover, and spring.

11. Install in reverse order. Inspect all parts carefully for wear or distortion, and replace as

Troubleshooting the Power Steering Gear

Problem	Cause	Solution
Hissing noise in steering gear	• There is some noise in all power steering systems. One of the most common is a hissing sound most evident at standstill parking. There is no relationship between this noise and performance of the steering. Hiss may be expected when steering wheel is at end of travel or when slowly turning at standstill.	• Slight hiss is normal and in no way affects steering. Do not replace valve unless hiss is extremely objectionable. A replacement valve will also exhibit slight noise and is not always a cure. Investigate clearance around flexible coupling rivets. Be sure steering shaft and gear are aligned so flexible coupling rotates in a flat plane and is not distorted as shaft rotates. Any metal-to-metal contacts through flexible coupling will transmit valve hiss into passenger compartment through the steering column.
Rattle or chuckle noise in steering gear	• Gear loose on frame	• Check gear-to-frame mounting screws. Tighten screws to 88 N·m (65 foot pounds) torque.
	• Steering linkage looseness	• Check linkage pivot points for wear. Replace if necessary.
	• Pressure hose touching other parts of car	• Adjust hose position. Do not bend tubing by hand.
	• Loose pitman shaft over center adjustment	• Adjust to specifications
	NOTE: A slight rattle may occur on turns because of increased clearance off the "high point." This is normal and clearance must not be reduced below specified limits to eliminate this slight rattle.	
	• Loose pitman arm	• Tighten pitman arm nut to specifications
Squawk noise in steering gear when turning or recovering from a turn	• Damper O-ring on valve spool cut	• Replace damper O-ring
Poor return of steering wheel to center	• Tires not properly inflated	• Inflate to specified pressure
	• Lack of lubrication in linkage and ball joints	• Lube linkage and ball joints
	• Lower coupling flange rubbing against steering gear adjuster plug	• Loosen pinch bolt and assemble properly
	• Steering gear to column misalignment	• Align steering column
	• Improper front wheel alignment	• Check and adjust as necessary
	• Steering linkage binding	• Replace pivots
	• Ball joints binding	• Replace ball joints
	• Steering wheel rubbing against housing	• Align housing
	• Tight or frozen steering shaft bearings	• Replace bearings
	• Sticking or plugged valve spool	• Remove and clean or replace valve
	• Steering gear adjustments over specifications	• Check adjustment with gear out of car. Adjust as required.
	• Kink in return hose	• Replace hose
Car leads to one side or the other (keep in mind road condition and wind. Test car in both directions on flat road)	• Front end misaligned	• Adjust to specifications
	• Unbalanced steering gear valve	• Replace valve
	NOTE: If this is cause, steering effort will be very light in direction of lead and normal or heavier in opposite direction	

Troubleshooting the Power Steering Gear (cont.)

Problem	Cause	Solution
Momentary increase in effort when turning wheel fast to right or left	• Low oil level • Pump belt slipping • High internal leakage	• Add power steering fluid as required • Tighten or replace belt • Check pump pressure. (See pressure test)
Steering wheel surges or jerks when turning with engine running especially during parking	• Low oil level • Loose pump belt • Steering linkage hitting engine oil pan at full turn • Insufficient pump pressure • Pump flow control valve sticking	• Fill as required • Adjust tension to specification • Correct clearance • Check pump pressure. (See pressure test). Replace relief valve if defective. • Inspect for varnish or damage, replace if necessary
Excessive wheel kickback or loose steering	• Air in system • Steering gear loose on frame • Steering linkage joints worn enough to be loose • Worn poppet valve • Loose thrust bearing preload adjustment • Excessive overcenter lash	• Add oil to pump reservoir and bleed by operating steering. Check hose connectors for proper torque and adjust as required. • Tighten attaching screws to specified torque • Replace loose pivots • Replace poppet valve • Adjust to specification with gear out of vehicle • Adjust to specification with gear out of car
Hard steering or lack of assist	• Loose pump belt • Low oil level **NOTE:** Low oil level will also result in excessive pump noise • Steering gear to column misalignment • Lower coupling flange rubbing against steering gear adjuster plug • Tires not properly inflated	• Adjust belt tension to specification • Fill to proper level. If excessively low, check all lines and joints for evidence of external leakage. Tighten loose connectors. • Align steering column • Loosen pinch bolt and assemble properly • Inflate to recommended pressure
Foamy milky power steering fluid, low fluid level and possible low pressure	• Air in the fluid, and loss of fluid due to internal pump leakage causing overflow	• Check for leak and correct. Bleed system. Extremely cold temperatures will cause system aeriation should the oil level be low. If oil level is correct and pump still foams, remove pump from vehicle and separate reservoir from housing. Check welsh plug and housing for cracks. If plug is loose or housing is cracked, replace housing.
Low pressure due to steering pump	• Flow control valve stuck or inoperative • Pressure plate not flat against cam ring	• Remove burrs or dirt or replace. Flush system. • Correct
Low pressure due to steering gear	• Pressure loss in cylinder due to worn piston ring or badly worn housing bore • Leakage at valve rings, valve body-to-worm seal	• Remove gear from car for disassembly and inspection of ring and housing bore • Remove gear from car for disassembly and replace seals

Troubleshooting the Power Steering Pump

Problem	Cause	Solution
Chirp noise in steering pump	• Loose belt	• Adjust belt tension to specification
Belt squeal (particularly noticeable at full wheel travel and stand still parking)	• Loose belt	• Adjust belt tension to specification
Growl noise in steering pump	• Excessive back pressure in hoses or steering gear caused by restriction	• Locate restriction and correct. Replace part if necessary.
Growl noise in steering pump (particularly noticeable at stand still parking)	• Scored pressure plates, thrust plate or rotor • Extreme wear of cam ring	• Replace parts and flush system • Replace parts
Groan noise in steering pump	• Low oil level • Air in the oil. Poor pressure hose connection.	• Fill reservoir to proper level • Tighten connector to specified torque. Bleed system by operating steering from right to left—full turn.
Rattle noise in steering pump	• Vanes not installed properly • Vanes sticking in rotor slots	• Install properly • Free up by removing burrs, varnish, or dirt
Swish noise in steering pump	• Defective flow control valve	• Replace part
Whine noise in steering pump	• Pump shaft bearing scored	• Replace housing and shaft. Flush system.
Hard steering or lack of assist	• Loose pump belt • Low oil level in reservoir **NOTE:** Low oil level will also result in excessive pump noise • Steering gear to column misalignment • Lower coupling flange rubbing against steering gear adjuster plug • Tires not properly inflated	• Adjust belt tension to specification • Fill to proper level. If excessively low, check all lines and joints for evidence of external leakage. Tighten loose connectors. • Align steering column • Loosen pinch bolt and assemble properly • Inflate to recommended pressure
Foaming milky power steering fluid, low fluid level and possible low pressure	• Air in the fluid, and loss of fluid due to internal pump leakage causing overflow	• Check for leaks and correct. Bleed system. Extremely cold temperatures will cause system aeriation should the oil level be low. If oil level is correct and pump still foams, remove pump from vehicle and separate reservoir from body. Check welsh plug and body for cracks. If plug is loose or body is cracked, replace body.
Low pump pressure	• Flow control valve stuck or inoperative • Pressure plate not flat against cam ring	• Remove burrs or dirt or replace. Flush system. • Correct
Momentary increase in effort when turning wheel fast to right or left	• Low oil level in pump • Pump belt slipping • High internal leakage	• Add power steering fluid as required • Tighten or replace belt • Check pump pressure. (See pressure test)
Steering wheel surges or jerks when turning with engine running especially during parking	• Low oil level • Loose pump belt • Steering linkage hitting engine oil pan at full turn • Insufficient pump pressure	• Fill as required • Adjust tension to specification • Correct clearance • Check pump pressure. (See pressure test). Replace flow control valve if defective.

Troubleshooting the Power Steering Pump (cont.)

Problem	Cause	Solution
Steering wheel surges or jerks when turning with engine running especially during parking (cont.)	• Sticking flow control valve	• Inspect for varnish or damage, replace if necessary
Excessive wheel kickback or loose steering	• Air in system	• Add oil to pump reservoir and bleed by operating steering. Check hose connectors for proper torque and adjust as required.
Low pump pressure	• Extreme wear of cam ring • Scored pressure plate, thrust plate, or rotor • Vanes not installed properly • Vanes sticking in rotor slots • Cracked or broken thrust or pressure plate	• Replace parts. Flush system. • Replace parts. Flush system. • Install properly • Freeup by removing burrs, varnish, or dirt • Replace part

necessary. Pack multipurpose grease into the bearing on the suspension support. Torque a *new* rod nut to 30–40 ft.lb.; the upper support nuts to 45–50 ft.lb.; the lower control arm nuts are torqued to 152 ft.lb.

Lower Ball Joints
INSPECTION

Jack up the lower suspension arm. Check the front wheel play. Replace the lower ball joint if the play at the wheel rim exceeds 1mm vertical motion or 2mm horizontal motion. Be sure that the dust covers are not torn and they are securely glued to the ball joints.

REMOVAL AND INSTALLATION

NOTE: *On models equipped with upper and lower ball joints-if both ball joints are to be removed, always remove the lower and then the upper ball joint.*

1. Raise the front of the vehicle and support it with jackstands. Remove the wheel.
2. Remove the two bolts attaching the ball joint to the steering knuckle.
3. Remove the stabilizer nut, retainer and cushion.
4. Jack up the opposite wheel until the body of the car just lifts off the jackstand.
5. Loosen the lower control arm mounting bolt, wiggle the arm back and forth and then remove the bolt. Disconnect the lower control arm from the stabilizer bar.

NOTE: *When removing the lower control arm, be careful not to lose the caster adjustment spacer.*

6. Carefully mount the lower control arm in a vise and then, using a ball joint removal tool,

disconnect the ball joint removal tool, disconnect the ball joint from the arm.

7. Installation is in the reverse order of removal. Please note the following:

a. Tighten the ball joint-to-control arm nut to 67 ft.lb. and use a new cotter pin.

b. Tighten the steering knuckle-to-control arm bolts to 83 ft.lb.

c. Before tightening the stabilizer bar nuts, mount the wheels and lower the car. Bounce the car several times to settle the suspension and then tighten the stabilizer bolts to 66–90 ft.lb. Tighten the control arm-to-body bolts to 83 ft.lb.

d. Check the front end alignment.

Lower Control Arm
REMOVAL AND INSTALLATION

1. Raise and support the front end with jackstands under the frame.
2. Remove the two bolts holding the ball joint to the knuckle. Disconnect the lower arm from the knuckle.
3. Disconnect the stabilizer from the lower arm.
4. Unbolt and remove the arm.
5. Installation is the reverse of removal. Observe the following torques:
•Ball joint nut: 67 ft.lb.
•Steering knuckle-to-arm: 83 ft.lb.
•Stabilizer bar nut: 86 ft.lb.
•Lower arm-to-body: 83 ft.lb.

Front End Alignment

Front end alignment measurements require the use of special equipment. Before measuring alignment or attempting to adjust it, always check the following points:

1. Be sure that the tires are properly inflated.

2. Ensure that the wheels are properly balanced.

3. Check the ball joints to determine if they are worn or loose.

4. Check front wheel bearing adjustment.

5. Be sure that the car is on a level surface.

6. Check all suspension parts for tightness.

CASTER AND CAMBER ADJUSTMENTS

NOTE: *Caster and camber adjustments do not apply to vehicles with MacPherson strut front suspension. If measurements are incorrect, there is distortion or severe wear in the system and part(s) must be replaced. Toe-in is adjusted as described below.*

TOE-IN ADJUSTMENT

Measure the toe-in. Adjust it, if necessary, by loosening the tie rod end clamping bolts and rotating the tie rod adjusting tubes. Tighten the clamping bolts when finished.

NOTE: *Both tie rods should be the same length. If they are not, perform the adjustment until the toe-in is within specifications and the tie rod ends are equal in length.*

REAR SUSPENSION

MacPherson Struts

REMOVAL AND INSTALLATION

1. On 4-door sedan, remove the package tray and vent duct.

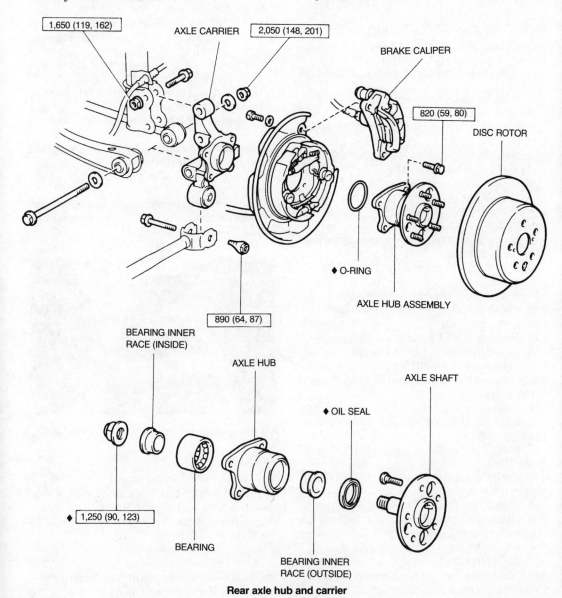

Rear axle hub and carrier

2. On hatchback, remove the speaker grilles.

3. Disconnect the brake line from the wheel cylinder.

4. Remove the brake line from the brake hose.

5. Disconnect the brake hose from its bracket on the strut.

6. Loosen, but do not remove, the nut holding the suspension support to the strut.

7. Unbolt the strut from the rear arm.

8. Unbolt the strut from the body.

9. Installation is the reverse of removal. Torque the strut-to-body bolts to 17 ft.lb.; the strut-to-rear arm bolts to 105 ft.lb.; suspension support-to-strut nut to 36 ft.lb.

10. Refill and bleed the brake system.

Rear Axle Hub and Bearing
REMOVAL AND INSTALLATION

1. Raise and support the rear end on jackstands.

2. Remove the rear wheels.

3. Remove the brake drums.

4. Disconnect the brake line from the wheel cylinder and plug it to prevent fluid loss.

5. Remove the four hub-to-carrier bolts and slide the hub off. Remove the O-ring.

6. Unbolt the carrier from the strut.

7. Unbolt the carrier from the suspension arms.

8. Remove the carrier.

9. Using a cold chisel, loosen the staked part of the hub nut and remove the nut.

10. Using a puller, remove the axle shaft from the hub.

11. Remove the bearing inner race.

12. Using a puller, remove the bearing outer race from the shaft.

13. Remove the oil seal.

14. Drive the bearing from the hub.

15. Position a new outer race on the bearing and press a new seal into the hub. Coat the seal lip with grease.

16. Position a new inner race on the bearing and press the hub and bearing assembly onto the shaft.

17. Install the nut and torque it to 90 ft.lb. Stake the nut.

18. Position the carrier on the strut tube and torque the bolts to 119 ft.lb.

19. Install the bolts attaching the carrier to the suspension arms, finger tight only at this point. Make sure that the lip of the nut is in the hole in the arm.

20. Insert the strut rod-to-carrier bolt so that the lip of the nut is in the groove of the rod.

21. Install a new O-ring on the carrier.

22. Install the hub and backing plate. Torque the bolts to 59 ft.lb.

23. Connect the brake line, install the drum and bleed the brakes.

24. Lower the car to the ground. Bounce it a few times to set the suspension and torque the suspension arm fasteners to 64 ft.lb.

STEERING

Steering Wheel
REMOVAL AND INSTALLATION
Three-Spoke

CAUTION: *Do not attempt to remove or install the steering wheel by hammering on it. Damage to the energy absorbing steering column could result.*

1. Unfasten the horn and turn signal multiconnector(s) at the base of the steering column shroud.

2. Loosen the trim pad retaining screws from the back side of the steering wheel.

3. Lift the trim pad and horn button assembly(ies) from the wheel.

4. Remove the steering wheel hub retaining nut.

5. Scratch matchmarks on the hub and shaft to aid in correct installation.

6. Use a steering wheel puller to remove the steering wheel.

7. Installation is performed in the reverse order of removal. Tighten the wheel retaining nut to 15–22 ft.lb.

Removing the four-spoke wheel with a puller

Two-Spoke

The two-spoke steering wheel is removed in the same manner as the three-spoke, except that the trim pad should be pried off with a screwdriver. Remove the pad by lifting it toward the top of the wheel.

Four-Spoke

CAUTION: *Do not attempt to remove or install the steering wheel by hammering on it.*

Damage to the energy absorbing steering column could result.

1. Unfasten the horn and turn signal multiconnectors at the base of the steering column shroud (underneath the instrument panel).

2. Gently pry the center emblem off the front of the steering wheel.

3. Insert a wrench through the hole and remove the steering wheel retaining nut.

4. Scratch matchmarks on the hub and shaft to aid installation.

5. Use a steering wheel puller to remove the steering wheel.

6. Installation is the reverse of removal. Tighten the steering wheel retaining nut to 15–22 lbs.

Turn Signal Switch
REMOVAL AND INSTALLATION

1. Disconnect the negative (–) battery cable.

2. Remove the steering wheel, as outlined in the appropriate preceding section.

3. Unfasten the screws which secure the upper and lower steering column shroud halves.

4. Unfasten the screws which retain the turn signal switch and remove the switch from the column.

5. Installation is performed in the reverse order of removal.

Ignition Lock/Switch
REMOVAL AND INSTALLATION

1. Disconnect the negative battery cable.

2. Unfasten the ignition switch multiconnector underneath the instrument panel.

3. Remove the screws which secure the upper and lower halves of the steering column cover.

4. Turn the lock cylinder to the ACC position with the ignition key.

5. Push the lock cylinder stop in with a small, round object (cotter pin, punch, etc).

NOTE: *On some models it may be necessary to remove the steering wheel and turn signal switch first.*

6. Withdraw the lock cylinder from the lock housing while depressing the stop tab.

7. To remove the ignition switch, unfasten its securing screws and withdraw the switch from the lock housing.

8. Align the locking cam with the hole in the ignition switch and insert the switch in the lock housing.

9. Secure the switch with its screw(s).

10. Make sure that both the lock cylinder and the column lock are in the ACC position. Slide the cylinder into the lock housing until the stop tab engages the hole in the lock.

11. The rest of installation is performed in the reverse order of removal.

Steering Gear
REMOVAL & INSTALLATION

1. Open the hood. Remove the two set bolts, and remove the sliding yoke from between the steering rack housing and the steering column shaft.

2. Remove the cotter pin and nut holding the knuckle arm to the tie rod end. Using a tie rod puller, disconnect the tie rod end from the knuckle arm.

3. Tag and disconnect the power steering lines if equipped. Remove the steering housing brackets and remove the housing.

4. Installation is the reverse of removal. Torque the rack housing mounting bolts to 43 ft.lb. and the tie rod set nuts to 36 ft.lb. Use a new cotter pin.

Power Steering Pump
REMOVAL AND INSTALLATION

1. Remove the fan shroud.

2. Unfasten the nut from the center of the pump pulley.

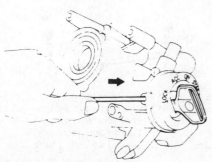

Ignition lock/switch removal

Power steering pump removal showing (1) front mounting bolts and (2) pump

NOTE: *Use the drive belt as a brake to keep the pulley from rotating.*

3. Withdraw the drive belt.

4. Remove the pulley and the woodruff key from the pump shaft.

5. Detach the intake and outlet hoses from the pump reservoir.

NOTE: *Tie the hose ends up high, so that the fluid cannot flow out of them. Drain or plug the pump to prevent fluid leakage.*

6. Remove the bolt from the rear mounting brace.

7. Remove the front bracket bolts and withdraw the pump.

8. Installation is performed in the reverse order of removal. Note the following, however:

    a. Tighten the pump pulley mounting bolt to 25–39 ft.lb.

    b. Adjust the pump drive belt tension. The belt should deflect 8–10mm when 22 lbs. pressure is applied midway between the air pump and the power steering pump.

    c. Fill the reservoir with Dexron®II automatic transmission fluid. Bleed the air from the system, as detailed following.

BLEEDING

1. Raise the front of the car and support it securely with jackstands.

2. Fill the pump reservoir with DEXRON®II automatic transmission fluid.

3. Rotate the steering wheel from lock-to-lock several times. Add fluid as necessary.

4. With the steering wheel turned fully to one lock, crank the starter while watching the fluid level in the reservoir.

NOTE: *Disconnect the high tension lead from the coil. Do not start the engine. Operate the starter with a remote starter switch or have an assistant do it from inside of the car. Do not run the starter for prolonged periods.*

5. Repeat Step 4 with the steering wheel turned to the opposite lock.

6. Start the engine. With the engine idling, turn the steering wheel from lock-to-lock two or three times.

7. Lower the front of the car and repeat Step 6.

8. Center the wheel at the midpoint of its travel. Stop the engine.

9. The fluid level should not have risen more than 5mm. If it does, repeat Step 7 again.

10. Check for fluid leakage.

Steering Linkage
REMOVAL AND INSTALLATION

1. Raise the front of the vehicle and support it with jackstands.

CAUTION: *Be sure that the vehicle is securely supported. Do not support it by the lower control arms.*

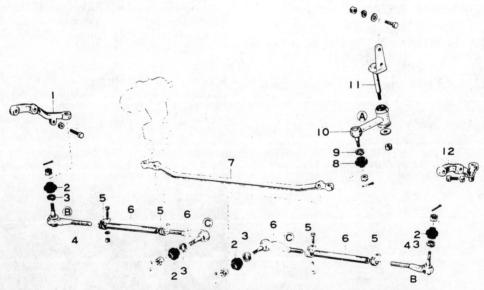

1. Steering knuckle arm—right-hand	6. Tie-rod adjusting tube	11. Idler arm support
2. Dust seal	7. Steering relay rod	12. Steering knuckle arm—left-hand
3. Clip	8. Dust seal	A. Idler arm assembly
4. Tie-rod end	9. Lock ring	B. Tie-rod end assembly
5. Tie-rod end clamp	10. Steering idler arm	C. Tie-rod adjusting tube

Steering linkage components (typical)

Wheel Alignment Specifications

Year	Caster		Camber		Toe-in (in.)	Steering Axis inclination	Wheel Pivot Ratio (deg)	
	Range (deg)	Pref Setting (deg)	Range (deg)	Pref Setting (deg)			Inner Wheel	Outer Wheel
1983–85	①	②	0–1P	½P	⑤	12½P	—	—
1986	⁷⁄₁₆P–1¾P	1P	³⁄₁₆N–1¼P	⁹⁄₁₆P	0–0.16	12½	38	30

① Man. Str.: ½P–1½P
   Pwr. Str.: 2P–3P
② Man. Str.: 1P
   Pwr. Str.: 2½P
③ Man. Str.: 0
   Pwr. Str.: 0.08

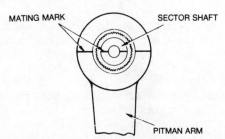

MATING MARK   SECTOR SHAFT

PITMAN ARM

Align the marks on the pitman arm and the sector shaft

2. Remove the gravel shields if they prevent access to the steering linkage.

3. Unfasten the nut and, using a puller, disconnect the pitman arm from the sector shaft.

4. Unfasten the idler arm support securing bolts and remove the support from the frame.

5. Detach the tie rod ends with a puller after removing the cotter pins and castellated nuts.

6. Remove the steering linkage as an assembly.

7. Installation is performed in the reverse order of removal. Note the following however:

a. Tighten the linkage parts to the torque figures given in the Steering Linkage Torque Specifications chart.

b. Align the marks on pitman arm and sector shaft before installing the pitman arm.

c. The self locking nut used on some models, on the idler arm, may be reused if it cannot be turned by hand when fitted to the bolt.

d. Adjust the toe-in to specifications after completing the steering linkage installation procedure.

Brakes

BRAKE SYSTEM

Understanding the Brakes

HYDRAULIC SYSTEM

Basic Operating Principles

Hydraulic systems are used to actuate the brakes of all modern automobiles. The system transports the power required to force the frictional surfaces of the braking system together from the pedal to the individual brake units at each wheel. A hydraulic system is used for two reasons. First, fluid under pressure can be carried to all parts of an automobile by small hoses, some of which are flexible, without taking up a significant amount of room or posing routing problems. Second, a great mechanical advantage can be given to the brake pedal end of the system, and the foot pressure required to actuate the brakes can be reduced by making the surface area of the master cylinder pistons smaller than that of any of the pistons in the wheel cylinders or calipers.

The master cylinder consists of a fluid reservoir and either a single or double cylinder and piston assembly. Double type master cylinders are designed to separate the front and rear braking systems hydraulically in case of a leak.

Steel lines carry the brake fluid to a point on the vehicle's frame near each of the vehicle's wheels. The fluid is then carried to the wheel cylinders by flexible tubes in order to allow for suspension and steering movements.

Each wheel cylinder contains two pistons, one at either end, which push outward in opposite directions. In disc brake systems, the cylinders are part of the calipers. One or four cylinders are used to force the brake pads against the disc, but all cylinders contain one piston only. All pistons employ some type of seal, usually made of rubber, to minimize fluid leakage. A rubber dust boot seals the outer end of the cylinder against dust and dirt. The boot fits around the outer end of the piston on disc brake calipers, and around the brake actuating rod on wheel cylinders.

The hydraulic system operates as follows: When at rest, the entire system, from the piston(s) in the master cylinder to those in the wheel cylinders or calipers, is full of brake fluid. Upon application of the brake pedal, fluid trapped in front of the master cylinder piston(s) is forced through the lines to the wheel cylinders. Here, it forces the pistons outward, in the case of drum brakes, and inward toward the disc, in the case of disc brakes. The motion of the pistons is opposed by return springs mounted outside the cylinders in drum brakes, and by internal springs or spring seals, in disc brakes.

Upon release of the brake pedal, a spring located inside the master cylinder immediately returns the master cylinder pistons to the normal position. The pistons contain check valves and the master cylinder has compensating ports drilled in it. These are uncovered as the pistons reach their normal position. The piston check valves allow fluid to flow toward the wheel cylinders or calipers as the pistons withdraw. Then, as the return springs force the brake pads or shoes into the released position, the excess fluid reservoir through the compensating ports. It is during the time the pedal is in the released position that any fluid that has leaked out of the system will be replaced through the compensating ports.

Dual circuit master cylinders employ two pistons, located one behind the other, in the same cylinder. The primary piston is actuated directly by mechanical linkage from the brake pedal. The secondary piston is actuated by fluid trapped between the two pistons. If a leak develops in front of the secondary piston, it moves forward until it bottoms against the front of the master cylinder, and the fluid trapped between the pistons will operate the rear brakes. If the rear brakes develop a leak, the primary piston will move forward until direct contact with the secondary piston takes place, and it will force the secondary piston to actuate the front brakes. In either case, the brake pedal moves farther when the brakes are applied, and less braking power is available.

All dual circuit systems use a switch to warn the driver when only half of the brake system is operational. This switch is located in a valve body which is mounted on the firewall or the frame below the master cylinder. A hydraulic piston receives pressure from both circuits, each circuit's pressure being applied to one end of the piston. When the pressures are in balance, the piston remains stationary. When one circuit has a leak, however, the greater pressure in that circuit during application of the brakes will push the piston to one side, closing the switch and activating the brake warning light.

In disc brake systems, this valve body also contains a metering valve and, in some cases, a proportioning valve. The metering valve keeps pressure from traveling to the disc brakes on the front wheels until the brake shoes on the rear wheels have contacted the drums, ensuring that the front brakes will never be used alone. The proportioning valve controls the pressure to the rear brakes to avoid rear wheel lock-up during very hard braking.

Warning lights may be tested by depressing the brake pedal and holding it while opening one of the wheel cylinder bleeder screws. If this does not cause the light to go on, substitute a new lamp, make continuity checks, and, finally, replace the switch as necessary.

The hydraulic system may be checked for leaks by applying pressure to the pedal gradually and steadily. If the pedal sinks very slowly to the floor, the system has a leak. This is not to be confused with a springy or spongy feel due to the compression of air within the lines. If the system leaks, there will be a gradual change in the position of the pedal with a constant pressure.

Check for leaks along all lines and at wheel cylinders. If no external leaks are apparent, the problem is inside the master cylinder.

DISC BRAKES

Basic Operating Principles

Instead of the traditional expanding brakes that press outward against a circular drum, disc brake systems utilize a disc (rotor) with brake pads positioned on either side of it. Braking effect is achieved in a manner similar to the way you would squeeze a spinning phonograph record between your fingers. The disc (rotor) is a casting with cooling fins between the two braking surfaces. This enables air to circulate between the braking surfaces making them less sensitive to heat buildup and more resistant to fade. Dirt and water do not affect braking action since contaminants are thrown off by the centrifugal action of the rotor or scraped off the by the pads. Also, the equal clamping action of the two brake pads tends to ensure uniform, straight line stops. Disc brakes are inherently self-adjusting.

There are three general types of disc brake:
1. A fixed caliper.
2. A floating caliper.
3. A sliding caliper.

The fixed caliper design uses two pistons mounted on either side of the rotor (in each side of the caliper). The caliper is mounted rigidly and does not move.

The sliding and floating designs are quite similar. In fact, these two types are often lumped together. In both designs, the pad on the inside of the rotor is moved into contact with the rotor by hydraulic force. The caliper, which is not held in a fixed position, moves slightly, bringing the outside pad into contact with the rotor. There are various methods of attaching floating calipers. Some pivot at the bottom or top, and some slide on mounting bolts. In any event, the end result is the same.

DRUM BRAKES

Basic Operating Principles

Drum brakes employ two brake shoes mounted on a stationary backing plate. These shoes are positioned inside a circular drum which rotates with the wheel assembly. The shoes are held in place by springs. This allows them to slide toward the drums (when they are applied) while keeping the linings and drums in alignment. The shoes are actuated by a wheel cylinder which is mounted at the top of the backing plate. When the brakes are applied, hydraulic pressure forces the wheel cylinder's actuating links outward. Since these links bear directly against the top of the brake shoes, the tops of the shoes are then forced against the inner side of the drum. This action forces the bottoms of the two shoes to contact the brake drum by rotating the entire assembly slightly (known as servo action). When pressure within the wheel cylinder is relaxed, return springs pull the shoes back away from the drum.

Most modern drum brakes are designed to adjust themselves during application when the vehicle is moving in reverse. This motion

Troubleshooting the Brake System

Problem	Cause	Solution
Low brake pedal (excessive pedal travel required for braking action.)	• Excessive clearance between rear linings and drums caused by inoperative automatic adjusters	• Make 10 to 15 alternate forward and reverse brake stops to adjust brakes. If brake pedal does not come up, repair or replace adjuster parts as necessary.
	• Worn rear brakelining	• Inspect and replace lining if worn beyond minimum thickness specification
	• Bent, distorted brakeshoes, front or rear	• Replace brakeshoes in axle sets
	• Air in hydraulic system	• Remove air from system. Refer to Brake Bleeding.
Low brake pedal (pedal may go to floor with steady pressure applied.)	• Fluid leak in hydraulic system	• Fill master cylinder to fill line; have helper apply brakes and check calipers, wheel cylinders, differential valve tubes, hoses and fittings for leaks. Repair or replace as necessary.
	• Air in hydraulic system	• Remove air from system. Refer to Brake Bleeding.
	• Incorrect or non-recommended brake fluid (fluid evaporates at below normal temp).	• Flush hydraulic system with clean brake fluid. Refill with correct-type fluid.
	• Master cylinder piston seals worn, or master cylinder bore is scored, worn or corroded	• Repair or replace master cylinder
Low brake pedal (pedal goes to floor on first application—o.k. on subsequent applications.)	• Disc brake pads sticking on abutment surfaces of anchor plate. Caused by a build-up of dirt, rust, or corrosion on abutment surfaces	• Clean abutment surfaces
Fading brake pedal (pedal height decreases with steady pressure applied.)	• Fluid leak in hydraulic system	• Fill master cylinder reservoirs to fill mark, have helper apply brakes, check calipers, wheel cylinders, differential valve, tubes, hoses, and fittings for fluid leaks. Repair or replace parts as necessary.
	• Master cylinder piston seals worn, or master cylinder bore is scored, worn or corroded	• Repair or replace master cylinder
Decreasing brake pedal travel (pedal travel required for braking action decreases and may be accompanied by a hard pedal.)	• Caliper or wheel cylinder pistons sticking or seized	• Repair or replace the calipers, or wheel cylinders
	• Master cylinder compensator ports blocked (preventing fluid return to reservoirs) or pistons sticking or seized in master cylinder bore	• Repair or replace the master cylinder
	• Power brake unit binding internally	• Test unit according to the following procedure: (a) Shift transmission into neutral and start engine (b) Increase engine speed to 1500 rpm, close throttle and fully depress brake pedal (c) Slow release brake pedal and stop engine (d) Have helper remove vacuum check valve and hose from power unit. Observe for backward movement of brake pedal. (e) If the pedal moves backward, the power unit has an internal bind—replace power unit

Troubleshooting the Brake System (cont.)

Problem	Cause	Solution
Spongy brake pedal (pedal has abnormally soft, springy, spongy feel when depressed.)	• Air in hydraulic system • Brakeshoes bent or distorted • Brakelining not yet seated with drums and rotors • Rear drum brakes not properly adjusted	• Remove air from system. Refer to Brake Bleeding. • Replace brakeshoes • Burnish brakes • Adjust brakes
Hard brake pedal (excessive pedal pressure required to stop vehicle. May be accompanied by brake fade.)	• Loose or leaking power brake unit vacuum hose • Incorrect or poor quality brake-lining • Bent, broken, distorted brakeshoes • Calipers binding or dragging on mounting pins. Rear brakeshoes dragging on support plate. • Caliper, wheel cylinder, or master cylinder pistons sticking or seized • Power brake unit vacuum check valve malfunction • Power brake unit has internal bind • Master cylinder compensator ports (at bottom of reservoirs) blocked by dirt, scale, rust, or have small burrs (blocked ports prevent fluid return to reservoirs). • Brake hoses, tubes, fittings clogged or restricted • Brake fluid contaminated with improper fluids (motor oil, transmission fluid, causing rubber components to swell and stick in bores • Low engine vacuum	• Tighten connections or replace leaking hose • Replace with lining in axle sets • Replace brakeshoes • Replace mounting pins and bushings. Clean rust or burrs from rear brake support plate ledges and lubricate ledges with molydisulfide grease. **NOTE:** If ledges are deeply grooved or scored, do not attempt to sand or grind them smooth—replace support plate. • Repair or replace parts as necessary • Test valve according to the following procedure: (a) Start engine, increase engine speed to 1500 rpm, close throttle and immediately stop engine (b) Wait at least 90 seconds then depress brake pedal (c) If brakes are not vacuum assisted for 2 or more applications, check valve is faulty • Test unit according to the following procedure: (a) With engine stopped, apply brakes several times to exhaust all vacuum in system (b) Shift transmission into neutral, depress brake pedal and start engine (c) If pedal height decreases with foot pressure and less pressure is required to hold pedal in applied position, power unit vacuum system is operating normally. Test power unit. If power unit exhibits a bind condition, replace the power unit. • Repair or replace master cylinder **CAUTION:** Do not attempt to clean blocked ports with wire, pencils, or similar implements. Use compressed air only. • Use compressed air to check or unclog parts. Replace any damaged parts. • Replace all rubber components, combination valve and hoses. Flush entire brake system with DOT 3 brake fluid or equivalent. • Adjust or repair engine

Troubleshooting the Brake System (cont.)

Problem	Cause	Solution
Grabbing brakes (severe reaction to brake pedal pressure.)	• Brakelining(s) contaminated by grease or brake fluid	• Determine and correct cause of contamination and replace brakeshoes in axle sets
	• Parking brake cables incorrectly adjusted or seized	• Adjust cables. Replace seized cables.
	• Incorrect brakelining or lining loose on brakeshoes	• Replace brakeshoes in axle sets
	• Caliper anchor plate bolts loose	• Tighten bolts
	• Rear brakeshoes binding on support plate ledges	• Clean and lubricate ledges. Replace support plate(s) if ledges are deeply grooved. Do not attempt to smooth ledges by grinding.
	• Incorrect or missing power brake reaction disc	• Install correct disc
	• Rear brake support plates loose	• Tighten mounting bolts
Dragging brakes (slow or incomplete release of brakes)	• Brake pedal binding at pivot	• Loosen and lubricate
	• Power brake unit has internal bind	• Inspect for internal bind. Replace unit if internal bind exists.
	• Parking brake cables incorrrectly adjusted or seized	• Adjust cables. Replace seized cables.
	• Rear brakeshoe return springs weak or broken	• Replace return springs. Replace brakeshoe if necessary in axle sets.
	• Automatic adjusters malfunctioning	• Repair or replace adjuster parts as required
	• Caliper, wheel cylinder or master cylinder pistons sticking or seized	• Repair or replace parts as necessary
	• Master cylinder compensating ports blocked (fluid does not return to reservoirs).	• Use compressed air to clear ports. Do not use wire, pencils, or similar objects to open blocked ports.
Vehicle moves to one side when brakes are applied	• Incorrect front tire pressure	• Inflate to recommended cold (reduced load) inflation pressure
	• Worn or damaged wheel bearings	• Replace worn or damaged bearings
	• Brakelining on one side contaminated	• Determine and correct cause of contamination and replace brakelining in axle sets
	• Brakeshoes on one side bent, distorted, or lining loose on shoe	• Replace brakeshoes in axle sets
	• Support plate bent or loose on one side	• Tighten or replace support plate
	• Brakelining not yet seated with drums or rotors	• Burnish brakelining
	• Caliper anchor plate loose on one side	• Tighten anchor plate bolts
	• Caliper piston sticking or seized	• Repair or replace caliper
	• Brakelinings water soaked	• Drive vehicle with brakes lightly applied to dry linings
	• Loose suspension component attaching or mounting bolts	• Tighten suspension bolts. Replace worn suspension components.
	• Brake combination valve failure	• Replace combination valve
Chatter or shudder when brakes are applied (pedal pulsation and roughness may also occur.)	• Brakeshoes distorted, bent, contaminated, or worn	• Replace brakeshoes in axle sets
	• Caliper anchor plate or support plate loose	• Tighten mounting bolts
	• Excessive thickness variation of rotor(s)	• Refinish or replace rotors in axle sets
Noisy brakes (squealing, clicking, scraping sound when brakes are applied.)	• Bent, broken, distorted brakeshoes	• Replace brakeshoes in axle sets
	• Excessive rust on outer edge of rotor braking surface	• Remove rust

Troubleshooting the Brake System (cont.)

Problem	Cause	Solution
Noisy brakes (squealing, clicking, scraping sound when brakes are applied.) (cont.)	• Brakelining worn out—shoes contacting drum of rotor	• Replace brakeshoes and lining in axle sets. Refinish or replace drums or rotors.
	• Broken or loose holdown or return springs	• Replace parts as necessary
	• Rough or dry drum brake support plate ledges	• Lubricate support plate ledges
	• Cracked, grooved, or scored rotor(s) or drum(s)	• Replace rotor(s) or drum(s). Replace brakeshoes and lining in axle sets if necessary.
	• Incorrect brakelining and/or shoes (front or rear).	• Install specified shoe and lining assemblies
Pulsating brake pedal	• Out of round drums or excessive lateral runout in disc brake rotor(s)	• Refinish or replace drums, re-index rotors or replace

causes both shoes to rotate very slightly with the drum, rocking an adjusting lever, thereby causing rotation of the adjusting screw.

POWER BRAKE BOOSTERS

Power brakes operate just as standard brake systems except in the actuation of the master cylinder pistons. A vacuum diaphragm is located on the front of the master cylinder and assists the driver in applying the brakes, reducing both the effort and travel he must put into moving the brake pedal.

The vacuum diaphragm housing is connected to the intake manifold by a vacuum hose. A check valve is placed at the point where the hose enters the diaphragm housing, so that during periods of low manifold vacuum brake assist vacuum will not be lost.

Depressing the brake pedal closes off the vacuum source and allows atmospheric pressure to enter on one side of the diaphragm. This causes the master cylinder pistons to move and apply the brakes. When the brake pedal is released, vacuum is applied to both sides of the diaphragm, and return springs return the diaphragm and master cylinder pistons to the released position. If the vacuum fails, the brake pedal rod will butt against the end of the master cylinder actuating rod, and direct mechanical application will occur as the pedal is depressed.

The hydraulic and mechanical problems that apply to conventional brake systems also apply to power brakes, and should be checked for if the tests below do not reveal the problem.

Test for a system vacuum leak as described below:

1. Operate the engine at idle without touching the brake pedal for at least one minute.

2. Turn off the engine, and wait one minute.

3. Test for the presence of assist vacuum by depressing the brake pedal and releasing it several times. Light application will produce less and less pedal travel, if vacuum was present. If there is no vacuum, air is leaking into the system somewhere.

Test for system operation as follows:

1. Pump the brake pedal (with engine off) until the supply vacuum is entirely gone.

2. Put a light, steady pressure on the pedal.

3. Start the engine, and operate it at idle. If the system is operating, the brake pedal should fall toward the floor if constant pressure is maintained on the pedal.

Power brake systems may be tested for hydraulic leaks just as ordinary systems are tested.

Adjustments
REAR DRUM BRAKES

All Models

These models are equipped with self-adjusting rear drum brakes. No adjustment is possible or necessary.

FRONT DISC BRAKES

Front disc brakes require no adjustment, as hydraulic pressure maintains the proper brake pad-to-disc contact at all times.

NOTE: *The brake fluid level should be checked regularly. (See Chapter 1).*

Master Cylinder
REMOVAL AND INSTALLATION

1. Unfasten the hydraulic lines from the master cylinder.

2. Detach the hydraulic fluid pressure differential switch wiring connectors. On models with ESP (brake fluid level warning device),

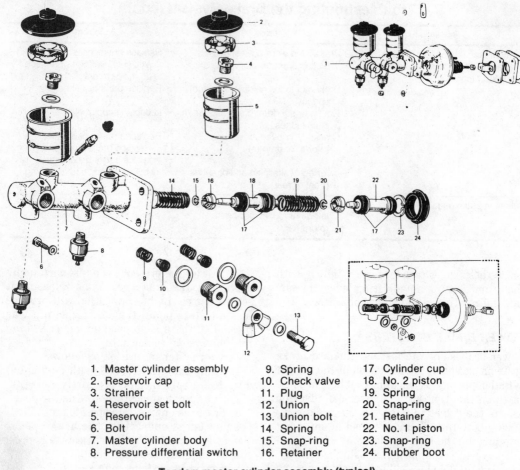

1. Master cylinder assembly
2. Reservoir cap
3. Strainer
4. Reservoir set bolt
5. Reservoir
6. Bolt
7. Master cylinder body
8. Pressure differential switch

9. Spring
10. Check valve
11. Plug
12. Union
13. Union bolt
14. Spring
15. Snap-ring
16. Retainer

17. Cylinder cup
18. No. 2 piston
19. Spring
20. Snap-ring
21. Retainer
22. No. 1 piston
23. Snap-ring
24. Rubber boot

Tandem master cylinder assembly (typical)

disconnect the fluid level sensor wiring connectors, as well.

3. Unfasten the nuts and remove the master cylinder assembly from the power brake unit.

4. Installation is performed in the reverse order of removal. Note the following, however:

a. Before tightening the master cylinder mounting nuts or bolts, screw the hydraulic line into the cylinder body, a few turns.

b. After installation is completed, bleed the master cylinder and the brake system.

OVERHAUL

1. Remove the reservoir caps and floats. Unscrew the bolts and secure the reservoirs to the main body.

2. Remove the pressure differential warning switch assembly (if equipped). Then, working from the rear of the cylinder, remove the boot, snapping, stop washer, piston No. 1, spacer, cylinder cup, spring retainer, and spring, in that order.

NOTE: *Depending on the model, it may be*

necessary to remove the side mounted stop bolt before the pistons can be removed.

3. Remove the endplug and gasket from the front of the cylinder, then remove the front piston stop-bolt from underneath. Pull out the spring, retainer, piston No. 2, spacer, and the cylinder cup.

4. Remove the two outlet fittings, washers, check valves and springs.

5. Remove the piston cups from their seats only if they are to be replaced.

6. After washing all parts in clean brake fluid, dry them with compressed air (if available). Inspect the cylinder bore for wear, scuff marks, or nicks. Cylinders may be honed slightly, but the limit is 0.15mm. In view of the importance of the master cylinder, it is recommended that it is replaced rather than overhauled if worn or damaged.

7. Assembly is performed in the reverse order of disassembly. Absolute cleanliness is important. Coat all parts with clean brake fluid prior to assembly.

Bleed the hydraulic system after the master cylinder is installed, as detailed following.

Proportioning Valve

A proportioning valve is used to reduce the hydraulic pressure to the rear brakes because of weight transfer during high speed stops. This helps to keep the rear brakes from locking up by improving front-to-rear brake balance.

REMOVAL AND INSTALLATION

1. Disconnect the brake lines from the valve unions.
2. Unfasten the valve mounting bolt, if used.
3. Remove the proportioning valve assembly.
   NOTE: *If the proportioning valve is defective, it must be replaced as an assembly. It cannot be rebuilt.*
4. Installation is the reverse of removal. Bleed the brake system after it is completed.

Bleeding

CAUTION: *Do not reuse brake fluid which has been bled from the brake system.*
1. Insert a clear vinyl tube into the bleeder plug on the master cylinder or the wheel cylinders.
   NOTE: *If the master cylinder has been overhauled or if air is present in it, start the bleeding procedure with the master cylinder. Otherwise (and after bleeding the master cylinder), start with the wheel cylinder which is farthest from the master cylinder.*
2. Insert the other end of the tube into a jar which is half filled with brake fluid.
3. Slowly depress the brake pedal (have an assistant do it) and turn the bleeder plug $\frac{1}{3}$–$\frac{1}{2}$ of a turn at the same time.
   NOTE: *If the brake pedal is depressed too fast, small air bubbles will form in the brake fluid which will be very difficult to remove.*
4. Bleed the cylinder before hydraulic pressure decreases in the cylinder.
5. Repeat this procedure until the air bubbles are removed and then go on to the next wheel cylinder.
   CAUTION: *Add brake fluid to the master cylinder reservoir, so that it does not completely drain during bleeding.*

FRONT DISC BRAKES

INSPECTION

An inspection slot is provided, in most cases, in the top of the caliper for checking the brake pad thickness. However, if the thickness seems

Bleeding the disc brake caliper

marginal, the pads should be removed from the caliper and checked.
   NOTE: *Always replace the pads on both front wheels. When inspecting or replacing the brake pads, check the surface of the disc rotors for scoring, wear and runout. The rotors should be resurfaced if badly scored or replaced if badly worn.*

Fixed Caliper Type Disc Brakes

The fixed caliper design uses two pistons mounted on either side of the disc rotor. The caliper is rigidly mounted and does not move.

Sliding Caliper Type Disc Brake

The sliding caliper design uses one piston mounted on the inboard side of the disc rotor. The caliper, which is not held in a fixed position, moves slightly when the brake is applied. The movement of the caliper brings the outside brake pad into contact with the disc rotor.

Disc Brake Pads
REMOVAL AND INSTALLATION
Fixed Caliper

1. Loosen the front wheel lugs slightly, then raise and safely support the front of the car. Remove the front wheel(s).
2. Remove the center spring, the retaining clips and the mounting pins from the caliper.
3. Remove the brake pads and antisqueal shims. A pair of locking pliers will help when you are pulling the pads from the caliper.
4. Remove the master cylinder cap and take a small amount of brake fluid from the reservoir. Force the pistons back into their bores to accommodate the greater thickness of the new brake pads.
5. Clean all caliper and pad locating parts.
6. Check the disc rotor for excessive runout. (See following section on disc rotors).
7. Apply a light coating of grease on the shims and on the metal backing of the pad.

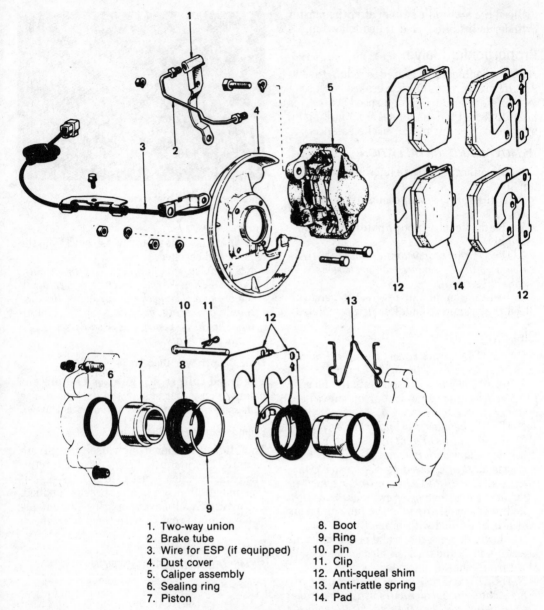

1. Two-way union
2. Brake tube
3. Wire for ESP (if equipped)
4. Dust cover
5. Caliper assembly
6. Sealing ring
7. Piston
8. Boot
9. Ring
10. Pin
11. Clip
12. Anti-squeal shim
13. Anti-rattle spring
14. Pad

Fixed caliper disc brake (typical)

8. Install the brake pads with the antisqueal shims (be sure the arrows are pointed in the right direction), the retaining pins and clips and the center spring in the reverse order of removal.

9. Pump the brake pedal several times to adjust the caliper pistons. Road test the car. If the brake pedal feels soft, it may be necessary to bleed the system.

Sliding Caliper

1. Loosen the front wheel lugs slightly, then raise and safely support the front of the car. Remove the front wheel(s).

2. Remove the guide key retainers. Apply light pressure to the caliper housing and slide the guide keys from (between) the caliper housing and the pad support.

3. Remove the caliper housing. Suspend the housing (with wire) so there is no strain on the brake hose.

4. Remove the brake pads and the support springs. Note the various positions of the parts removed.

5. Clean all of the parts that will be used over again. Remove the master cylinder cap and take a small amount of brake fluid from the reservoir. Force the piston back into the

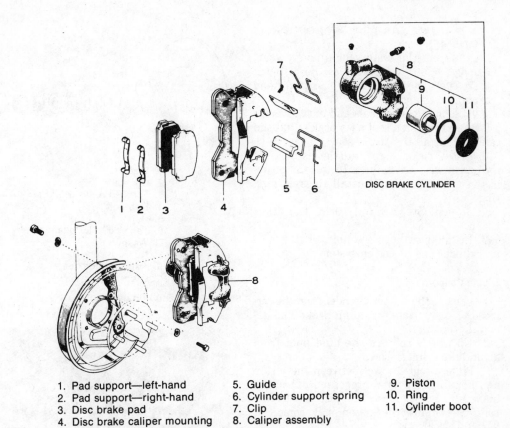

DISC BRAKE CYLINDER

1. Pad support—left-hand
2. Pad support—right-hand
3. Disc brake pad
4. Disc brake caliper mounting
5. Guide
6. Cylinder support spring
7. Clip
8. Caliper assembly
9. Piston
10. Ring
11. Cylinder boot

Sliding caliper disc brake (typical)

caliper bore to accommodate the greater thickness of the new brake pads.

6. Install the support springs, the brake pads, and the antirattle clips into the pad support.

7. Position the caliper housing on the support and install the guide keys and retainers.

8. Pump the brake pedal several times to adjust the caliper piston. Road test the car. If the brake pedal feels soft, it may be necessary to bleed the system.

Disc Brake Caliper

REMOVAL AND INSTALLATION

1. Remove the disc brake pads as previously described.

2. Disconnect the brake hose from the caliper. The fixed caliper is mounted by two bolts, cut the safety wire and remove the bolts. Remove the caliper. The sliding caliper support is held on by two mounting bolts, cut the safety wire and remove the bolts. Remove the caliper support.

3. Installation is the reverse of removal. Be sure to safety wire the mounting bolts. Torque the mounting bolts to 65 ft.lb.

OVERHAUL

Fixed Caliper

1. Remove the caliper as previously described.

CAUTION: *The caliper halves must not be separated. If brake fluid leaks from the bridge seal, replace the caliper assembly.*

2. Clean the caliper assembly of all accumulated mud and dust.

3. Remove the retaining rings. Remove the dust covers.

4. Hold one piston with a finger so that it will not come out and gradually apply air pressure to the brake line fitting. This should cause the other piston to come out, but if the piston you are holding begins moving before the other, switch your finger over and remove the more movable one first.

5. Carefully remove the other piston.

6. With a finger, carefully remove both piston seals.

7. Thoroughly clean all parts in brake fluid.

8. Inspect, as follows:

a. Check cylinder walls for damage or excessive wear. Light rust, etc. should be removed with fine emery paper. If the wall is heavily rusted, replace the caliper assembly.

b. Inspect the pad, as previously described.

c. Inspect the piston for uneven wear, damage or any rust. Replace the piston if there is any rust, as it is chrome plated and cannot be cleaned.

d. Replace piston seals and dust covers.

9. Coat the piston seal with brake fluid and carefully install the piston seal.

10. Install the dust seal onto the piston. Coat the piston with brake fluid. Install the piston and seal assembly and install the retaining ring.

11. Repeat Steps 9 and 10 for the other piston.

12. Install the caliper assembly. Fill the master cylinder and bleed the system.

Sliding Caliper

1. Remove the caliper cylinder from the car. (See the appropriate preceding Brake Pad Removal procedure).

2. Carefully remove the dust boot from around the cylinder bore.

3. Place a folded towel between the piston and housing. Apply compressed air to the brake line union to force the piston out of its bore. Be careful, the piston may come out forcefully.

4. Remove the seal from the piston. Check the piston and cylinder bore for wear and/or corrosion. Replace components as necessary. Assembly is performed in the following order:

1. Coat all components with clean brake fluid.

2. Install the seal and piston in the cylinder bore, after coating them with the rubber lubricant supplied in the rebuilding kit. Seat the piston in the bore.

3. Fit the boot into the groove in the cylinder bore.

4. Install the caliper cylinder assembly on to the support.

5. Fill the master cylinder and bleed the system.

Brake Disc (Rotor)
REMOVAL AND INSTALLATION

1. Remove the brake pads and caliper, or caliper and support as previously described.

2. Check the disc runout with a dial indicator, if available. See the rotor inspection section for details.

3. Remove the grease cap from the center of the hub. Remove the cotter pin and the castellated nut.

4. Remove the wheel hub with the disc rotor attached.

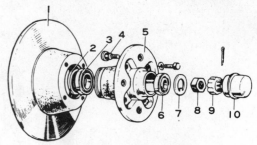

1. Disc
2. Oil seal
3. Tapered roller bearing
4. Hub bolt
5. Hub
6. Tapered roller bearing
7. Washer
8. Nut
9. Adjusting lock cap
10. Grease cap

Brake disc and hub assembly

Checking disc run-out

5. Inspect the rotor. See the rotor inspection section for details.

6. Check the wheel bearings, repack them with grease if necessary.

7. Installation is the reverse of removal. Before installation, coat the hub oil seal with multipurpose grease. Install the hub and disc rotor. Adjust the wheel bearing preload. See the wheel bearing section.

INSPECTION

Examine the disc. If it is worn, warped or scored, it must be replaced. Check the thickness of the disc against the specifications given in the Disc and Pad Specifications chart. If it is below specifications, replace it. Use a micrometer to measure the thickness.

The disc run-out should be measured before the disc is removed and again, after the disc is installed. Use a dial indicator mounted on a stand to determine run-out. If run-out exceeds 0.15mm (all models), replace the disc.

NOTE: *Be sure that the wheel bearing nut is*

CHILTON'S
AUTO BODY
REPAIR TIPS

Tools and Materials • Step-by-Step Illustrated Procedures
How To Repair Dents, Scratches and Rust Holes
Spray Painting and Refinishing Tips

With a little practice, basic body repair procedures can be mastered by any do-it-yourself mechanic. The step-by-step repairs shown here can be applied to almost any type of auto body repair.

TOOLS & MATERIALS

You may already have basic tools, such as hammers and electric drills. Other tools unique to body repair — body hammers, grinding attachments, sanding blocks, dent puller, half-round plastic file and plastic spreaders — are relatively inexpensive and can be obtained wherever auto parts or auto body repair parts are sold. Portable air compressors and paint spray guns can be purchased or rented.

Auto Body Repair Kits

The best and most often used products are available to the do-it-yourselfer in kit form, from major manufacturers of auto body repair products. The same manufacturers also merchandise the individual products for use by pros.

Kits are available to make a wide variety of repairs, including holes, dents and scratches and fiberglass, and offer the advantage of buying the materials you'll need for the job. There is little waste or chance of materials going bad from not being used. Many kits may also contain basic body-working tools such as body files, sanding blocks and spreaders. Check the contents of the kit before buying your tools.

BODY REPAIR TIPS

Safety

Many of the products associated with auto body repair and refinishing contain toxic chemicals. Read all labels before opening containers and store them in a safe place and manner.

• Wear eye protection (safety goggles) when using power tools or when performing any operation that involves

the removal of any type of material.

• Wear lung protection (disposable mask or respirator) when grinding, sanding or painting.

Sanding

1 Sand off paint before using a dent puller. When using a non-adhesive sanding disc, cover the back of the disc with an overlapping layer or two of masking tape and trim the edges. The disc will last considerably longer.

2 Use the circular motion of the sanding disc to grind *into* the edge of the repair. Grinding or sanding away from the jagged edge will only tear the sandpaper.

3 Use the palm of your hand flat on the panel to detect high and low spots. Do not use your fingertips. Slide your hand slowly back and forth.

WORKING WITH BODY FILLER

Mixing The Filler

Cleanliness and proper mixing and application are extremely important. Use a clean piece of plastic or glass or a disposable artist's palette to mix body filler.

1 Allow plenty of time and follow directions. No useful purpose will be served by adding more hardener to make it cure (set-up) faster. Less hardener means more curing time, but the mixture dries harder; more hardener means less curing time but a softer mixture.

2 Both the hardener and the filler should be thoroughly kneaded or stirred before mixing. Hardener should be a solid paste and dispense like thin toothpaste. Body filler should be smooth, and free of lumps or thick spots.

Getting the proper amount of hardener in the filler is the trickiest part of preparing the filler. Use the same amount of hardener in cold or warm weather. For contour filler (thick coats), a bead of hardener twice the diameter of the filler is about right. There's about a 15% margin on either side, but, if in doubt use less hardener.

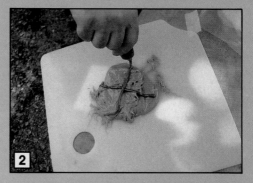

3 Mix the body filler and hardener by wiping across the mixing surface, picking the mixture up and wiping it again. Colder weather requires longer mixing times. Do not mix in a circular motion; this will trap air bubbles which will become holes in the cured filler.

Applying The Filler

1 For best results, filler should not be applied over 1/4″ thick.

Apply the filler in several coats. Build it up to above the level of the repair surface so that it can be sanded or grated down.

The first coat of filler must be pressed on with a firm wiping motion.

Apply the filler in one direction only. Working the filler back and forth will either pull it off the metal or trap air bubbles.

REPAIRING DENTS

Before you start, take a few minutes to study the damaged area. Try to visualize the shape of the panel before it was damaged. If the damage is on the left fender, look at the right fender and use it as a guide. If there is access to the panel from behind, you can reshape it with a body hammer. If not, you'll have to use a dent puller. Go slowly and work the metal a little at a time. Get the panel as straight as possible before applying filler.

1 This dent is typical of one that can be pulled out or hammered out from behind. Remove the headlight cover, headlight assembly and turn signal housing.

2 Drill a series of holes ½ the size of the end of the dent puller along the stress line. Make some trial pulls and assess the results. If necessary, drill more holes and try again. Do not hurry.

3 If possible, use a body hammer and block to shape the metal back to its original contours. Get the metal back as close to its original shape as possible. Don't depend on body filler to fill dents.

4 Using an 80-grit grinding disc on an electric drill, grind the paint from the surrounding area down to bare metal. Use a new grinding pad to prevent heat buildup that will warp metal.

5 The area should look like this when you're finished grinding. Knock the drill holes in and tape over small openings to keep plastic filler out.

6 Mix the body filler (see Body Repair Tips). Spread the body filler evenly over the entire area (see Body Repair Tips). Be sure to cover the area completely.

7 Let the body filler dry until the surface can just be scratched with your fingernail. Knock the high spots from the body filler with a body file ("Cheesegrater"). Check frequently with the palm of your hand for high and low spots.

8 Check to be sure that trim pieces that will be installed later will fit exactly. Sand the area with 40-grit paper.

9 If you wind up with low spots, you may have to apply another layer of filler.

10 Knock the high spots off with 40-grit paper. When you are satisfied with the contours of the repair, apply a thin coat of filler to cover pin holes and scratches.

11 Block sand the area with 40-grit paper to a smooth finish. Pay particular attention to body lines and ridges that must be well-defined.

12 Sand the area with 400 paper and then finish with a scuff pad. The finished repair is ready for priming and painting (see Painting Tips).

Materials and photos courtesy of Ritt Jones Auto Body, Prospect Park, PA.

REPAIRING RUST HOLES

There are many ways to repair rust holes. The fiberglass cloth kit shown here is one of the most cost efficient for the owner because it provides a strong repair that resists cracking and moisture and is relatively easy to use. It can be used on large and small holes (with or without backing) and can be applied over contoured areas. Remember, however, that short of replacing an entire panel, no repair is a guarantee that the rust will not return.

1 Remove any trim that will be in the way. Clean away all loose debris. Cut away all the rusted metal. But be sure to leave enough metal to retain the contour or body shape.

2 Grind away all traces of rust with a 24-grit grinding disc. Be sure to grind back 3-4 inches from the edge of the hole down to bare metal and be sure all traces of paint, primer and rust are removed.

3 Block sand the area with 80 or 100 grit sandpaper to get a clear, shiny surface and feathered paint edge. Tap the edges of the hole inward with a ball peen hammer.

4 If you are going to use release film, cut a piece about 2-3″ larger than the area you have sanded. Place the film over the repair and mark the sanded area on the film. Avoid any unnecessary wrinkling of the film.

5 Cut 2 pieces of fiberglass matte to match the shape of the repair. One piece should be about 1″ smaller than the sanded area and the second piece should be 1″ smaller than the first. Mix enough filler and hardener to saturate the fiberglass material (see Body Repair Tips).

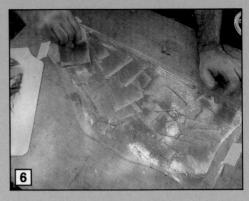

6 Lay the release sheet on a flat surface and spread an even layer of filler, large enough to cover the repair. Lay the smaller piece of fiberglass cloth in the center of the sheet and spread another layer of filler over the fiberglass cloth. Repeat the operation for the larger piece of cloth.

7 Place the repair material over the repair area, with the release film facing outward. Use a spreader and work from the center outward to smooth the material, following the body contours. Be sure to remove all air bubbles.

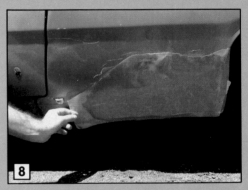

8 Wait until the repair has dried tack-free and peel off the release sheet. The ideal working temperature is 60°-90° F. Cooler or warmer temperatures or high humidity may require additional curing time. Wait longer, if in doubt.

9 Sand and feather-edge the entire area. The initial sanding can be done with a sanding disc on an electric drill if care is used. Finish the sanding with a block sander. Low spots can be filled with body filler; this may require several applications.

10 When the filler can just be scratched with a fingernail, knock the high spots down with a body file and smooth the entire area with 80-grit. Feather the filled areas into the surrounding areas.

11 When the area is sanded smooth, mix some topcoat and hardener and apply it directly with a spreader. This will give a smooth finish and prevent the glass matte from showing through the paint.

12 Block sand the topcoat smooth with finishing sandpaper (200 grit), and 400 grit. The repair is ready for masking, priming and painting (see Painting Tips).

Materials and photos courtesy Marson Corporation, Chelsea, Massachusetts

PAINTING TIPS

Preparation

1 SANDING — Use a 400 or 600 grit wet or dry sandpaper. Wet-sand the area with a 1/4 sheet of sandpaper soaked in clean water. Keep the paper wet while sanding. Sand the area until the repaired area tapers into the original finish.

2 CLEANING — Wash the area to be painted thoroughly with water and a clean rag. Rinse it thoroughly and wipe the surface dry until you're sure it's completely free of dirt, dust, fingerprints, wax, detergent or other foreign matter.

3 MASKING — Protect any areas you don't want to overspray by covering them with masking tape and newspaper. Be careful not get fingerprints on the area to be painted.

4 PRIMING — All exposed metal should be primed before painting. Primer protects the metal and provides an excellent surface for paint adhesion. When the primer is dry, wet-sand the area again with 600 grit wet-sandpaper. Clean the area again after sanding.

Painting Techniques

P aint applied from either a spray gun or a spray can (for small areas) will provide good results. Experiment on an old piece of metal to get the right combination before you begin painting.

SPRAYING VISCOSITY (SPRAY GUN ONLY) — Paint should be thinned to spraying viscosity according to the directions on the can. Use only the recommended thinner or reducer and the same amount of reduction regardless of temperature.

AIR PRESSURE (SPRAY GUN ONLY) — This is extremely important. Be sure you are using the proper recommended pressure.

TEMPERATURE — The surface to be painted should be approximately the same temperature as the surrounding air. Applying warm paint to a cold surface, or vice versa, will completely upset the paint characteristics.

THICKNESS — Spray with smooth strokes. In general, the thicker the coat of paint, the longer the drying time. Apply several thin coats about 30 seconds apart. The paint should remain wet long enough to flow out and no longer; heavier coats will only produce sags or wrinkles. Spray a light (fog) coat, followed by heavier color coats.

DISTANCE — The ideal spraying distance is 8″-12″ from the gun or can to the surface. Shorter distances will produce ripples, while greater distances will result in orange peel, dry film and poor color match and loss of material due to overspray.

OVERLAPPING — The gun or can should be kept at right angles to the surface at all times. Work to a wet edge at an even speed, using a 50% overlap and direct the center of the spray at the lower or nearest edge of the previous stroke.

RUBBING OUT (BLENDING) FRESH PAINT — Let the paint dry thoroughly. Runs or imperfections can be sanded out, primed and repainted.

Don't be in too big a hurry to remove the masking. This only produces paint ridges. When the finish has dried for at least a week, apply a small amount of fine grade rubbing compound with a clean, wet cloth. Use lots of water and blend the new paint with the surrounding area.

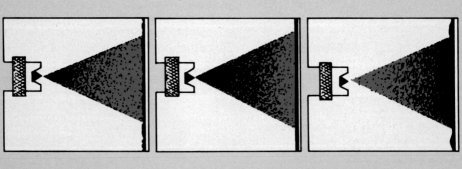

WRONG	CORRECT	WRONG
Thin coat. Stroke too fast, not enough overlap, gun too far away.	*Medium coat. Proper distance, good stroke, proper overlap.*	*Heavy coat. Stroke too slow, too much overlap, gun too close.*

Disc and Pad Specifications (in.)

New Disc Thickness	Disc Service Limit Thickness	Run-Out Limit	Pad Thickness Limit
0.86	0.83	0.006	0.040

properly tightened. If it is not, an inaccurate run-out reading may be obtained. If different run-out readings are obtained with the same disc, between removal and installation, this is probably the cause.

REAR DRUM BRAKES

Brake Drums

REMOVAL AND INSTALLATION

All Models

1. Remove the hub cap (if used) and loosen the lug nuts. Release the parking brake.
2. Block the front wheels, raise the rear of the car, and support it with jackstands.
CAUTION: *Support the car securely.*
3. Remove the lug nuts and the wheel.
4. Unfasten the brake drum retaining screws.
5. Tap the drum lightly with a mallet in order to free it. If the drum is difficult to remove use a puller. But first be sure that the parking brake is released.

CAUTION: *Don't depress the brake pedal once the drum has been removed.*
6. Inspect the brake drum as detailed following.
7. Brake drum installation is performed in the reverse order of removal.

INSPECTION

1. Clean the drum.
2. Inspect the drum for scoring, cracks, grooves and out-of-roundness. Replace or turn the drum, as required.
3. Light scoring may be removed by dressing the drum with fine emery cloth.
4. Heavy scoring will require the use of a brake drum lathe to turn the drum. The service limits of the drum inside diameter are 0.060" over original diameter.

Brake Shoes

REMOVAL AND INSTALLATION

1. Perform the Brake Drum Removal procedure as previously detailed.
2. Unhook the shoe tension springs from the shoes with the aid of a brake spring removing tool.
3. Remove the brake shoe securing springs.
4. Disconnect the parking brake cable at the parking brake shoe lever.

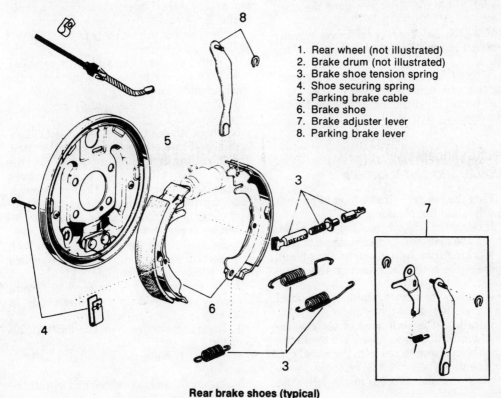

1. Rear wheel (not illustrated)
2. Brake drum (not illustrated)
3. Brake shoe tension spring
4. Shoe securing spring
5. Parking brake cable
6. Brake shoe
7. Brake adjuster lever
8. Parking brake lever

Rear brake shoes (typical)

5. Withdraw the shoes, complete with the parking brake shoe lever.

6. Unfasten the C-clip and remove the adjuster assembly from the shoes.

7. Inspect the shoes for wear and scoring. Have the linings replaced if their thickness is less than 1mm.

8. Check the tension springs to see if they are weak, distorted or rusted.

9. Inspect the teeth on the automatic adjuster wheel for chipping or other damage.

NOTE: *Grease the point of the shoe which slides against the backing plate. Do not get grease on the linings.*

10. Installation is performed in the following order:

a. Attach the parking brake shoe lever and the automatic adjuster lever to the rear side of the shoe.

b. Fasten the parking brake cable to the lever on the brake shoe.

c. Install the automatic adjuster and fit the tension spring on the adjuster lever.

d. Install the securing spring on the rear shoe and then install the securing spring on the front shoe.

NOTE: *The tension spring should be installed on the anchor, before performing Step d.*

e. Hook one end of the tension spring over the rear shoe with the tool used during removal. Hook the other end over the front shoe.

CAUTION: *Be sure that the wheel cylinder boots are not being pinched in the ends of the shoes.*

f. Test the automatic adjuster by operating the parking brake shoe lever.

g. Install the drum and adjust the brakes as previously detailed.

Wheel Cylinders

REMOVAL AND INSTALLATION

1. Plug the master cylinder inlet to prevent hydraulic fluid from leaking.

2. Remove the brake drums and shoes as detailed in the appropriate preceding section.

3. Working from behind the backing plate, disconnect the hydraulic line from the wheel cylinder.

4. Unfasten the screws retaining the wheel cylinder and withdraw the cylinder.

5. Installation is performed in the reverse order of removal. However, once the hydraulic line has been disconnected from the wheel cylinder, the union seat must be replaced. To replace the seat, proceed in the following manner:

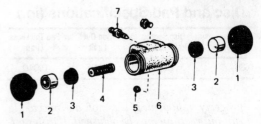

1. Wheel cylinder boot
2. Wheel cylinder piston
3. Cylinder cup
4. Compression spring
5. Union seat
6. Wheel cylinder body
7. Bleeder plug

Wheel cylinder assembly (typical)

1. Use a screw extractor with a diameter of 2.5mm and having reverse threads, to remove the union seat from the wheel cylinder.

2. Drive in the new union seat with a 8mm bar, used as a drift.

3. Remember to bleed the brake system after completing wheel cylinder, brake shoe and drum installation.

OVERHAUL

It is not necessary to remove the wheel cylinder from the backing plate if it is only to be inspected or rebuilt.

1. Remove the brake drum and shoes. Remove the wheel cylinder only if it is going to be replaced.

2. Remove the rubber boots from either end of the wheel cylinder.

3. Withdraw the piston and cup assemblies.

4. Take the compression spring out of the wheel cylinder body.

5. Remove the bleeder plug (and ball), if necessary.

6. Check all components for wear or damage. Inspect the bore for signs of wear, scoring, and/or scuffing. If in doubt, replace or hone the wheel cylinder (with a special hone). The limit for honing a cylinder is 0.127mm oversize. Wash all the residue from the cylinder bore with clean brake fluid and blow dry.

Assembly is performed in the following order:

1. Soak all components in clean brake fluid, or coat them with the rubber grease supplied in the wheel cylinder rebuilding kit.

2. Install the spring, cups (recesses toward the center), and pistons in the cylinder body, in that order.

3. Insert the boots over the ends of the cylinder.

4. Install the bleeder plug (and ball), if removed.

5. Assemble the brake shoes and install the drum.

PARKING BRAKE

ADJUSTMENTS

1. Ensure that the rear brake shoes are correctly adjusted.

2. Without depressing the button, pull the parking brake handle up slowly, and count the number of notches before the brake is applied. It should take 4–7 notches. If not, proceed with Step 3.

3. Working from underneath of the car, loosen the locknut on the parking brake equalizer.

4. Screw the adjusting nut in, just enough so that the parking brake cables have no slack.

5. Hold the adjusting nut in this position while tightening the locknut.

6. Check the rotation of the rear wheels, with the parking brake off, to be sure that the brake shoes aren't dragging.

Body and Trim

9

EXTERIOR

Doors

REMOVAL AND INSTALLATION

1. Matchmark the door-to-hinge position.
2. Have an assitant hold the door while you remove the door-to-hinge bolts.
3. Installation is the reverse of removal.

ADJUSTMENT

Fore and aft adjustment is done by loosening the hinge-to-body bolts and moving the door as required.

Up and down adjustment is done by loosening the hinge-to-door bolts and moving the door as required.

Make sure that the hinge adjustments are

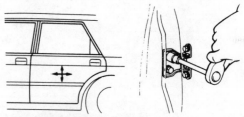

Front door striker adjustment. Rear door adjustment is identical

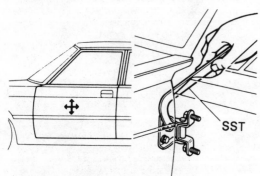

Front door fore/aft adjustment

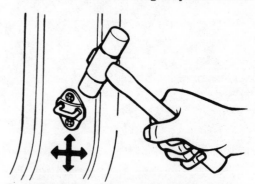

Rear door fore/aft adjustment

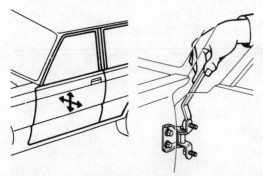

Front door up and down adjustment

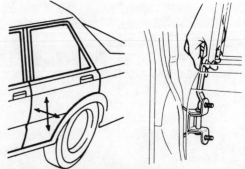

Rear door up and down adjustment

How to Remove Stains from Fabric Interior

For rest results, spots and stains should be removed as soon as possible. Never use gasoline, lacquer thinner, acetone, nail polish remover or bleach. Use a 3' x 3" piece of cheesecloth. Squeeze most of the liquid from the fabric and wipe the stained fabric from the outside of the stain toward the center with a lifting motion. Turn the cheesecloth as soon as one side becomes soiled. When using water to remove a stain, be sure to wash the entire section after the spot has been removed to avoid water stains. Encrusted spots can be broken up with a dull knife and vacuumed before removing the stain.

Type of Stain	How to Remove It
Surface spots	Brush the spots out with a small hand brush or use a commercial preparation such as K2R to lift the stain.
Mildew	Clean around the mildew with warm suds. Rinse in cold water and soak the mildew area in a solution of 1 part table salt and 2 parts water. Wash with upholstery cleaner.
Water stains	Water stains in fabric materials can be removed with a solution made from 1 cup of table salt dissolved in 1 quart of water. Vigorously scrub the solution into the stain and rinse with clear water. Water stains in nylon or other synthetic fabrics should be removed with a commercial type spot remover.
Chewing gum, tar, crayons, shoe polish (greasy stains)	Do not use a cleaner that will soften gum or tar. Harden the deposit with an ice cube and scrape away as much as possible with a dull knife. Moisten the remainder with cleaning fluid and scrub clean.
Ice cream, candy	Most candy has a sugar base and can be removed with a cloth wrung out in warm water. Oily candy, after cleaning with warm water, should be cleaned with upholstery cleaner. Rinse with warm water and clean the remainder with cleaning fluid.
Wine, alcohol, egg, milk, soft drink (non-greasy stains)	Do not use soap. Scrub the stain with a cloth wrung out in warm water. Remove the remainder with cleaning fluid.
Grease, oil, lipstick, butter and related stains	Use a spot remover to avoid leaving a ring. Work from the outisde of the stain to the center and dry with a clean cloth when the spot is gone.
Headliners (cloth)	Mix a solution of warm water and foam upholstery cleaner to give thick suds. Use only foam—liquid may streak or spot. Clean the entire headliner in one operation using a circular motion with a natural sponge.
Headliner (vinyl)	Use a vinyl cleaner with a sponge and wipe clean with a dry cloth.
Seats and door panels	Mix 1 pint upholstery cleaner in 1 gallon of water. Do not soak the fabric around the buttons.
Leather or vinyl fabric	Use a multi-purpose cleaner full strength and a stiff brush. Let stand 2 minutes and scrub thoroughly. Wipe with a clean, soft rag.
Nylon or synthetic fabrics	For normal stains, use the same procedures you would for washing cloth upholstery. If the fabric is extremely dirty, use a multi-purpose cleaner full strength with a stiff scrub brush. Scrub thoroughly in all directions and wipe with a cotton towel or soft rag.

correct. To adjust the striker, loosen the striker bolts and tap the striker with a wood or plastic mallet it achieve correct positioning.

Door Locks

REMOVAL AND INSTALLATION

Front or Rear Door

1. Remove the door panel and watershield.
2. Disconnect the door outside opening linkage.
3. Disconnect the lock cylinder control linkage.

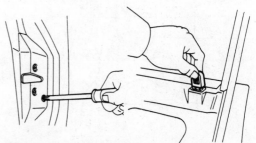

Removing the lock knob and lock assembly retaining screws

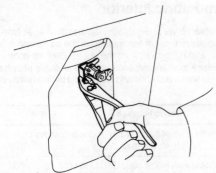

Removing the lock cylinder retaining clip

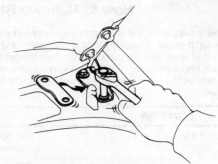

Removing or installing shims under the hinge

Hood latch adjustment

4. Remove the lock knob.
5. Remove the three lock assembly retaining screws and remove the door lock.
6. Remove the lock cylinder retaining clip with a pliers and remove the lock cylinder.
7. Installation is the reverse of removal.

Hood

REMOVAL AND INSTALLATION

1. Open the hood and matchmark the hood-to-hinge position.
2. Remove the hood-to-hinge bolts and lift off the hood.
3. Installation is the reverse of removal.

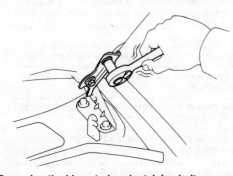

Removing the hinge-to-hood retaining bolts

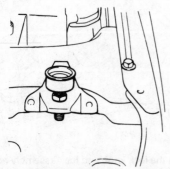

Hood leading edge adjuster

ADJUSTMENT

Hood position can be adjusted by adding or subtracting shims under the hood hinges and by adjusting the front hood bumper.

The hood latch can be adjusted by loosening the retaining bolts and moving the latch as required.

Rear Hatch Lid

REMOVAL AND INSTALLATION

1. Open the hatch completely.
2. Disconnect the damper from the hatch and swing the damper out of the way.
3. Matchmark the hatch-to-hinge position.
4. Remove the hatch-to-hinge bolts and lift off the hatch.
5. Installation is the reverse of removal.

ADJUSTMENTS

Fore/Aft and Left/Right adjustments are made by loosening the hinge bolts and positioning the hatch as required.

Vertical adjustment of the door edge is made by removing shims from, or adding shims to, the shim packs under the hinges.

Latch adjustments are made by removing the panel lower cover, loosening the latch bolts and moving the latch as required.

Sedan Trunk Lid
REMOVAL AND INSTALLATION

1. Slide the torsion bar from the center bracket.

2. Using tool SST 09804-22020, push down on the torsion bar at one end and pull the trunk lid off of the torsion bar.

3. Slowly lift the tool and remove the torsion bar from the bracket.

4. Repeat steps 2 and 3 for the other end.

5. Installation is the reverse of removal.

ADJUSTMENT

To adjust fore/aft and left/right position, loosen the hinge-to-trunk lid bolts and position the lid as required.

To adjust the vertical fit of the front edge of the trunk lid, increase or decrease the number of shims under the hinges.

Windshield
REMOVAL AND INSTALLATION

The windshield is installed with a urethane bonding agent and installation has to conform to Federal Motor Vehicle Safety Standards. Therefore, windhield replacement should be left to a professional shop.

Rear Window Glass
REMOVAL AND INSTALLATION
Sedan

1. Remove the rear seat.
2. Remove the roof side inner molding.
3. Remove the package tray trim panel.
4. Disconnect the rear defogger wiring.
5. Cover the painted surfaces adjacent to the rear window molding with tape.

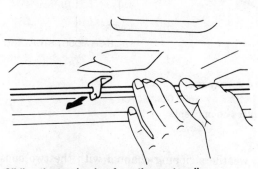

Sliding the torsion bar from the center clip

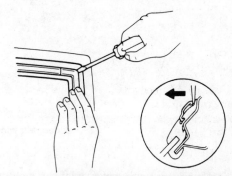

Sedan rear window molding joint cover removal

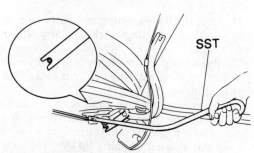

Installing the tool on the torsion bar

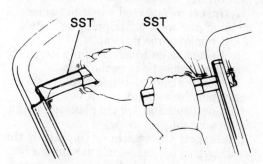

Sedan rear window molding removal

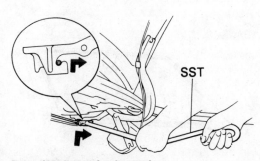

Releasing the torsion bar end

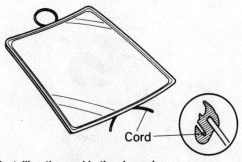

Installing the cord in the channel

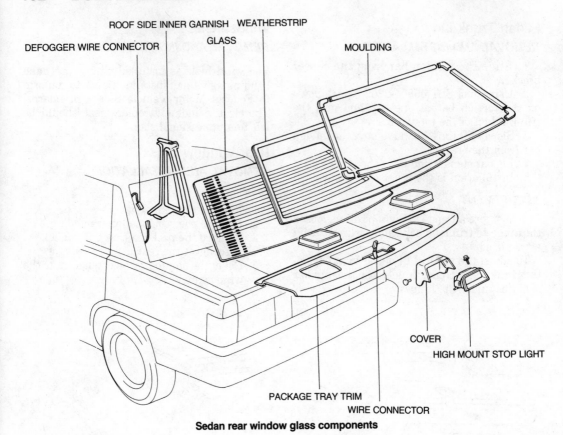

DEFOGGER WIRE CONNECTOR
ROOF SIDE INNER GARNISH
WEATHERSTRIP
GLASS
MOULDING
COVER
HIGH MOUNT STOP LIGHT
PACKAGE TRAY TRIM
WIRE CONNECTOR

Sedan rear window glass components

6. Using a screwdriver, pry off the molding joint covers.

7. Insert a flat wood wand between the molding and weatherstripping and slide it along, removing the molding.

8. Using a screwdriver, carefully loosen the weatherstripping lip from the body.

9. Working from the inside, force the weatherstripping lip outward.

10. Go outside and pull the glass and weatherstripping out.

11. Inspect the weatherstripping. If the weatherstripping has become hard and/or brittle, it should be replaced.

12. Insert a length of strong, thin cord in the weatherstripping channel with the two ends meeting at the bottom.

13. Fit the weatherstripping around the edge of the glass.

14. Coat the body opening and outer edge of the weatherstripping with a soapy water solution.

15. Press the glass assembly into position in the body opening with the two ends of the cord hanging inside the car.

16. Go inside the car, and, with someone pushing on the glass from the outside with a light, steady pressure, pull the ends of the cord to slip the weatherstripping lip over the body channel. Make sure that the glass is firmly in

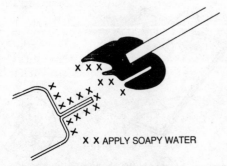

X X APPLY SOAPY WATER

Soapy water application

Installing the weatherstripping with the cord

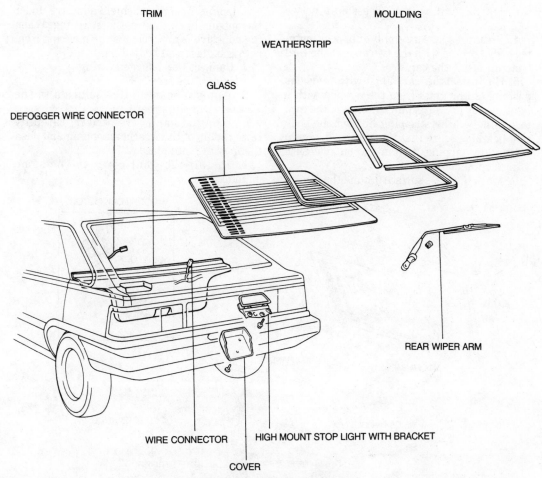

TRIM

MOULDING

WEATHERSTRIP

GLASS

DEFOGGER WIRE CONNECTOR

REAR WIPER ARM

WIRE CONNECTOR   HIGH MOUNT STOP LIGHT WITH BRACKET

COVER

Hatchback window components

position by tapping it from the outside with your open hand.

17. Mask the glass surface around the weatherstripping. Apply windshield adhesive under the outside lip of the weatherstripping. When the adhesive is dry, remove the masking from both the glass and body areas.

18. Connect the defogger wiring.

19. Install the package tray.

20. Install the roof molding.

21. Apply a soapy water solution to the weatherstripping groove.

22. Using a small screwdriver, carefully raise the lip of the weatherstripping and push the molding into place.

23. Install the joint cover in the same manner.

Hatchback

1. Remove the hatch trim panel by prying the retaining pins out with a screwdriver.

2. Remove the rear wiper arm, and, on 1986 models, the stop light.

3. Disconnect the defogger wiring.

4. Cover the painted surfaces adjacent to the rear window molding with tape.

5. Using a screwdriver, pry off the molding joint covers.

6. Insert a flat wood wand between the molding and weatherstripping and slide it along, removing the molding.

7. Using a screwdriver, carefully loosen the weatherstripping lip from the body.

8. Working from the inside, force the weatherstripping lip outward.

9. Go outside and pull the glass and weatherstripping out.

10. Inspect the weatherstripping. If the weatherstripping has become hard and/or brittle, it should be replaced.

11. Insert a length of strong, thin cord in the weatherstripping channel with the two ends meeting at the bottom.

12. Fit the weatherstripping around the edge of the glass.

13. Coat the body opening and outer edge of

the weatherstripping with a soapy water solution.

14. Press the glass assembly into position in the body opening with the two ends of the cord hanging inside the car.

15. Go inside the car, and, with someone pushing on the glass from the outside with a light, steady pressure, pull the ends of the cord to slip the weatherstripping lip over the body channel. Make sure that the glass is firmly in position by tapping it from the outside with your open hand.

16. Mask the glass surface around the weath-erstripping. Apply windshield adhesive under the outside lip of the weatherstripping. When the adhesive is dry, remove the masking from both the glass and body areas.

17. Connect the defogger wiring.

18. Install the trim.

19. Apply a soapy water solution to the weatherstripping groove.

20. Using a small screwdriver, carefully raise the lip of the weatherstripping and push the molding into place.

21. Install the joint cover in the same manner.

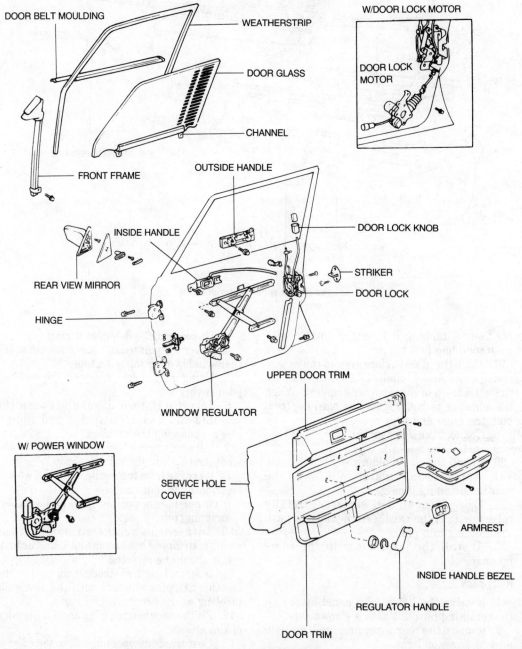

Front door components

INTERIOR

Door Panels

REMOVAL AND INSTALLATION

Front Door

1. Remove the inside door handle bezel.
2. Remove the armest.

3. Push inward on the door panel and pry off the window handle retaing pin.

4. Tape the end of a thin screwdriver and insert the screwdriver between the door panel and door. Slide the screwdriver until you hit a retaining pin, then, carefully, pry the pin out of the door. Do this with each pin until the panel is free.

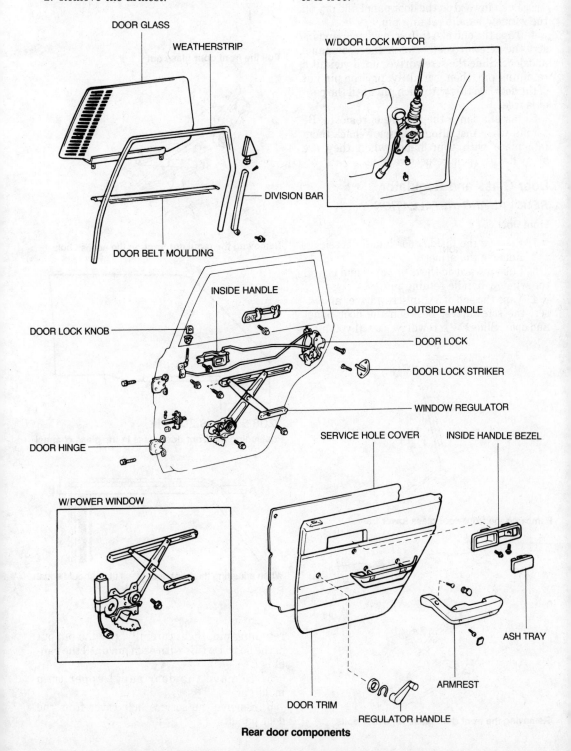

DOOR GLASS
WEATHERSTRIP
W/DOOR LOCK MOTOR
DIVISION BAR
DOOR BELT MOULDING
INSIDE HANDLE
OUTSIDE HANDLE
DOOR LOCK KNOB
DOOR LOCK
DOOR LOCK STRIKER
WINDOW REGULATOR
DOOR HINGE
SERVICE HOLE COVER
INSIDE HANDLE BEZEL
W/POWER WINDOW
ASH TRAY
ARMREST
DOOR TRIM
REGULATOR HANDLE

Rear door components

5. Installation is the reverse of removal. Be careful when installing the pins. Whack them into place with your hand, when they are aligned with their respective holes.

Rear Door

1. Remove the inside door handle bezel.
2. Remove the armest and ashtray.
3. Push inward on the door panel and pry off the window handle retaing pin.
4. Tape the end of a thin screwdriver and insert the screwdriver between the door panel and door. Slide the screwdriver until you hit a retaining pin, then, carefully, pry the pin out of the door. Do this with each pin until the panel is free.
5. Installation is the reverse of removal. Be careful when installing the pins. Whack them into place with your hand, when they are aligned with their respective holes.

Door Glass and Regulator
REMOVAL AND INSTALLATION
Front Door

1. Remove the inside door handle bezel.
2. Remove the armest.
3. Push inward on the door panel and pry off the window handle retaing pin.
4. Tape the end of a thin screwdriver and insert the screwdriver between the door panel and door. Slide the screwdriver until you hit a

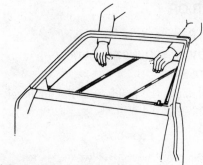

Pull the front door glass out

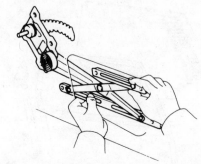

Removing the regulator through the access hole

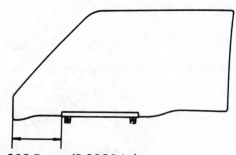

208.5 mm (8.2086 in.)
Positioning the front door glass in the glass channel

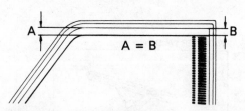

$A = B$

When adjusting the front door glass fit, A should equal B

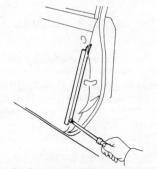

Removing the front door glass lower frame

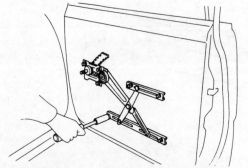

Removing the front door glass regulator bolts

retaining pin, then, carefully, pry the pin out of the door. Do this with each pin until the panel is free.
5. Remove the door panel upper trim molding.
6. Remove the service hole cover from the door panel.

7. Remove the retaining screw and remove the rear lower frame from the glass run.

8. Remove the two glass channel mount bolts.

9. Pull the glass up and out of the door.

10. Lower the regulator to the service hole position.

11. If equipped, disconnect the power window motor wiring connector.

12. Remove the equalizer arm bracket mounting bolts.

13. Remove the regulator mount bolts.

14. Remove the regulator (and motor) from the door.

15. Installation is the reverse of removal. Raise the glass to the almost closed position and make sure that the leading and trailing edges of the glass are equidistant from the top of the glass channel. If not, adjust the equalizer arm to achieve an even fit.

Rear Door

1. Remove the inside door handle bezel.

2. Remove the armest and ashtray.

3. Push inward on the door panel and pry off the window handle retaing pin.

4. Tape the end of a thin screwdriver and insert the screwdriver between the door panel and door. Slide the screwdriver until you hit a retaining pin, then, carefully, pry the pin out of the door. Do this with each pin until the panel is free.

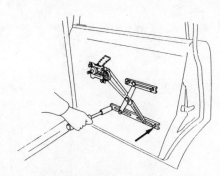

Removing the rear door glass regulator bolts

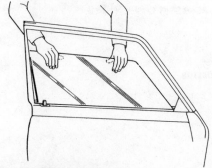

Pulling the rear door glass out

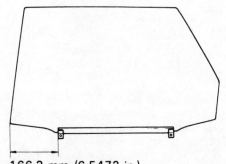

166.3 mm (6.5472 in.)

Installing the rear door glass into its channel

5. Remove the door panel upper trim molding.

6. Remove the division bar by removing the two screws under the weatherstripping, the screw from the panel and pulling the glass run from the division bar. Pull the bar from the door.

7. Remove the two glass channel mount bolts.

8. Pull the glass up and out of the door.

9. Lower the regulator to the service hole position.

10. If equipped, disconnect the power window motor wiring connector.

11. Remove the equalizer arm bracket mounting bolts.

12. Remove the regulator mount bolts.

13. Remove the regulator (and motor) from the door.

14. Installation is the reverse of removal. Raise the glass to the almost closed position and make sure that the leading and trailing edges of the glass are equidistant from the top of the glass channel. If not, adjust the equalizer arm to achieve an even fit.

Seats

REMOVAL AND INSTALLATION

Front seats are held to the floor with four bolts each.

The sedan rear seat is retained by two clips at the front and two bolts at the rear.

The hatchback rear seat cushion is retained by four bolts, while the seat back is bolted to its hinges.

When installing the seats, torque the front seat bolts to 27 ft.lb.; the sedan rear seat bolts to 9 ft.lb.; the hatchback seat cushion front bolts to 27 ft.lb.; the hatchback seat cushion rear bolts to 9 ft.lb.; the seat back-to-center hinge bolts to 65 in.lb.; the seat back-to-side hinge bolts to 13 ft.lb.

SEDAN

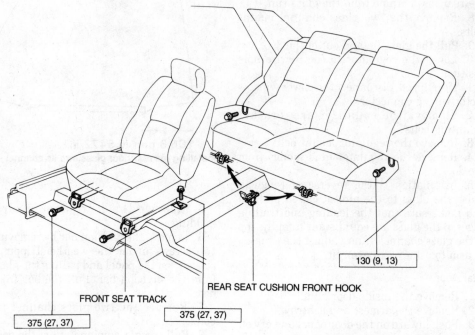

130 (9, 13)

REAR SEAT CUSHION FRONT HOOK

FRONT SEAT TRACK

375 (27, 37)

375 (27, 37)

LIFTBACK

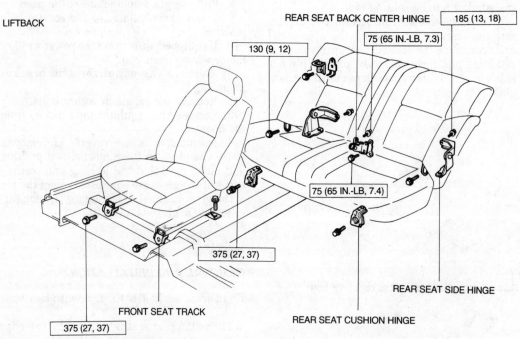

REAR SEAT BACK CENTER HINGE

185 (13, 18)

75 (65 IN.-LB, 7.3)

130 (9, 12)

75 (65 IN.-LB, 7.4)

REAR SEAT SIDE HINGE

REAR SEAT CUSHION HINGE

FRONT SEAT TRACK

375 (27, 37)

375 (27, 37)

KG-CM (FT-LB, N·M) : SPECIFIED TORQUE

Front and rear seat details

Mechanic's Data

General Conversion Table

Multiply By	To Convert	To	
LENGTH			
2.54	Inches	Centimeters	.3937
25.4	Inches	Millimeters	.03937
30.48	Feet	Centimeters	.0328
.304	Feet	Meters	3.28
.914	Yards	Meters	1.094
1.609	Miles	Kilometers	.621
VOLUME			
.473	Pints	Liters	2.11
.946	Quarts	Liters	1.06
3.785	Gallons	Liters	.264
.016	Cubic inches	Liters	61.02
16.39	Cubic inches	Cubic cms.	.061
28.3	Cubic feet	Liters	.0353
MASS (Weight)			
28.35	Ounces	Grams	.035
.4536	Pounds	Kilograms	2.20
—	To obtain	From	Multiply by

Multiply By	To Convert	To	
AREA			
.645	Square inches	Square cms.	.155
.836	Square yds.	Square meters	1.196
FORCE			
4.448	Pounds	Newtons	.225
.138	Ft./lbs.	Kilogram/meters	7.23
1.36	Ft./lbs.	Newton-meters	.737
.112	In./lbs.	Newton-meters	8.844
PRESSURE			
.068	Psi	Atmospheres	14.7
6.89	Psi	Kilopascals	.145
OTHER			
1.104	Horsepower (DIN)	Horsepower (SAE)	.9861
.746	Horsepower (SAE)	Kilowatts (KW)	1.34
1.60	Mph	Km/h	.625
.425	Mpg	Km/1	2.35
—	To obtain	From	Multiply by

Tap Drill Sizes

National Coarse or U.S.S.

Screw & Tap Size	Threads Per Inch	Use Drill Number
No. 5	40	39
No. 6	32	36
No. 8	32	29
No. 10	24	25
No. 12	24	17
1/4	20	8
5/16	18	F
3/8	16	5/16
7/16	14	U
1/2	13	27/64
9/16	12	31/64
5/8	11	17/32
3/4	10	21/32
7/8	9	49/64

National Coarse or U.S.S.

Screw & Tap Size	Threads Per Inch	Use Drill Number
1	8	7/8
1 1/8	7	63/64
1 1/4	7	1 7/64
1 1/2	6	1 11/32

National Fine or S.A.E.

Screw & Tap Size	Threads Per Inch	Use Drill Number
No. 5	44	37
No. 6	40	33
No. 8	36	29
No. 10	32	21

National Fine or S.A.E.

Screw & Tap Size	Threads Per Inch	Use Drill Number
No. 12	28	15
1/4	28	3
6/16	24	1
3/8	24	Q
7/16	20	W
1/2	20	29/64
9/16	18	33/64
5/8	18	37/64
3/4	16	11/16
7/8	14	13/16
1 1/8	12	1 3/64
1 1/4	12	1 11/64
1 1/2	12	1 27/64

Drill Sizes In Decimal Equivalents

Inch	Decimal	Wire	mm	Inch	Decimal	Wire	mm	Inch	Decimal	Wire & Letter	mm	Inch	Decimal	Letter	mm	Inch	Decimal	mm
1/64	.0156		.39		.0730	49			.1614		4.1		.2717		6.9		.4331	11.0
	.0157		.4		.0748		1.9		.1654		4.2		.2720	I		7/16	.4375	11.11
	.0160	78			.0760	48			.1660	19			.2756		7.0		.4528	11.5
	.0165		.42		.0768		1.95		.1673		4.25		.2770	J		29/64	.4531	11.51
	.0173		.44	5/64	.0781		1.98		.1693		4.3		.2795		7.1	15/32	.4688	11.90
	.0177		.45		.0785	47			.1695	18			.2810	K			.4724	12.0
	.0180	77			.0787		2.0	11/64	.1719		4.36	9/32	.2812		7.14	31/64	.4844	12.30
	.0181		.46		.0807		2.05		.1730	17			.2835		7.2		.4921	12.5
	.0189		.48		.0810	46			.1732		4.4		.2854		7.25	1/2	.5000	12.70
	.0197		.5		.0820	45			.1770	16			.2874		7.3		.5118	13.0
	.0200	76			.0827		2.1		.1772		4.5		.2900	L		33/64	.5156	13.09
	.0210	75			.0846		2.15		.1800	15			.2913		7.4	17/32	.5312	13.49
	.0217		.55		.0860	44			.1811		4.6		.2950	M			.5315	13.5
	.0225	74			.0866		2.2		.1820	14			.2953		7.5	35/64	.5469	13.89
	.0236		.6		.0886		2.25		.1850	13		19/64	.2969		7.54		.5512	14.0
	.0240	73			.0890	43			.1850		4.7		.2992		7.6	9/16	.5625	14.28
	.0250	72			.0906		2.3		.1870		4.75		.3020	N			.5709	14.5
	.0256		.65		.0925		2.35	3/16	.1875		4.76		.3031		7.7	37/64	.5781	14.68
	.0260	71			.0935	42			.1890		4.8		.3051		7.75		.5906	15.0
	.0276		.7	3/32	.0938		2.38		.1890	12			.3071		7.8	19/32	.5938	15.08
	.0280	70			.0945		2.4		.1910	11			.3110		7.9	39/64	.6094	15.47
	.0292	69			.0960	41			.1929		4.9	5/16	.3125		7.93		.6102	15.5
	.0295		.75		.0965		2.45		.1935	10			.3150		8.0	5/8	.6250	15.87
	.0310	68			.0980	40			.1960	9			.3160	O			.6299	16.0
1/32	.0312		.79		.0981		2.5		.1969		5.0		.3189		8.1	41/64	.6406	16.27
	.0315		.8		.0995	39			.1990	8			.3228		8.2		.6496	16.5
	.0320	67			.1015	38			.2008		5.1		.3230	P		21/32	.6562	16.66
	.0330	66			.1024		2.6		.2010	7			.3248		8.25		.6693	17.0
	.0335		.85		.1040	37		13/64	.2031		5.16		.3268		8.3	43/64	.6719	17.06
	.0350	65			.1063		2.7		.2040	6		21/64	.3281		8.33	11/16	.6875	17.46
	.0354		.9		.1065	36			.2047		5.2		.3307		8.4		.6890	17.5
	.0360	64			.1083		2.75		.2055	5			.3320	Q		45/64	.7031	17.85
	.0370	63		7/64	.1094		2.77		.2067		5.25		.3346		8.5		.7087	18.0
	.0374		.95		.1100	35			.2087		5.3		.3386		8.6	23/32	.7188	18.25
	.0380	62			.1102		2.8		.2090	4			.3390	R			.7283	18.5
	.0390	61			.1110	34			.2126		5.4		.3425		8.7	47/64	.7344	18.65
	.0394		1.0		.1130	33			.2130	3		11/32	.3438		8.73		.7480	19.0
	.0400	60			.1142		2.9		.2165		5.5		.3445		8.75	3/4	.7500	19.05
	.0410	59			.1160	32		7/32	.2188		5.55		.3465		8.8	49/64	.7656	19.44
	.0413		1.05		.1181		3.0		.2205		5.6		.3480	S			.7677	19.5
	.0420	58			.1200	31			.2210	2			.3504		8.9	25/32	.7812	19.84
	.0430	57			.1220		3.1		.2244		5.7		.3543		9.0		.7874	20.0
	.0433		1.1	1/8	.1250		3.17		.2264		5.75		.3580	T		51/64	.7969	20.24
	.0453		1.15		.1260		3.2		.2280	1			.3583		9.1		.8071	20.5
	.0465	56			.1280		3.25		.2283		5.8	23/64	.3594		9.12	13/16	.8125	20.63
3/64	.0469		1.19		.1285	30			.2323		5.9		.3622		9.2		.8268	21.0
	.0472		1.2		.1299		3.3		.2340	A			.3642		9.25	53/64	.8281	21.03
	.0492		1.25		.1339		3.4	15/64	.2344		5.95		.3661		9.3	27/32	.8438	21.43
	.0512		1.3		.1360	29			.2362		6.0		.3680	U			.8465	21.5
	.0520	55			.1378		3.5		.2380	B			.3701		9.4	55/64	.8594	21.82
	.0531		1.35		.1405	28			.2402		6.1		.3740		9.5		.8661	22.0
	.0550	54		9/64	.1406		3.57		.2420	C		3/8	.3750		9.52	7/8	.8750	22.22
	.0551		1.4		.1417		3.6		.2441		6.2		.3770	V			.8858	22.5
	.0571		1.45		.1440	27			.2460	D			.3780		9.6	57/64	.8906	22.62
	.0591		1.5		.1457		3.7		.2461		6.25		.3819		9.7		.9055	23.0
	.0595	53			.1470	26			.2480		6.3		.3839		9.75	29/32	.9062	23.01
	.0610		1.55		.1476		3.75	1/4	.2500	E	6.35		.3858		9.8	59/64	.9219	23.41
1/16	.0625		1.59		.1495	25			.2520		6.		.3860	W			.9252	23.5
	.0630		1.6		.1496		3.8		.2559		6.5		.3898		9.9	15/16	.9375	23.81
	.0635	52			.1520	24			.2570	F		25/64	.3906		9.92		.9449	24.0
	.0650		1.65		.1535		3.9		.2598		6.6		.3937		10.0	61/64	.9531	24.2
	.0669		1.7		.1540	23			.2610	G			.3970	X			.9646	24.5
	.0670	51		5/32	.1562		3.96		.2638		6.7		.4040	Y		31/32	.9688	24.6
	.0689		1.75		.1570	22		17/64	.2656		6.74	13/32	.4062		10.31		.9843	25.0
	.0700	50			.1575		4.0		.2657		6.75		.4130	Z		63/64	.9844	25.0
	.0709		1.8		.1590	21			.2660	H			.4134		10.5	1	1.0000	25.4
	.0728		1.85		.1610	20			.2677		6.8	27/64	.4219		10.71			

AIR/FUEL RATIO: The ratio of air to gasoline by weight in the fuel mixture drawn into the engine.

AIR INJECTION: One method of reducing harmful exhaust emissions by injecting air into each of the exhaust ports of an engine. The fresh air entering the hot exhaust manifold causes any remaining fuel to be burned before it can exit the tailpipe.

ALTERNATOR: A device used for converting mechanical energy into electrical energy.

AMMETER: An instrument, calibrated in amperes, used to measure the flow of an electrical current in a circuit. Ammeters are always connected in series with the circuit being tested.

AMPERE: The rate of flow of electrical current present when one volt of electrical pressure is applied against one ohm of electrical resistance.

ANALOG COMPUTER: Any microprocessor that uses similar (analogous) electrical signals to make its calculations.

ARMATURE: A laminated, soft iron core wrapped by a wire that converts electrical energy to mechanical energy as in a motor or relay. When rotated in a magnetic field, it changes mechanical energy into electrical energy as in a generator.

ATMOSPHERIC PRESSURE: The pressure on the Earth's surface caused by the weight of the air in the atmosphere. At sea level, this pressure is 14.7 psi at 32°F (101 kPa at 0°C).

ATOMIZATION: The breaking down of a liquid into a fine mist that can be suspended in air.

AXIAL PLAY: Movement parallel to a shaft or bearing bore.

BACKFIRE: The sudden combustion of gases in the intake or exhaust system that results in a loud explosion.

BACKLASH: The clearance or play between two parts, such as meshed gears.

BACKPRESSURE: Restrictions in the exhaust system that slow the exit of exhaust gases from the combustion chamber.

BAKELITE: A heat resistant, plastic insulator material commonly used in printed circuit boards and transistorized components.

BALL BEARING: A bearing made up of hardened inner and outer races between which hardened steel ball roll.

BALLAST RESISTOR: A resistor in the primary ignition circuit that lowers voltage after the engine is started to reduce wear on ignition components.

BEARING: A friction reducing, supportive device usually located between a stationary part and a moving part.

BIMETAL TEMPERATURE SENSOR: Any sensor or switch made of two dissimilar types of metal that bend when heated or cooled due to the different expansion rates of the alloys. These types of sensors usually function as an on/off switch.

BLOWBY: Combustion gases, composed of water vapor and unburned fuel, that leak past the piston rings into the crankcase during normal engine operation. These gases are removed by the PCV system to prevent the build-up of harmful acids in the crankcase.

BRAKE PAD: A brake shoe and lining assembly used with disc brakes.

BRAKE SHOE: The backing for the brake lining. The term is, however, usually applied to the assembly of the brake backing and lining.

BUSHING: A liner, usually removable, for a bearing; an anti-friction liner used in place of a bearing.

BYPASS: System used to bypass ballast resistor during engine cranking to increase voltage supplied to the coil.

CALIPER: A hydraulically activated device in a disc brake system, which is mounted straddling the brake rotor (disc). The caliper contains at least one piston and two brake pads. Hydraulic pressure on the piston(s) forces the pads against the rotor.

CAMSHAFT: A shaft in the engine on which are the lobes (cams) which operate the valves. The camshaft is driven by the crankshaft, via a belt, chain or gears, at one half the crankshaft speed.

CAPACITOR: A device which stores an electrical charge.

CARBON MONOXIDE (CO): a colorless, odorless gas given off as a normal byproduct of combustion. It is poisonous and extremely dangerous in confined areas, building up slowly to toxic levels without warning if adequate ventilation is not available.

CARBURETOR: A device, usually mounted on the intake manifold of an engine, which mixes the air and fuel in the proper proportion to allow even combustion.

CATALYTIC CONVERTER: A device installed in the exhaust system, like a muffler, that converts harmful byproducts of combustion into carbon dioxide and water vapor by means of a heat-producing chemical reaction.

CENTRIFUGAL ADVANCE: A mechanical method of advancing the spark timing by using flyweights in the distributor that react to centrifugal force generated by the distributor shaft rotation.

CHECK VALVE: Any one-way valve installed to permit the flow of air, fuel or vacuum in one direction only.

CHOKE: A device, usually a moveable valve, placed in the intake path of a carburetor to restrict the flow of air.

CIRCUIT: Any unbroken path through which an electrical current can flow. Also used to describe fuel flow in some instances.

CIRCUIT BREAKER: A switch which protects an electrical circuit from overload by opening the circuit when the current flow exceeds a predetermined level. Some circuit breakers must be reset manually, while other reset automatically

COIL (IGNITION): A transformer in the ignition circuit which steps of the voltage provided to the spark plugs.

COMBINATION MANIFOLD: An assembly which includes both the intake and exhaust manifolds in one casting.

COMBINATION VALVE: A device used in some fuel systems that routes fuel vapors to a charcoal storage canister instead of venting them into the atmosphere. The valve relieves fuel tank pressure and allows fresh air into the tank as fuel level drops to prevent a vapor lock situation.

COMPRESSION RATIO: The comparison of the total volume of the cylinder and combustion chamber with the piston at BDC and the piston at TDC.

CONDENSER: 1. An electrical device which acts to store an electrical charge, preventing voltage surges.
2. A radiator-like device in the air conditioning system in which refrigerant gas condenses into a liquid, giving off heat.

CONDUCTOR: Any material through which an electrical current can be transmitted easily.

CONTINUITY: Continuous or complete circuit. Can be checked with an ohmmeter.

COUNTERSHAFT: An intermediate shaft which is rotated by a mainshaft and transmits, in turn, that rotation to a working part.

CRANKCASE: The lower part of an engine in which the crankshaft and related parts operate.

CRANKSHAFT: The main driving shaft of an engine which receives reciprocating motion from the pistons and converts it to rotary motion.

CYLINDER: In an engine, the round hole in the engine block in which the piston(s) ride.

CYLINDER BLOCK: The main structural member of an engine in which is found the cylinders, crankshaft and other principal parts.

CYLINDER HEAD: The detachable portion of the engine, fastened, usually, to the top of the cylinder block, containing all or most of the combustion chambers. On overhead valve engines, it contains the valves and their operating parts. On overhead cam engines, it contains the camshaft as well.

DEAD CENTER: The extreme top or bottom of the piston stroke.

DETONATION: An unwanted explosion of the air fuel mixture in the combustion chamber caused by excess heat and compression, advanced timing, or an overly lean mixture. Also referred to as "ping".

DIAPHRAGM: A thin, flexible wall separating two cavities, such as in a vacuum advance unit.

DIESELING: A condition in which hot spots in the combustion chamber cause the engine to run on after the key is turned off.

DIFFERENTIAL: A geared assembly which allows the transmission of motion between drive axles, giving one axle the ability to turn faster than the other.

DIODE: An electrical device that will allow current to flow in one direction only.

DISC BRAKE: A hydraulic braking assembly consisting of a brake disc, or rotor, mounted on an axle, and a caliper assembly containing, usually two brake pads which are activated by hydraulic pressure. The pads are forced against the sides of the disc, creating friction which slows the vehicle.

DISTRIBUTOR: A mechanically driven device on an engine which is responsible for electrically firing the spark plug at a predetermined point of the piston stroke.

DOWEL PIN: A pin, inserted in mating holes in two different parts allowing those parts to maintain a fixed relationship.

DRUM BRAKE: A braking system which consists of two brake shoes and one or two wheel cylinders, mounted on a fixed backing plate, and a brake drum, mounted on an axle, which revolves around the assembly. Hydraulic action applied to the wheel cylinders forces the shoes outward against the drum, creating friction and slowing the vehicle.

DWELL: The rate, measured in degrees of shaft rotation, at which an electrical circuit cycles on and off.

ELECTRONIC CONTROL UNIT (ECU): Ignition module, module, amplifier or igniter. See Module for definition.

ELECTRONIC IGNITION: A system in which the timing and firing of the spark plugs is controlled by an electronic control unit, usually called a module. These systems have not points or condenser.

ENDPLAY: The measured amount of axial movement in a shaft.

ENGINE: A device that converts heat into mechanical energy.

EXHAUST MANIFOLD: A set of cast passages or pipes which conduct exhaust gases from the engine.

FEELER GAUGE: A blade, usually metal, of precisely predetermined thickness, used to measure the clearance between two parts. These blades usually are available in sets of assorted thicknesses.

F-Head: An engine configuration in which the intake valves are in the cylinder head, while the camshaft and exhaust valves are located in the cylinder block. The camshaft operates the intake valves via lifters and pushrods, while it operates the exhaust valves directly.

FIRING ORDER: The order in which combustion occurs in the cylinders of an engine. Also the order in which spark is distributed to the plugs by the distributor.

FLATHEAD: An engine configuration in which the camshaft and all the valves are located in the cylinder block.

FLOODING: The presence of too much fuel in the intake manifold and combustion chamber which prevents the air/fuel mixture from firing, thereby causing a no-start situation.

FLYWHEEL: A disc shaped part bolted to the rear end of the crankshaft. Around the outer perimeter is affixed the ring gear. The starter drive engages the ring gear, turning the flywheel, which rotates the crankshaft, imparting the initial starting motion to the engine.

FOOT POUND (ft.lb. or sometimes, ft. lbs.): The amount of energy or work needed to raise an item weighing one pound, a distance of one foot.

FUSE: A protective device in a circuit which prevents circuit overload by breaking the circuit when a specific amperage is present. The device is constructed around a strip or wire of a lower amperage rating than the circuit it is designed to protect. When an amperage higher than that stamped on the fuse is present in the circuit, the strip or wire melts, opening the circuit.

GEAR RATIO: The ratio between the number of teeth on meshing gears.

GENERATOR: A device which converts mechanical energy into electrical energy.

HEAT RANGE: The measure of a spark plug's ability to dissipate heat from its firing end. The higher the heat range, the hotter the plug fires.

HUB: The center part of a wheel or gear.

HYDROCARBON (HC): Any chemical compound made up of hydrogen and carbon. A major pollutant formed by the engine as a byproduct of combustion.

HYDROMETER: An instrument used to measure the specific gravity of a solution.

INCH POUND (in.lb. or sometimes, in. lbs.): One twelfth of a foot pound.

INDUCTION: A means of transferring electrical energy in the form of a magnetic field. Principle used in the ignition coil to increase voltage.

INJECTION PUMP: A device, usually mechanically operated, which meters and delivers fuel under pressure to the fuel injector.

INJECTOR: A device which receives metered fuel under relatively low pressure and is activated to inject the fuel into the engine under relatively high pressure at a predetermined time.

INPUT SHAFT: The shaft to which torque is applied, usually carrying the driving gear or gears.

INTAKE MANIFOLD: A casting of passages or pipes used to conduct air or a fuel/air mixture to the cylinders.

JOURNAL: The bearing surface within which a shaft operates.

KEY: A small block usually fitted in a notch between a shaft and a hub to prevent slippage of the two parts.

MANIFOLD: A casting of passages or set of pipes which connect the cylinders to an inlet or outlet source.

MANIFOLD VACUUM: Low pressure in an engine intake manifold formed just below the throttle plates. Manifold vacuum is highest at idle and drops under acceleration.

MASTER CYLINDER: The primary fluid pressurizing device in a hydraulic system. In automotive use, it is found in brake and hydraulic clutch systems and is pedal activated, either directly or, in a power brake system, through the power booster.

MODULE: Electronic control unit, amplifier or igniter of solid state or integrated design which controls the current flow in the ignition primary circuit based on input from the pickup coil. When the module opens the primary circuit, the high secondary voltage is induced in the coil.

NEEDLE BEARING: A bearing which consists of a number (usually a large number) of long, thin rollers.

OHM: (Ω) The unit used to measure the resistance of conductor to electrical flow. One ohm is the amount of resistance that limits current flow to one ampere in a circuit with one volt of pressure.

OHMMETER: An instrument used for measuring the resistance, in ohms, in an electrical circuit.

OUTPUT SHAFT: The shaft which transmits torque from a device, such as a transmission.

OVERDRIVE: A gear assembly which produces more shaft revolutions than that transmitted to it.

OVERHEAD CAMSHAFT (OHC): An engine configuration in which the camshaft is mounted on top of the cylinder head and operates the valve either directly or by means of rocker arms.

OVERHEAD VALVE (OHV): An engine configuration in which all of the valves are located in the cylinder head and the camshaft is located in the cylinder block. The camshaft operates the valves via lifters and pushrods.

OXIDES OF NITROGEN (NOx): Chemical compounds of nitrogen produced as a byproduct of combustion. They combine with hydrocarbons to produce smog.

OXYGEN SENSOR: Used with the feedback system to sense the presence of oxygen in the exhaust gas and signal the computer which can reference the voltage signal to an air/fuel ratio.

PINION: The smaller of two meshing gears.

PISTON RING: An open ended ring which fits into a groove on the outer diameter of the piston. Its chief function is to form a seal between the piston and cylinder wall. Most automotive pistons have three rings: two for compression sealing; one for oil sealing.

PRELOAD: A predetermined load placed on a bearing during assembly or by adjustment.

PRIMARY CIRCUIT: Is the low voltage side of the ignition system which consists of the ignition switch, ballast resistor or resistance wire, bypass, coil, electronic control unit and pick-up coil as well as the connecting wires and harnesses.

PRESS FIT: The mating of two parts under pressure, due to the inner diameter of one being smaller than the outer diameter of the other, or vice versa; an interference fit.

RACE: The surface on the inner or outer ring of a bearing on which the balls, needles or rollers move.

REGULATOR: A device which maintains the amperage and/or voltage levels of a circuit at predetermined values.

RELAY: A switch which automatically opens and/or closes a circuit.

RESISTANCE: The opposition to the flow of current through a circuit or electrical device, and is measured in ohms. Resistance is equal to the voltage divided by the amperage.

RESISTOR: A device, usually made of wire, which offers a preset amount of resistance in an electrical circuit.

RING GEAR: The name given to a ring-shaped gear attached to a differential case, or affixed to a flywheel or as part a planetary gear set.

ROLLER BEARING: A bearing made up of hardened inner and outer races between which hardened steel rollers move.

ROTOR: 1. The disc-shaped part of a disc brake assembly, upon which the brake pads bear; also called, brake disc.
2. The device mounted atop the distributor shaft, which passes current to the distributor cap tower contacts.

SECONDARY CIRCUIT: The high voltage side of the ignition system, usually above 20,000 volts. The secondary includes the ignition coil, coil wire, distributor cap and rotor, spark plug wires and spark plugs.

SENDING UNIT: A mechanical, electrical, hydraulic or electromagnetic device which transmits information to a gauge.

SENSOR: Any device designed to measure engine operating conditions or ambient pressures and temperatures. Usually electronic in nature and designed to send a voltage signal to an on-board computer, some sensors may operate as a simple on/off switch or they may provide a variable voltage signal (like a potentiometer) as conditions or measured parameters change.

SHIM: Spacers of precise, predetermined thickness used between parts to establish a proper working relationship.

SLAVE CYLINDER: In automotive use, a device in the hydraulic clutch system which is activated by hydraulic force, disengaging the clutch.

SOLENOID: A coil used to produce a magnetic field, the effect of which is produce work.

SPARK PLUG: A device screwed into the combustion chamber of a spark ignition engine. The basic construction is a conductive core inside of a ceramic insulator, mounted in an outer conductive base. An electrical charge from the spark plug wire travels along the conductive core and jumps a preset air gap to a grounding point or points at the end of the conductive base. The resultant spark ignites the fuel/air mixture in the combustion chamber.

SPLINES: Ridges machined or cast onto the outer diameter of a shaft or inner diameter of a bore to enable parts to mate without rotation.

TACHOMETER: A device used to measure the rotary speed of an engine, shaft, gear, etc., usually in rotations per minute.

THERMOSTAT: A valve, located in the cooling system of an engine, which is closed when cold and opens gradually in response to engine heating, controlling the temperature of the coolant and rate of coolant flow.

TOP DEAD CENTER (TDC): The point at which the piston reaches the top of its travel on the compression stroke.

TORQUE: The twisting force applied to an object.

TORQUE CONVERTER: A turbine used to transmit power from a driving member to a driven member via hydraulic action, providing changes in drive ratio and torque. In automotive use, it links the driveplate at the rear of the engine to the automatic transmission.

TRANSDUCER: A device used to change a force into an electrical signal.

TRANSISTOR: A semi-conductor component which can be actuated by a small voltage to perform an electrical switching function.

TUNE-UP: A regular maintenance function, usually associated with the replacement and adjustment of parts and components in the electrical and fuel systems of a vehicle for the purpose of attaining optimum performance.

TURBOCHARGER: An exhaust driven pump which compresses intake air and forces it into the combustion chambers at higher than atmospheric pressures. The increased air pressure allows more fuel to be burned and results in increased horsepower being produced.

VACUUM ADVANCE: A device which advances the ignition timing in response to increased engine vacuum.

VACUUM GAUGE: An instrument used to measure the presence of vacuum in a chamber.

VALVE: A device which control the pressure, direction of flow or rate of flow of a liquid or gas.

VALVE CLEARANCE: The measured gap between the end of the valve stem and the rocker arm, cam lobe or follower that activates the valve.

VISCOSITY: The rating of a liquid's internal resistance to flow.

VOLTMETER: An instrument used for measuring electrical force in units called volts. Voltmeters are always connected parallel with the circuit being tested.

WHEEL CYLINDER: Found in the automotive drum brake assembly, it is a device, actuated by hydraulic pressure, which, through internal pistons, pushes the brake shoes outward against the drums.

ABBREVIATIONS AND SYMBOLS

A: Ampere

AC: Alternating current

A/C: Air conditioning

A-h: Ampere hour

AT: Automatic transmission

ATDC: After top dead center

μA: Microampere

bbl: Barrel

BDC: Bottom dead center

bhp: Brake horsepower

BTDC: Before top dead center

BTU: British thermal unit

C: Celsius (Centigrade)

CCA: Cold cranking amps

cd: Candela

cm^2: Square centimeter

cm^3, cc: Cubic centimeter

CO: Carbon monoxide

CO_2: Carbon dioxide

cu.in., in^3: Cubic inch

CV: Constant velocity

Cyl.: Cylinder

DC: Direct current

ECM: Electronic control module

EFE: Early fuel evaporation

EFI: Electronic fuel injection

EGR: Exhaust gas recirculation

Exh.: Exhaust

F: Fahrenheit

F: Farad

pF: Picofarad

μF: Microfarad

FI: Fuel injection

ft.lb., ft. lb., ft. lbs.: foot pound(s)

gal: Gallon

g: Gram

HC: Hydrocarbon

HEI: High energy ignition

HO: High output

hp: Horsepower

Hyd.: Hydraulic

Hz: Hertz

ID: Inside diameter

in.lb.; in. lb.; in. lbs: inch pound(s)

Int.: Intake

K: Kelvin

kg: Kilogram

kHz: Kilohertz

km: Kilometer

km/h: Kilometers per hour

kΩ: Kilohm

kPa: Kilopascal

kV: Kilovolt

kW: Kilowatt

l: Liter

l/s: Liters per second

m: Meter

mA: Milliampere

mg: Milligram

mHz: Megahertz

mm: Millimeter

mm^2: Square millimeter

m^3: Cubic meter

$M\Omega$: Megohm

m/s: Meters per second

MT: Manual transmission

mV: Millivolt

μm: Micrometer

N: Newton

N-m: Newton meter

NOx: Nitrous oxide

OD: Outside diameter

OHC: Over head camshaft

OHV: Over head valve

Ω: Ohm

PCV: Positive crankcase ventilation

psi: Pounds per square inch

pts: Pints

qts: Quarts

rpm: Rotations per minute

rps: Rotations per second

R-12: A refrigerant gas (Freon)

SAE: Society of Automotive Engineers

SO_2: Sulfur dioxide

T: Ton

t: Megagram

TBI: Throttle Body Injection

TPS: Throttle Position Sensor

V: 1. Volt; 2. Venturi

μV: Microvolt

W: Watt

∞: Infinity

<: Less than

>: Greater than

Index

Chilton's Repair & Tune-Up Guides

The Complete line covers domestic cars, imports, trucks, vans, RV's and 4-wheel drive vehicles.

RTUG Title	Part No.	RTUG Title	Part No.
AMC 1975-82 Covers all U.S. and Canadian models	7199	**Corvair 1960-69** Covers all U.S. and Canadian models	6691
Aspen/Volare 1976-80 Covers all U.S. and Canadian models	6637	**Corvette 1953-62** Covers all U.S. and Canadian models	6576
Audi 1970-73 Covers all U.S. and Canadian models.	5902	**Corvette 1963-84** Covers all U.S. and Canadian models	6843
Audi 4000/5000 1978-81 Covers all U.S. and Canadian models including turbocharged and diesel engines	7028	**Cutlass 1970-85** Covers all U.S. and Canadian models	6933
Barracuda/Challenger 1965-72 Covers all U.S. and Canadian models	5807	**Dart/Demon 1968-76** Covers all U.S. and Canadian models	6324
Blazer/Jimmy 1969-82 Covers all U.S. and Canadian 2- and 4-wheel drive models, including diesel engines	6931	**Datsun 1961-72** Covers all U.S. and Canadian models of Nissan Patrol; 1500, 1600 and 2000 sports cars; Pick-Ups; 410, 411, 510, 1200 and 240Z	5790
BMW 1970-82 Covers all U.S. and Canadian models	6844	**Datsun 1973-80 Spanish**	7083
Buick/Olds/Pontiac 1975-85 Covers all U.S. and Canadian full size rear wheel drive models	7308	**Datsun/Nissan F-10, 310, Stanza, Pulsar 1977-86** Covers all U.S. and Canadian models	7196
Cadillac 1967-84 Covers all U.S. and Canadian rear wheel drive models	7462	**Datsun/Nissan Pick-Ups 1970-84** Covers all U.S and Canadian models	6816
Camaro 1967-81 Covers all U.S. and Canadian models	6735	**Datsun/Nissan Z & ZX 1970-86** Covers all U.S. and Canadian models	6932
Camaro 1982-85 Covers all U.S. and Canadian models	7317	**Datsun/Nissan 1200, 210, Sentra 1973-86** Covers all U.S. and Canadian models	7197
Capri 1970-77 Covers all U.S. and Canadian models	6695	**Datsun/Nissan 200SX, 510, 610, 710, 810, Maxima 1973-84** Covers all U.S. and Canadian models	7170
Caravan/Voyager 1984-85 Covers all U.S. and Canadian models	7482	**Dodge 1968-77** Covers all U.S. and Canadian models	6554
Century/Regal 1975-85 Covers all U.S. and Canadian rear wheel drive models, including turbocharged engines	7307	**Dodge Charger 1967-70** Covers all U.S. and Canadian models	6486
Champ/Arrow/Sapporo 1978-83 Covers all U.S. and Canadian models	7041	**Dodge/Plymouth Trucks 1967-84** Covers all $^{1}/_{2}$, $^{3}/_{4}$, and 1 ton 2- and 4-wheel drive U.S. and Canadian models, including diesel engines	7459
Chevette/1000 1976-86 Covers all U.S. and Canadian models	6836	**Dodge/Plymouth Vans 1967-84** Covers all $^{1}/_{2}$, $^{3}/_{4}$, and 1 ton U.S. and Canadian models of vans, cutaways and motor home chassis	6934
Chevrolet 1968-85 Covers all U.S. and Canadian models	7135	**D-50/Arrow Pick-Up 1979-81** Covers all U.S. and Canadian models	7032
Chevrolet 1968-79 Spanish	7082	**Fairlane/Torino 1962-75** Covers all U.S. and Canadian models	6320
Chevrolet/GMC Pick-Ups 1970-82 Spanish	7468	**Fairmont/Zephyr 1978-83** Covers all U.S. and Canadian models	6965
Chevrolet/GMC Pick-Ups and Suburban 1970-86 Covers all U.S. and Canadian $^{1}/_{2}$, $^{3}/_{4}$ and 1 ton models, including 4-wheel drive and diesel engines	6936	**Fiat 1969-81** Covers all U.S. and Canadian models	7042
Chevrolet LUV 1972-81 Covers all U.S. and Canadian models	6815	**Fiesta 1978-80** Covers all U.S. and Canadian models	6846
Chevrolet Mid-Size 1964-86 Covers all U.S. and Canadian models of 1964-77 Chevelle, Malibu and Malibu SS; 1974-77 Laguna; 1978-85 Malibu; 1970-86 Monte Carlo; 1964-84 El Camino, including diesel engines	6840	**Firebird 1967-81** Covers all U.S. and Canadian models	5996
Chevrolet Nova 1986 Covers all U.S. and Canadian models	7658	**Firebird 1982-85** Covers all U.S. and Canadian models	7345
Chevy/GMC Vans 1967-84 Covers all U.S. and Canadian models of $^{1}/_{2}$, $^{3}/_{4}$, and 1 ton vans, cutaways, and motor home chassis, including diesel engines	6930	**Ford 1968-79 Spanish**	7084
Chevy S-10 Blazer/GMC S-15 Jimmy 1982-85 Covers all U.S. and Canadian models	7383	**Ford Bronco 1966-83** Covers all U.S. and Canadian models	7140
Chevy S-10/GMC S-15 Pick-Ups 1982-85 Covers all U.S. and Canadian models	7310	**Ford Bronco II 1984** Covers all U.S. and Canadian models	7408
Chevy II/Nova 1962-79 Covers all U.S. and Canadian models	6841	**Ford Courier 1972-82** Covers all U.S. and Canadian models	6983
Chrysler K- and E-Car 1981-85 Covers all U.S. and Canadian front wheel drive models	7163	**Ford/Mercury Front Wheel Drive 1981-85** Covers all U.S. and Canadian models Escort, EXP, Tempo, Lynx, LN-7 and Topaz	7055
Colt/Challenger/Vista/Conquest 1971-85 Covers all U.S. and Canadian models	7037	**Ford/Mercury/Lincoln 1968-85** Covers all U.S. and Canadian models of FORD Country Sedan, Country Squire, Crown Victoria, Custom, Custom 500, Galaxie 500, LTD through 1982, Ranch Wagon, and XL; MERCURY Colony Park, Commuter, Marquis through 1982, Gran Marquis, Monterey and Park Lane; LINCOLN Continental and Towne Car	6842
Corolla/Carina/Tercel/Starlet 1970-85 Covers all U.S. and Canadian models	7036	**Ford/Mercury/Lincoln Mid-Size 1971-85** Covers all U.S. and Canadian models of FORD Elite, 1983-85 LTD, 1977-79 LTD II, Ranchero, Torino, Gran Torino, 1977-85 Thunderbird; MERCURY 1972-85 Cougar,	6696
Corona/Cressida/Crown/Mk.II/Camry/Van 1970-84 Covers all U.S. and Canadian models	7044		

continued on next page

RTUG Title	Part No.	RTUG Title	Part No.
1983-85 Marquis, Montego, 1980-85 XR-7; LINCOLN 1982-85 Continental, 1984-85 Mark VII, 1978-80 Versailles		Mercedes-Benz 1974-84 Covers all U.S. and Canadian models	6809
Ford Pick-Ups 1965-86 Covers all $1/2$, $3/4$ and 1 ton, 2- and 4-wheel drive U.S. and Canadian pick-up, chassis cab and camper models, including diesel engines	6913	Mitsubishi, Cordia, Tredia, Starion, Galant 1983-85 Covers all U.S. and Canadian models	7583
		MG 1961-81 Covers all U.S. and Canadian models	6780
Ford Pick-Ups 1965-82 Spanish	7469	Mustang/Capri/Merkur 1979-85 Covers all U.S. and Canadian models	6963
Ford Ranger 1983-84 Covers all U.S. and Canadian models	7338	Mustang/Cougar 1965-73 Covers all U.S. and Canadian models	6542
Ford Vans 1961-86 Covers all U.S. and Canadian $1/2$, $3/4$ and 1 ton van and cutaway chassis models, including diesel engines	6849	Mustang II 1974-78 Covers all U.S. and Canadian models	6812
		Omni/Horizon/Rampage 1978-84 Covers all U.S. and Canadian models of DODGE omni, Miser, 024, Charger 2.2; PLYMOUTH Horizon, Miser, TC3, TC3 Tourismo; Rampage	6845
GM A-Body 1982-85 Covers all front wheel drive U.S. and Canadian models of BUICK Century, CHEVROLET Celebrity, OLDSMOBILE Cutlass Ciera and PONTIAC 6000	7309		
		Opel 1971-75 Covers all U.S. and Canadian models	6575
GM C-Body 1985 Covers all front wheel drive U.S. and Canadian models of BUICK Electra Park Avenue and Electra T-Type, CADILLAC Fleetwood and deVille, OLDSMOBILE 98 Regency and Regency Brougham	7587	Peugeot 1970-74 Covers all U.S. and Canadian models	5982
		Pinto/Bobcat 1971-80 Covers all U.S. and Canadian models	7027
		Plymouth 1968-76 Covers all U.S. and Canadian models	6552
GM J-Car 1982-85 Covers all U.S. and Canadian models of BUICK Skyhawk, CHEVROLET Cavalier, CADILLAC Cimarron, OLDSMOBILE Firenza and PONTIAC 2000 and Sunbird	7059	Pontiac Fiero 1984-85 Covers all U.S. and Canadian models	7571
		Pontiac Mid-Size 1974-83 Covers all U.S. and Canadian models of Ventura, Grand Am, LeMans, Grand LeMans, GTO, Phoenix, and Grand Prix	7346
GM N-Body 1985-86 Covers all U.S. and Canadian models of front wheel drive BUICK Somerset and Skylark, OLDSMOBILE Calais, and PONTIAC Grand Am	7657		
		Porsche 924/928 1976-81 Covers all U.S. and Canadian models	7048
		Renault 1975-85 Covers all U.S. and Canadian models	7165
GM X-Body 1980-85 Covers all U.S. and Canadian models of BUICK Skylark, CHEVROLET Citation, OLDSMOBILE Omega and PONTIAC Phoenix	7049	Roadrunner/Satellite/Belvedere/GTX 1968-73 Covers all U.S. and Canadian models	5821
		RX-7 1979-81 Covers all U.S. and Canadian models	7031
GM Subcompact 1971-80 Covers all U.S. and Canadian models of BUICK Skyhawk (1975-80), CHEVROLET Vega and Monza, OLDSMOBILE Starfire, and PONTIAC Astre and 1975-80 Sunbird	6935	SAAB 99 1969-75 Covers all U.S. and Canadian models	5988
		SAAB 900 1979-85 Covers all U.S. and Canadian models	7572
		Snowmobiles 1976-80 Covers Arctic Cat, John Deere, Kawasaki, Polaris, Ski-Doo and Yamaha	6978
Granada/Monarch 1975-82 Covers all U.S. and Canadian models	6937		
Honda 1973-84 Covers all U.S. and Canadian models	6980	Subaru 1970-84 Covers all U.S. and Canadian models	6982
International Scout 1967-73 Covers all U.S. and Canadian models	5912	Tempest/GTO/LeMans 1968-73 Covers all U.S. and Canadian models	5905
Jeep 1945-87 Covers all U.S. and Canadian CJ-2A, CJ-3A, CJ-3B, CJ-5, CJ-6, CJ-7, Scrambler and Wrangler models	6817	Toyota 1966-70 Covers all U.S. and Canadian models of Corona, MkII, Corolla, Crown, Land Cruiser, Stout and Hi-Lux	5795
		Toyota 1970-79 Spanish	7467
Jeep Wagoneer, Commando, Cherokee, Truck 1957-86 Covers all U.S. and Canadian models of Wagoneer, Cherokee, Grand Wagoneer, Jeepster, Jeepster Commando, J-100, J-200, J-300, J-10, J20, FC-150 and FC-170	6739	Toyota Celica/Supra 1971-85 Covers all U.S. and Canadian models	7043
		Toyota Trucks 1970-85 Covers all U.S. and Canadian models of pick-ups, Land Cruiser and 4Runner	7035
		Valiant/Duster 1968-76 Covers all U.S. and Canadian models	6326
Laser/Daytona 1984-85 Covers all U.S. and Canadian models	7563	Volvo 1956-69 Covers all U.S. and Canadian models	6529
Maverick/Comet 1970-77 Covers all U.S. and Canadian models	6634	Volvo 1970-83 Covers all U.S. and Canadian models	7040
Mazda 1971-84 Covers all U.S. and Canadian models of RX-2, RX-3, RX-4, 808, 1300, 1600, Cosmo, GLC and 626	6981	VW Front Wheel Drive 1974-85 Covers all U.S. and Canadian models	6962
		VW 1949-71 Covers all U.S. and Canadian models	5796
Mazda Pick-Ups 1972-86 Covers all U.S. and Canadian models	7659	VW 1970-79 Spanish	7081
Mercedes-Benz 1959-70 Covers all U.S. and Canadian models	6065	VW 1970-81 Covers all U.S. and Canadian Beetles, Karmann Ghia, Fastback, Squareback, Vans, 411 and 412	6837
Mereceds-Benz 1968-73 Covers all U.S. and Canadian models	5907		

Chilton's Repair & Tune-Up Guides are available at your local retailer or by mailing a check or money order for **$13.50** plus **$2.50** to cover postage and handling to:

Chilton Book Company
Dept. DM
Radnor, PA 19089

NOTE: When ordering be sure to include your name & address, book part No. & title.